Knowledge Governance

Knowledge Governance

Processes and Perspectives

Nicolai J. Foss and Snejina Michailova

Great Clarendon Street, Oxford OX2 6DP

Oxford University Press is a department of the University of Oxford.
It furthers the University's objective of excellence in research, scholarship,
and education by publishing worldwide in

Oxford New York

Auckland Cape Town Dar es Salaam Hong Kong Karachi
Kuala Lumpur Madrid Melbourne Mexico City Nairobi
New Delhi Shanghai Taipei Toronto

With offices in

Argentina Austria Brazil Chile Czech Republic France Greece
Guatemala Hungary Italy Japan Poland Portugal Singapore
South Korea Switzerland Thailand Turkey Ukraine Vietnam

Oxford is a registered trade mark of Oxford University Press
in the UK and in certain other countries

Published in the United States
by Oxford University Press Inc., New York

First published 2009

British Library Cataloguing in Publication Data

Data available

Library of Congress Cataloging in Publication Data

Data available

Typeset by SPI Publisher Services, Pondicherry, India
Printed on acid-free paper
by the MPG Books Group
in the UK

ISBN 978–0–19–923592–6 (Hbk)

10 9 8 7 6 5 4 3 2 1

Contents

List of Figures

List of Tables

List of Contributors

Kenneth Amaeshi is a Research Fellow at Warwick Business School

Linda Argote is the Carnegie Bosch Professor of Organizational Behavior and Theory, Tepper School of Business, Carnegie-Mellon University, and the Editor-in-Chief, *Organization Science*

Michael Christensen is a post doc at the Strategic Organization Design Unit at the Southern Denmark University

Kirsten Foss is a Professor of Organization and Strategy at the Norwegian School of Economics and Management

Nicolai J. Foss is a Professor of Strategy and Organization at the Copenhagen Business School, the Director of CBS' Center for Strategic Management and Globalization, and a Professor of Knowledge-based Firm Organization at the Norwegian School of Economics and Management

Anna Grandori is Professor of Organization and Management, Bocconi University

Bruce Heimann is Assistant Professor of Management, College of Business

Kenneth Husted is Professor of Innovation and Research Management at the University of Auckland Business School

Aimée A. Kane is an Assistant Professor of Management and Organizations at New York University Stern School of Business

Thorbjørn Knudsen is Professor of Strategic Organization Design, and the Director of the Strategic Organization Design Unit at the Southern Denmark University

Snejina Michailova is Professor of International Business at the University of Auckland Business School

Jackson Nickerson is the Frahm Family Professor of Organization and Strategy, the Olin Business School, Washington University

Margit Osterloh is Professor at the University of Zurich, Institute for Organization and Administrative Science

Harry Scarbrough is Professor in Warwick Business School

Antoinette Weibel is Assistant Professor at the University of Zurich, Institute for Organization and Administrative Science

Todd Zenger is the Robert and Barbara Frick Professor of Business Strategy, the Olin Business School, Washington University

1

Knowledge governance: themes and questions

Snejina Michailova and Nicolai J. Foss

1.1. Introduction: The Interface Between Knowledge and Organization

Various arguments, both research- and practice-driven, have given significant impetus to the use of the concept of knowledge in management research over the last few decades. It is conventionally claimed that ours is a knowledge economy, a notion that may be fuzzy but that clearly seems to capture important phenomena and tendencies. Among these tendencies—actual, alleged, and imagined—are the growing value of human capital inputs, the greater than ever importance of immaterial assets and scientific knowledge in production, the need to control in-house an increasing number of technologies (even if product portfolios are shrinking) (Brusoni, Prencipe, and Pavitt 2001), and to tap an increasing number of knowledge nodes, not only internally but also through alliances and networks with other firms and institutions. These tendencies profoundly impact economic organization and competitive advantages and highlight the role of organization as the context of the creation of knowledge-based competitive advantages.

A conspicuous manifestation of this is that the number of knowledge-intensive firms is rapidly growing. These are firms where workers have a high level of expertise in specific domains, which, when deployed in an integrated fashion to deliver strategically placed value-added products and services, leads to competitive positioning. More generally, however, management academics have strongly stressed the role of organizational factors in the process of building knowledge-based strategies that are able to bring sustained competitive advantage (Grant 1996; Nonaka and Takeuchi 1995). For example, firms are argued to adopt 'network organization' (Miles and Snow 1992) and engage in 'corporate disaggregation' (Zenger and Hesterly 1997), so as to become 'information age organizations' (Mendelsson and Pillai 1999) that can build the 'dynamic capabilities' (Teece, Pisano, and Shuen 1997) required for competing in the knowledge economy. In other words, organization is designed to foster certain knowledge-related outcomes.

1.1.1. *The Rise of the Knowledge (Management) Movement*

The concept of 'knowledge' is complex, multilayered, and multifaceted (Blackler 1995). The role of knowledge, considered both as a dependent variable and as an independent variable, has been a major research focus for several fields in management studies. The academics' interest in 'knowledge management' is clearly evidenced in the fact that various theoretical disciplines, such as philosophy, information and library science, strategic management, organizational economics, sociology, organization theory, organizational behavior, and cognitive psychology, all have contributed to the theoretical debates centered around 'knowledge' and its 'management.' Jointly, they have established a very broad body of discourse. Since the 1960s, social scientists and others have tried to utilize 'knowledge' as a unit of analysis starting from simple attempts to categorize knowledge to the complex formulations existing today. Hull (2000: 59) summarized this development in the following way:

> ...the notion that knowledge is an important entity, a unit of analysis, which presents particular types of problem which can no longer be left purely to philosophers, but which require the attention of various other experts. This provides for a variety of concepts, linkages, investigations, commentaries, labels, new language and re-definitions of old language, and changes in practices and techniques.

Among those 'various other experts' are countless management researchers who give rise to a knowledge movement that cuts across traditionally separate disciplines in management research. The movement is based on the shared view that the management of knowledge is increasingly becoming a critical issue for competitive dynamics, international strategy, the accumulation and deployment of resources, the boundaries of firms, and many other issues. Underpinning this is a reconceptualization of the business firm as a knowledge-creating and -integrating entity

(Drucker 1999; Grant 1996; Hedlund 1994; Nonaka 1994; Spender 1996*c*; Tsoukas 1996). The interest in knowledge assets, knowledge processes, and knowledge work has moved beyond the phase of knowledge management being a management fad or fashion. The interest is remaining strong and is growing; it will likely endure even if the label might change (Drucker 1993).

The *strategic management* field has developed a number of approaches emphasizing knowledge (Grant 1996) and giving knowledge assets a center stage. While the resource-based view (Barney 1991; Wernerfelt 1984) applies to *any* resource, a number of later, strongly overlapping approaches (the knowledge-based view of the firm, the dynamic capabilities approach, etc.) clearly highlight knowledge assets. 'The essence of the firm in the new economy,' says David Teece (2000: 29), '. . . is its ability to create, transfer, assemble, integrate, protect, and exploit knowledge assets.' Competitive advantages may be enjoyed from superior management of each one of these processes.

The *international business* field is developing a view of the multinational corporation as a knowledge-based entity (Gupta and Govindarajan 1991, 2000; Hedlund 1994; Kogut and Zander 1993; Nielsen and Michailova 2007; Schulz 2003; Szulanski 1996). The field is concerned with various knowledge-related issues in the multinational corporation context and/or in a broader cross-border context. The issues that have been examined so far can be clustered into four groups: (*a*) characteristics, types, and dimensions of knowledge (Madhok and Liu 2006; Minbaeva 2007; Schulz 2003); (*b*) characteristics of actors involved in the knowledge processes (Fang et al. 2007; Gupta and Govindarajan 2000; Kostova 1999; Schulz 2003; Szulanski, Cappetta, and Jensen 2004); (*c*) characteristics of the relationships between the actors involved in the knowledge processes (Hansen, Mors, and Løvås 2005; Jensen and Szulanski 2004; Kostova and Roth 2002; Li 2005); and (*d*) outcomes of knowledge processes (Fang et al. 2007; Hansen 2002; Hansen, Mors, and Løövås 2005; Kostova and Roth 2002).

Network ideas emphasizing connections between knowledge nodes—often, although not exclusively, based on sociology ideas on network ties—have been and continue being influential (Kogut 2000; Powell 1990). The literature on collaborative networks highlights the importance of, to mention but a few issues, social capital and exchange (Tsai and Ghoshal 1998), network position and absorptive capacity (Tsai 2001), and coordination, competition, and innovation/knowledge sharing (Powell, Koput, and Smith-Doerr 1996; Teece 1992; Tsai 2002). Relevant for the context of this book is the fact that while (interorganizational) networks have often been studied in isolation from governance approaches, there are studies that testify to the fruitfulness of combining ideas and insights from both approaches (Gerlach 1992; Lomi and Grandi 1997; Nohria and Garcia-Pont 1991).

Knowledge management has become not only a huge body of research literature but also a widespread organizational practice (Easterby-Smith and Lyles 2003). It highlights the personal and contextual dimensions of knowledge and knowing (Blackler 2000; Brown and Duguid 1991; Cook and Brown 1999; Lave and Wenger 1991; Polanyi 1967; Weick 1977), and underlines the indeterminate nature of organizational knowledge (Tsoukas 1996): nobody can know in advance of using it what knowledge is needed (Merali 2000; Polanyi 1967; Tsoukas 1996; Weick 1995). Not surprisingly, the knowledge literature in management studies has arrived at numerous taxonomies and distinctions. Winter (1987) documented an early and particularly important contribution with the distinctions between knowledge tacitness versus explicitness, system-quality versus stand-alone, teachability versus nonteachability, and complexity versus noncomplexity. The Winter distinctions have been the basis for significant subsequent empirical work (Birkinshaw, Nobel, and Ridderstråle 2002; Kogut and Zander 1993).

The above notions concerning the importance of knowledge, and especially tacit knowledge, for constituting competitive advantage, organizational performance, and organizational success have been put forward by, among others, Bartlett and Ghoshal (1989), Nonaka and Takeuchi (1995), Grant (1996), Spender (1996*a*, 1996*b*), Stewart (1997), Bennett (1998), and Chakravarthy et al. (2003). They have clearly been taken very seriously in the corporate landscapes. Executives introduce formalized knowledge management systems materializing the conviction that managing knowledge assets is increasingly important for their organizations (Nielsen and Michailova 2007; Offsey 1997) even if their organizations are not necessarily knowledge-intensive firms (Newman 1997). According to a KPMG Knowledge Management Survey from early 2000s, 80 percent of the surveyed organizations had at that time some knowledge management projects in place, 40 percent had a formal knowledge management program, and 25 percent had appointed a Chief Knowledge Officer (Skyrme 2001).

The knowledge movement has seriously engaged business and management consultants also. The consultancy business has not only stepped into the game but also contributed much to the establishment of the knowledge movement. The first management conference in the United States which explicitly focused upon knowledge—beyond theories of artificial intelligence—was entitled 'Managing the Knowledge Asset into the 21st Century,' and was convened by Digital Equipment Corporation and the Technology Transfer Society at Purdue University in 1987.[1] The second one was on 'Knowledge Productivity' and was coordinated by Steelcase North America and EDS in April 1992. McKinsey and Company initiated their Knowledge Management Practice during the same time frame. According to Hull (2000: 49), the focus on knowledge and its management was an ideal opportunity for consultancy firms to restore their tarnished image associated with the numerous problems due to the business process reengineering fad.

1.1.2. *The Rise of the Knowledge Economy and Changing Organization*

Another impetus to the knowledge governance approach has been the many ways in which knowledge and organization have been linked in various discussions of the 'knowledge economy.' To be sure, getting analytically to grips with the construct of the 'knowledge economy' is, to put it mildly, an undertaking of very considerable complexity, because the number of relevant variables would seem to be overwhelming and causality would seem to be so complicated that any model can only capture select processes and mechanisms. Indeed, most social scientists have treated the knowledge economy as a sort of overall framing vision, and have focused on select mechanisms, for example, how organization is affected by information and communication technologies (ICT), the increasing importance of human capital inputs, and the increasingly distributed nature of knowledge. Consider these in turn.

Virtually all discussions of the knowledge economy invoke ICT as a main driver and primary characteristic of the knowledge economy. Many see ICT as the heartbeats that animate the knowledge economy—ICT makes information cheaper to process, store, and transmit. For example, arguments are put forward that ICT drives productivity increases, facilitates the formation of networks within and between firms, flattens hierarchies, reduces overall firm size, facilitates (external and internal) scale economies, eases the modularization of production, etc. (Brynjolfsson et al. 1994; Culnan, Armstrong, and Hitt 1999; Garicano

[1] Source: www.entovation.com/momentum/momentum.htm.

and Rossi-Hansberg 2003; Paganetto 2004). Given the context of knowledge economy, it may seem more reasonable to look at those tendencies that are knowledge rather than information related. Many writers have stressed the distinction between information and knowledge (e.g., Boisot 1998; Nonaka and Takeuchi 1995; Spender 1996*a*; Teece 2001). Knowledge is seen as a partly tacit and context-dependent capacity to select, interpret, and aggregate information which, in turn, is explicit and less contextual. As Teece (2001: 130) puts it: 'A Bloomberg or Reuters newsfeed is information. The opinions of the leading analysts and commentators, putting the news into context and enabling it to be used to create value, are more akin to knowledge.' The knowledge economy is indeed remarkable by the growing importance of not only information but also knowledge.

A manifestation of this is the strongly growing importance of human capital. Acquiring human capital is largely a matter of reducing the costs of selecting, interpreting, and aggregating information and knowledge.[2] In management research, the increasing importance of human capital has been reflected in notions of 'knowledge workers' (Zuboff 1988) and 'knowledge-intensive firms' (Starbuck 1992), as mentioned earlier. Many argue that such firms are differentiated from 'traditional' firms in terms of organizational control by relying less on direction through the exercise of authority, eschewing high-powered performance incentives, and embracing 'culture' and 'clan' modes of organizational control (Adler 2001; Child and McGrath 2001).

While information is becoming continuously cheaper to process, store, and transmit (Garicano and Rossi-Hansberg 2003), an increasingly influential argument asserts that the knowledge needed to create value is becoming increasingly dispersed, either in direct geographical terms (e.g., Doz, Santos, and Williamson 2001) or in terms of technological

[2] A number of studies and indicators suggest that the importance of human capital has increased massively. Thus, in terms of overall impressionistic figures, the proportion of knowledge workers, such as managers, professionals, and technical workers, increased from 10% of the US workforce in 1900 to 17% in 1950 to 33% in 1999. Creative workers, such as engineers and architects, artists and entertainers, increased from 1% in 1900 to 2% in 1950 to 5.7% in 1999. Large-scale econometric studies provide the same message. Jorgenson and Fraumeni (1995) show that in the US economy, human capital overwhelms physical capital in terms of contributing to value added and that its weight has been continuously increasing. Machin and van Reenen (1998) present evidence that the relative demand for skilled labor has increased in the 1990s in the seven OECD countries they investigate. Berman, Bound, and Griliches (1994) find a similar tendency in the US economy, as do sector and industry-specific studies. For example, Demsetz (1996) shows that the share of high-skilled employees in US banking has strongly increased (around 8 percentage points from 1983 to 1995), the most pronounced increase in any US industry.

disciplines (Brusoni, Prencipe, and Pavitt 2001; Coombs and Metcalfe 2000; Granstrand, Patel, and Pavitt 1997; Matusik and Hill 1998). Firms need to build and maintain an increasing number of 'knowledge nodes' with lead users, universities, technical service institutes, user communities (e.g., Brusoni, Prencipe, and Pavitt 2001; Coombs and Metcalfe 2000; Granstrand, Patel, and Pavitt 1997; Hodgson 1998; Smith 2000; Von Hippel 1988; Wang and von Tunzelmann 2000). Because firms increasingly need to rely on a growing number of knowledge specialists, whether employees or outside knowledge agents, they also need to have the absorptive capacity to *potentially* source an increasing number of technologies. In fact, it is arguable that many knowledge nodes, particularly to universities, are established in order to create this absorptive capacity (Pavitt 1991). The tendency for many firms to have an increasing number of technological disciplines in-house, even if product portfolios are shrinking, may also be a reflection of the need to increase absorptive capacity in the face of an increasingly complex division of labor in science and technology (Brusoni, Prencipe, and Pavitt 2001).

This tendency is seen as having strong transformative implications for economic organization, notably the employment relations, internal organization structure, and the boundaries of the firm. For example, the increasing reliance on 'knowledge workers,' specialists, expert talent, etc. that is seen to accompany the increasingly distributed nature of productive knowledge challenges traditional authority relations (because knowledge workers have much more bargaining power, Rajan and Zingales 2001) and makes extensive delegation of decision rights necessary in firms' internal organizations (so as to colocate rights with knowledge; Mendelsson and Pillai 1999). With respect to 'external organization' (to use Marshall's 1920 phrase), firms increasingly engage in relational forms of contracting that can simultaneously keep opportunism at bay and create the rich interfaces that are necessary for sharing and integration of complementary knowledge (Heiman and Nickerson 2002; Helper, McDuffie, and Sabel 2000). Thus, a picture is emerging of new kinds of firms that '...tend to be non-vertically integrated, human-capital-intensive organisations that operate in a highly competitive environment' (Zingales 2000: 1643), yet are still strongly networked to other firms and to knowledge institutions.

Virtually all of those who have written on the subject agree that tasks and activities in the knowledge economy need to be coordinated in a manner that is different from the management of traditional manufacturing activities (as portrayed in, for example, Chandler 1962). Similarly, there are numerous arguments around that the boundaries of firms change under the impact of the need to make better use of existing knowledge, source new knowledge, etc. These accounts usually treat knowledge as a kind of contingency factor that affects organization. The focus of the knowledge governance approach that this collection of essays contributes to is rather to take organization as the independent variable, treating the outcomes of knowledge processes as the dependent variable. However, the two approaches are two sides of the same coin, a coin that is made up of the intersection of knowledge (processes) and organization.

1.1.3. *The Knowledge Governance Approach*

The 'knowledge governance approach' (Foss 2007; Foss et al. 2003) which is highlighted in this book represents an emerging attempt to think systematically about the intersection of knowledge and organization. 'Governing knowledge processes' means choosing governance structures (e.g., markets, hybrids, hierarchies) (Williamson 1996) and governance and coordination mechanisms (contracts, directives, reward schemes, incentives, trust, management styles, organizational culture, etc.), so as to favorably influence processes of transferring, sharing, integrating, using, and creating knowledge. Such structures and mechanisms matter to organizational-level knowledge processes because they define the incentives and coordinate the actions of organizational members in knowledge processes (Foss and Mahnke 2003).

By 'governance mechanisms' we make reference to the specific apparatus that is deployed to influence organizational members' behaviors, particularly in relation to their engagement in knowledge processes. The governance mechanisms can be both formal, such as goal setting, planning, directives, rules and regulations, and residual rights of control (Bensaou and Venkatraman 1995; Grandori 2001; Kumar and Seth 1998), and informal, such as trust, management styles, organizational cultures, communication flows, and channels (Arrow 1974; Michailova and Husted 2003). Formal and informal mechanisms often are applied simultaneously. They can, to mention but a few interaction options, complement or substitute each other (Poppo and Zenger 2002), reinforce each other's effects (Grandori and Soda 1995), weaken each other's application (Edelman et al. 2004), enhance some of each other's features (Gulati and Singh 1998), or moderate each other's scope (Gulati 1995; Uzzi 1997).

Thus, the knowledge governance approach addresses such issues as, what is the impact of different kinds of (systems and strength of) incentives on knowledge sharing, integration, and creation, and how does this work through individual level motivation and cognition? What combinations of governance mechanisms are best suited for promoting knowledge sharing, integration, and creation within and between firms? What are the organizational and exchange hazards of knowledge processes, and how does the deployment of governance mechanisms remedy such hazards? Knowledge governance scholars address these issues on the basis of explicit micro-foundations, that is, explicit assumptions about the individual motivation, preferences, expectations, cognitive styles, etc. These scholars trace the causal processes running from organization (macro) to individuals and their interaction (micro) and explore how these micro-processes give rise to organization-level knowledge-related outcomes, that is, organization-level knowledge utilization, sharing, creation, etc. We will provide a fuller picture of the knowledge governance approach in the concluding chapter, and instead, pose some of the open questions, as we see them, and the contributions made by the chapters in this book.

1.1.4. *Governing Knowledge Processes: Some Open Questions*

This book's starting point is that knowledge processes can be governed. This book attempts to box the compass on knowledge governance and, hopefully, stake out a prominent position in this developing field by articulating a detailed examination of various knowledge governance mechanisms. All contributions to this book deal with particular mechanisms, explain these mechanisms' essence, nature, and specific features, and theorize about their advantages and disadvantages in relation to particular knowledge processes and, where appropriate, in relation to alternative governance mechanisms.

Looking across the chapters in this book, it appears that a fundamental issue that still remains unresolved, neither academically nor in practice, is whether in the new economy the knowledge workers have reversed the traditional relationship between employer and employee. In a detailed discussion of this issue, Frank (2000: 2002–4) concluded that a positive answer to this question is not substantiated in any way. Journalists and popular management writers alike, for example, Peters and Waterman (1982) and Handy (1997), fuel the impression that the company management and power is essentially in the knowledgeable employees' hands.

Executives are remarkably silent, probably because such an impression, as far as it stays at the impression level, suits well the fact that they manage and are paid for managing their knowledge workers. Our argument is that the increasing importance of knowledge workers suggests the need for new governance mechanisms that recognize the fact that it is increasingly the employees who possess the knowledge able to generate wealth rather than that the employees are equipped with the power to manage because they are knowledge owners.[3] Yet, the issue remains whether governance mechanisms, even new/innovative ones, do/will change the employer–employee relationship in its fundamental nature.

We have several times referred to knowledge governance mechanism in general as a particular management/administrative apparatus. However, it is worth questioning such a position and extending the box that has so far framed much of the thinking in relation to governance mechanisms. For instance, is it worth considering the entrepreneurial functions of the firms rather than the administrative ones? If so, do entrepreneurial functions provide the basis of some unique governance mechanisms, are those compatible with mechanisms associated with the administrative functions, can the coexistence of various functions open the possibility for particular combinations of governance mechanisms, etc.? The problem-finding problem-solving perspective discussed by Heiman et al. in this volume provides important hints in this direction by outlining implications of this perspective for examining entrepreneurship and the entrepreneurial firm.

Another unresolved question is whether knowledge governance primarily aims at optimizing the cost of the processes of managing knowledge or whether there is more to it. This raises associated questions, such as whether this cost is determinable at all and what role time plays in conducting a particular knowledge process and applying specific governance mechanisms and observing effects from it. The relation between knowledge processes and governance issues is an under-researched area, both theoretically and empirically, in comparison with writings concerning the characteristics of knowledge, knowledge taxonomies, how knowledge may be disseminated within and between organizations and the philosophical foundations of knowledge. To date there has been little consideration of research heuristics linking governance and knowledge.

[3] For a discussion of the advantages and drawbacks of different kinds of control for managing knowledge workers, for example, structural, ideological, technocratic, and sociological control mechanisms, see Ray (1986).

An issue that does not transpire through the chapters, at least not explicitly and strongly enough, is context. Context, defined at different levels, is important for examining any issues relevant to organizations. In relation to knowledge governance, obviously, the issues and challenges we have identified will not simultaneously confront all firms at the same time in the same manner. Organizations embedded in certain national cultural and institutional contexts will deal with knowledge governance issues differently from those located in other macro environments. Industry matters as well and so does the particular organizational context. Taking context seriously will allow testing of the robustness of the proposed theories and analytical frameworks.

The chapters in this book extend considerably the list of unanswered questions and unresolved issues. The chapters' introductions and concluding sections outline existing gaps and suggest potential fruitful avenues for future research, respectively. It becomes apparent that the knowledge governance field is hungry for and ready to absorb theoretical and empirical examination of various causal mechanisms and contextual factors in relations among knowledge processes and ways of their governing.

The contributions to this book demonstrate convincingly that the governance of knowledge processes can be investigated in many different ways. As editors, we opted intentionally for perspectives from different disciplines and fields, and so we let rather different voices speak on the knowledge governance theme.

The different bodies of theory that we consider in this book vary on numerous dimensions and have correspondingly different implications for the understanding of the governance of knowledge processes. Part of the motivation of this book was to see whether the different bodies of knowledge would substitute, complement, build on, overlap, or conflict each other. We find this to be an appropriate objective. Although it might be tempting to aim at overcoming the fragmentation in the field, it seems achieving such an aim is still premature. This in itself explains the idea behind an edited volume. Once a particular research field has somewhat already taken shape, coherent works that take a sharp and original cut through a particular set of issues seem to be most desirable. But when the field itself is still inchoate, collected volumes seem to have a certain advantage. Precisely because the counters of the field are not yet clearly demarcated, the natural divergences of a collected volume are better suited to exploring a large part of the idea-space.[4]

[4] We thank one of the OUP anonymous advisors for making this observation.

1.1.5. *The Contributions to this Book*

While the chapters in this book vary on several dimensions, they are united by the main overall idea, namely, to identify and examine knowledge governance mechanisms. An important theme that unites the chapters in this book is the question of *which knowledge processes are influenced by governance mechanisms*. Some chapters are concerned with knowledge generation and growth (Osterloh and Weibel), others relate to knowledge sharing (Husted and Michailova), a third cluster of chapters addresses both knowledge creation and sharing (Heiman et al., Grandori, Argote, and Kane), and a final group focuses on knowledge utilization (Christensen and Knudsen, Foss and Foss). Figure 1.1 positions the contributions along two dimensions: the type of knowledge processes addressed and the type of governance mechanisms examined in terms of the formal–informal dichotomy.

This leads us to the second dimension that goes across the contributions in this book, namely, the *type of knowledge governance mechanisms*. While some authors discuss exclusively informal mechanisms (Foss and Foss, Argote and Kane, Husted and Michailova), others examine in detail how

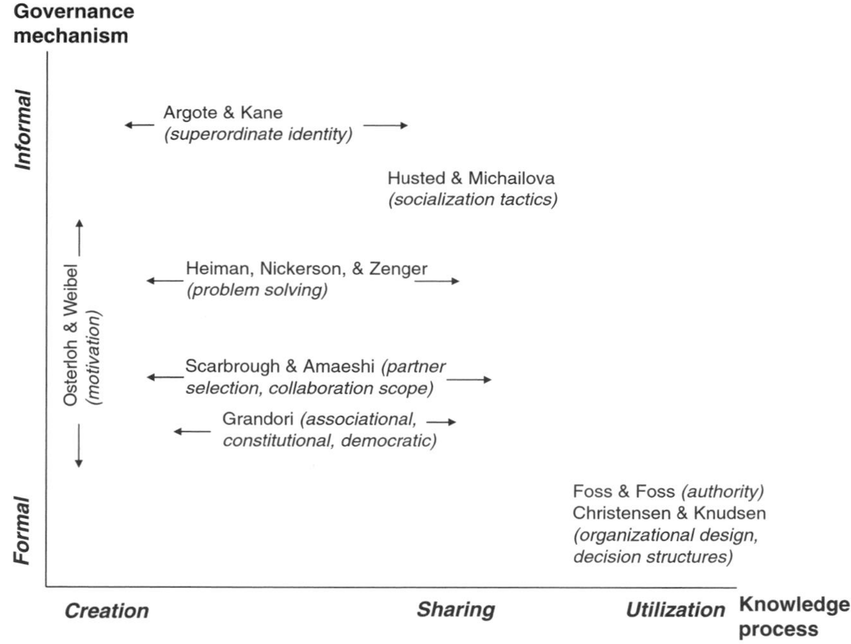

Figure 1.1. Knowledge processes and type of governance mechanisms

formal governance mechanisms are employed to influence knowledge processes (Christensen and Knudsen). A third group of authors discuss mechanisms that spread between the poles of the formal–informal continuum. For instance, Osterloh and Weibel's chapter takes seriously both extrinsic and intrinsic motivation; Heiman et al.'s problem-identification–problem-solving perspective includes both formal and informal elements; and Garndori's associational, constitutional, and democratic governance mechanisms, too, spread over the continuum between formal and informal mechanisms. An interesting, and related, dimension of several contributions is the interaction effects that are likely to appear due to the application of particular mechanisms. For instance, some informal mechanisms, for example superordinate identity (Argote and Kane), are argued to act as substitute to monitoring, and socialization tactics (Husted and Michailova) is recommended to be applied as a substitute to detailed and expensive formalized contracts.

The chapters in this book are positioned differently in terms of the *scope of the governance mechanisms* they address, from intraorganizational to interorganizational. As illustrated in Figure 1.2, some chapters specifically

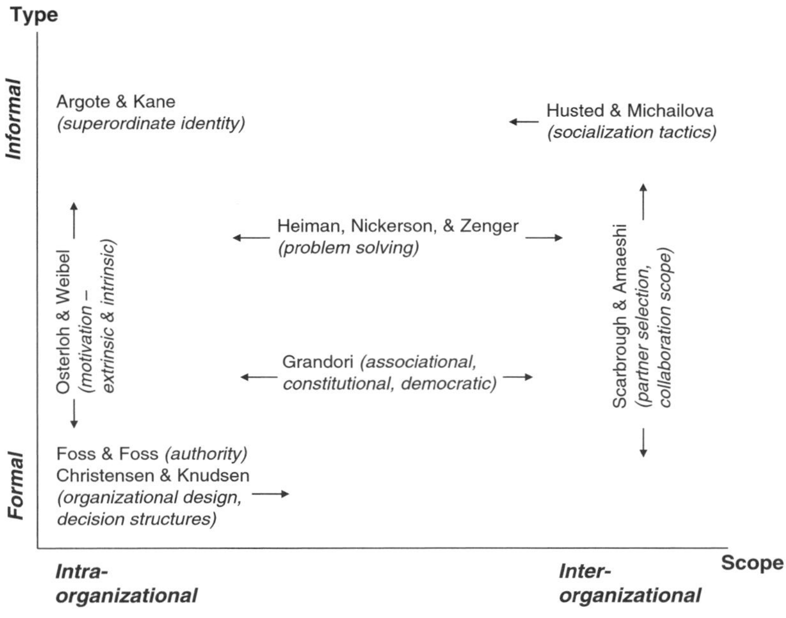

Figure 1.2. Type and scope of knowledge governance mechanisms

focus on either intra- (Christensen and Knudsen, Foss and Foss, Osterloh and Weibel, Argote and Kane) or interorganizational settings (Husted and Michailova) while others (Grandori, Heiman et al.) theorize about knowledge governance issues in both intra- and interorganizational contexts.

This book is a mosaic of *theoretical* and *empirical* contributions. Among the latter group of contributions are Argote and Kane's chapter based on a field study and experiments and Scarbrough and Amaeshi's chapter which presents a detailed case study of a major collaborative research program in the European aerospace industry. Christensen and Knudsen's chapter, too, relies on several cases to argue the application of their proposed analytical framework.

The chapters discuss knowledge governance from *different disciplinary and theoretical perspectives*. Grandori's and Foss and Foss's chapters are both grounded in organizational economics, the latter also taking a point of departure in the problem-solving perspective. The questions addressed in Heiman et al.'s chapter and their extension of the problem-solving perspective are embedded in the strategic management literature. Christensen and Knudsen's framework is grounded in formal organizational theory. Osterloh and Weibel's analysis relies largely on social psychology and psychological economics. The organizational behavior literature is taken seriously in Argote and Kane's and in Husted and Michailova's contributions. This variety of disciplines and theoretical orientations is a fortunate, but also a largely intended result of our initial fundamental organizing idea as editors to present multidisciplinary perspectives on knowledge governance in one volume. Exposing the reader to multiple voices from various disciplines seems necessary and fruitful to understand knowledge governance in its complex entirety. Yet, there can be different interpretations of the fact that there is no core group of theories that seem to be preferred by the contributors to this book. One possible interpretation can be that the field is at a multiparadigmatic, multitheoretical stage of development. An alternative interpretation could be that research in the field is slow to take seriously the opportunities for some consolidation, bridging, and dialogue among the seemingly diverse theoretical orientations and contributions. Felin and Spender's chapter offers a beautiful illustration of the fertility of explicit dialogues and exchange of ideas embedded in different theoretical preferences, in this case organizational theory and economics. To quote the very ending of their chapter,

> ...maybe it is the conversation that is most important, that we continue to interact across artificial disciplinary boundaries (language games), and resist the temptation to talk only to the members of our own community, thereby separating what we do and whatever intelligence we produce from the really important questions that concern those whose life is not lived in the ivory tower, the people who create real value and the real conditions of live.

We now turn to a brief presentation of the key contribution of each chapter.

The chapter by Heiman, Nickerson, and Zenger departs from and builds largely on Nickerson and Zenger's problem-solving perspective (2004) on knowledge governance. The authors review this emergent approach focused around organizing to discover valuable problems and efficient searching for solutions. The chapter elevates the existing literature in this stream by (*a*) summarizing both the problem finding and the problem solving of the earlier suggested perspective and (*b*) moving beyond laying out the elements of the perspective and discussing gaps and new potentially rewarding research trajectories. The chapter suggests several research programs that might create value for researchers and practitioners alike.

The claim that understanding organizations within the knowledge economy requires a firmer grip on the way knowledge held by individuals can be aggregated into organizational knowledge is a starting point in Christensen and Knudsen's chapter 'The architecture of knowledge organization.' Indeed, this is a serious issue that has been pointed out numerous times in the knowledge management literature and Christensen and Knudsen present a framework of how this aggregation can actually be achieved. They examine the fundamental relation between organizational design and the utilization of knowledge resources. Through several examples the authors illustrate how their framework can be used to analyze simultaneous decision-making in complex settings (like the UN Security Council) and to capture sequential decision processes. The chapter considers flexible decision structures facing a turbulent environment and fixed decision structures facing a stable, but complex task environment and in this way, it addresses various important problems emphasized in the knowledge management literature.

Similarly to Heiman et al., the chapter by Grandori also examines creation of valuable new knowledge, however, extending the notion by discussing knowledge growth, that is, the generation/production of new valid knowledge. She, too, develops her arguments in both intra- (innovative firms) and interfirm (innovative alliances) contexts. Drawing from contributions in organization theory and organizational economics, Grandori argues that constitutional and democratic governance mechanisms, while under-researched, are particularly important for the governance of innovation. She concludes that governing knowledge growth is associated with a combination of mechanisms linked to market-like, firm-like, and communitarian attributes.

The chapter by Foss and Foss focuses on knowledge utilization and raises the issue of whether knowledge that is distributed (i.e., is not possessed by any single mind, but that belongs to a group of interacting agents) is misaligned with authority as a governance mechanism. In other words, the authors question the argument that authority cannot be an efficient coordination mechanism in the presence of distributed knowledge. Relying on ideas from organizational economics (like Grandori in this book) and on problem solving (like Heiman et al. in this book), Foss and Foss differentiate between two types of authority and conclude that some manifestations of authority are an efficient governance mechanism under conditions of distributed knowledge.

Similarly to Heiman et al. and Grandori in this volume, Osterloh and Weibel's chapter analyzes knowledge production. Borrowing from social psychology and psychological economics, the authors frame explorative knowledge production as a social dilemma. They compare solutions to social dilemmas for exploitative and explorative knowledge work and conclude that the differences between the two are mainly with respect to cognitive distance or cognitive overlap and are crucial for the solutions that can be applied to overcome social dilemmas. The authors further argue that extrinsic motivation—predisposing transactional solutions—cannot sufficiently solve social dilemmas associated with exploration.

The next two chapters, by Argote and Kane and by Husted and Michailova, are both inspired by the organizational behavior literature. They each examine particular organizational behavior concepts, superordinate identity and socialization tactics, respectively, and argue that these are two efficient and relatively low-cost knowledge governance mechanisms. On the basis of a field study and laboratory experiments, Argote and Kane prove that the sense of belonging to a higher order unit—a superordinate social identity—facilitates knowledge creation and transfer among employees and across units in a firm and elevates receptivity to innovations. In other words, knowledge creation and knowledge transfer tend to be greater across units that share such identity than across units that are not part of such a relationship. The authors also demonstrate that the benefits of subscribing to a superordinate social identity are more pronounced when knowledge is not demonstrable or easily recognized. The authors predict that superordinate identity can be a mechanism that efficiently substitutes monitoring/close supervision.

The chapter by Husted and Michailova proposes socialization tactics as an informal and relatively low-cost knowledge governance mechanism. The authors argue that in contexts where it is difficult to codify all important issues in formal contracts, socialization tactics appears to be an attractive alternative. Their chapter has an interesting twist: they examine socialization tactics as a mechanism that managers can apply within their firm in order to influence the knowledge-sharing behavior of knowledge workers involved in interorganizational R&D collaborations. Socialization tactics appears as an efficient mechanism for dealing with R&D employees' dual allegiance, for example these employees being loyal to both their own organization and the collaboration. The authors develop the distinction between four types of R&D workers—lonely wolfs, company soldiers, gone native, and gatekeepers—and argue that managers should apply different socialization tactics to govern these workers' participation in external collaborative networks.

Like Husted and Michailova, Scarbrough and Amaeshi, too, take the R&D collaboration as the context of their study. This empirical study discusses the distinctive challenges the open approach to innovation processes poses to knowledge governance. These challenges, the authors argue, go some way beyond the problem of absorbing knowledge because open innovation involves a qualitative shift in the way the firm creates, exploits, and organizes knowledge. This has wide-ranging implications for the way the focal firm manages itself and its knowledge base. At the very least, open innovation implies a reduced dependence on internal R&D functions and a greater willingness to trade knowledge with external collaborators. More broadly, though, the serious pursuit of open innovation is likely to extend to radical changes in the structure and management practices of the firm to foster greater interactivity with the expanding ecology of knowledge providers. Scarbrough and Amaeshi also discuss the dilemma between stability and change in the form of governance adopted. Examining the European Union-funded mega-project MOZART they conclude that because innovation proceeds sporadically and sometimes erratically from existing knowledge to new knowledge, it is difficult to sustain a particular governance solution over the course of the whole process. They demonstrate how, in the case of MOZART, this dilemma is exacerbated by the scope and complexity of the work involved.

The chapter by Felin and Spender is 'an exchange of ideas on knowledge governance.' The two authors engage in a dialogue on the epistemological foundations of knowledge management in general and knowledge governance in particular. The duo's starting point is a discussion of what they call 'first principles': the need for micro- (individual level) foundations of knowledge-related arguments, the aggregation of macro- into macro-elements/processes/phenomena which requires moving from macro to micro explanations, and finally, the importance of collective action and interaction among individuals in their context. This chapter problematizes some of the knowledge governance foundations and poses important questions that require further clarifying and refining.

Our concluding chapter (Chapter 11) takes stock on the extent to which these questions have been addressed by the chapters and where the knowledge governance approach is likely to head in the future.

References

Adler, P. S. 2001. 'Market, hierarchy, and trust: The knowledge economy and the future of capitalism,' *Organization Science* 12(2): 215–34.

Arrow, K. J. 1974. *The Limits of Organization*. New York: Norton.

Barney, J. 1991. 'Firm resources and sustained competitive advantages,' *Journal of Management* 17(1): 99–120.

Bartlett, C. A. and S. Ghoshal. 1989. *Managing Across Borders: The Transnational Solution*. Massachusetts, Boston: Harvard Business School Press.

Bennett, R. H., III. 1998. 'The importance of tacit knowledge in strategic deliberations and decisions,' *Management Decision* 36(9): 589–97.

Bensaou, B. M. and R. V. Venkatraman. 1995. 'Configurations of interorganizational relationships: A comparison between U.S. and Japanese automakers,' *Management Science* 41(9): 1471–93.

Berman, E., J. Bound, and Z. Griliches. 1994. 'Changes in the demand for skilled labor within U.S. manufacturing: Evidence from the annual survey of manufacturing,' *Quarterly Journal of Economics* 109(2): 367–98.

Birkinshaw, J., R. Nobel, and J. Ridderstråle. 2002. 'Knowledge as a contingency variable: Do the characteristics of knowledge predict organization structure?,' *Organization Science* 13(3): 274–90.

Blackler, F. 1995. 'Knowledge, knowledge work and organizations: An overview and interpretation,' *Organization Studies* 16(6): 1020–46.

—— 2000. 'Collective wisdom,' *People Management* 6(13): 61–3.

Boisot, M. 1998. *Knowledge Assets, Securing Competitive Advantage in the Information Economy*. Oxford: Oxford University Press.

Brown, J. S. and P. Duguid. 1991. 'Organization learning and communities of practice: Towards a unified view of working, learning and innovation,' *Organization Science* 2(1): 40–57.

Brusoni, S., A. Prencipe, and K. Pavitt. 2001. 'Knowledge specialization, organizational coupling, and the boundaries of the firm: Why do firms know more than they make?,' *Administrative Science Quarterly* 46(4): 597–621.

Brynjolfsson, E., T. W. Malone, V. Gurbaxani, and A. Kambil. 1994. 'Does information technology lead to smaller firms?,' *Management Science* 40(12): 1628–44.

Chakravarthy, B., S. McEvily, Y. Doz, and D. Rau. 2003. 'Knowledge management and competitive advantage,' in M. Easterby-Smith and M. A. Lyles (eds.) *Handbook of Organizational Learning and Knowledge Management*. Massachusetts, Oxford: Blackwell Publishers.

Chandler, A. D. 1962. *Strategy and Structure*. Massachusetts, Cambridge: MIT Press.

Child, J. and R. G. McGrath. 2001. 'Organizations unfettered: Organizational form in an information intensive economy,' *The Academy of Management Journal* 44(6): 1135–48.

Cook, S. D. N. and J. S. Brown. 1999. 'Bridging epistemologies: The generative dance between organizational knowledge and organizational knowing,' *Organization Science* 10(4): 381–400.

Coombs, R. and S. Metcalfe. 2000. 'Organizing for innovation: Co-ordinating distributed innovation capabilities,' in N. J. Foss and V. Mahnke (eds.) *Competence, Governance, and Entrepreneurship*. Oxford: Oxford University Press.

Culnan, M. J., P. K. Armstrong, and L. M. Hitt. 1999. 'Information technology and firm boundaries: Evidence from panel data,' *Information Systems Research* 10(2): 134–49.

Demsetz, R. 1996. *The Re-tooling of the Banking Industry: Evidence from the Labor Force*. Working paper, Federal Reserve Bank of New York.

Doz, Y., J. Santos, and P. Williamson. 2001. *From Global to Metanational*. New York: Harvard Business School Press.

Drucker, P. F. 1993. *Post-Capitalist Society*. Oxford: Butterworth-Heinemann.

—— 1999. 'Knowledge-worker productivity: The biggest challenge,' *California Management Review* 41(2): 79–94.

Easterby-Smith, M. and M. A. Lyles. 2003. *Handbook of Organizational Learning and Knowledge management*. Massachusetts, Oxford: Blackwell Publishing.

Edelman, L. F., M. Bresnen, S. Newell, H. Scarbrough, and J. Swan. 2004. 'The benefits and pitfalls of social capital: Empirical evidence from two organizations in the United Kingdom,' *British Journal of Management* 15: 59–69.

Fang, Y., M. Wade, A. Delios, and P. W. Beamish. 2007. 'International diversification, subsidiary performance, and the mobility of knowledge resources,' *Strategic Management Journal* 28(10): 1053–64.

Foss, N. J. 2007. 'The emerging knowledge governance approach: Challenges and characteristics,' *Organization* 14: 29–52.

——and V. Mahnke. 2003. 'Knowledge management: What does organizational economics contribute?,' in M. Easterby-Smith and M. A. Lyles (eds.) *Handbook of Knowledge Management*. Massachusetts, Oxford: Blackwell Publishing.

——K. Husted, S. Michailova, and T. Pedersen. 2003. *Governing Knowledge Processes: Theoretical Foundations and Research Opportunities*. Working paper no. 1, Center for Knowledge Governance, Copenhagen Business School.

Frank, U. 2000. 'Multi-perspective enterprise models as a conceptual foundation for knowledge management,' *Proceedings of the Hawaii International Conference on System Sciences* 3.

Garicano, L. and E. Rossi-Hansberg. 2003. *Organization and Inequality in the Knowledge Economy*. Working paper, University of Chicago.

Gerlach, M. L. 1992. 'The Japanese corporate network: A block model analysis,' *Administrative Science Quarterly* 37(1): 105–39.

Grandori, A. 2001. 'Neither hierarchy nor identity: Knowledge governance mechanisms and the theory of the firm,' *Journal of Management and Governance* 5(3–4): 381–99.

——and G. Soda. 1995. 'Inter-firm networks: Antecedents, mechanisms and forms,' *Organization Studies* 16(2): 184–214.

Granstrand, O., P. Patel, and K. L. R. Pavitt. 1997. 'Multi-technology corporations: Why they have "distributed" rather than "distinctive core" competencies,' *California* Management Review 39(4): 8–25.

Grant, R. M. 1996. 'Toward a knowledge-based theory of the firm,' *Strategic Management Journal* 17: 109–22.

Gulati, R. 1995. 'Does familiarity breed trust? The implications of repeated ties for contractual choice in alliances,' *The Academy of Management Journal* 38(1): 85–112.

——and H. Singh. 1998. 'The architecture of cooperation: Managing coordination costs and appropriation concerns in strategic alliances,' *Administrative Science Quarterly* 43(4): 781–814.

Gupta, A. K. and V. Govindarajan. 1991. 'Knowledge flows and the structure of control within multinational corporations,' *Academy of Management Review* 18(4): 768–92.

————2000. 'Knowledge flows within MNCs,' *Strategic Management Journal* 21(8/9): 473–96.

Handy, C. B. 1997. *The Hungry Spirit*. London: Hutchinson.

Hansen, M. T. 2002. 'Knowledge networks: Explaining effective knowledge sharing in multiunit companies,' *Organization Science* 13(3): 232–48.

——M. L. Mors and B. Løvås. 2005. 'Knowledge sharing in organizations: Multiple networks, multiple Phases,' *Academy of Management Journal* 48(5): 776–93.

Hedlund, G. 1994. 'A model of knowledge management in the N-form corporation,' *Strategic Management Journal* 15: 73–91.

Heiman, B. and J. A. Nickerson. 2002. 'Towards reconciling transaction cost economics and the knowledge-based view of the firm: The context of inter-firm collaborations,' *International Journal of the Economics of Business* 9(1): 97–116.

Helper, S., J. P. McDuffie, and C. Sabel. 2000. 'Pragmatic collaborations: Advancing knowledge while controlling opportunism,' *Industrial and Corporate Change* 9(3): 443–87.

Hodgson, G. 1998. *Economics and Utopia*. London: Routledge.

Hull, R. 2000. 'Knowledge management and the conduct of expert labor,' in C. Prichard, R. Hull, M. Chumer and H. Willmott (eds.) *Managing Knowledge: Critical Investigations of Work and Learning*. Hampshire: Macmillan Press.

Jensen, R. and G. Szulanski. 2004. 'Stickiness and the adaptation of organizational practices in cross-border knowledge transfers,' *Journal of International Business Studies* 35(6): 508–23.

Jorgenson, D. W. and B. M. Fraumeni. 1995. 'Investment in education and U.S. economic growth,' in D. W. Jorgenson (eds.) *Productivity and Postwar US Economic Growth*. Massachusetts, Cambridge: MIT Press.

Kogut, B. 2000. 'The network as knowledge: Generative rules and the emergence of structure,' *Strategic Management Journal* 21(3): 405–25.

——and U. Zander. 1993. 'Knowledge of the firm and the evolutionary theory of the multinational corporation,' *Journal of International Business Studies* 24(4): 625–45.

Kostova, T. 1999. 'Transnational transfer of strategic organizational practices: A contextual perspective,' *Academy of Management Review* 24(2): 308–24.

——and K. Roth. 2002. 'Adoption of an organizational practice by subsidiaries of multinational corporations: Institutional and relational effects,' *Academy of Management Journal* 45(1): 215–33.

Kumar, S. and A. Seth. 1998. 'The design of coordination and control mechanisms for managing joint venture-parent relationships,' *Strategic Management Journal* 19(6): 579–99.

Lave, J. and E. Wenger. 1991. *Situated Learning: Legitimate Peripheral Participation*. Cambridge: Cambridge University Press.

Li, L. 2005. 'The effects of trust and shared vision on inward knowledge transfer in subsidiaries' intra- and inter-organizational relationships,' *International Business Review* 14(1): 77–95.

Lomi, A. and A. Grandi. 1997. 'The network structure of inter-firm relationships in the southern Italian mechanical industry,' in M. Ebers (eds.) *The Formation of Inter-Organizational Networks*. Oxford: Oxford University Press.

Machin, S. and J. van Reenen. 1998. 'Technology and changes in skill structure evidence from seven OECD countries,' *Quarterly Journal of Economics* 113(4): 1215–44.

Madhok, A. and C. Liu. 2006. 'A coevolutionary theory of the multinational firm,' *Journal of International Management* 12(1): 1–21.

Matusik, S. F. and C. W. L. Hill. 1998. 'The utilization of contingent work, knowledge creation and competitive advantage,' *Academy of Management Review* 23(4): 680–97.

Mendelsson, H. and R. R. Pillai. 1999. 'Information age organizations, dynamics, and performance,' *Journal of Economic Behavior and Organization* 38(1): 253–81.

Merali, Y. 2000. 'The organic metaphor in knowledge management,' *Emergence* 2(4): 14–22.

Michailova, S. and K. Husted. 2003. 'Knowledge sharing hostility in Russian firms,' *California Management Review* 45(3): 59–77.

Miles, R. E. and C. C. Snow. 1992. 'Causes of failure in network organizations,' *California Management Review* 34(4): 53–72.

Minbaeva, D. B. 2007. 'Knowledge transfer in multinational corporations,' *Management International Review* 47(4): 567–93.

Newman, V. 1997. 'Redefining knowledge management to deliver competitive advantage,' *Journal of Knowledge Management* 1(2): 123–8.

Nickerson, J. A. and T. R. Zenger. 2004. 'A knowledge-based theory of a firm—the problem solving perspective,' *Organization Science* 15(6): 617–32.

Nielsen, B. B. and S. Michailova. 2007. 'Knowledge management systems in multinational corporations: Typology and transitional dynamics,' *Long Range Planning* 40(3): 314–40.

Nohria, N. and C. Garcia-Pont. 1991. 'Global strategic linkages and industry structure,' *Strategic Management Journal* 12(4): 105–24.

Nonaka, I. 1994. 'A dynamic theory of organizational knowledge creation,' *Organization Science* 5(1): 14–37.

—— and H. Takeuchi. 1995. *The Knowledge-Creating Company: How Japanese Companies Create the Dynamics of Innovation*. New York: Oxford University Press.

Offsey, S. 1997. 'Knowledge management: Linking people to knowledge for bottom line results,' *Journal of Knowledge Management* 1(2): 113–22.

Paganetto, L. 2004. *Knowledge Economy, Information Technologies and Growth*. Aldershot: Ashgate Publishing Company.

Pavitt, K. 1991. 'What makes basic research economically useful?,' *Research Policy* 20(2): 109–19.

Peters, T. J. and R. H. Waterman, Jr. 1982. *In Search of Excellence: Lessons from America's Best-Run Companies*. New York: Warner Books.

Polanyi, M. 1967. *The Tacit Dimension*. Garden City: Anchor Books.

Poppo, L. and T. Zenger. 2002. 'Do formal contracts and relational governance function as substitutes or complements?,' *Strategic Management Journal* 23(8): 707–25.

Powell, W. W. 1990. 'Neither market nor hierarchy: Network forms of organization,' *Research in Organizational Behavior* 12: 295–336.

——, K. W. Koput, and L. Smith-Doerr. 1996. 'Interorganizational collaboration and the locus of innovation: Networks of learning in biotechnology,' *Administrative Science Quarterly* 41(1): 116–45.

Rajan, R. and L. Zingales. 2001. *The Great Reversals: The Politics of Financial Development in the Twentieth Century*. Working paper no. 526, Center for Research in Security Prices, University of Chicago GSB.

Ray, C. A. 1986. 'Corporate culture: The last frontier of control,' *Journal of Management Studies* 23(3): 287–97.

Schulz, M. 2003. 'Pathways of relevance: Exploring inflows of knowledge into subunits of multinational corporations,' *Organization Science* 14(4): 440–59.

Skyrme, D. J. 2001. *Capitalizing on Knowledge, from e-Business to k-Business*. Butterworth-Heinemann.

Smith, K. 2000. *What is the 'Knowledge Economy'? Knowledge-Intensive Industries and Distributed Knowledge Bases*. Working paper, STEP group, Oslo.

Spender, J. C. 1996*a*. 'Organizational knowledge, learning and memory: Three concepts in search of a theory,' *Journal of Organizational Change Management* 9(1): 63–78.

—— 1996*b*. 'Competitive advantage from tacit knowledge? Unpacking the concept and its strategic implications,' in B. Moingeon and A. Edmondson (eds.) *Organizational Learning and Competitive Advantage*. London: Sage.

—— 1996*c*. 'Making knowledge the basis of a dynamic theory of the firm,' *Strategic Management Journal* 17(10): 45–62.

Starbuck, W. H. 1992. 'Learning by knowledge intensive firms,' *Journal of Management Studies* 29(6): 147–75.

Stewart, T. A. 1997. *Intellectual Capital: The New Wealth of Organizations*. New York: Doubleday.

Szulanski, G. 1996. 'Exploring internal stickiness: Impediments to the transfer of best practice within the firm,' *Strategic Management Journal* 17: 27–43.

—— R. Cappetta, and R. J. Jensen. 2004. 'When and how trustworthiness matters: Knowledge transfer and the moderating effect of causal ambiguity,' *Organization Science* 15(5): 600–13.

Teece, D. J. 1992. 'Competition, cooperation, and innovation: Organizational arrangements for regimes of rapid technological progress,' *Journal of Economic Behavior and Organization* 18(1): 1–25.

—— 2000. *Managing Intellectual Capital: Organizational, Strategic and Policy Dimensions*. Oxford: Oxford University Press.

—— 2001. 'Strategies or managing knowledge assets: The role of firm structure and industrial context,' in I. Nonaka and D. J. Teece (eds.) *Managing Industrial Knowledge: Creation Transfer and Utilization*. London: Sage.

——, G. Pisano, and A. Shuen. 1997. 'Dynamic capabilities and strategic management,' *Strategic Management Journal* 18(7): 509–33.

Tsai, W. 2001. 'Knowledge transfer in intraorganizational networks: Effects of network position and absorptive capacity on business unit innovation and performance,' *Academy of Management Journal* 44(5): 996–1004.

—— 2002. 'Social structure of "coopetition" within a multiunit organization: Coordination, competition, and intraorganizational knowledge sharing,' *Organization Science* 13(2): 179–90.

—— and S. Ghoshal. 1998. 'Social capital and value creation: The role of intrafirm networks,' *Academy of Management Journal* 41(4): 464–76.

Tsoukas, H. 1996. 'The firm as a distributed knowledge system: A constructivist approach,' *Strategic Management Journal* 17: 11–25.

Uzzi, B. 1997. 'Social structure and competition in interfirm networks: The paradox of embeddedness,' *Administrative Science Quarterly* 42(1): 35–67.

Von Hippel, E. 1988. *The Sources of Innovation*. New York: Oxford University Press.

Wang, K. Q. and N. von Tunzelmann. 2000. 'Complexity and the functions of the firm: Breadth and depth,' *Research Policy* 29(7–8): 805–18.

Weick, K. 1977. 'Enactment Processes in Organizations,' in B. M. Staw and G. R. Salancik (eds.) *New Directions in Organizational Behavior.* Chicago: St Clair Press.

Weick, K. E. 1995. *Sensemaking in Organizations*. Thousand Oaks: Sage Publications.

Wernerfelt, B. 1984. 'A resource-based view of the firm,' *Strategic Management Journal* 5(2): 171–80.

Williamson, O. E. 1996. *The Mechanisms of Governance*. Oxford: Oxford University Press.

Winter, S. G. 1987. 'Knowledge and competence as strategic assets,' in D. J. Teece (ed.) *The Competitive Challenge*. Massachusetts, Cambridge: Ballinger.

Zenger, T. and W. S. Hesterly. 1997. 'The disaggregation of corporations: Selective intervention, high-powered incentives, and molecular units,' *Organization Science* 8(3): 209–22.

Zingales, L. 2000. 'In search of new foundations,' *Journal of Finance* 55(4): 1623–53.

Zuboff, S. 1988. *In the Age of the Smart Machine*. New York: Heinemann.

2

Governing knowledge creation: a problem-finding and problem-solving perspective

Bruce Heiman, Jackson Nickerson, and Todd Zenger

2.1. Introduction

The formation of knowledge has long been recognized as a key driver of value creation both within firms and within economies (e.g., see the work of Nelson and Winter 1982, as well as recent work by Furman, Porter, and Stern 2002, and Von Hippel and Tyre 1993). While knowledge formation has received much attention, the mechanisms by which knowledge and its formation are governed until recently have been largely ignored. Theories of governance and organization have directed their focus elsewhere on topics of exchange, knowledge transfer, and production efficiency. Rather limited attention has been directed at how firms and markets efficiently organize (govern) the process of creating new knowledge.

This neglect of knowledge governance in general and the governance of knowledge formation in particular partly reflects choices about the unit of analysis in existing theories of organization. For instance, these theories explore how firms efficiently govern an identified exchange (e.g., Williamson), organize to execute an industry-driven strategy (e.g., Porter 1980), or organize to accomplish particular activities or tasks (starting with Taylor (1911), and including much of the micro-organizational behavior literature). All of these approaches implicitly begin with the value-creating knowledge already in hand and ask how the firm can best organize to generate value from this knowledge. If, however, we are to directly tackle the question of how to organize to create value or create knowledge, we must begin with a unit of analysis that focuses squarely on the question of interest. We argue that problems form a useful unit of analysis upon which to build an organizational theory of value creation. We argue that the central task of leaders, whether managers or entrepreneurs, is to identify valuable problems to solve and then organize an efficient solution search. Firms, which are effective in problem finding and problem solving, create value.

The purpose of this chapter is to review an emergent approach to governing knowledge formation that is focused around organizing to discover valuable problems and efficiently searching for solutions, which builds largely on Nickerson and Zenger (2004). Our review of this problem-finding and problem-solving perspective (PFPS) begins by contrasting the conventional questions of strategy research with the questions raised by focusing on problem finding and solution discovery. In particular, this perspective departs from the more traditional question of finding sustainable competitive advantage and explores instead questions dealing with how leaders find new problems that yield substantial, continuing value streams. Put differently, we are interested in exploring an economizing logic of managerial choice to maximize expected value. These questions ultimately focus on organizing to effectively find problems and then, based on the attributes of the problem, organizing an effective solution search.

We begin our discussion of the perspective by focusing first on problem finding. Problem finding in this perspective is concerned with methods by which leaders describe in broad terms the knowledge, which, if discovered, would create value. The way a problem is defined can profoundly influence the type of solution discovered. For instance, a microprocessor manufacturer recently defined their problem as developing a new architecture to integrate all of the electronics for a portable computer on a single chip. After announcing failure to solve this problem, management then recast their motivating agenda to a problem more easily solved: developing the next level in portable computer performance by extending their existing microprocessor architecture. Thus, problems define opportunities for value creation. In finding problems, leaders may also frame and formulate the problem in a way that involves implicit assumptions about required categories of knowledge and the likely need for and nature of knowledge recombination required to solve the problem. Our discussion emphasizes mechanisms, processes, and organizational approaches that overcome impediments to effective problem finding. Surprisingly, problem finding is a topic that has not been widely addressed in the literature especially in the strategic management and governance literatures. Perhaps the most closely related literature is on opportunity discovery in entrepreneurship. For an overview we recommend consulting a *Journal of Management Studies* special issue (volume 44, issue 7) on the entrepreneurial theory of the firm. This literature, however, says very little about how a leader can deliberately organize to find, frame, and formulate problems.

Our discussion continues with problem solving. Our basic premise is that firms must organize to match the attributes of the problems they seek to solve. The attributes of a problem are first identified: for example, degree of complexity and ill-structuredness (Simon 1973). While problem attributes describe one aspect of the problem-solving challenge, characteristics of the knowledge required to search for valuable solutions also influence knowledge recombination. For instance, the attributes of the problem-solving context, such as the tacitness of knowledge and the extent to which knowledge is dispersed across many individuals (knowledge dispersion), can pose challenges for knowledge creation. Thus, these problem-level and knowledge environmental factors interact in the process of searching for valuable solutions. The PFPS perspective predicts that these attributes are matched in an economizing way with different organizational structures thereby enabling efficient solution search. Such matching increases the likelihood of finding increasingly valuable solutions at lower cost.

After laying out these basic elements of the problem-finding and problem-solving perspective we proceed by discussing gaps in and future directions for research. These gaps allow us to prospectively suggest several research programs that might create value for researchers and practitioners alike, especially those interested in a knowledge governance approach to creating value.

It is important to note that this chapter is not meant to provide a comprehensive review of all literature related to problem solving and problem finding. Indeed, because the perspective is interdisciplinary in nature, it connects to wide ranging set of literatures that can be accessed by reading the original research contributions. Rather, this chapter is more narrowly designed to present the central tenets of an approach to value creation that focuses on problem finding and problem solving, and conclude by highlighting the substantial potential for research that adopts this perspective. We encourage interested readers to visit the primary research that forms the basis of our review.

2.2. Motivating Questions in Strategic Management Research

The central goal of leaders, as we view it, is to create value or streams of rents that the firm can then strategically capture. However, strategy research conventionally focuses on several broad goals of firms, all of which pertain primarily to value capture from existing value streams. For instance, firms maximizing profits via monopoly or monopoly-like rents (Kreps 1990; Porter 1980; Smith 1976), accessing and exploiting resources that generate rents (Barney 1991; Dierickx and Cool 1989; Wernerfelt 1984), and minimizing operational and governance costs (Williamson 1985). None of these approaches focus on specific ways in which leaders can create value. Similarly, industrial organization economics, which underlies many of these approaches to strategy, suffers from the same problem: present and future supply and demand curves are assumed known. With these assumptions, value capture scholars ask how firms might best (*a*) block entry and manipulate competitors to set prices or to price discriminate, (*b*) obtain and/or deploy resources to increase rents captured, and/or (*c*) minimize all types of costs (operational and governance) to increase profitability. Thus, much of strategy research emphasizes the capturing of value from pre-identified sources of advantage (e.g., Porter 1980).

The goal of value capture, while undoubtedly a necessary condition, is not a sufficient condition to consistently generate profitability let alone grow profits. Neglected is the vital role of value creation. In all of the aforementioned perspectives, value is assumed to have been created by someone or some organization, and the central challenge for managers is to secure a portion of the created value, in excess of costs, for the firm. Other more dynamic views of competition, firms, and markets (e.g., Nelson and Winter 1982; Schumpeter 1942) acknowledge the importance of value creation but suffer another weakness. This literature on economic change and evolution treats innovation and creativity as largely simple, replicable industrial routines to be optimized (Nelson and Winter 1982). Details about actual processes of how leaders create value are omitted, despite sophisticated discussions of how the environment for value creation changes over time (Schumpeter 1942). Existing economic views of value creation assume that managers somehow either automatically know how to create value or are consistently lucky at finding it.

Other perspectives like the resource-based view of the firm acknowledge the role played by rare, inimitable, and valuable assets in generating value.

However, even in this perspective, value creation is largely assumed. For instance, the resource-based view does not predict which asset or asset combinations are likely to be valuable. Nor does it imply when these combinations are likely to be valuable. Instead, the resource-based view argues that firms must find valuable, rare, inimitable, resources and organize them appropriately (Barney and Hesterly 2006). The resource-based view of the firm thus offers rather few specific recommendations to leaders on how they can organize to continuously create value.

Thus, fundamentally lacking in the strategic management literature is a focus on the simple fact that value requires creation before capture. While much of the literature in strategy is focused on maintaining, protecting, and defending rents, less well developed is an understanding of how to organize to deliberately and continuously create value—how to organize the production of valuable new knowledge. Obviously, discovering new streams of rents or new sources of value is central to increasing the value of the firm. This is true in part because entry, competition, technological innovation, shifting preferences, and other competitive threats emerge and eventually undermine almost any firm's current sources of rents (e.g., Chesbrough 1997; Schumpeter 1942). Moreover, even if the firm persists in capturing value from existing rent streams, increasing the value of the firm, as desired by investors, requires the firm to constantly reveal new sources of value from which the firm then strategically captures rents. Without discovering new growth opportunities, focusing efforts solely on value capture and defending a position are ultimately fatal to the organization. Creating value is therefore vital to strategic management.

Creating value, and doing so continuously, is ultimately an organizational and strategic issue. For instance, consistently creating new value requires leaders and organizations to identify new problems that both (*a*) are amenable to a firm's unique abilities to assemble knowledge to solve problems, and (*b*) yield substantial economic value when solved. Thus, the challenge for leaders is to structure an organization that continuously and deliberately creates new value.

2.3. Deliberate Value Creation

We maintain that the potential for deliberate value creation lies in finding and solving problems. Of course, deliberately identifying a problem involves forethought about the firm's ability to assemble knowledge sets to solve the problem (whether knowledge is internal to the firm or not), as well as its ability to capture value from the solution. Leaders should not want to select problems for which they have little chance of cost effectively discovering a solution, or for which their firm has little chance of capturing value. Problem choice therefore should be influenced by solution search and value capture possibilities. With much of the research in strategy already focused on value capture, below we suppress detailed discussion of the influence of value capture in finding and solving problems.

We begin by discussing organizational approaches to problem finding or identification. The key question for *problem finding* is: how can managers organize a search to identify and select a problem whose resolution can be expected to generate significant value? We suggest that an effective approach to problem identification examines individual, group, and organizational characteristics that facilitate or impede problem identification, with a strong focus on processes. Our approach seeks to understand how various processes affect the finding, framing, and formulation of various kinds of problems. Thus, we adopt problem search as an appropriate unit of analysis and study how and why processes shape the nature of problems identified.

The key question for *problem solving* is: how can managers organize an efficient search for high value solutions to an identified problem? The efficient approach to solution search depends on the complexity or non-decomposability of the problem, the extent to which non-decomposability generates hazards or social dynamics that impede knowledge-formation, and the efficacy of various governance mechanisms for encouraging searches appropriate for the level of problem complexity. Some problems can be solved through the combination of independent, modular searches, and consequently require minimal organizational control. Other problems require knowledge sharing across actors as well as coordinated search; for such problems, various forms or hierarchy are optimal to efficiently manage the attendant knowledge-formation hazards. The recent literature in this perspective is reviewed below to illuminate both problem finding and problem solving.

2.3.1. *Problem Finding*

As discussed above, deliberate efforts at value creation begin with first finding a problem to solve. This problem may be a customer or supplier problem, or a problem embedded in a value chain, production process, or service delivery operation. Much like scientific discovery, effectively finding a valuable problem is often more critical than effectively discovering solutions. In regard to scientific discovery, Einstein and Infeld (1938: 92) claim that '[t]he formulation of a problem is often more essential than its solution.... To raise new questions, new possibilities, to regard old questions from a new angle, requires creative imagination and marks real advance in science.' The same may be true for nonscientific discovery as well.

Given the importance of problem finding for knowledge creation, it is surprising that few managerial theories focus on the processes that support problem finding, framing, and formulation. In fact, theories in strategic management and organization often skip over this step by assuming the existence of a problem and then explore the question of how to solve it. For instance, Cyert and March (1963) in their treatise on the behavioral theory of the firm assume a problem has been identified and explore how to organize the firm to solve these problems. The primary problems of interest to Cyert and March can be described as decomposable and operational problems. Transaction cost economics assumes a transaction and asks how it should be governed. The question left unasked is how the firm decides on which transactions, presumably value-creating transactions, to pursue and thereby ignores considering the choice of problem to solve. The resource-based and knowledge-based theories of the firm specify that value derives from resources that are rare inimitable, and valuable. This definition presupposes that value is already created and therefore says little or nothing about processes (and problems) involved in value creation. The absence of consideration of choice of problem also runs throughout the network, trust, and management literatures. For instance, the trust literature does not study how trust expands or narrows a firm's capacity for problem formulation. Network analyses typically examine existing networks without reference to why they were formed or to what problem formulations they influence. While the management literature largely from the 1970s and early 1980s (e.g., Mitroff and Lyles 1980) began to document issues of problem formulation, little progress in developing theory and mechanisms for improving problem formulation were made. Even though little progress has been made on enhancing our understanding of problem formulation, it is widely recognized that raising new questions—finding a new problem—is difficult and rare but valuable, which resonates with Einstein and Infeld's perspective.

It is precisely this point of problem finding that Nickerson, Silverman, and Zenger (2007) address. They argue that searching for a problem resembles a search for an 'unknown unknown.' That is, while solving a problem involves searching for a solution on a largely unseen knowledge landscape, searching for a problem involves searching for landscapes. In the context of such uncertainty, their discussion focuses on a variety of impediments that undermine and contaminate efforts to find, frame, and formulate problems. While these impediments are normally explored from an individual or group level unit of analysis, these impediments can be readily recast and viewed using the problem as the unit of analysis.

Impediments arise in the individual as well as group levels of analysis. Nickerson, Silverman, and Zenger (2007) largely focus on impediments in groups in part because groups may hold the promise of mitigating individual biases. They categorize common impediments into cognitive, motivational, and informational impediments. The specific biases and group dynamics in these categories as described by Nickerson, Silverman, and Zenger (2007) include the well-known biases of anchoring, perceptual bias, information distortion and sampling, dominance, groupthink, primacy, satisficing, and conflicts of interest, among others. Such biases, whether cognitive, motivational, or informational, if not counteracted, can contaminate problem discovery and identification. For instance:

- *Anchoring* refers to sticking to the way something has been done in the past—letting path dependence drive thinking. For example, an anchored group would reject the possibility of rotational molding techniques if they have always employed other (e.g., injection molding) techniques.
- *Perceptual bias* refers to distinct cognitive frames possessed by individuals and their lack of ability to see beyond the frames they possess. For example, the cognitive frame of a nuclear engineer might make it unlikely for that engineer to start a solar photovoltaic energy company.
- *Information distortion* refers to the inaccuracy of internal or external data available to a project team. For example, many firms regret that they did not correctly see the size of the market for a completely touch screen-based telephone like Apple's iPhone. *Information sampling,* a variation on information distortion, arises when individuals share knowledge they have in common, but fail to share information that they do not have in common.

- *Dominance* describes the condition when a top manager asserts authority or a highly talkative individual dominates conversation in such a way as to discourage discourse and contributions from others.
- *Groupthink* is a highly popularized phenomenon in which groups quickly get locked in to inferior decisions or perspectives.
- *Primacy* arises when events that happen first color or overshadow what comes later.
- *Satisficing* was identified by Simon (1945). It implies that decision-makers meet a criterion for adequacy rather than meet an optimality criterion. Participants engage in satisficing when the problem they choose is viewed as 'good enough.' For example, in the last part of the twentieth century, large American steel firms clearly focused on solving problems related to optimizing their existing assets. In the process they ignored alternative problems framed around how to craft flexible, inexpensive-to-reconfigure, low-cost milling operations. This alternative problem framing resulted in the highly successful minimills. The large steal manufacturers simply viewed their current manufacturing approaches as 'good enough,' and the key problems focused on incremental refinements.
- *Conflicts of interest* arise when a team member pursues subgoals that do not align with the goals of the project, team, or the organization. For example, team members may engage in politics with the goal of advancing their career or functional organization at the cost of others.

From a problem-finding perspective, these impediments are related to the knowledge environment factors (heterogeneous teams) from which the biases and dynamics are generated. In particular, it is the heterogeneity of motivations, cognitive schema, and information by actors involved in finding, framing, and formulating problems that stimulate these group biases and dynamics. Therefore, a preliminary approach is to identify attributes of group heterogeneity and the knowledge environment from which attributes are constructed to determine the method for expanding the range of problem formulations. The following paragraphs sketch out the relationship between at least some of these group biases and dynamics and the methods available for overcoming them for various problem contexts.

Focusing on these impediments, Nickerson, Silverman, and Zenger (2007) argue that these group biases and dynamics can be mitigated by the use of structured processes to find, frame, and formulate problems. They define structured processes as comprising a set of facts, circumstances, or experiences that are or can be observed and described, and are marked by gradual changes through a series of measurable states. This definition focuses on observability, which suggests that strictly cognitive processes are outside the scope of their perspective. Relying on observability of a process suggests that the process can be designed, evaluated, and improved upon—important features that ultimately can give rise to organizational advantages that lead to continually creating value.

Nickerson, Silverman, and Zenger (2007) suggest that organizations utilize two broad classes of processes in identifying problems: analytic and synthetic. While the problem remains are unit of analysis, they posit that the problems identified depend on the nature of the processes utilized to find them. Analytic process comprises a set of structured and detailed process steps through which organizations find, frame, and formulate problems to solve. The key features of this class of processes are that they disassemble and decompose the value chain. Their effective application requires an environment in which (*a*) production is repeated, (*b*) the production process can be defined and characterized, and (*c*) customers have experience with the product or service. Classic examples of analytic processes include Six Sigma, lean manufacturing, statistical process control (SPC), and Quality Function Deployment. These analytic processes identify deviations that arise in specific tasks and activities and frame and formulate problems around improving the specific task and activity. Such processes appear to mitigate the impediments described above and have thus been both profitably applied and widely adopted. Such problems and their corresponding solutions, however, tend to yield rather incremental innovation and value creation based on the existing architecture of production. By disassembling and decomposing the value chain, problems that are found are generally localized. On the margin, solutions to these problems increase value often by lowering cost or increasing quality but only incrementally within the localized part of the value chain that is the focus of the analytic process.

Synthetic processes, the second broad class of processes identified by Nickerson, Silverman, and Zenger (2007), are similar to analytic processes to the extent they represent a structured sequence of state-changing steps that produce stimuli which can lead to problem identification. However, whereas analytic processes disassemble and decompose, synthetic processes focus on recombining and expanding to generate inductive, exploratory synthesis. Essential differences between analytic and synthetic processes are the (*a*) nature of stimuli that launch problem identification and (*b*) choice of problem to solve. In the case of the former, synthetic processes involve stimuli from less-structured or unstructured environments whereas analytic processes rely on stimulation from deviations and waste from repeated activities. In the case of the later, analytic processes identify problems that generally are well-structured such as eliminating production bottlenecks, shrinking work in process inventories, or reducing output variability. Synthetic processes, by contrast, are less constrained and problem identification is less certain and more ill-structured. In selecting problems, managers must decide not only which questions represent design challenges to create value but also which problems their organizations have a reasonable likelihood of solving at a low enough cost to create and capture value.

In summary, research on problem finding from a process perspective is nascent and the future development of this perspective remains unclear. Nonetheless, what is clear is that problem finding, framing, and formulating is strategic and may continuously generate new value if organizations develop capabilities in the area of problem identification. This perspective offers at least one particular approach for achieving continuous value creation. The perspective posits that various cognitive, motivational, and informational impediments undermine problem formulation. These impediments may also preclude the finding of new problems. The perspective's key insight is that it may be possible to design structured processes that mitigate or at least attenuate impediments thereby enhancing an organizations' problem-finding ability. Theory remains under development for exploring the relationships between various impediments and the mechanisms, notably processes, able to mitigate or at least attenuate these biases. Nonetheless, the early work by Nickerson, Silverman, and Zenger (2007) provides at least one avenue for developing a new approach to theorizing about problem finding.

2.3.2. *Problem-Solving Perspective*

The value of a problem is of course ultimately defined by the value of the discovered solution. Hence, with a well-formulated problem in hand, the critical managerial task is organizing an effective solution discovery effort. In much the same way that group and individuals biases hinder problem finding, solution discovery is plagued by impediments to knowledge sharing or what we term, knowledge formation hazards. The problem-solving perspective then argues that organizing solution discovery involves efficiently overcoming these impediments. How this is efficiently done depends on the attributes of the problem, specifically the complexity of a problem.

Following Simon (1962), problem complexity is categorized into decomposable, nearly decomposable, and non-decomposable problems based on the extent to which the relevant knowledge sets may interact to produce a valuable solution. As the name suggests, decomposable problems are problems decomposable into subproblems. Solving such problems requires little or no knowledge sharing and hence, impediments to knowledge sharing are unimportant. Each subproblem of the larger aggregate problem can be efficiently outsourced to specialists in the market who search for a solution to their subproblem. Decomposability implies that the solutions to each subproblem are additive, which means that optimal solutions for each subproblem combine to form a global optimum for the original problem. Nickerson and Zenger (2004) use the illustration of designing a desktop personal computer that is not cutting edge in technology to highlight this situation.

On the other extreme of complexity are problems which cannot be easily decomposed into subproblems and where rich and extensive interactions across those possessing various categories of knowledge are required. To solve such problems requires extensive knowledge recombination as individuals seek to develop theories to guide solution search. For such problems, impediments to knowledge sharing or knowledge formation hazards greatly hinder solution discovery. The perspective highlights two hazards in particular. The first hazard is a knowledge appropriation hazard that arises from the well-known Arrow (1974) information paradox in which specialists are unlikely to share and transfer knowledge without some way of safeguarding its use and further transmission. The second hazard is referred to by Nickerson and Zenger (2004) as strategic knowledge accumulation. This hazard arises because individuals possess incentives to strategically alter the path of search to disproportionately benefit their own knowledge accumulation and value with respect to others. Strategic knowledge accumulation also can manifest in terms of keeping knowledge from others. For instance, Cyert and Kumar (1996) discuss the (negative) incentives of technological gatekeepers to strategically filter out knowledge into the firm that is too distant from the knowledge they control themselves. Nickerson and Zenger argue that a team with the features of being vertically integrated, investing in horizontal communication channels and codes, and facing low individual incentive intensity, using consensus for determining the sequence of search trials, can more efficiently form knowledge for solving such complex problems than other forms of organization. Investment in and maintenance of horizontal communication channels and codes makes this mode of organization comparatively quite costly. Nickerson and Zenger (2004) use the illustration of designing and building a leading edge microprocessor circuit that demands numerous knowledge sets that extensively interact in determining the value of solutions to represent such non-decomposable problems.

Intermediate levels of problem complexity represent a nearly decomposable system in which subproblems can be identified but vital interdependencies among the subproblems remain. The aforementioned knowledge hazards are present in such nearly decomposable situations but to a much lesser degree. Nickerson and Zenger (2004) argue that the logic of efficiency leads to the adoption of authority-based organizational structure. In this structure, low-powered individual incentives are used in conjunction with a central manager who partitions the problem into subproblems. Specialists search within their knowledge domains for solutions to their assigned subproblems. Specialists' solutions are transmitted vertically to the manager who makes choices about constraints and directs the specialists to search further given the set of constraints. This iterated structure requires investment and maintenance of vertical communication channels and codes instead of horizontal ones. In this case, it is the manager who engages in knowledge formation. This governance mode diminishes in efficacy as the cognitive capacity of the manager to form new knowledge spanning the scope of the problem is reached. That is, problems with higher levels of problem complexity lead such authority-based hierarchies to be inefficient for solutions search compared to consensus-based hierarchies.

While this perspective recognizes the importance of governance, the critical unit for value creation is the problem, not the transaction, as in Williamson's (1985) paradigm of transaction cost economics. While focusing on the governance of transactions is not unrelated to value creation, we contend the approach is better suited to questions of value appropriation/capture. That said, in some instances the two units of analysis coincide. For instance, Nickerson and Zenger's theory paper (2004) introduces archetypical organizational forms of the market, authority-based hierarchy, and consensus-based hierarchy. Yet, other organizational modes are relevant. Heiman and Nickerson (2002) developed propositions regarding effects of complexity and knowledge tacitness (problem attributes) on the governance choice for interfirm collaboration. Such hybrid cases were not considered by Nickerson and Zenger. Heiman and Nickerson (2004: 401) empirically explore these propositions for between-firm collaborations using the CATI database of interfirm cooperation by exploring the relationship between attributes of the exchange/problem—knowledge tacitness and problem-solving complexity—and the types of knowledge management practices and, ultimately, formal governance structures adopted to support the exchange/problem. Their key finding is that knowledge management practices such as high-bandwidth communication channels and the development of co-specialized communication codes are chosen to economically respond to the challenges of increasing tacitness and complexity. Moreover, they found that adoption of these knowledge management practices is supported by governance commitments such as equity-based joint ventures. This research stream provides an early exploration of the relationship between problem attributes and governance mechanisms and structures between firms in which the problem and transaction are coincident units of analysis.

Heiman and Nickerson (2002, 2004) suggest that attributes of the knowledge context may influence problem solving and governance choice. As mentioned above, knowledge tacitness is one such attribute. They also define and empirically measure knowledge dispersion, which reflects how '... "spread-out" knowledge is among different [firms] in a collaboration. The more dispersed knowledge is, the more difficult knowledge sharing becomes as the cost for knowledge sharing increases' (p. 408). Empirical evidence suggests that a high degree of knowledge dispersion is associated with applying progressively more costly knowledge management practices and that dispersion-related affects are exacerbated in the presence of complexity and tacitness. While only preliminary, this research suggests that attributes of the knowledge environment such as knowledge tacitness and knowledge dispersion may be important to consider when designing efficient governance structures for knowledge creation.

Another application and extension of problem solving was developed by Macher (2006). He extended the problem-solving perspective by further dimensionalizing attributes of the problem. In addition to problem complexity, his research examines how solutions of well- versus ill-structured problems are governed. Following Simon (1973), Macher's well-structured problems have well understood initial states and end states and involve familiar elements including approaches for solving while ill-structured problems lack these properties (Macher 2006: 828). His

work also empirically supports the hypothesized links between problem attributes and governance choice. The paper finds that within the semiconductor industry, '[i]ntegrated firms realize performance advantages when problem solving in technological development is ill-structured and complex, while the same is true for specialized firms when problem solving in technological development is well-structured and simple [i.e., non-complex]' (p. 826). The theme of governing the problem-solving activity, based on another attribute of problems (well- vs. ill-structuredness) provides a new and important avenue for understanding how firms organize to create value.

The PFPS perspective has particular application in examining entrepreneurship and the entrepreneurial firm (Hsieh, Nickerson, and Zenger 2007). The perspective offers three useful insights for scholars of entrepreneurship. First, the concept of opportunity discovery, which is central to much of the entrepreneurship literature, is usefully divided into two distinct activities: problem finding and problem solving. Separating opportunity discovery into these two distinct activities helps highlight important avenues for spawning entrepreneurship. Second, the type of organization an entrepreneur builds to solve a chosen problem depends on the nature of the problem. Entrepreneurs may choose to outsource problem solving for highly decomposable problems, choose consensus-based hierarchy for highly non-decomposable problems, and choose authority-based hierarchy for nearly decomposable hierarchy. Third, entrepreneurs (and leaders) differ in their cognitive capacities to combine knowledge which influences the efficient form of organization. Acknowledging this factor introduces a shift parameter into the governance choice calculus. Entrepreneurs who possess expansive cognitive capabilities increase the range of complexity over which authority-based hierarchy provides an efficient match. In contrast, entrepreneurs with more limited cognitive capabilities are more likely to outsource for low complexity problems and adopt a consensus-based organization for more complex problems. The perspective offers a theory for organizing the entrepreneurial firm.

In summary, the problem-solving perspective introduced by Nickerson and Zenger (2004) views the central role of leaders as creating value by organizing in a way that facilitates the forms of knowledge exchange appropriate for a given problem. Initial empirical work by Macher (2006) finds support for this approach. Moreover, the perspective has rich implications for choice of organizing both *within* and *between* firms and predicts not only whether to use a firm or a market for knowledge creation but also specifies the type of internal organizational structure a firm should adopt for efficient knowledge formation. Similarly, these insights apply to entrepreneurs' decisions whether or not to form a new firm and, if so, what organizational form this new firm should take. The perspective also offers highlights regarding how an individual entrepreneur's or leader's cognitive capacity can affect these organizational decisions. Notably, predictions about the use of markets, authority-based hierarchy, and consensus-based hierarchy go far beyond typical make or buy prescriptions of alternative internal organizational structures to provide a broad array of organizational choices.

An antecedent assumption noted in the problem-solving perspective is that management has chosen a proper problem to solve. Thus, Nickerson and Zenger (2004) briefly discuss how managers must choose problems with an eye toward their ability to efficiently solve them and their ability to capture value from the solution they discover. While a theory concerning the governance of problem solving and value appropriation acts as a useful starting point for understanding how to organize value creation, the question of problem finding was left largely unexplored in this initial treatment. Nickerson, Silverman, and Zenger (2007) investigate problem finding in more detail, and rename the perspective the problem-finding and problem-solving (PFPS) perspective to reflect the importance of problem finding.

2.3.3. *Research Opportunities*

Properly governing knowledge associated with solving and identifying problems is a crucial, but perennially neglected part of creating high performance organizations. Until now, a good organizing framework for unpacking problems, impediments, and processes has been lacking. The problem-solving perspective articulated by Heiman and Nickerson (2002, 2004), Hsieh, Nickerson, and Zenger (2007), Macher (2006), Nickerson and Zenger (2004), and Nickerson, Silverman, and Zenger (2007) is clearly nascent but represents at least one path to increasing our understanding of problem-related issues that abound in value creation activities.

Research to date has laid out core mechanisms for relating the unit of analysis and the nature of problems to the costs and benefits of alternative forms of organization for solving these problems. By doing so, this research has opened the possibility of several potentially rewarding new research streams. For instance, the problem-solving theory presently focuses on three archetypal organizational structures: market, authority-based hierarchy, and consensus-based hierarchy. Heiman and Nickerson explored other structures related to interfirm organization. These structures are unlikely to span the entire space of alternative organizational forms available either within the firm or between firms. Moreover, while empirical evidence is supportive, it is limited. Heiman and Nickerson (2004) work with a large database (CATI) with a limited number of variables and with a second dataset rich in descriptive variables but of limited size. Macher's study (2006) offers a richer set of data that investigates just one industry, semiconductors, and one class of problems. While providing a useful vector, much more theoretical and empirical research is needed to flush out a problem-solving perspective. What additional attributes are appropriate for characterizing problems? What additional contextual attributes like knowledge dispersion are useful to incorporate into the theory? What other alternative organizational structures are available within the firm or between firms? What are the costs and competencies of various choices for mitigating knowledge formation hazards? What specific steps should leaders undertake to implement alternative governance modes?

An underlying assumption in the problem-solving perspective is that the problems managers select to solve are independent. While this assumption may initially be useful for theory development, it misses opportunities to theoretically identify important sources of competitive advantage. For instance, having invested in a consensus-based hierarchy to organize search by recombining a particular set of knowledge, leaders may be better off selecting problems that take advantage of the knowledge and organizational structure assembled from prior problems. Thus, there may be a path dependence to problem selection that arises from prior organizational and knowledge investments. Under what conditions should leaders choose problems similar in character to past problems? When should leaders choose problems that require knowledge and organizational mechanisms that differ from what the organization presently has in place? While competition may play an important role in addressing these questions, it is likely not the only important factor. Moreover, even if competition is central, literature on competition generally does not focus on choice of problems to solve.

Another potential research stream arises from Nickerson and Zenger's assertion that dynamics are inherent in problems. Problems that initially are ill-structured and non-decomposable (e.g., design the next top-selling portable consumer electronics gadget) eventually progress to structured and decomposable problems as the product or service is designed and manufactured. For instance, designing the architecture for a new advanced microprocessor is an ill-structured highly complex problem. Yet, once the architecture is developed, the problem becomes more structured and less non-decomposable, which suggests that as the problem solving needs change through various steps of development so too will knowledge formation demands and the organizational structures needed to efficiently support these demands.

Literatures from other fields span at least some of these issues. Research from the product development literature seems the most promising for advancing our understanding of proper organizing. Several scholars explore the nexus of task nature and organizational structure in product development (e.g., Beckman and Barry 2007; Eppinger et al. 2005; Tidd and Bodley 2002). Nonetheless, little research adopts the problem as the unit of analysis and explores how changing knowledge formation demands relate to organizational management and structure, which raises several questions. Do new product/process development organizations match up with knowledge formation demands of particular problems? If so, when should alternative organizational structures be adopted with respect to the changing knowledge formation demands of a problem as its solution advances? Understanding of problem life cycles is embryonic and presents interesting future challenges for unpacking the role of problem solving in value creation. Revisiting the product development literature through a problem-finding and problem-solving perspective may open up new questions about the management of innovation.

With an eye toward understanding the role of industry life cycles on problem finding and problem solving, Nickerson and Zenger (2004) also speculate that the emergence of a dominant design affects problem complexity. A dominant design implies that new problems leaders find are likely to be decomposable or nearly decomposable rather than non-decomposable with respect to the accepted dominant architecture. Dominant design emergence may impact not only the attributes of problems (more decomposable problems than before), thereby affecting the choice or organization for problem solving, but also by impacting the location and dispersion of knowledge. To the extent that dominant designs enable large product markets, we might expect that some knowledge is widely available while other knowledge becomes more specialized and dispersed across the economy. If so, how will the changing knowledge environment impact the problems managers choose to solve? How should the choice of organizational structure change in response to the location and dispersion of knowledge in the economy?

While the aforementioned questions may appear to be focused on existing firms, many of these questions also apply to entrepreneurship. At present no empirical research evaluates predictions generated by Hsieh, Nickerson, and Zenger's (2007) entrepreneurial theory of the firm. The research on entrepreneurship generally does not explore the nature of problems entrepreneurs are trying to solve nor does this research explore the structure of entrepreneurial firms at their formation. Therefore, a bevy of empirical opportunities exist for evaluating problem-solving predictions of entrepreneurial firms. New theoretical opportunities are also available. To what extent do different types of problems or their corresponding organizations impact growth of entrepreneurial enterprises? Do problem attributes impact capital formation? Governance? Current and future growth?

Problem finding offers another set of potential research trajectories. Clearly, theory predicting which biases and group dynamics are present in various situations is needed. More importantly, theory that provides insight into what kinds of structured processes mitigate biases and group dynamics is needed. Yet, as Nickerson, Silverman, and Zenger (2007) explain, most studies of process in strategic management and organization investigate how problems are solved rather than how they are identified and chosen, or study processes from a perspective of organizational change. Even in those instances where valuable structured processes like lean manufacturing and Six Sigma are known, the literature provides neither a behavioral theory about when and why these processes are beneficial nor a theoretical apparatus for assessing the benefits of alternative processes (p. 222). What processes lead to finding problems that when solved confer competitive advantage? How can firms develop processes that continually provide them with unique streams of problems that yield rents?

2.4. Conclusion

One of the most vital challenges in governing knowledge is the formation of knowledge that creates value. Unfortunately, until recently the strategy literature has not provided a systematic knowledge governance approach for persistently creating new knowledge. The problem-finding problem-solving perspective offers a new lens for theoretically and empirically exploring how leaders can persistently create value. This perspective begins with adopting the problem as the unit of analysis, which differs from much of the extant literature in management. It also focuses attention on how problems can be found, framed, and formulated instead of taking a problem as given as in much of the extant literature.

This chapter summarized both the problem-finding and problem-solving aspects of the perspective. It described how problem finding is enabled by adopting structured processes that overcome a variety of cognitive, motivational, and informational biases and group dynamics. These impediments inhibit finding problems unless mechanisms such as structured processes are adopted to overcome them. The chapter also described how problem solving is enabled by matching alternative governance structures with attributes of the problem and knowledge environment in a discriminating way. Problems, depending on their complexity, engender knowledge formation hazards that impede solution search especially for complex and ill-structured problems in which knowledge is tacit and dispersed. Matching governance structures in an economizing way can efficiently overcome these knowledge formation impediments.

Perhaps the greatest value of this chapter is its contribution in identifying a variety of potential research trajectories that build off of the PFPS perspective. Theoretical and empirical opportunities to build on this literature abound. Numerous questions around problem finding as well as problem solving are identified, which we hope scholars will find useful as they dig deeper into researching issues of knowledge governance.

References

Arrow, K. J. 1974. *Organization and Information. The Limits of Organization.* New York: W.W. Norton & Co.: 33–43.

Barney, J. B. 1991. 'Firm Resources and Sustainable Competitive Advantage,' *Journal of Management* 17: 99–120.

—— and W. Hesterly. 2006. *Strategic Management and Competitive Advantage: Concepts and Cases.* New York: Prentice-Hall (Pearson).

Beckman, S. L. and M. Barry. 2007. 'Innovation as a Learning Process: Embedding Design Thinking,' *California Management Review* 50: 1–33.

Chesbrough, H. 1997. *Dynamic Coordination and Creative Destruction: A Comparative Analysis of Incumbent Success and Failure in the Worldwide Hard Disk Drive Industry.* Dissertation: Haas School of Business, UC Berkeley.

Cyert, R. M. and P. Kumar. 1996. 'Economizing by firms through learning and adaptation,' *Journal of Economic Behavior & Organization* 29(2): 211–31.

—— and J. G. March. 1963. *A Behavioral Theory of the Firm: Chapter 6*. Cambridge, Mass.: Blackwell Business.

Dierickx, I., K. Cool, and J. B. Barney. 1989. 'Asset Stock Accumulation and Sustainability of Competitive Advantage; Comment; Reply,' *Management Science* 35(12): 1504–14.

Einstein, A., and L. Infeld. 1938. *The evolution of physics*. New York: Simon & Schuster.

Eppinger, S. D., D. E. Whitney, R. P. Smith, D. A. Gebala. 2005. 'A model-based method for organizing tasks in product development,' *Research in Engineering Design* 6(1): 1–13.

Furman, J., M. Porter, and S. Stern. 2002. 'The determinants of national innovative capacity,' *Research Policy* 31: 899–933.

Heiman, B. A. and J. A. Nickerson. 2002. 'Towards Reconciling Transaction Cost Economics and the Knowledge-Based View of the Firm: The Context of Interfirm Collaborations,' *International Journal of the Economics of Business* 9(1): 97–116.

—— —— 2004. 'Empirical Evidence Regarding the Tension between Knowledge Sharing and Knowledge Expropriation in Collaborations,' *Managerial and Decision Economics* 25: 401–20.

Hsieh, C., J. A. Nickerson, and T. R. Zenger. 2007. 'Opportunity Discovery, Problem Solving and the Entrepreneurial Theory of the Firm,' *Journal of Management Studies* 44: 1255–77.

Kreps, D. 1990. 'Modeling Competitive Situations,' in *A Course in Microeconomic Theory*. Princeton: Princeton University Press.

Macher, J. T. 2006. 'Technological Development and the Boundaries of the Firm: A Knowledge-Based Examination in Semiconductor Manufacturing,' *Management Science* 52(6): 826–43.

Mitroff, I. I. and M. A. Lyles. 1980. 'Organizational Problem Formulation: An Empirical Study,' *Administrative Science Quarterly* 25: 102–19.

Nelson, R. R. and S. G. Winter. 1982. *An Evolutionary Theory of Economic Change*. Cambridge: Belknap Press.

Nickerson, J. A. and T. R. Zenger. 2004. 'A Knowledge-Based Theory of Governance Choice: A Problem-Solving Approach,' Working paper, St. Louis: Olin School of Business, forthcoming in Organization Science.

—— B. S. Silverman, and T. R. Zenger. 2007. 'The "Problem" of Creating and Capturing Value,' *Strategic Organization* 5(3): 211–25.

Oxley, J. 1997. 'Appropriability Hazards and Governance in Strategic Alliances: A Transaction Cost Approach,' *Journal of Law Economics & Organization* 13(2): 387–409.

Porter, M. E. 1980. *Competitive Strategy*. New York: Free Press.

Schumpeter, J. A. 1942. *Capitalism, Socialism and Democracy*. London: G. Allen & Unwin Ltd.

Simon, H. 1945. *Administrative Behavior*. New York: Free Press.

Simon, H. A. 1962. 'The Architecture of Complexity,' *Proceedings of the American Philosophical Society* 106(6): 467–82.

—— 1973. 'The Structure of Ill Structured Problems,' *Artificial Intelligence* 4: 181–201.

Smith, A. 1976. *An Inquiry into the Nature and Causes of the Wealth of Nations*. Chicago: University of Chicago Press.

Taylor, F. W. 1911. *The Principles of Scientific Management*. New York: Harper & Brothers.

Tidd, J. and K. Bodley. 2002. 'The Influence of Project Novelty on the New Product Development Process,' *R&D Management* 32: 127–38.

Von Hippel, E. and M. Tyre. 1993. 'How Learning by Doing is Done: Problem Identification in Novel Process Equipment,' *Research Policy*: 1–12.

Wernerfelt, B. 1984. 'A Resource-Based View of the Firm,' *Strategic Management Journal* 12: 75–94.

Williamson, O. E. 1985. *The Economic Institutions of Capitalism*. New York: Free Press.

3

The architecture of knowledge organization

Michael Christensen and Thorbjørn Knudsen

3.1. Introduction: The Architecture of Knowledge Organization

In recent years, the creation, development, and capturing of value from knowledge has emerged as a critical issue in many firms and industries. This development has led to a burst of attention to knowledge assets in the management, organization, and strategy literatures (Foss and Pedersen 2002; Foss et al. 2005; Grant 1996; Hedlund 1994). Yet, little systematic thinking has been offered about the ways in which organizations choose and adapt their structure in order to better meet the new challenges associated with the knowledge economy, such as lower communication costs, increased connectivity of various media, and increased turbulence in international markets. A particularly important new challenge that must be addressed is that both good and bad alternatives travel faster in the knowledge economy (Collins and Chow 1998). Little advice has been offered in the way of designing organizations that meet this challenge.

More generally, there is a fundamental relation between organizational design and the utilization of knowledge resources. Even when abstracting from issues of motivation, organizational structure will influence both the quality of the decisions that get made and the way individuals acquire new knowledge. Very little is known about such issues. We believe that the lack of useful models of knowledge organizations lie at the heart of these gaps in our knowledge. In particular, we find that a critical gap in our understanding of organizations within the knowledge economy concerns the way in which knowledge residing at the level of individuals is aggregated into knowledge at the organizational level.

The purpose of this chapter is to meet the challenge of modeling the organization of knowledge. We draw on recent extensions of the Sah and Stiglitz (1986, 1988) characterization of organizational architectures to provide a general framework with which individual beliefs can be aggregated into organizational-level knowledge (Christensen and Knudsen 2004, 2007; Knudsen and Levinthal 2007). Sah (1991) and Stiglitz (2002) provide an overview of this literature. Christensen and Knudsen (2004, 2007), Csaszar (2007), and Koh (1992*a*, 1992*b*, 1994*a*, 1994*b*) add in a number of ways to the basic models of Sah and Stiglitz (1986, 1988). A simple sketch of the argument is provided in Augier and Knudsen (2004).

An organizational architecture comprises the following fundamental building blocks: organizational members, channels through which the members can pass information or control to each other, and a set of rules that help define the flow of information or control among them. The organizational-level knowledge is endogenously defined as an aggregate derived from the fundamental building blocks. The individual organizational members are represented by their beliefs about quality. That is, we focus on aggregate belief structures as an important aspect of knowledge organizations. Below, we offer illustrations that explain how aggregate structures are formally derived.

Using the proposed analytical platform, we explain how the organization of knowledge impacts the quality of the decisions that get made. To illustrate this point, a number of applications of the proposed framework are considered. These include models of learning and adaptation that trace how the organization of knowledge impacts the absorption of new knowledge in complex task environments (Knudsen and Levinthal 2007), and how the design of flexible forms of organization can help firms in turbulent markets (Christensen and Knudsen 2008). Further issues addressed by the proposed analytical platform include choice among more than two alternatives and upgrading knowledge within the context of other learners. These topics are briefly considered in the conclusion.

3.2. Decision-Making in Knowledge Organizations

Knowledge workers often cooperate. They occupy positions in organizations and they produce flows of information to each other. The knowledge organization may experience success or failure because of structural properties, because of the processes that take place within the confines of the current structure, or because of the proficiency and enthusiasm with which individuals engage in their tasks. We characterize knowledge in terms of individual beliefs about quality. A knowledge organization is a joint operation comprising a number of individuals. The following example highlights our thinking about knowledge organizations.

Our example considers credit evaluation in Bank2, one of the many activities that engage knowledge workers in today's society. While computers are often used for credit evaluation (e.g., by generating credit scores), the actual decision to accept or reject a client is made by one or more human actors. Each employee of Bank2 has gained specialized knowledge through formal education and experience on the job. The employees vary in their position in the organization, the number of years they have spent in that position, and the overall number of years they have been employed in the bank.

Bank2 has a number of local branches where credit advisors (CAs) evaluate applications from business clientele. The evaluations result in immediate approval, rejection, or, as is often the case, referral to a credit officer (CO) in the bank's central credit unit. The CO can approve, reject, consult with a colleague at the same level, or refer the credit application to the next layer. We are here considering credit applications of modest size (approximately US$1 million) that occur rather frequently (about 60–100 per year). It should be emphasized that screening applicants for credits is a major source of differential success in the banking industry.

The common measure of the efficacy of a bank's credit evaluation is the number of defaults, a term that refers to the frequency of losses (error rates). The bank has a good estimate of Type II error (defaults), but little information on Type I error (rejecting good applications). The error rate for this bank is approximately 0.5 percent and there are significant differences among comparable banks. The official policy of Bank2 is to 'caution all evaluators to be mindful of the balance between risk and reward.' In practice, this translates into a conservative policy of evaluating a number of indicators that are thought to correlate with risk of default. The employees at Bank2 are instilled with a sense of caution and the organizational structure further provides a 'safety filter,' which reduces the overall probability of accepting risk. Our main point is that we need theory to disentangle the contributions of the organization, and the individual employees toward the overall performance of the knowledge organization.

The organization in Bank2 impacts on the quality of the decisions that get made in the aggregate. Even rather subtle changes in the flow of information at Bank2 could result in significant gains or losses. Our concern here is to provide a framework with which we can model the way individual knowledge is aggregated into organizational-level knowledge, that is, how individual beliefs about credit applications are expressed at the organizational level. Our perspective on knowledge focuses on decision-making. The organization of knowledge is here thought of as an architecture that may help boundedly rational agents make better choices. While other dimensions of knowledge deserve attention, we find that this is a useful place to begin modeling knowledge organizations.

We now leave Bank2, that is, until we reach the conclusion where the case will serve to add perspective to the material covered in this chapter. We first outline a general modeling framework and then move on to illustrate how our framework can be used to understand the organization of decisions in the UN Security Council and among editors and reviewers in academic journals. Our tour of applications includes a treatment of search processes in complex landscapes and decision-making in turbulent markets. Even though there is a logical structure to the development of the argument, we have made each section rather self-contained in order to facilitate engagement with the material according to interest and preference.

3.3. The Modeling Framework

Our characterization of knowledge organizations focuses on alternative evaluation. Issues relating to creation of new alternatives are black-boxed for the purposes of simplifying the exposition. In considering applications of our framework, we shall indicate how the properties of organizational architectures influence the way knowledge workers generate new alternatives. We shall further consider how organizational architectures influence the way individual knowledge workers accumulate experience. The perspective points to an intricate interplay between organizational architectures, the development of individual capabilities, and possible tensions between short-term and longer term objectives.

3.3.1. *Organizational Architectures*

An organizational architecture is a structure comprising organizational members, channels through which the members can pass information or control to each other, and a set of rules that help define the flow of information or control among them. The purpose of an organization, as considered here, is to make decisions regarding whether to accept or reject alternatives, and these decisions have economic consequences. Decision rights are introduced as the right of an individual agent to ultimately accept an alternative on behalf of the architecture. Note that an agent can be an individual organization member, or a collection of organization members.

The process of making a decision goes as follows. An organizational architecture will (repeatedly) be confronted with an alternative drawn from an initial portfolio **I**, representing the currently available alternatives (and thus the current state of the business environment). The alternative enters the structure through one of its agents and traverses the structure until it is either rejected or accepted on behalf of the organization. Rejection means that nothing is altered; the alternative is terminated and dumped in a wastebin **T**. In this case, there is no direct economic consequence for the organization. Acceptance means that the organization realizes the preferred alternative, which, according to its quality, creates economic value. In this case, there is a direct economic consequence. This is symbolized by storing the alternative in a final portfolio **F**. In both cases, a cost is paid for making the decision.

If an alternative capable of producing income is rejected, then the organization made an error, denoted a Type I error. If, on the other hand, the organization accepts an alternative producing a negative income, it is said to have made a Type II error. In both of these cases, the decision was a failure, and in all other cases, it was a success. The ultimate fate of the alternative depends on how the agents are interconnected, thereby motivating the study of different organizational architectures.

The structures we refer to as the two-member hierarchy and polyarchy, are the simplest possible structures. Figure 3.1 provides an overview of the hierarchy and its environment, the initial portfolio **I**, and the final portfolio **F** in which accepted alternatives are stored. The termination node **T** is a wastebin where the rejected alternatives are dumped. The two-member hierarchy represents a serial processing of alternatives. It is straightforward to generalize it to *n*-member hierarchies simply by adding nodes to the sequence between **I** and **F**. In contrast to the simple hierarchy, Figure 3.2 portrays the extreme flat organization, also known as a polyarchy. It is a structure representing a parallel processing of alternatives. The polyarchy can be generalized by adding nodes to the sequence between **I** and **F**.

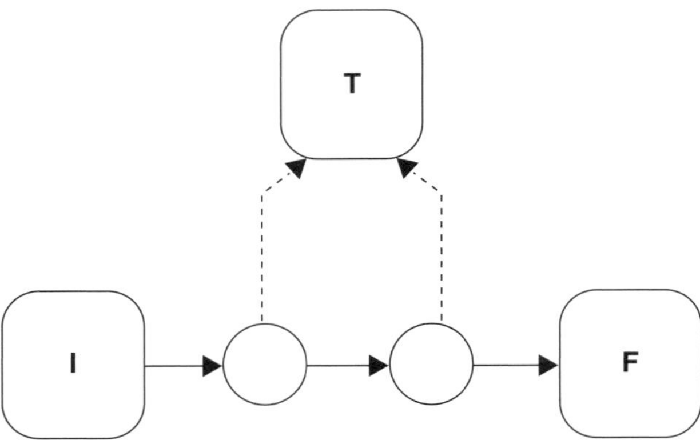

Figure 3.1. A two-member hierarchy

The two basic structures can be used as building blocks to construct any possible hybrid form of organization engaged in sequential decision-making. Even further elaborations are possible if we allow nondeterministic information flows. That is, agents may dispatch alternatives to each other on a more or less random basis. The point is that our modeling framework admits any possible form of organization engaged in sequential decision-making. What about simultaneous decision-making?

So far, we have considered sequential decision-making. A unifying substructure called a committee of n members and consensus $k$provides a useful generalization that captures *simultaneous decision-making*. This substructure is constructed by picking a polyarchical structure and supplying a dynamic rule according to which the organization accepts an alternative

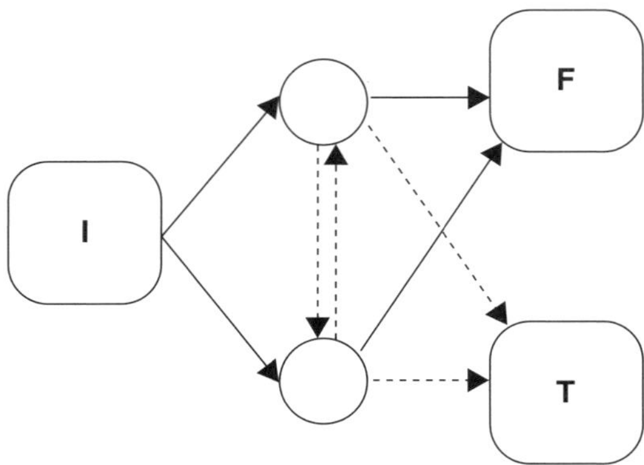

Figure 3.2. A two-member polyarchy

if k or more agents evaluate the project positively (e.g., $k \geq n/2$ represents a simple majority rule).

3.3.2. *Aggregation*

A single agent has a screening function of $f(x)$. The agent screening function represents the agent's beliefs about a quality distribution. Probabilities are assigned to accepting proposals that vary in their quality. These probabilities can be viewed as the agent's current beliefs, for example about the quality of a credit application. In unknown territory, the agent is prone to make more mistakes. The agent screening function takes this into account as an expression of the limits that characterize the decision-maker. In a turbulent and complex environment, the agent screening function may not be monotonous, it can be very ugly and it can even represent choice by the flipping of a coin.

The organization as an entity has a screening function of $F = q[f(x)]$. In order to derive the organization-level screening function, the organization is modeled as a graph (more precisely a directed, finite, and connected graph). The graph-screening function F represents the level of knowledge as a function of the individual members' cognitive skills and the choice of architecture, the organization structure that defines the flow of information among the organization members. Methods to derive the organization-level screening function F have been provided in Christensen and Knudsen (2004). In the following, we draw on these methods to illustrate how the knowledge structure of architectures can be represented (Figure 3.3).

In the general case, we suggest that knowledge organizations are characterized in terms of an external environment that provides a distribution of inputs **X**. Our basic framework does not consider inputs that originate inside the organization. A more elaborate treatment will allow for modification of both inputs and impressions about inputs. Such elaborations capture the fact that agents often influence (or manipulate) each other's beliefs about quality without changing the underlying asset. A further elaboration of our framework would also allow for generation (rather than modification) of inputs and beliefs within the organization.

The organization processes inputs and produces outputs **Z** and **Y**, where **Z** is a distribution of rejected alternatives and **Y** is a distribution of accepted alternatives. The knowledge organization is modeled as a graph comprising a collection of organizational members, a collection of channels through which the members can pass information or control to each

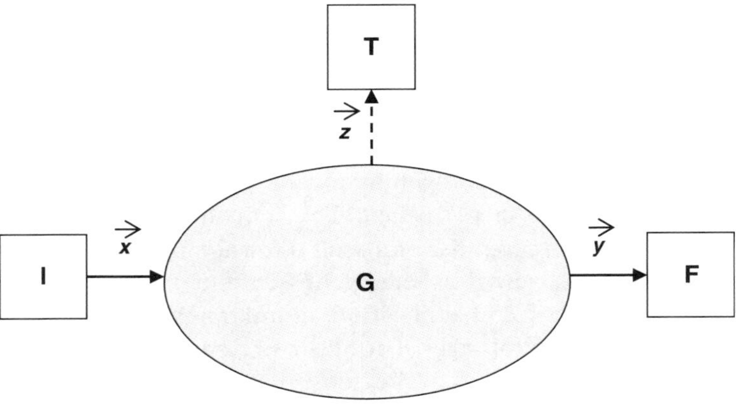

Figure 3.3. The general characterization of a knowledge organization

other, a topology that defines the overall pattern of connections among organizational members, and a set of dynamic rules that help define the flow of information or control that can be admitted by the topology.

The inputs that the knowledge organization receives are often transformed during its activity. Working with an alternative often improves the understanding of its quality. Also, features of an alternative may be added, removed, or improved. Thus, the input distribution **X** is different from the output distributions **Z** and **Y**. In order to better get a grip on this rather abstract discussion, we now illustrate the modeling framework with a number of examples.

3.4. Illustrative Example of the Basic Framework

In all of our examples, the agents have reasonable, but far from perfect, cognitive skills. Let us consider an important and commonly known organization, namely, the UN Security Council. The Security Council is composed of 5 permanent members and 10 temporary members (two-year terms).[1] The acceptance of a UN resolution relating to substantive matters

[1] The information provided here is publicly available at the UN as is the outcome of voting in the UN Security Council. According to Article 27 of Chapter V of the UN Charter, each member of the Security Council shall have one vote. Decisions of the Security Council on procedural matters shall be made by an affirmative vote of nine members. Decisions of the Security Council on all other matters shall be made by an affirmative vote of nine members including the concurring votes of the permanent members. The permanent seats are held by China, France, Russia, the UK, and the United States.

requires 9 out of 15 affirmative votes in addition to concurrent votes from the 5 permanent members. That is, the five permanent members hold veto power over substantive resolutions. A negative vote cast by a single permanent member will lead to rejection of a resolution even if meets the requirement of nine affirmative votes.

The UN Security Council is an example of joint decision-making, or voting. Decisions of the Security Council on procedural matters shall be made by an affirmative vote of nine members. The acceptance of a resolution on all other matters requires that two conditions are fulfilled: nine out of 15 members must accept a resolution and none out of the 5 permanent members must reject a resolution. Figure 3.4 shows how this plays out. It is much more likely that decisions on procedural matter can be made than it is to get a resolution on other matters accepted. The veto of the five permanent members introduces a very conservative bias, which will tend to preserve the status quo.

So far, we have illustrated how our framework can be used to model knowledge organizations engaged in simultaneous decision-making. We

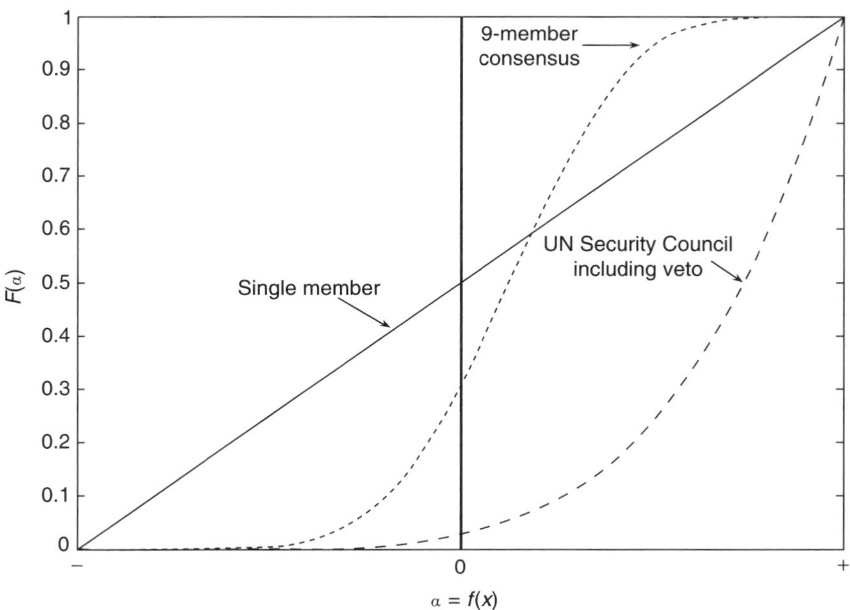

Figure 3.4. Aggregation of decision-making in the UN Security Council

now show how our framework can be applied when organizations try to absorb new knowledge in complex task environments.

3.5. Absorption of New Knowledge in Complex Task Environments[2]

We use the NK model for organizational analysis and extend it to study the impact of imperfect evaluation on organizational performance. At a basic level, evaluation of alternatives can suffer from two possible errors: Type I errors of rejecting a superior alternative and Type II errors of accepting an inferior alternative.

Different organizational structures vary in their proclivity to make one type of error or the other. In particular, hierarchical structures, in which a proposal needs to be validated by successive ranks of the hierarchy in order to be approved, will tend to reduce the likelihood that an inferior alternative will be adopted (hierarchy reduces Type II error). In contrast, the polyarchy is a flat organizational structure in which approval by any one actor in a series of decision-makers is sufficient for an alternative to be approved. Polyarchies will therefore tend to minimize the probability of rejecting a superior alternative (polyarchy reduces Type I error).

Using this analytical platform, we examine how alternative organizations of evaluators would move on a space of possible alternatives. In particular, we use the structure of fitness landscapes (Kauffman 1993; Wright 1931) to characterize a sense in which alternatives are more or less proximate to one another. As in Levinthal (1997), a process of local search is modeled as examining, at random, one of the adjacent points in the space of alternatives. The value of points in adjacent locations in fitness landscapes are correlated, with the degree of correlation being 'tuned' by the intensity of the interdependencies among the *N* attributes that contribute to the fitness of a given alternative. Changing the level of interdependencies also impacts the overall structure of the landscape in that the number of local peaks increases with the degree of interdependencies (Kauffman 1993). The presence of local peaks poses particular challenges to a process of local search, as a decision-maker at a local peak will be unable to identify superior alternatives that may be present on the broader landscape.

[2] The following material is an extraction from Knudsen and Levinthal (2007). We refer to that article for elaborations.

3.5.1. *Model*

The model structure has three basic elements: the characterization of individual evaluation of alternatives, how individual evaluators are aggregated into an organizational form, and the specification of the task environment or the space of alternatives.

3.5.2. *Individual Evaluation of Alternatives*

Individual evaluators are characterized as being able to distinguish between a proposed action alternative and the status quo with more or less reliability. A perfect evaluator would, with certainty, distinguish between inferior and superior alternatives no matter how small the value differences are among two proposals. However, decision-makers are unlikely to conform to such high standards. Actors are likely to make errors in identifying which, among a pair of alternatives, are, in fact, superior. However, one would expect that the likelihood of making a false classification is a decreasing function of the actual differences in value between the alternatives. That is, one may frequently misclassify pairs of alternatives that vary in payoff by only a small amount. In contrast, if the payoff to the two alternatives is substantially different, then the probability of making a misclassification would certainly be less than in the former case.

These properties are reflected in the screening functions represented in Figure 3.5. The horizontal axis indicates the actual difference in payoffs between a currently held alternative and a proposed alternative (current fitness minus new fitness), ranging from large negative differences in value to large positive values. The vertical axis indicates the probability that an evaluator would accept the proposed alternative. Obviously, an intelligent screening function should have an upward slope such that superior alternatives are more likely to be accepted than inferior alternatives. In the extreme, with a perfect evaluator, the curve would have a point of discontinuity at zero, such that proposed alternatives with a payoff less than the current alternative (yielding a negative fitness difference) would be rejected with probability 1 and those with higher payoff (positive fitness difference) accepted with certainty.

We specify a family of screening functions $f(x)$ that takes the difference, x, of current fitness minus new fitness as an argument. The particular functional form used in the present work is a linear screening function, $f(x) = \alpha x + \beta$. The slope of the line, indicated by the variable α, can be

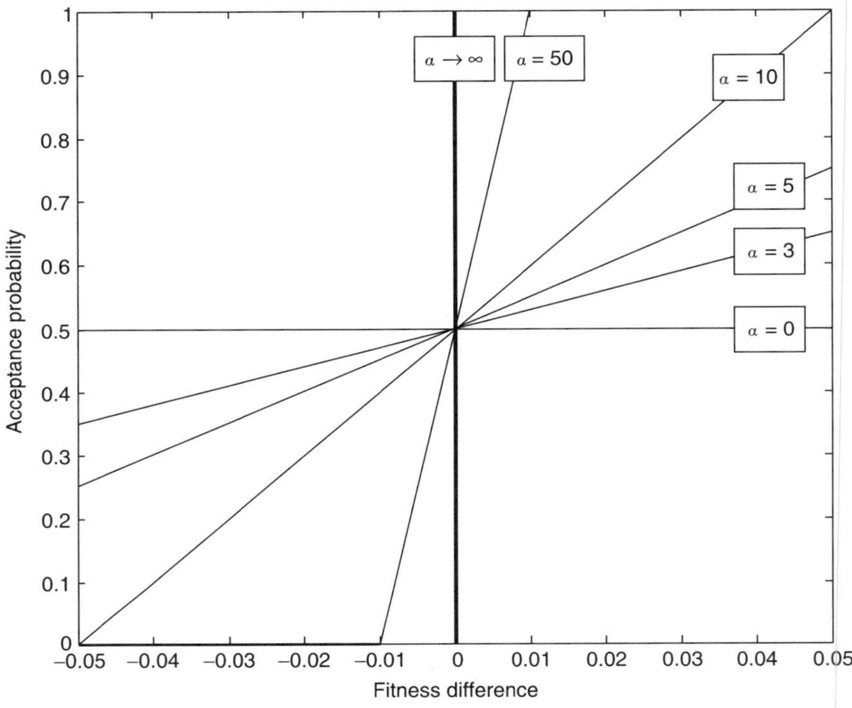

Figure 3.5. Six levels of screening ability for an evaluator, ranging from completely random screening ($\alpha = 0$) to perfect screening ($\alpha \to \infty$)

interpreted as the screening capability of the evaluator. A steeper slope, or higher value of α, implies that the probability of accepting a proposal is more sensitive to changes in its actual value. The cut-off of the line, indicated by the variable β, can be interpreted as the bias of the evaluator's error. We restrict our attention to those that are unbiased. Thus, we have symmetric errors, $\beta = 0$ and the screening function becomes $f(x) = \alpha x$. As α becomes arbitrary large ($\alpha \to \infty$), the screening function approximates that of a perfect evaluator.

3.5.3. *Results for Individual Evaluators*

To provide some initial understanding of the nature of the adaptive search process modeled here, we first consider the behavior of individual evaluators and then, in the subsequent analysis, model the behavior of alternative organizational structures. All results reported here are based on simulations of landscapes with $N = 10$. We use $K = 3$ as a baseline case. Unless indicated otherwise, our results reflect the average of 100 entities searching on each of a 100 distinct landscapes, resulting in 10,000 unique runs obtained from 100 different landscapes. Each of these landscapes has the same structure in terms of K, the degree of interdependence among attributes in contributing to performance, but represents a distinct draw on the common underlying probability generating structure. At the beginning of each of the 10,000 runs, attribute sets are randomly assigned to the individual entities.

To enhance the comparison across these families of landscapes, we normalize the performance level on each surface so that average performance equals 0.5 and maximum performance equals 1. That is, the crude fitness measure à la Kauffman were normalized in order to compare the results across different values of K. Using this normalized instead of the crude fitness measure does not alter the results in a qualitative sense.

Figure 3.6 indicates the performance of two types of evaluators who vary according to the accuracy of their evaluation function. For the sake of a baseline comparison, we model one as being a perfect evaluator; in this setting, only alternatives that enhance the actual pay-off will be accepted. In contrast, the other evaluator ($\alpha = 10$) exhibits some intelligence in evaluation (i.e., $\alpha > 0$), with the probability of accepting a more favorable alternative increasing as a linear function of the performance increases associated with that alternative; however, this evaluator will at times mistakenly accept alternatives that in fact offer inferior performance and in other instances reject alternatives that could enhance the organization's performance (i.e., α is finite). We see that the perfect evaluator quickly asymptotes in the performance that is achieved, while the imperfect evaluator not only outperforms the perfect evaluator, but also, if additional periods are examined, continues to exhibit modest but steady performance improvement. Perfect evaluation leads to the rapid identification of a local peak and the perfect evaluation function will lead the actor to maintain that position for the remainder of the simulation, while imperfect evaluation leads to persistence in search.

We would expect, however, that imperfect evaluation would suffer from two possible downsides. First, it is natural to expect that an imperfect evaluator would experience a slower rate of ascent in initial performance gains as an imperfect evaluator, by definition, will at times make downward moves. Even though the perfect evaluator converges faster to the local optimum than does the imperfect evaluator, the difference in the initial rate of progress between the imperfect and the perfect evaluator is

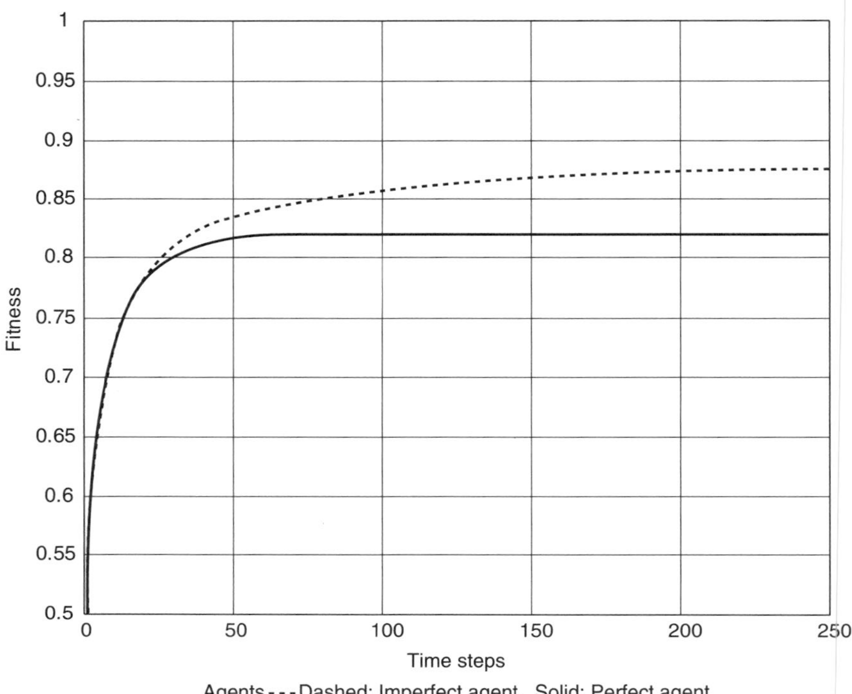

Figure 3.6. Fitness for perfect evaluator and imperfect evaluator ($K = 3$, $\alpha = 10$, 10,000 evaluators. One hundred distinct landscapes with 100 evaluators on each)

too slight to be visible in the comparison shown in Figure 3.5. However, around period 40, we start to see a divergence in the two performance curves as the performance of the imperfect evaluator continues on an upward gradient while that of the perfect evaluator begins to asymptote. With less ability of the imperfect evaluator or larger values of N, the faster convergence of the perfect evaluator to a local optimum becomes more pronounced.

The other 'penalty' that imperfect evaluation might exhibit is with respect to a limited ability to maintain, over extended periods of time, the attractive alternatives that have been identified. Given the noise in his or her evaluation process, even if a global peak is identified, there is a chance of mistakenly being seduced off of it by an alternative that appears superior.

Imperfect evaluators do not to wander too far off from the attractive peaks that they identify. We do not often see a situation in which slightly inferior alternatives are adopted and, then from this new lower base, even more inferior alternatives are mistakenly adopted. It is certainly possible for evaluators to take such a two-step 'walk' from an attractive peak and on occasion they will do so. However, the fact that the screening process, while imperfect, is nonetheless intelligent, in that more favorable alternatives are more likely to be accepted than less favorable ones, implies that mistakes, walks away from superior alternatives, will tend to be self-correcting. After accepting an inferior alternative that takes him or her away from an attractive peak, it is more likely that the subsequent move will be back to this same peak rather than a move that takes the evaluator even further away from this location.

Our main result is driven by the fact that in high K worlds, firms that do local search (with perfect evaluation) will get stuck on one of the myriad of local peeks that exist. A general claim that noise (perturbations and mutations) is beneficial in complex landscapes is not very novel. Scholars have long recognized that in complex environments some degree of perturbation or mutation leads to broader search and better outcomes. Our claim goes further, however, by considering what may be called 'intelligent noise.' Mutation probabilities are (usually) identical for all of the alternatives and thus insensitive to fitness differences. In contrast, the screening function introduced in the present work is sensitive to the goodness of possible alternatives. An alternative that has much lower fitness than the current alternative will be accepted with a (very) low probability. Similarly, alternatives with much higher fitnesses will be accepted with a (very) high probability. Finally, alternatives that only differ marginally are accepted with a probability of about 1/2. Thus, imperfect evaluation introduces intelligent search in the sense that error probabilities depend on the performance of a new proposed alternative relative to the current.

Because the search effort of our imperfect evaluator (e.g., $\alpha = 10$, $N = 10$, $K = 3$) is characterized by 'intelligent noise,' she can outperform perfect evaluators even if they benefit from (slight) random mutations. The reason is that random mutations lead to broader search at the cost of occasional detours to inferior points in the fitness landscape. A screening function, by contrast, can be devised to favor broad search with a much lower probability of experiencing such detours. Even though we have used a linear screening function, our framework allows the screening function to take on any shape. This has two important implications. First, we can model a much larger family of disturbances that may influence the search process than is feasible with perturbations or mutations of bit-strings. Second, and related, we can capture any kind of deviations from perfect evaluation, including symmetric or nonsymmetric evaluation (as in Prospect Theory), and other kinds of misguided evaluation. This is an important property of our framework because it admits a straightforward way to model cognitive biases and evaluation errors emphasized in the behavioral literature (e.g., Prospect Theory).

3.5.4. *Organizational Evaluation of Alternatives*

The beliefs of individual evaluators can be aggregated into organizational-level belief structures. In particular, organizations can be characterized by the number of evaluators within them, but also more subtly by the nature of decision authority within them. Following Sah and Stiglitz (1986), we focus on whether a given actor has the authority to approve or reject a proposed alternative, or is merely authorized to pass the proposed initiative along within a broader chain of command. In particular, consider the flow of decisions in six distinct organizational forms shown in Figure 3.7.

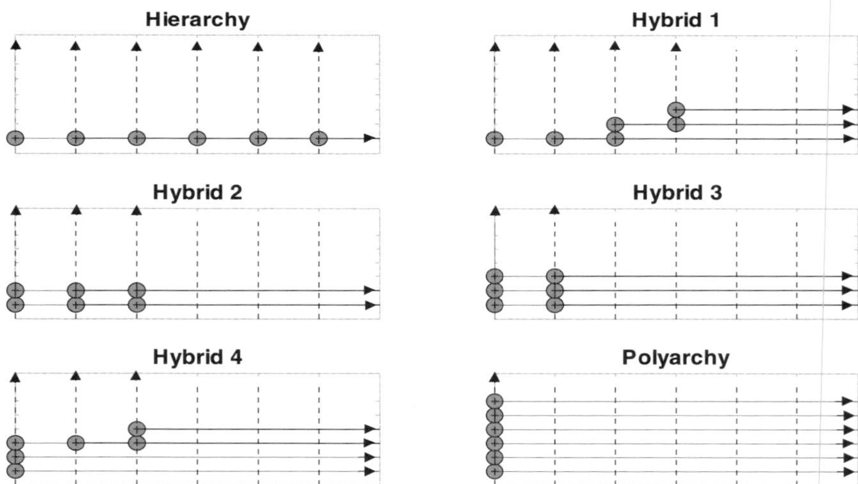

Figure 3.7. Flow of decisions in six stylized organizational forms each with six members. In each of the six organizational forms shown here, proposals enter with the actor in the lower left corner and then flow from the left toward the right. Dashed lines show rejection of proposals and solid lines show acceptance. Proposals that exit to the right are adopted by the organization. The organizational-level screening function, F, is a polynomial in the individual-level screening function, $f(x)$, under the assumption that all members of an organization have identical screening functions

In analyzing the role of alternative organizational forms, we wish to distinguish between the effect of individual differences in screening ability and the impact of the structure of the relationship among evaluators within the organization. Therefore, we treat organizations as being homogeneous in the screening ability of the individual evaluators that comprise the organization, though we examine the impact of varying this homogeneous level.

Figure 3.7 indicates the effective screening properties of six alternative organizational forms, all composed of six evaluators with an α value of 10. Using methods outlined in Christensen and Knudsen (2007), we derived an organizational-level screening function, F, which is a mathematical representation of the flow of decisions in an organizational form (as shown in Figure 3.6). In order to examine the effect of changing organizational structure, we assume that all members in an organization have identical ability. That is, we assume that the individual-level screening function, $f(x)$, the probability that an individual accepts an alternative, is the same for all members of an organization.

The particular functional form of F represents an aggregation of beliefs in the organization under consideration. The organization-level screening function of an n-member hierarchy is $F = f(x)^n$ and the organization-level screening function of an n-member polyarchy is $F = 1 - [1 - f(x)]^n$. For example, accepting an alternative in the six-member hierarchy requires that all of its six members accept the alternative. Therefore, the organizational-level screening function of the hierarchy (shown in Figure 3.7) is given by $F = f(x)^6$, which is the probability that this structure accepts the alternative in question. In a similar way, it is easy to see that the organizational-level screening function of the polyarchy (shown in Figure 3.7) is given by $F = 1 - [1 - f(x)]^6$, that is, the probability that at least one out of the six polyarchy members accepts an alternative. The screening functions of the four hybrids, shown in Figure 3.7, were derived in a similar way. As a point of reference, in Figure 3.8, we also include for comparison the evaluation function of a single perfect evaluator. The issue of organizational form is not relevant in the case of perfect evaluators as each perfect evaluator in the organization would simply replicate the decision of others.

3.5.5. *Results for the Organizational Level*

What is the effect of organizational architecture on search processes? We see that the hierarchical form has many of the properties of the perfect

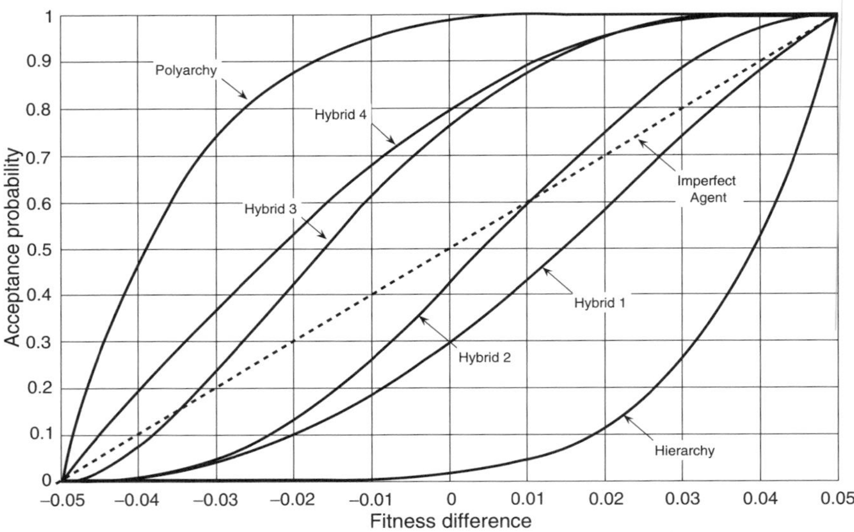

Figure 3.8. Ability of imperfect evaluator compared to six organizational forms, each built of six identical imperfect evaluators. The figure represents the case where $n = 6$ and $\alpha = 10$. The ability of the six hybrid organizational forms were derived according to the procedure shown in Appendix 1

evaluator. Such organizations tend only to 'walk' uphill, albeit slowly, as they tend only to accept new alternatives that do in fact lead to an increase in performance. Thus, as with perfect evaluators, they tend to be 'prisoners' of their starting positions, identifying local peaks but not exploring more broadly in the landscape. Further we find that our intermediate forms can offer an effective mix of exploration and exploitation (March 1991; Holland 1975). Elements of polyarchy enhance the breadth of search, but some degree of hierarchy facilitates the organization's ability to reliably sustain an attractive position in the landscape once identified. However, given that even a population of single evaluators is able to cluster rather closely to the most attractive peaks in the landscape, only a modest degree of hierarchy is needed to reliably sustain an attractive position in the performance landscape.

Reflecting these trade-offs between the search inducing polyarchy forms and the inertia generating hierarchical forms, we find an important complementarity between organizational form and screening ability of the evaluators who comprise the organization. However, it is also important to note that some of the six organizational forms would result in a lower performance than could be generated by an individual member of the organization (i.e., the imperfect evaluator shown with square markers). Organizations have the potential to compensate for weaknesses of individual screeners (hierarchy potentially helping to reduce the extensiveness of search in the case of highly inaccurate screeners and polyarchy forms usefully enhancing the degree of search for more accurate screeners), but the inappropriate organizational form may exacerbate the pathologies associated with an individual evaluator.

For very imperfect screening ability (α values of 1 and 2), the hierarchy yields a substantially higher level of performance relative to the polyarchy form. Hierarchy is a useful complement to very imperfect screeners. Individuals who evaluate alternatives with considerable noise naturally induce considerable breadth of search. Breadth of search has the virtuous quality of preventing organizations from locking in prematurely to inferior peaks. Sustained breadth of search, however, has the liability of generating a more dispersed distribution of organizations around the superior alternatives that come to be identified in the long run. Thus, highly imperfect evaluators, even if placed in a hierarchical structure, are likely to generate broad ranging search, but the hierarchical form will enhance the ability of such organizations to retain the attractive solutions that are identified.

Conversely, polyarchy is a desired complement to organizations composed of highly accurate screeners (α values of 6 or more). Accurate screeners are likely to rapidly identify a local peak in the landscape. Polyarchy, a form that permits any individual within the organization to approve an alternative, only requires one of the six actors in the organization to view an alternative as favorable in order to result in its adoption. Thus, as long as the evaluation of the individual evaluators composing the organization has some possibility of error, polyarchy compounds the likelihood of accepting an alternative that results in an immediate decline in performance; at the same time, however, polyarchy offers the possibility of broadening search to new regions of the performance landscape. If actors are highly accurate in their individual screening, such organizations do not pay a significant price for their pro-acceptance bias of the polyarchy form in that, in the long run, the distribution of organizations is still tightly packed around the superior peaks in the performance landscape.

For modest α values, some hybrid form dominates both the hierarchy and the polyarchy: Hybrid 2 dominates at α values of 2 and 3, Hybrid 3 dominates at α of 4, and Hybrid 3 dominates at α of 4. The effect of Hybrid 2 is to somewhat narrow down the breadth of search while producing a sharper ability to discriminate between alternatives (as shown in Figure 3.8). This effect is critical at values of α that are modest, but not extremely low (α value of 1). As the discriminatory ability sharpens at values of α above 3, less hierarchical forms that broaden search are favored, that is Hybrid 3 and Hybrid 4, and then, with α values of 6 or more, the polyarchy. Interestingly, the very similar results produced by Hybrid 1 and Hybrid 2 reflect the trade-off between narrowing down the breadth of search (Hybrid 1) and sharpening the discriminatory ability (Hybrid 2).

Indeed, these results suggest that organizational forms must be designed to fit the contingencies of the available workforce (screening ability) as well as the task environment (level of uncertain evaluation and interdependencies among policy attributes). Thus, in the same task environment, the more able are the individual evaluators composing the organization, the more that organizational form should shift toward the permissiveness of the polyarchy form. Very able evaluators need a structure that accepts and empowers the divergent views of organizational members. Conversely, evaluators who are less able and therefore less discriminating require the repeated checks on behavior that hierarchical elements provide. Note that, as evaluators become near-perfect screeners, performance becomes insensitive to the specification of organizational form. In the limit, with perfect screeners, evaluators would simply replicate each others' evaluation decision; thus, in the limit, performance is invariant to organizational form and the number of evaluators engaged in evaluation. Thus, a perfect evaluator would not benefit from being member of an organization.

More generally, our analyses imply that knowledge organizations can always be designed to remedy the actions of imperfect decision-makers that are not in tune with the contingencies they face (Christensen and Knudsen 2007). Our framework thus offers answers to some of the open questions relating to the design of knowledge organizations.

3.6. The Advantage of Flexible Organization Structures[3]

We now turn to illustrating our framework within the context of turbulent markets. According to both scholarly and popular works, it appears to be a stylized fact that flexibility is beneficial in turbulent markets, but we do

[3] The following material is an extraction from Christensen and Knudsen (2008). We refer to that article for elaborations.

not really know why. To address this gap in our knowledge, we examine whether flexible decision teams can be designed to reduce mistakes and thus increase profits, as MNCs decide to enter and exit turbulent international markets. Such markets offer interesting opportunities, but they are also risky adventures because of irrecoverable entry and exit costs. Under turbulent conditions, a promising market opportunity can turn sour. Mistakes get made when firms leave a market too early, or too late. Such mistakes are costly, and increased market turbulence can lead to both more frequent and more severe mistakes.

We here explain how a simple extension of our modeling structure allows comparison of industry entry and exit under alternative assumptions of managerial ability and different levels of market turbulence. Three types of decision-makers—the optimizer, the local searcher, and the fallible evaluator—were compared in a generic entry–exit model where turbulent market conditions are modeled as fluctuating short-run profits. The optimizer uses a dynamic programming approach to extract the optimal critical levels of operating profit from the Bellman equation.[4] Individual agents capable of using such methods can identify and use a proposed optimal profit level to trigger industry entry and exit. These would be very close to perfection, but real-world decision-makers are unlikely to achieve such high standards. Local search is modeled as examining a profit level of zero. If operating profits is above zero, the agent enters the market and if profit is below zero it exits. In this way, such agents search for new markets that satisfy some minimum performance criteria (potential profit should be at least zero).

The fallible evaluator has imperfect discriminating ability. This type of decision-maker behaves like a local searcher, but is not capable of making sharp evaluations of short-run profit for the reasons proffered in the literature on new organizational forms and elsewhere (ambiguity, complex interactions, limited information, limited computation power, etc.). That is, our fallible evaluator behaves in accordance with the stylized description of real-world decision-makers offered in much of the organization and management literature (Knudsen and Levinthal 2007). The discriminating ability of the fallible evaluator is modeled as a linear screening function of the type previously illustrated in Figure 3.5. The slope of the screening function captures fallibility, and fallibility translates

[4] The Bellman equation is a common numerical method used to extract information on optimal expected rewards from a Markov decision process such as the one considered here. This method, also known as dynamic programming, was developed by Bellman (1957) and Howard (1960).

into a wider zone of uncertainty as regards entry and exit decisions. A wide zone of uncertainty is a mixed blessing. The lower the slope, the more fallible is the decision-maker, and the wider is the zone of uncertainty within which costly reversals of prior decisions can occur. On the other hand, a wider zone of uncertainty spans multiple trigger points.

In our case, the observed levels of profit that lead to successful decisions are far apart when firms pay an irrecoverable fee to enter and exit. Costly entry and exit decisions introduce multiple decision criteria because they require consideration of two trigger points for observed profit. In a sense there is a trade-off between treatment of multiple decision criteria and certain quality discrimination. The local searcher can make extremely sharp judgments about quality but this virtue goes hand in hand with a zone of uncertainty that shrinks to a single point, that is, the local searcher is unable to consider more than one trigger point.

It is disturbing that the characterization of the local searcher in most of our formal models does not match the empirical reality in entry and exit decisions (as regards multiple decision criteria). As sunk costs increase, the individual agent is less able to handle the conflicting demands of multiple decision criteria and certain quality discrimination. The way out is to structure costly entry decisions in decision teams.[5]

3.6.1. *Decision Teams*

We use our recent extension of the Sah and Stiglitz (1985, 1986, 1988) characterization of organizational architectures to model evaluation in teams. This modeling approach was recently extended to the study of imperfect evaluation within the context of NK models (Knudsen and Levinthal 2007). The problem we are considering here is different from those problems for which the NK model is best suited (as illustrated in the previous section). The NK model has become the standard tool for organizational analysis of complex spaces where alternatives are hard to locate even though the payoff for each particular configuration remains fixed, once and for all. In contrast, the problem we are addressing relates to fluctuating payoffs.

The intuition in what follows is that fallible evaluators can (always) benefit from being placed in flexible teams whereas local searchers are

[5] More generally, the structuring of decision flows among multiple agents becomes a critical issue when imperfect agents face a difficult trade-off between treatment of multiple decision criteria and certain quality discrimination. A more comprehensive guide to designing decision structures is provided in Christensen and Knudsen (2007).

beyond help because they discriminate perfectly. Ironically, imperfect discrimination of fallible agents is a source of flexibility that can be utilized by designing appropriate decision teams. As we shall see, this gives rise to the surprising result that flexible teams with relatively few fallible decision-makers can outdo the so-called 'optimizer.' Notably, the fallible decision-makers in our model are modeled as uncertain 'local searchers' and thus, in accordance with much of the literature on organizations and management, are quite realistic.

Local searchers are limited in their ability to search for new alternatives, but once identified, they are capable of perfect discrimination. Within the present context, local search approaches optimality when the critical levels of operating profit become a single point—say, optimal entry (exit) for non-negative (negative) operating profit. This happens when entry and exit costs go to zero. In contrast to local searchers, fallible agents are not capable of perfect discrimination. However, in a turbulent market with significant entry (and exit) costs, the optimal points of entry and exit are located far apart, that is, firms only enter if operating profits are (very) high and they only exit if operating profits are (very) low. To help fallible agents overcome the inbuilt rigidity that narrows their focus to a single point of operating profit, we are led to consider the possible advantage of using flexible evaluation structures. In particular, we consider two extreme forms of evaluation structure. One is the hierarchy, in which a proposal to enter (or exit) a market is validated at successively higher levels in the team. Only if the proposal is accepted at each level, will the MNC enter a new market. The second form is a polyarchy, a flat, decentralized structure in which acceptance by any one actor is sufficient for the proposal to be approved. A flexible decision team is modeled by shifting between the two forms of organization.

The effect of locating fallible evaluators (e.g., $\alpha = 0.05$) in a hierarchical form is shown in Figure 3.8. In what we term a hierarchy, the short-run profit is initially considered by a member of the decision team. If the proposal is rejected by that team member, it is eliminated from further consideration and the business unit discontinues its activities (or remains inactive). Alternatively, if the proposal is approved by that decision-maker, then it is passed on to the next decision-maker in the chain of command. A proposal is acted upon only if it has been positively vetted by all of the evaluators in the team.

Figure 3.8 compares the effect of locating fallible agents in hierarchical decision teams with 2 (H2), 5 (H5), or 10 (H10) members, and also compares these structures to the optimizer and the local searcher. The single fallible agent is represented by a dashed line and we use a linear screening function with a slope of $\alpha = 0.05$ for the purpose of illustration. H5 is a hierarchy employing five such agents. We can read off the probability of entry for the hierarchical teams on the y-axis and compare these to the single fallible agent, the optimizer, and the local searcher. Suppose the observed profit is 5. In that case, the local searcher enters with probability $p = 1$, the single fallible agent enters with probability $p = 0.75$, and H5 enters with a probability of $p = 0.24$. The hierarch tones down a positive vetting made by a single fallible team member (reducing the entry probability from 0.75 to 0.24). The effect is to reinforce the status quo unless a very promising observation is made. As the size of the hierarchy increases, its screening function approaches a vertical line. Figure 3.9 illustrates this effect by mapping out the change in screening functions from H2 over H5 to H10.

The effect of locating fallible evaluators (e.g., $\alpha = 0.05$) in a flat team, also known as a polyarchy, is exactly the mirror image of Figure 3.9 and therefore not shown here. In the flat team, a proposed alternative can be adopted by any of the members of the decision team. Only if all decision-makers in succession reject an alternative is it dismissed.

3.6.2. *Flexible Decision Teams*

The aim of our model is to examine whether teams of fallible evaluators can benefit from being located in flexible organizations, for example, from shifting between hierarchical and flat, polyarchical modes of organization. This case could also be viewed as the consistent use of a hierarchical form with shifting targets (accepting entry vs. accepting exit).

Note how the local searcher in Figure 3.9 is represented by a single vertical line ($\alpha \to \infty$) while the optimizer is represented by two vertical lines computed by dynamic programming. Costly entry and exit decisions require consideration of two trigger points for observed profit. These two points represent the challenge of balancing two kinds of error. One is the error of staying in the market despite a downturn in the business cycle and the second is the error of missing an upturn in the business cycle by remaining inactive.

A flexible use of teams that shift between entry decisions in hierarchical teams and exit decisions in flat, polyarchical teams will effectively mimic the optimizer's use of two decision criteria. For example, using H5 in Figure 3.9 in the case of an entry decision and then delegating the exit decision to a flat, polyarchical, team would shift between the H5 curve

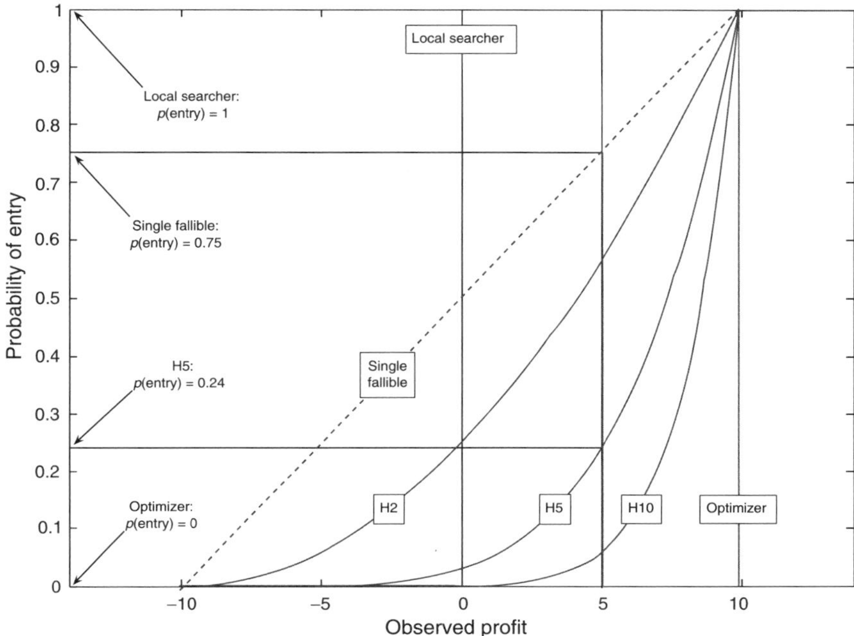

Figure 3.9. Levels of ability for hierarchical decision teams with 2 (H2), 5 (H5), or 10 (H10) fallible members compared to the optimizer and the local searcher. The teams employ fallible agents who are represented with a dashed line in our example ($\alpha = 0.05$). H5 is a hierarchy with five such employees. We can read off the probability of entry at the y-axis for hierarchical teams and then compare these to the single fallible agent, the optimizer, and the local searcher. For example, the optimal point for entry is shown when $\sigma = 4$, $\gamma = 0.90$, $K_{\text{Exit}} = 10$, and $K_{\text{Entry}} = 10$. If observed profit is 5, then the optimizer will not enter the market. By contrast, the single fallible agent would enter with $p = 0.24$, H5 with $p = 0.75$, and the local searcher with $p = 1$

and its mirror image, a curve for a five-member polyarchy (not shown here). This leads to the surprising result that simple flexible decision structures comprising 4–5 imperfect people can outdo the entirely superhuman performance of the 'optimal' agent (an encouraging result as regards realism).

It also turns out that the organizational structure that best helps the myopic decision-maker in our model is a flexible team of quite realistic size (4–5 members). The reason that larger teams, such as H10 in Figure 3.9, are inferior is that they span a narrower zone of uncertainty. In Figure 3.9, H10 is closer to the straight line of the perfect agent than H5.

More generally, as more agents are included in the decision team, the hierarchy (and polyarchy) approaches a straight line. However, our results show that in turbulent markets, some zone of uncertainty, as represented by a nonlinear trigger point in Figure 3.9, is superior to perfect discrimination represented by a straight line.

3.6.3. *The Nature of the Environment*

The local environment for the MNC subsidiary is more or less turbulent and the MNC considers whether its subsidiary should operate. More precisely, short-run profit is a random walk with normally distributed shocks, $N(\mu, \sigma^2)$. A parameter γ determines the rate of reversal toward the mean. The following analyses set average profits to zero, but vary the volatility parameter σ in order to examine alternative levels of turbulence in international markets. Higher volatility σ increases turbulence. This is shown in Figure 3.10, where the lower panel illustrates a highly turbulent task environment ($\sigma = 10$), while the upper panel illustrates a less turbulent environment ($\sigma = 4$).

Figure 3.10 shows the optimal entry and exit points computed by dynamic programming (these points are identical to the examples from Figures 3.1 and 3.2). Only if observed profit is at least 9.89 does the optimizer enter the market and become active. Once active, the optimizer exits only if observed profit falls below −9.90. The *actual* entry and exit decisions for the optimizer are shown in the panels of Figure 3.10. The upper panel of Figure 3.9 also shows a period where H5 has comparative advantage over the optimizer (from $t = 13$ to $t = 36$). The underlying reasoning is subtle. As depicted in Figure 3.9, the optimal evaluator uses a single linear trigger point, but the organization comprising fallible agents has a curvilinear set of trigger points. This curvilinear set of trigger points can effectively work as a confidence interval around the exit and entry points used by the optimizer. Supposing the observed profit is positive, H5 enters with a positive probability. On average, therefore, H5 would be active during some of the periods between $t = 13$ and $t = 36$ (upper panel of Figure 3.10). During this time, the net profit is positive. Therefore, H5 earns an expected positive profit. By contrast, the optimizer earns a profit of zero during the same period because it remains inactive (until $t = 36$).

But why is H5 superior to the fallible agent? Again, it is useful to refer back to Figure 3.9. If the observed profit is 5, the single fallible agent enters with probability $p = 0.75$ and H5 enters with a probability of $p = 0.24$. The single fallible agent is quick to enter and once active in the market, it is

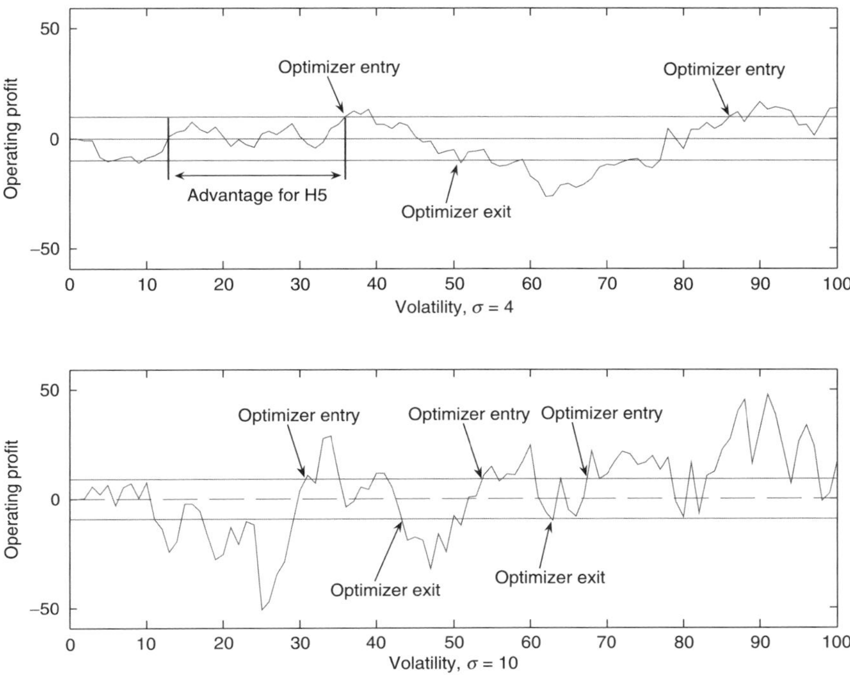

Figure 3.10. Examples of profit distributions with low ($\sigma = 4$) and high volatility ($\sigma = 10$). In both cases, the autoregression, γ, is 0.90. Optimal entry points for $K_{\text{Exit}} = 10$, $K_{\text{Entry}} = 10$ are also shown. The entry and exit decisions for the optimizer are shown in both panels. The upper panel also shows a period where H5 has a comparative advantage over the optimizer. In this period, H5 would earn a positive profit whereas the optimizer is inactive and earns a profit of 0

also quick to reverse the decision, and exit. As profits fluctuate the single fallible agent will make many reversals of prior decisions. When exit and entry are costly, the net result is diminished profits when compared to the steadier course of H5. Some restraint is required before the firm enters and that is exactly what H5 provides. If more agents were included, however, the restraint would become excessive. The move from H5 to H10 in Figure 3.9 illustrates this effect.

3.6.4. *The Decision to Enter and Become Active*

The MNC observes the next period's potential profit and its current operational status. It then takes an action about whether it should operate in the next period. In consequence, the MNC earns a reward that depends on the current state of the economic system, the current operational state of the MNC, and the action taken. In addition, an unknown exogenous shock influences the next period's potential profit. If the MNC is not operating and decides to enter the international market under consideration, it pays a fixed entry cost, K_{Entry}. Should the MNC be operating in an international market and then decide to exit, there is a shutdown cost of K_{Exit}. In all simulations, K_{Entry} was set at 10 and K_{Exit} was set at 10 (our results hold for a broad range of these values).

3.6.5. *Estimation of Critical Levels of Short-Run Profit*

The optimal value of the business unit, given an observed short-run profit and operational status, is estimated by the Bellman equation. This unrealistic dynamic programming approach is only available to the 'optimizer.' The local searcher and the fallible agents simply compare short run to a criterion for satisficing performance. If short-run profits are too low, it will stay out (or exit in the case that it is active). The fallible decision-maker behaves exactly like the local searcher. The only difference is that the fallible decision-maker sometimes makes a wrong decision, that is, exits when the firm should have remained active according to the satisficing criterion. The critical profit levels extracted for a particular example of $\sigma = 4$, and $\gamma = 0.90$ are shown in Figures 3.1 and 3.2. Figure 3.11 shows the results obtained for this particular example, with $\sigma = 4$, and $\gamma = 0.90$. A similar result is obtained for a broad range of parameter values.

3.6.6. *Results*

We compared the performances of the three types of decision-makers in a 'horse race' over 1,000 periods. On the basis of 1,000 samples, we found that optimizers always outperform local searchers and single fallible evaluators.[6] Generally, local searchers, who are perfect evaluators using a wrong decision rule (critical profit level of $\pi = 0$, in the case of both entry and exit), also outperform single fallible evaluators (as shown in Figures 3.3 and 3.4). The single fallible evaluator does not perform well, tending to promote frequent (and costly) reversals of prior decisions. Since entry and exit, in each case, are associated with a non-recoverable cost, the many mistakes impose a considerable cumulative cost.

[6] As described below in the text, all results reported here were confirmed through comprehensive additional tests.

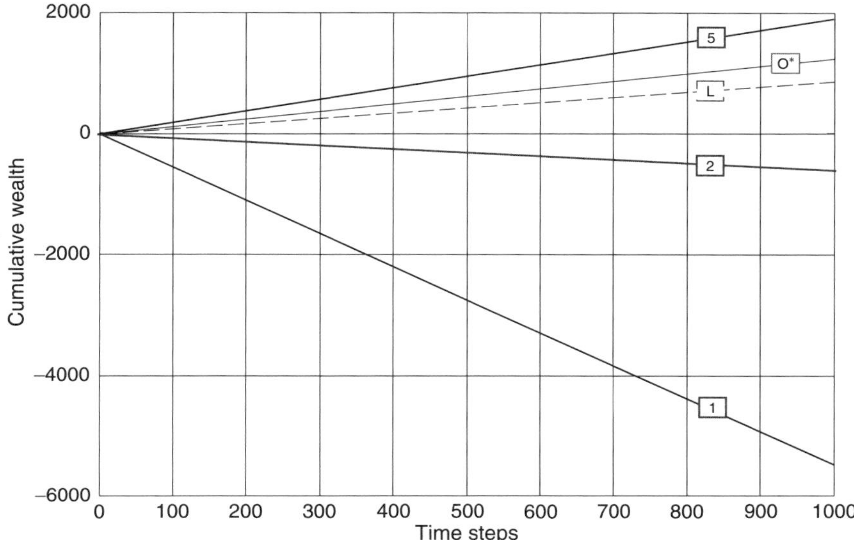

Figure 3.11. Performance of the optimizer, the local searcher, and a single fallible evaluator ($\alpha = 0.10$), compared with the performance of flexible decision teams with two or five fallible members. Example for $\sigma = 4$, $\gamma = 0.90$, $K_{\text{Exit}} = 10$, $K_{\text{Entry}} = 10$

The performance of the local searcher shown in Figure 3.10 is markedly higher than the performance of the single fallible decision-maker and even a flexible team comprising two fallible decision-makers. As more decision-makers are added to the team, the quality of the decisions further improves until it comprises five members. As further members are added, however, there would be a marginal decline in performance.[7]

The critical values of short-run profit used in the simulation reported in Figure 3.11 are the same as those in Figure 3.9. From Figure 3.9, it can be seen that the effect of adding members to the hierarchical decision team is to push a portion of the screening function to the southeast of the critical entry value. Adding members implies that the screening function of the decision team begins to approximate the optimal entry level. At some point, however, the screening function is pushed too far to the east, beyond the optimal level. The exit case is perfectly symmetrical to the case of entry and therefore not shown here. By switching between the hierarchy when entry opportunities are evaluated and the flat, polyarchy when

[7] Results are not shown here, but available upon request.

exit options are considered, a team of fallible evaluators can approximate the two optimal values of entry and exit.

The most surprising result is that fallible decision-makers who use flexible decision-making structures are generally superior to the so-called 'optimal' decisions based on a dynamic programming approach.[8] Figure 3.9 shows the cause of this surprising result: the optimal evaluator uses a single linear trigger point, but the organization comprising fallible agents has a curvilinear set of trigger points. The set of curvilinear trigger points effectively works as a confidence interval around the optimizer's exit and entry point. A team of fallible decision-makers would exit before the operating profit plunges to the negative level required by an optimizer.

So, it is the nonlinearity induced by the joint effect of individual evaluators that produces curvilinear trigger points. This nonlinearity gives our small teams an edge. Thus, flexible teams of fallible agents become a source of competitive advantage in a turbulent environment.[9] The effect is most pronounced in moderately volatile task environments. In a highly volatile environment, the shifts from low profits to high-profit peaks are much sharper (see Figure 3.10) and the shifts that trigger entry and exit will therefore tend to be the same for the optimizer and H5. In consequence, the advantage of H5 over the optimizer shrinks as volatility increases (in our analyses, from $\sigma = 4$ to $\sigma = 10$). The only exception to the surprising advantage of H5 over the optimizer is a very low volatility of $\sigma = 1$. In that case, the optimizer will never enter (since entry and exit costs are substantial at $K_{\text{Exit}} = 10$ and $K_{\text{Entry}} = 10$). By contrast, H5 will on average earn negative profits because it occasionally will enter and then discover that the operating profits cannot cover the entry cost. However, our flexible teams of simple fallible agents are generally superior to the so-called optimizer when task environments become more volatile ($\sigma > 1$). In a world with increasingly turbulent international markets, our results generally suggest why small flexible decision teams are beneficial.

[8] The so-called 'optimal' decisions based on a dynamic programming approach are superior only if there is very modest turbulence—or very low entry/exit costs.

[9] We use the hierarchy and the flat structure to simplify the analysis, but the results can be obtained for any flexible decision structure that changes from 'more' to 'less' centralized. This is shown in additional robustness checks available upon request. This proposition is valid within the modeling framework suggested here. It is due to the general property that centralized decision structures are more 'conservative' and decentralized decision structures more 'optimistic.'

3.7. Conclusion

We have introduced a general framework with which individual beliefs can be aggregated into organizational-level knowledge. Through examples, we have illustrated how our framework lends itself to analyzing simultaneous decision-making in committees, such as the UN Security Council. More detailed examples illustrated how our framework can be used to capture sequential decision processes. We considered both flexible decision structures facing a turbulent environment and fixed decision structures facing a stable, but complex task environment. These applications of our framework illustrate how it can be used to capture some of the most important problems emphasized in the literature on knowledge management.

While offering a very general framework, a number of simplifying assumptions eased the exposition. First, we assumed that agents were identical. Even if any conceivable shape of subjective beliefs could be captured by an individual-level screening function, we have not (yet) considered the possibility of heterogeneous beliefs. Second, we have only considered what amounts to deterministic organization structures. In a deterministic structure, a proposal is definitely sent to a particular successor (or accepted/rejected by the organization). In a stochastic organization structure, a proposal is definitely sent to two or more successors, but the likelihood of sending a project to any of these is determined by a set of weights (a probability distribution over possible receivers). Third, we have only considered what is known as acyclical structures. In acyclical structures, proposals do not return to an agent for a second evaluation. By contrast, cyclical organization structures allow that a proposal circulates among a number of agents, at least for a number of rounds, before they are finally processed. None of the simplifying assumptions are binding, so our framework can readily admit such extensions (at the cost of engaging with some technical complications).

It is time now to return to the example of Bank2 which opened this chapter. In this case study, we extracted the actual average screening function of 40 employees in Bank2 by sending around 'fake' applications of varying quality. The experiment included five gradations of quality (in terms of uncovered losses on loan applications) and since the parameters were known, we could estimate the average evaluation function for all of the 40 employees involved in the study. Under the assumption of homogeneity we could then assess how the organizational structure impacted on the quality of the decisions that get made. As we uncovered, the way credit evaluations are processed in Bank2, it first appeared as a four-member hierarchy. Additional information implied that the credit evaluation structure (of Bank2) was stochastic rather than deterministic. Credit applications could be accepted, rejected, or sent to a successor (we estimated the likelihood of each option from 209 projects). It also became clear that Bank2 used a cyclical evaluation structure. Quite often, an application was returned to a lower level for a second vetting. Overall, the bank had organized its evaluation process so it reduced the probability of accepting losses at the cost of forgoing good applications. It had a conservative effect similar to other hierarchical structures considered in this chapter. Surprisingly, only very minor changes to the assumptions suggested that Bank2 could incur significant losses without realizing the cause.

Further issues emerged as we continued to examine the data from Bank2. Most importantly, it turned out that lower level and higher level employees had very different abilities to assess loan applications. This observation raised the issue of heterogeneous beliefs and led to further exciting discoveries relating to experiential learning. Briefly, it appeared that lower level employees were better judges of poor quality because they more frequently had opportunity to assess bad loan applications. As bad loan applications would tend to be rejected at lower levels, higher level folks were robbed of the opportunity to experience such applications. Apparently, higher level employees became more 'rusty' and gradually lost their ability to evaluate a bad application when they very occasionally were presented with one.

Our engagement with Bank2 indicates how our framework can be used in real-world cases with potential benefits to practice. This example is only indicative of possible applications. Organizations that frequently evaluate a similar class of proposals, such as insurance companies, various financial operations, intelligence operations, and procuring, are obvious examples of knowledge organizations that would benefit from our framework. Our framework not only applies to operations that aim to reduce error. As illustrated above, it also provides guidance for knowledge organizations that wish to 'tune' the level of exploration that its search processes induces.

Even though our framework can be extended to real-world cases, it is important to be clear about its limitations. A number of issues remain open. First, there are issues relating to heterogeneity in the workforce. It is an open question, for example, in what position the organization would benefit most from the least able employee. Should the genius be placed at the top of the organization? Second, it is unclear how organizational structures impact on experiential learning within the context of other learners. Will very able employees at lower levels rob higher level managers of learning opportunities? Will geniuses at the bottom of the organization therefore create idiots at the top? Could job rotation alter such perverse learning outcomes? Third, how do knowledge organizations manage the trade-off between careful judgment and quick processing of high volume? Finally, how do issues relating to motivation and incentives interfere with beliefs and judgement?

In closing we would like to return to the challenge we identified at the beginning of the chapter. Our claim was that understanding organizations within the knowledge economy requires a firmer grip on the way knowledge held by individuals can be characterized and aggregated into knowledge at the organizational level. As a first step, we have offered an analytical platform, which accomplishes this for a broad class of evaluation problems. Even though important issues remain open, it is conceivable that our framework can be extended to address most of them.

References

Augier, M. and T. Knudsen. 2004. 'The Architecture and Design of the Knowledge Organization,' *Journal of Knowledge Management* 8(4): 6–20.

Bellman, R. E. 1957. *Dynamic Programming*. New Jersey, Princeton: Princeton University Press.

Christensen, M. and T. Knudsen. 2004. *The Architecture of Economic Organization: Toward a General Framework*, LINK Working Paper.

———2007. *The Human Version of Moore-Shannon's Theorem: The Design of Reliable Economic Systems*, Available at SSRN: http://ssrn.com/abstract=996311.

———2008. 'Entry and Exit Decisions in Flexible Teams,' *Journal of International Business Studies*, forthcoming.

Collins, J. J. and C. C. Chow. 1998. 'It's a Small World,' *Nature* 393: 409–10.

Csaszar, F. A. 2007. *An Efficient Frontier in Organization Design*, Available at SSRN: http://ssrn.com/abstract=985322.

Foss, N. J. and T. Pedersen. 2002. 'Sources of Subsidiary Knowledge and Organizational Means of Knowledge Transfer,' *Journal of International Management* 8: 49–67.

—— et al. 2005. *Governing Knowledge Processes: Theoretical Foundations and Research Opportunities*, Unpublished Manuscript, Copenhagen: Copenhagen Business School.

Grant, R. M. 1996. 'Towards a Knowledge-Based Theory of the Firm,' *Strategic Management Journal* 17: 109–22.

Hedlund, G. 1994. 'A Model of Knowledge Management and the N-Form Corporation,' *Strategic Management Journal* 15: 73–91.

Holland, J. H. 1975. *Adaptation in Natural and Artificial Systems*. Ann Arbor: University of Michigan Press.

Howard, R. 1960. *Dynamic Programming and Markov Processes*. Cambridge: The MIT Press.

Kauffman, S. A. 1993. *The Origins of Order: Self-Organization and Selection in Evolution*. New York: Oxford University Press.

Knudsen, T. and D. A. Levinthal. 2007. 'Two Faces of Search: Alternative Generation and Alternative Evaluation,' *Organization Science* 18: 39–54.

Koh, W. T. H. 1992*a*. 'Variable Evaluation Costs and the Design of Fallible Hierarchies and Polyarchies,' *Economic Letters* 38: 313–18.

—— 1992*b*. 'Human Fallibility and Sequential Decision-Making: Hierarchy versus Polyarchy,' *Journal of Economic Behavior and Organization* 18: 317–45.

—— 1994*a*. 'Making Decisions in Committees: A Human Fallibility Approach,' *Journal of Economic Behavior and Organization* 23: 195–214.

—— 1994*b*. 'Fallibility and Sequential Decision Making,' *Journal of Institutional and Theoretical Economics* 150(2): 362–74.

Levinthal, D. A. 1997. 'Adaptation on Rugged Landscapes,' *Management Science* 43: 934–50.

March, J. G. 1991. 'Exploration and Exploitation in Organizational Learning,' *Organization Science* 2: 71–87.

Sah, R. 1991. 'Fallibility in Human Organizations and Political Systems,' *Journal of Economic Perspectives* 5: 67–88.

Sah, R. K. and J. E. Stiglitz. 1985. 'Human Fallibility and Economic Organization,' *American Economic Review* 75: 292–7.

————. 1986. 'The Architecture of Economic Systems: Hierarchies and Polyarchies,' *American Economic Review* 76: 716–27.

————. 1988. 'Committees, Hierarchies and Polyarchies,' *Economic Journal* 98: 451–70.

Stiglitz, J. E. 2002. 'Information and the Change in the Paradigm of Economics,' *American Economic Review* 92: 460–501.

Volberda, H. W. 1996. 'Toward the Flexible Form: How to Remain Vital in Hypercompetitive Environments,' *Organization Science* 7(4): 359–74.

—— 1998. *Building the Flexible Firm*. Oxford: Oxford University Press.

Wright, S. 1931. 'Evolution in Mendelian Populations,' *Genetics* 16: 97–159.

4

Poliarchic governance and the growth of knowledge

Anna Grandori

4.1. Introduction

Innovation is increasingly important in modern economies. This fact has stimulated a flourishing of contributions analyzing knowledge related processes in economic activities. As pointed out in recent reviews of the field (Foss 2007), though, those advances have been mostly concerned with the problem of what types of knowledge are more or less difficult to transfer and share, and which organizational and governance mechanisms are more or less useful in facilitating knowledge exchange or sharing. Important as it is, this is not the entire problem. Knowledge must be produced, in addition to be transferred and shared. The production of knowledge, and more precisely the production of new valid knowledge (to which the term 'growth of knowledge' refers), has been a core concern in modern philosophy of science (Lakatos and Musgrave 1970), including various ideas on how to organize systems of collective action able to be highly innovative (Popper 1945: 66).

Instead, albeit lying at the core of innovation, the growth of knowledge in that sense has received limited attention in economic and administrative sciences, and even less attention has been devoted to the comparative assessment of governance structures for knowledge generation.

The work on innovation and governance in economics and management has been treating the issue in a limited way, in at least four respects:

- As said, it focused mostly on knowledge transfers, rather than also on knowledge production.

- It mostly addressed the *ex post* processes: the commercialization of innovation and the availability of complementary resources (Teece 1986); the competitive implications of the unequal development of knowledge resources in different systems (Nelson 1993).
- It mostly addressed the incentive and motivational side of knowledge production rather than the cognitive side: for example, issues of appropriability of results and incentive to invest in 'research' (e.g., Hennart 1988; Ouchi and Bolton 1988) rather than the research process itself.
- It rarely linked knowledge generation processes with governance mechanisms in a fine-grained way, beyond the general understanding that the 'openness' of firms to interfirm knowledge exchanges and interfirm networks are conducive to innovation (Chesbrough 2004; Powell 1996).

In organization and strategic management research, governance and coordination mechanisms have been considered in a more detailed way (e.g., Grant 1996; Kogut and Zander 1996; Nonaka and Takeuchi 1995). The emphasis here has been not only on knowledge transferring but also and especially on knowledge sharing; but still not much on knowledge generation. When considered, knowledge production has been mostly analyzed through the lenses of the sociology of knowledge and of science—describing how scientific communities are structured in practice, and how difficult it is to construct and communicate knowledge in a rational, logically sound way; rather than of philosophy of science and the logic of discovery—how to generate new reliable and valid knowledge, in spite of the difficulties (Grandori and Kogut 2002). Arguably, however, the latter type of approach would be all the more conducive to draw implications for the effective governance of innovation. For example, if from the 'rational reconstruction' of the history of science we derive the idea that the competition between research programs is a regime particularly conducive to the growth of knowledge (Lakatos 1970), then we can derive the implication that systems organized so as to allow that kind of process have better chances to produce innovation. If from epistemology we derive the idea that 'valid knowledge' is not 'objective knowledge' but it is knowledge produced through sound hypotheses formulation and testing procedures (Hanson 1958; Popper 1935; Simon 1977), then we can try to devise organizational arrangements that are supportive to experimentation and unbiased learning (Popper 1989; Weick 1979). If we acknowledge that sources of uncertainty are not limited to 'exogenous variance,' 'unspecifiable probabilities,' and 'unforeseeable contingencies,' but can involve structural, 'epistemic uncertainty' about what the relevant problems and cause–effect relations are (Grandori 1984; Langlois 1986; Shackle 1972), then we can revisit the implications of uncertainty for governance, for example we might appraise and design contracts in quite a different way from trying to minimize their 'incompleteness' (Grandori 1999, 2005; Loasby 1976).

Hence, in this chapter, knowledge growth is intended as knowledge production as contrasted with knowledge exchange; and as production of valid, empirically corroborated, logically sound knowledge as contrasted with biased, superstitious, or otherwise false beliefs. Second, the notion of knowledge growth used here, as in the philosophy of knowledge, includes both incremental and radical ('normal' or 'revolutionary') discovery, and includes 'rejections' and 'forgetting' (getting rid of past falsified or obsolete beliefs) as part of the growth. The knowledge considered is economically applicable knowledge, and the level of analysis (the learning system) is not that of societies or communities of knowledge, but that of organized systems based on 'continued association of dedicated assets' (Demsetz 1991), such as firms and networks of firms.

The contribution of the chapter is a reassessment of governance mechanisms in their capacity of governing knowledge generation. Governance issues arise when the relevant knowledge for economic action is disseminated among different actors (Hayek 1945). This condition is arguably more the rule than the exception, and even a condition for knowledge growth, in modern economies. In fact, as products and production processes have become more complex, technology intensive, based on scientific and cultural advances in a variety of fields, the input components can less and less be mastered by any single actor, even if collective, like a group or a firm. Specialization becomes not only possible and efficient but also cognitively unavoidable (Arora and Gambardella 1994; Pisano 1991). Hence, systems with high knowledge growth potential can be characterized as being 'distributed knowledge systems,' in the sense of differentiated and partitioned across different actors.

A comparative (re)assessment of the main governance mechanisms in their capacity of sustaining knowledge growth is outlined in Section 4.1 of this chatper. In the second part, relevant available evidence on the organization and governance of innovative firms and innovation-oriented interfirm networks will be brought into the picture, to provide initial evidence of which new (and old) facts the framework can predict.

4.2. An Organizational Failures Framework for the Growth of Knowledge

4.2.1. *Market Failures, Hierarchical Failures, and Innovation*

In organizational economics, the 'Organizational Failures Framework' (Williamson 1975), started out by recognizing, with Hayek, the 'marvel' of market mechanisms in orienting the use of resources 'in the right direction,' without anyone knowing the whole picture, only on the basis of local knowledge of the condition of production and of the 'sufficient statistics of prices.' Whereas exchanges are not instantaneous, uncertainty, intended as lack of knowledge about possible future contingencies and about the value of what is delivered, has been then indicated as a source of market failure, as it impairs the writing and enforcement of complete contracts. Hence, the argument goes, if objective alignment cannot be assumed, and contracts provide incomplete protection, then some alternative governance mechanism, allowing adaptive decision-making as circumstances become observable should be devised to regulate exchanges of goods and services *'ex post.'* Hierarchical governance, intended as authority-based decision-making and control, coupled with unilateral ownership of the mean of production ('capitalistic' governance) has been indicated as the most effective among those devices under a range of conditions.

The main line of this argument has generally become codified and diffused as a general statement that uncertainty coupled with conflict of interests among unreplaceable actors, conceived as mostly due to asset specificity, favor hierarchical as opposed to market-like governance. This summary view is however highly imprecise.

To start with, the comparative assessment of governance mechanisms is always conducted *under some conditions*. In some writings, these conditions are spelled out very clearly. For example, Williamson (1980) highlighted that the superior efficiency and adaptiveness of a 'capitalistic' property right assignment (unilateral ownership of technical assets separated from ownership of human assets) combined with centralized contract negotiation and coordination by authority in the organization of work,[1] is contingent to at least the following conditions:

[1] To our purposes, it is worthwhile noticing that Williamson (1980) also admits and actually stresses that different configurations of asset ownership (capitalistic, entrepreneurial, and collective) can be coupled with more than one decision and coordination mechanisms

- Stages of production are separable through inventories and can proceed independently of each other; in addition economies of specialization are realized within each stage.
- The type of uncertainty to which the system should 'adapt' is of the 'exogenous variance' type, and not of the 'lack of knowledge' type ('aleatory uncertainty' rater than 'epistemic uncertainty' in modern decision science parlance).
- Performance can be monitored.
- The preference of agents as to tasks to be performed and having the right of selecting them are:
  - randomly distributed; and
  - investments for expansion and innovation are ignored, only 'routine replacement' is assumed.

In spite of the rhetorical (or perhaps initial) emphasis on the virtues of authority, therefore, the technical details of Williamson's comparative assessment of governance modes as referred to human assets and work services reveal that the conditions under which coordination by authority may be deemed to be effective are not particularly wide, or are becoming less and less common in the knowledge-intensive economy. Actually, the conditions characterizing knowledge growth are almost the opposite:

- The action system is not well represented by a set of separable stage of production, but by a set of interdependent knowledge nodes. Provided that some connection gets established among those differentiated knowledge nodes, distributed knowledge nurtures knowledge growth. A well-established result in organizational research is in fact that 'differentiated and integrated' organizational forms have maximal innovation potential (Burns and Stalker 1961; Lawrence and Dyer 1983). Recent research focused on knowledge growth at the industry level suggests that this principle is valid across time and type of system of innovation considered. For example, Carnabuci (2005) set out to answer the question of why certain domains of technological knowledge advance faster than others. Based on all knowledge patented between 1975 and 1999 in the United States, he showed that the higher the number

(e.g., authority, joint decision-making, individual incentives) and with more or less centralized contract negotiation; resulting in more or less hierarchical and tightly coupled governance combinations).

of connections a technological domain has with other domains at a given point in time positively affects its subsequent growth prospects.

- The type of uncertainty characterizing research for new products, services, processes is first and foremost 'epistemic' or 'structural' (Grandori 1984; Langlois 1986): it concerns how to define the problem, which the cause–effect relations between alternatives and consequences might be, rather than just 'aleatory' or 'parametric' on what conditions will occur.
- Performance is difficult to monitor by any central agent, as typically behaviors are poorly observable and results are poorly measurable (Williamson 1981).
- Preferences on tasks to be performed are systematic, rather than random, as intrinsic motivation is a typical and precious trait of knowledge-intensive work (Baron and Kreps 1999).
- Objectives cannot be supposed to be 'aligned,' but this condition does not necessarily imply high conflict of interests and opportunism potential, especially in innovation games. In fact, distributed and differentiated knowledge is likely to be associated to different interpretations of situations and different preferences, not only among independent actors but even within the same organization (Lawrence and Lorsch 1967). Hence, potential conflict of interests among the players of innovation games should be assumed. However, the type of conflict is unlikely to be of the constant sum variety that is sensible to play with the minimax logic of the 'opportunism assumption'—that is, 'not knowing how the others will behave, assume that all will be uncooperative.' Partners for innovation are selected on the basis of partner-specific knowledge, performance records, third party certifications, within reputation bound arenas. In addition, the union of complementary competences generate surplus to be divided, conditional to effective contributions of knowledge, whereby if parties do not contribute, they do not learn and do not discover anything. Finally, the differentiation and even the conflict among objectives need not be a negative feature, a 'misalignment,' or 'subgoal pursuit' to be reduced as almost universally assumed in organizational economics. Rather, as organizational and negotiation research has repeatedly shown, conflict is a powerful stimulus to search for ingenious solutions, hence a source of innovation in itself (Bazerman and Neale 1992).

A similar contingency restatement of the virtues of hierarchy can be given of other core contributions in organizational economics, such as property rights theory.

In early seminal contributions (Alchian and Demsetz 1972; Holmstrom 1982), the emergence of hierarchy has been linked to conditions of 'team-production,' where knowledge cannot be acquired about which the contributions of different agents in a collective output are. However, the goodness of a hierarchical solution (centralized residual control and reward rights) was admittedly contingent upon the condition that behaviors are knowable (observable). If that cannot be assumed, and as uncertainty not only about agents' output but also about agents' input behavior (difficult to observe or evaluate) increases, then not only market-like exchange contracts become increasingly ineffective, but so do decision and control by authority. The reasons are traced especially in control problems: if not only output is poorly observable and measurable but also input behavior is largely so, as in many professional and knowledge-intensive activities, 'control' by authority, aimed at establishing how good the action was, would basically require the 'boss' to redo the work (examples in the legal profession are given). In other terms, a centralized monitor would not be able to develop better proxies of inputs than those of which the team of coworkers is capable (Alchian and Demsetz 1972).

In more recent property right theory, the contingency argument is applied to proprietary regimes, through the proposition that property rights should be allocated according to the criticality of investments; the consequence being that they may end up to be allocated to the providers of technical assets, or of social and human capital, giving rise to different governance arrangements (e.g., from the classical capitalistic firm, to the modern public company, to work cooperatives) (Hansman 1996; Hart and Moore 1990); even without considering knowledge effects, that is, the possibility that an actor contributing critical resources may be better off if other actors hold decision and control rights, if those other actors know more and are more expert than he is.

The failures of hierarchy recognized, organizational economics has typically admitted a 'third mode,' alternative to both 'hierarchy' and 'market' coordination, supposedly more suitable for governing highly uncertain knowledge and research intensive actions and transactions. The characterization of that third mode has been, however, very composite, to say the least: it has been conceived and named differently, as governance by 'clans,' 'collectives,' 'relational team,' 'communities,' 'culture,' relational contracting, and 'trust.' Section 4.2.2 will be devoted to better clarify which fundamental types of governance mechanisms may lie behind all these governance modes, so as to assess more precisely their distinctive properties in the governance of innovation.

Before turning to that, another set of propositions about the role of market-like and bureaucratic governance in knowledge-intensive, innovative activities should be highlighted, developed in organization theory.

The proposition that bureaucracy, in both its main dimensions of hierarchy/centralization and of planning and structuring of activities, is rather ineffective in the governance of knowledge-intensive activities and innovation is a classic in organization theory and research. The reasons provided are complementary to those identified in organizational economics. In fact, in the above-reviewed organizational economics studies, the conditions under which hierarchical governance is expected to fail have been linked to lack of knowledge especially along the dimension of performance measurement and treated mostly on a motivational side. Organization theory analyzed the cognitive side of hierarchical failure, reinforcing and qualifying the notion of hierarchical failure under uncertainty and distributed knowledge. Here, it has always been clear that uncertainty has two main components, one linked to exogenous variability (often called 'environmental uncertainty'), and a second component linked to the lack of models of cause–effect relations, schemes, and methods for solving problems, observation, and measurements difficulties (often called 'task complexity') (Perrow 1967). Variability is considered to be especially disturbing for planning and programming (as it impairs forecasting), while task complexity is expected to be especially disturbing for authority-based coordination (as it makes less likely that any one actor can master sufficient information) (Galbraith 1974; Grandori 1999). Planning and authority-based coordination have been supposed to leave the way to decentralized allocations of decision rights, colocated with relevant knowledge, where coordination is achieved in a 'team-like' way (Burns and Stalker 1961; Hedlund 1986; Thompson 1967) and/or to 'cultural' alignment and sharing of objectives and of knowledge (Grant 1996; Kogut and Zander 1996; Ouchi 1979). However, again, the types of governance mechanisms lying behind all these 'communitarian' and 'decentralized' governance forms, their commonalities and differences, and their distinctive properties (including why precisely they are needed) in the governance of innovation have not been clearly specified.

To complicate the picture, those classic organizational solutions have been more recently further sided by, and/or mixed up with, organizational practices that are conceived as 'market' elements 'infused' into firms (Lindkvist 2004; Zenger and Hesterley 1997): pay for performance in all its forms, entitlement of organizational units with property rights, free internal labor markets, free recombination of resources into projects. Hence a further question emerges on whether all these market-like and communitarian governance mechanisms cluster into discrete, mutually exclusive, structural alternatives, each made up of mechanisms that are consistent in that they are inspired to the same logic, qualitatively similar, that is, 'similar in kind' (Roberts 2004; Williamson 2004); or they provide practices that are complementary and can be combined into superior arrangements, precisely because they are 'different in kind' (Grandori 1997, Grandori and Furnari 2008).

4.2.2. *Innovation Deficits of Relational and Communitarian Governance*[2]

Relational governance has been seen as an alternative to both markets and hierarchies in the context of high uncertainty and distributed knowledge, as it is supposed to provide 'flexibility.' However, it encompasses a variegated range of tools with somehow different properties as to the management of uncertainty and innovation. To the purpose of assessing those properties more precisely, Grandori (2006) has distinguished among different meanings of the term 'relational governance.' Two of them are mostly used. In organizational economics, these contracts are thought of as 'self-enforceable' agreements (Baker, Gibbons, and Murphy 2002), whereas trust in lack of externally enforceable contracts stems from perception of positive payoffs from collaboration of any origin (from complementarities to repeated games with reputation). The other notion, mostly used in organization studies, can be called a view of relational contracts as 'socially enforceable' agreements. In fact, the core mechanism providing confidence in compliant behavior is social norms and social control on their application (Ouchi 1980). I have earlier argued that neither one is particularly well suited for governing highly innovative, distributed knowledge activities:

> In sum, relational contracting as informal socially enforceable or self-enforceable contracting, is contrasted with *formal* governance. The predictions that can be derived from both these views of relational contracting concern the circumstances where we may expect exchange and cooperation not to be regulated by formal

[2] This section is based on Grandori (2006).

contracts because more efficient substitutes are available, either ready for use social norms or built in incentives to cooperation. (Grandori 2006: 129)

Considering what these circumstances are though, we should note that relational contracting of both the above types seems to be applicable only in situations of limited uncertainty. In socially enforceable contracting, it should be known what behaviors are appropriate to what tasks and relevant contingencies and behaviors should be observable (at least once they materialize). In self-enforceable contracts, the logic of incentives relieves reliance on control and a somewhat greater uncertainty can be dealt with (unobservability of behaviors). However, observability of results and *ex ante* knowledge of payoffs is required. Then, both these types of RG seem to be unable to provide powerful mechanisms for dealing with the core type of uncertainty to be managed in innovation.

In a third meaning, governance is called relational because it regulates the *relation* among partners rather than the *content* of transactions (Goldberg 1976; Macauley 1963; Macneil 1978; Vanberg 1994). In this sense, relational governance can be either formal or informal; the main point is that the contract is procedural (how parties are going to interact) rather than substantive (what they have to deliver). In that meaning, we are going to argue, relational governance is an important governance mechanism in innovative settings, provided that some further qualifications on the *types* of procedures employed are added.

In fact, the above-mentioned approaches tend to conceive 'rules' and 'procedures' as a unitary coordination mode. Indeed, rules as such do have common properties if contrasted with ad hoc decision-making (Brennan and Buchanan 1985; Vanberg 1994). However, precisely because rule following involves the suspension of case-by-case decision-making and the prescription of behaviors to be followed in all cases, rules are more or less rigid and compatible with uncertainty depending on the level of generality versus detail and action-specificity of their prescriptions. More precisely, only high-level, procedural, constitutional rules, specifying how to make decisions, are a flexible mechanism, capable of coordinating action under uncertainty (Grandori 1999), as contrasted with applied, substantive, detailed rules, such as 'programs' or 'routines,' specifying which actions to perform under what circumstances (Cohen et al. 1996).

A neighboring set of governance mechanisms has been described under the heading of 'communitarian' governance, and has also been highlighted as particularly well suited for knowledge governance almost by definition, as based on common identity and common knowledge

(Brown and Duguid 1991; Kogut and Zander 1996; Ouchi 1980). However, it has also been argued that only some *types* of communities are actually conducive to the growth of knowledge: open, epistemic communities of knowledge, rather than close, routine-based communities of practices (Cohendet et al. 2004; Grandori 2001; Lindkvist 2005); internally diversified and mobile groups rather than homogeneous and stable teams (Meyerson, Weick, and Kramer 1996); collectives informed by meta-norms of originality and deviance with respect to any substantive behavioral norm, rather than by any substantive objective alignment (Lampel 2004; Wilkins and Ouchi 1983).

In sum, relational and communitarian governance encompasses at least two classes of mechanisms that differ in kind and governance properties: rule-like mechanisms and team-like mechanisms; and, within each of these two classes, only some mechanisms are actually well suited to governance for the growth of knowledge and innovation: high-level, general rules and norms (rather than detailed); and diversified and epistemic communities and groups (rather than clans and communities of practices). Hence, we shall let the term 'relational' and 'communitarian' governance identify the class of self-enforceable and socially enforceable informal devices (including culture homogenizing devices); while we shall focus and reexamine the mechanisms that might govern the cooperation of actors with heterogeneous knowledge and preferences, in highly uncertain and innovative tasks. The result will be the definition of a class of governance mechanisms that can be claimed to be specifically well tailored to the governance of knowledge-intensive, knowledge-generating activities.

4.2.3. *Associational Governance and Connected Poliarchy*

A starting and founding insight can still be found in Hayek's lesson: under efficiency, no large system of action can be centrally governed, by authority and planning; and this holds for cognitive reasons, no matter how large the bases of 'power' which the central actor may sit on. Actually, the argument goes the other way around: a consequence of the Hayekian law is that in large complex system of action, it is inefficient to allocate property and decision rights so that a unilateral power is constituted. A poliarchic rather than hierarchic order is required (Sah and Stiglitz 1985). This principle on the 'use of knowledge in society' has been widely winning as far as national economic systems and the inefficiency of allocating property and decision rights to a central government are concerned; while, in spite of its generality, it is still limitedly applied and limitedly accepted in the organization of other large economic systems, such as large firms.

Other classic contributions in economics and organization science have pointed in the same direction, though. Most prominently, in his seminal contribution on 'employment' contracts rather than 'labor-sale' contracts, Simon (1951) indicated in the shift from an agreement on tasks (as in sale contracts) to an agreement *on the procedures* for selecting tasks, the essential difference. Simon also indicated that authority is one of these possible procedural agreements, Pareto-efficient under particular conditions of agents' indifference over task. What is often forgotten is that Simon also extended the model to the more general case in which agents' preferences are systematic and defined (rather than undefined or randomly distributed) and they are different from those of the 'employing' party. Simon concludes that if both uncertainty and diversity of preferences are high, a distributed allocation of residual decision rights to the different parties involved is superior to their allocation to one party only. In other words, the procedure of letting some tasks be chosen by a 'boss' and some by 'the workers,' or even empowering the workers as to the choice of tasks, is superior to the procedure of letting a central agent selecting tasks. Simon linked the distribution of rights and the departure from an authority relation to the intensity of preferences of the different parties, but the location of the relevant *competencies* provides a less subjective and more cogent condition. In fact, in that case, it is in the interest of everybody that tasks are selected by the most competent party, and parties who provide other resources than competence—that is, typically financial and technical resources—are those in the position of being indifferent over task selection, provided that the results are good. Hence, in such conditions, there should be no 'boss': just multiple resource providers, each entitled to a share of residual decision rights. Empirically, in fact, in knowledge-intensive and professional activities, where not only task and contingencies are not foreseeable, and agents derive important benefits from performing one task rather than another (something common to other settings, where nevertheless authority prevails), but they have most of the relevant knowledge about proper task selection, decision rights over task selection are entirely attributed to agents or 'workers' who are linked into a firm through partnership-like contracts.

Given diffused discretion, a diffused allocation of residual reward rights is also to be expected, although tempered by the different attitudes toward risks, and by the amount and substitutability of the invested resources

(Hart and Moore 1990; Jensen and Meckling 1976). Hence, as a general pattern, one would expect that more residual reward rights are allocated to the more diversified risk-neutral investors (e.g., financial capital providers); and more decision and control rights to the less diversified and more competent knowledge providers.

In sum, in addition to reinforcing Hayek's argument in favor of decentralization under uncertainty, Simon's model also helps in qualifying a type of 'connected poliarchy,' different from the 'unconnected poliarchy' of market. In the latter, decisions are taken separately on the basis of local knowledge and price-like signals, so that the system moves in the 'right direction' without anyone exchanging knowledge and knowing the whole picture. In the former, decision rights are shared and allocated according to actors' preferences and knowledge, and decisions are taken jointly or according to a deliberate division of labor, so that local knowledge is 'connected' in deliberately directed new directions that have better chances of being 'right' than separate trial and error.

The relevance of procedural contracting in uncertain activities has also been highlighted in constitutional political economics. Contracts, under uncertainty on the terms of exchange, incorporate a 'shift of attention from the specification of the terms of agreement to a more general statement of the process of adjusting the terms over time—the establishment, in effect, of a "constitution" governing the on-going relationship' (Goldberg 1976: 428). Three types of 'rules' have been singled out as fundamental component of the contract (Vanberg 1994: 220):

> As a member of an organization, an individual submits certain of his resources—simultaneously with contributions made by other participants—to some kind of joint control or authority. The inclusive social contract among the members defines the terms of their participation in the arrangement, in particular in three regards. It specifies the resources that participants are to contribute to the common pool; it specifies the way decisions are to be made on the use of the combined resources; and it specifies how the participants share in the benefits produced by the joint endeavour.

The procedural, rule-like, constitutional 'contract' is however only a component of a governance regime conducive to knowledge growth through the discovery of projects and activities. In fact, the identity of partners matters and is actually crucial in the 'bet' that their combined resources will generate something good and novel. Hence, the procedural agreement needs to be complemented by a substantive agreement (which arguably is not a rule itself) about *who* the associating parties are, who will own the invested resources, and at what conditions they can enter and might exit from the 'ongoing relationship' (Grandori and Furlotti 2006*a*). To our purposes, then, is important to keep the substantive associational contract distinct from the procedural constitutional contract, as only the coupling between associational and constitutional contracting, and multiparty joint decision-making governance, can be expected to have the proper features, on the basis of the argument developed thus far. In fact, in less knowledge-intensive conditions, where the discovery of new action is not so central, we can also envisage combinations of associational contracting with price-like governance (e.g., resource-pooling associations providing common services to the associates); or combinations of exchange contracts coupled with constitutional ordering and joint decision-making coordination (as found, for example, in industrial districts or in long-term repeated buyer–seller exchanges).

In sum, an array of governance mechanisms (or 'syndrome of attributes') that seems to be particularly well suited to sustain and regulate the growth of knowledge in economic activities can be expected to be an 'associational,' 'constitutional,' and 'democratic' governance regime, whereas:

- *Associational governance* specifies who the associating parties are, which resources they are going to commit, who holds which rights over the invested resources, at what conditions parties can exit and withdraw resources, and how the surplus generated by the cooperation is going to be divided (rather than the tasks to be performed); and can be contrasted with transactional governance.
- *Constitutional governance* specifies which party holds what decision and control rights, and which procedures should be used on what matters, how voice and information is guaranteed (rather than the terms of exchange or cooperation); that is, procedural and framing governance that can be contrasted with substantive and task-specific governance.
- *Democratic governance* indicates that the regime is democratic rather than authoritarian, that is, decision procedures and residual decision and reward right allocations prefigure joint direct or representative decision-making and negotiation, majority or unanimity voting schemes, only residual use of 'third party' neutral arbitration authority; and distributed ownership of assets and residual reward, rather than residual decision and reward rights assigned to one party.

4.3. Empirical Evidence

The growth of knowledge in the economy, in its implications for governance, can be observed in settings such as new firms in emerging sectors or based on product and process innovations, firms that are not new themselves but show high innovation performances, and interfirm alliances for innovation.

The empirical evidence summarized in this section consistently indicates that the prevailing governance profiles in those setting indeed intensively employ associational contracting and democratic governance. However, it also indicates that these components of governance are typically further complemented by selected mechanisms of other type, especially for guaranteeing the conditions for democratic governance to operate effectively and efficiently.

4.3.1. *Knowledge Governance in Innovative Firms*

Empirical evidence on the internal organization of highly innovative, knowledge-intensive firm abounds.

The most obvious case in which the growth of knowledge is produced and governed by means of firm organization is the founding of new firms based on innovation. Theory and research on the effective organization of knowledge-intensive start-ups has typically reconstructed a governance profile featuring the following key aspects:

- Diverse resources are provided by a plurality of investors, in particular the providers of human and financial capital are rather differentiated subjects (Castilla 2003); property rights shares are carefully divided among all of them, in particular human capital providers are intensively involved in ownership through shareholding and stock options, and through positions in boards (Kaplan and Stromberg 2003).
- The internal organization is highly horizontal and team-like (Aoki 2004; Baker 2000; Baron and Kreps 1999).
- The providers of knowledge assets are highly mobile through series of projects (Meyerson, Weick, and Kramer 1996); at the same time, human capital investments do not get withdrawn but remain as ownership of the firm, while human capital investors appropriate monetary returns on those investments (Blair 1996).

The occurrence of sustained innovation performances in established firms can also be considered as a case in the successful growth of economic knowledge. Research on innovative corporations have consistently highlighted the importance of deregulation, deburocratization, decentralization, and 'disaggregation' of the enterprise (Burns and Stalker 1961; Miles et al. 1997; Volberda 1998; Zenger and Hesterley 1997). In particular, the recent 'corporate disaggregation movement' bears some parallel with that of 'deregulation' and reduced state intervention in national economies. In fact, the aim is similar, being the former intended to promote entrepreneurship and innovation in the excessively planned and bureaucratic, and not so 'mini,' 'miniature economies' of large firms (Cowen and Parker 1997; Jensen and Meckling 1992). The set of governance and organizational practices used in firms championing in performance is pretty large. Evidence from both in-depth case studies and wide surveys indicates that at least the following mechanisms are important in the achievement of high performance in innovation respects.

Roberts (2004) examines in considerable detail the organizational practices sustaining innovation in large established firms such as Nokia, 3M, Lincoln Electric, BP. Building on those, as well as on practices described in other case-based studies (e.g., Zenger and Hesterley 1997) he lists the profile of the 'disaggregated corporation' as follows (p. 232):

- discrete, self-contained, small units operating autonomously and accountable for results;
- incentives for performance at individual and unit level;
- reduction of hierarchy through delayering and open horizontal communication and linkages; and
- high investments in the development of human capital through training.

Analogous features are detected by other authors. For example, drawing on exemplary cases in highly professionalized, knowledge-intensive, innovative companies such as Acer, Apple, Oticon, and Semco, Miles et al. (1997) identify the key features of the observed, emerging networked form of organizing in 'entrepreneurial responsibility' (entitlement to residual rewards and decision rights), 'self-organization' (freedom of resource recombination), and 'member ownership' (asset ownership).

In the light of the argument advanced in this chapter, these data can be reanalyzed in the following way.

All cases describe systems that are focused on a twofold problem: devising organizational architectures that allow free recombinations among differentiated knowledge 'nodes,' and the discovery of new projects and activities; and that provide the proper incentives for actors to behave entrepreneurially in that game. The stylized nature of those systems, therefore, seems to conform to a game played with distributed knowledge assets; with the aim of finding combinations among them with high potential for the discovery of new successful activities.

The problems caused by the 'partial use' of the formula, as in the much debated Oticon case (Foss 2003), can be read as cases having mastered the cognitive side of knowledge management (opening channels of communication, free association and self-organization, deregulation, erase of hierarchy) but not the incentive side (residual rewards and property rights over innovations).

Some lessons on the issue of complementarities among governance mechanisms in the generation of innovation can also be learned.

First, in contrast with a dominant view in organizational economics (Roberts 2004; Williamson 2004), the 'list' of good governance practices for innovation clearly includes governance mechanisms that are 'different' rather than 'similar' in kind, and their very joint application in the same firm seems to be crucial for success. Evidence, thus interpreted, suggests that the menu of 'structural alternatives' is not isomorphic with the classes of governance mechanisms that may be considered 'of the same kind' (Grandori 1997; Grandori and Furnari 2008). In practice, and in the particular case of organizing for innovation, the problem need not and should not be framed as a choice between an 'incentive-driven' or a 'communitarian' model, but as a problem of detecting and combining complementary practices that often belong to those two different classes.

Second, with the aim of contributing in identifying those complementary practices in the case of innovation, we should notice that the differences among the mechanisms that are typically combined in innovative firms do not seem to reduce to the twofold conceptualization of mixing market and hierarchy elements, as transaction cost inspired leading contributions in this field have prospected (Zenger and Hesterley 1997). Practices like the intensive use of teamwork and horizontal communication arguably bring about 'infusion of community'; and practices like empowerment, and employee ownership arguably bring about 'infusions of democracy' more than bringing about 'infusions of market' (Grandori and Furnari 2008).

Third, the practices usually gathered under the heading of 'highly powered incentives' are usually considered 'market-like,' but this categorization seems questionable and even paradoxical: the core mechanisms of entitling internal 'molecular units' to the residual rewards produced by internal entrepreneurial venturing do institute strong monetary incentives; but they do so by means of reallocating property rights inside a firm (creating islands of shared property rights within island of shared property rights). Whether these internal 'island' are immersed in a sea of market-like relations—to quote Richardson (1972)—is a different question. In fact, those islands can be and often are connected by relations of other type (joint decision-making and problem solving, constitutions, plans, voting, hostages, negotiations, and coalitions; and inside contracting of various sort). Hence, the creation of molecular units is more a matter of the locus of ownership within the firm, of an 'infusion of democracy,' rather than an 'infusion of market.'

However, other mechanisms and practices characterized as 'highly powered incentives' do infuse market-like dynamics in the analyzed firms.

To the extent that internal entrepreneurs compete for attracting investments of human and financial capital, internal capital and labor markets are indeed instituted; to the extent that the new knowledge produced is patented for circulation within the firm internal knowledge markets are established; to the extent that inter-unit transfers are regulated by transfer prices and cost imputations, and 'pay for performance' is shaped according to a contingent contracting model internal miniature markets for good and services are set up.

If the observed governance practices are thus reclassified, we can draw the preliminary conclusion that the democratic governance of the firm has an important role in innovation; that some democratic practices such as diffused residual rewards holding have benefits both in terms of knowledge exchange and growth and in terms of motivation and incentives to engage in it; and that those practices seem to be complementary with some market-like mechanisms.

Evidence from large databases on organizational and HRM practices connected to innovation square well with that conjecture. For example, in the HRM area, it has repeatedly been found that the joint use of teamwork and knowledge management together with incentive pay is positively related to the performance of firms in highly innovative sectors (Laursen and Manke 2001) and to productivity and quality of output at the work group level (Ichniowski and Shaw 1997).

Research conducted on the organizational practices employed at the macro-organizational level has also found that the joint use of practices infusing market (e.g., contingent pay, highly mobile internal labor markets), community (e.g., culture and knowledge management in the usual practical definition of these practices), and democracy (flat allocations of residual reward and decision rights) are necessary (albeit not sufficient) conditions for achieving high performance on innovation parameters (Grandori and Furnari 2008).

4.3.2. *Knowledge Governance in Innovative Alliances*

Empirical studies on interfirm networks have generally indicated that when different partners engage in collaboration geared to innovation, and tasks are relatively complex, both informal agreements (social networks) and obligational contracting including a lot of job descriptions, contingent claim clauses and hierarchical provisions (bureaucratic networks) tend to fail, and proprietary networks prevail; and, among those, 'team-like,' parity-based arrangements, if interdependence is particularly intense (Grandori 1997).

Building on that general indication provided by network research, more recent studies have provided preliminary but directly relevant results on the role of associational contracting and democratic governance in knowledge-intensive collaborations, through both case studies and large data set analyses of interfirm alliance agreements.

Grandori and Furlotti (2006*a*, 2006*b*) content analyze the text of R&D alliance contracts and use complementary information on the collaborating firms to detect what type of agreements regulate these knowledge-intensive, knowledge-pooling activities. It turns out that:

- the specification of the output to be reached and the activities to be performed is low, but property rights over any output may be reached are highly specified into enforceable contracts;
- formal contracts extensively specify the resources to be provided, and the property rights over those inputs;
- formal contracts typically mention general principles and codes of conduct that should inspire behaviors (good faith, due diligence, noncompetition); procedures for conflict resolution (negotiation procedures, type of mediation, and arbitration admitted); and procedures for decision-making (joint steering committees, specialized areas in

which different partners may decide autonomously, information rights, and obligations); and

- property rights over assets and outputs, residual rewards and decision, and control rights are typically shared among alliance partners.

Similar results are obtained by analyzing large databases. Thus, in a systematic documental analysis of about a hundred R&D biotech alliance, Furlotti (2007) found that:

- In over 80 percent of cases, a permanent structure or a permanent role (distinct from the contractual parties) is assigned decision-making rights over important activities of the alliance.
- Such structure is always (98.5%) a joint-steering committee; the representation in such committee is always egalitarian; there is moderate use of even arbitration authority to solve matters where the Committee cannot reach a majority decision (in 32% of cases).
- Residual reward rights allocations are more proportional to the relative value of parties' contributions.
- The *identity* of the parties matters. The agreements often contain restrictions to transfer rights to third parties (also in case of takeovers of one of the parties). The restrictions to the transfer of rights are usually more severe for the party that contributes the core technological expertise.
- In over 70 percent of cases alliance agreement explicitly grants the right to terminate without cause, but also put heavy taxes on that. In most cases the terminating party loses rights over the intellectual property developed by the alliance.
- Non-negligible contingent task specifications are included in less than 50 percent of the cases.

This evidence is consistent with what the few other detailed empirical studies available on the content of contract clauses in interfirm alliances. For example, Lerner and Merges (1998) conducted a detailed content-analysis of a sample of joint venture contracts in the US biotechnology industry. In a footnote, the authors make an observation on their finding that is peripheral to their argument but is central to our own:

> The detailed control rights assigned in alliance contracts are aspects of ownership that must be distinguished from mere contractual contingencies. They do not spell out a myriad of possible world-states, dictating outcomes under each of many

scenarios. Instead, they are discrete aspects of the fundamental ownership right over the research results (p. 134).

Other surveys on interfirm knowledge-intensive collaborations further qualify the mix of governance mechanisms that are used and the extent to which they are formalized into contracts or kept extra-contractual. An interesting regularity is that two classes of governance mechanisms seem to be most intensively formalized in interfirm contracts for innovation: shared property right allocations among partners; and prices, fees, milestone payments, warranties, and indemnities (Grandori and Furlotti 2007, Hagedoorn and Hesen 2007). In other terms, those contracts include and formalize both the core 'firm-like' attribute of unified property rights (in a shared rather than unilateral form) and the core 'market-like' attribute of prices.

In sum, the governance arrangements of interfirm alliances oriented to knowledge generation is predominantly poliarchic, and combine elements of connected poliarchy with elements of disconnected poliarchy. We could say that, if those governance solutions qualify as 'hybrid,' they are hybrids between market and democracy, more than hybrids between market and hierarchy.[3]

4.4. Conclusions

In conclusion, governance for the growth of knowledge is a combination of mechanisms in which selected mechanisms of different kind play a central role, in particular high and free mobility of resources (arguably a 'market-like' attribute); diffused and shared property rights (arguably a 'firm-like' attribute, but of a democratic and entrepreneurial sort); and team knowledge production (arguably a 'communitarian' attribute). This seems to hold for both intra-firm and interfirm innovative organization, confirming the conjecture that what matters most for innovation is a poliarchic and networked governance architecture rather than the internal/external divide (Grandori 1999).

This way of reading governance models for innovation has a bearing for some contemporary debates on knowledge governance. Puzzles like 'is an incentive-driven or a communitarian solution' better for innovation; or 'is selective intervention possible,' derive from anchoring the

[3] The underlying problem is the popular but incorrect identification between the institution of the firm and the coordination mechanism of hierarchy.

analysis to 'discrete structural alternatives' as packages of attributes that are thought to be consistent either because they are 'similar in kind,' or just because they have been frequently occurring together in practice in the past. Neither of these assumptions, however, is a particularly strong basis for a 'theory of complementarity' among governance mechanisms (Grandori and Furnari 2008). If the crafting of governance and organizational solutions is framed in a 'zero-based design' approach (Grandori 1999), whereby single mechanisms are evaluated both in a stand-alone mode and in combination with others in relation to the production of specified outcomes, then a wider variety of effective combinations might be predicted; and mechanisms that are 'underused' but possibly very effective may be detected. In the specific case of innovation outcomes, the 'discrete,' if not 'adversarial' view of governance and organizational arrangements, as well as the attraction toward solutions that are just frequently applied in practice (a case of the naturalistic fallacy?), have apparently produced an overstatement of the virtues of hierarchy in the governance of uncertainty, an overstatement of the role of communitarian and market-like governance in the promotion of innovation, and an understatement of the role of democratic governance for knowledge growth.

References

Alchian, A. A. and H. Demsetz. 1972. 'Production, Information Costs and Economic Organization,' *American Economic Review* 62: 777–95.

Aoki, M. 2004. 'Comparative Institutional Analysis of Corporate Governance,' in A. Grandori (ed.) *Corporate Governance and Firm Organization*, Oxford: Oxford University Press.

Arora, A. and A. Gambardella. 1994. 'The Changing Technology of Technological Change: General and Abstract Knowledge and the Division of Labour,' *Research Policy* 23: 523–32.

Baker, G. 2000. 'Human Capital, Learning and the Internet in the Modern Economy,' Milan, Wonderland, 2000 Conference.

—— R. Gibbons, and K. J. Murphy. 2002. 'Relational Contracts and the Theory of the Firm,' *Quarterly Journal of Economics* February: 39–84.

Baron, J. N. and D. M. Kreps. 1999. 'HRM in Emerging Companies,' in J. N. Baron and D. M. Kreps (eds.) *Strategic Human Resources*, New York: Wiley.

Bazerman, M. and M. Neale. 1992. *Negotiating Rationally*. New York: Free Press.

Blair, M. 1996. *Wealth creation and wealth sharing: A colloquium on corporate governance and investments in human capital*. Washington, DC: Brookings Institute.

Brennan, G. H. and J. M. Buchanan. 1985. *The Reasons of Rules*. Cambridge: Cambridge University Press.

Brown, J. S. and P. Duguid. 1991. 'Organizational Learning and Communities-of-Practice: Toward a Unified View of Working, Learning, and Innovation,' *Organization Science* 2: 40–57.

Burns, T. and G. M. Stalker. 1961. *The Management of Innovations*. London: Tavistock Publications.

Carnabuci, G. 2005. *A Theory of Knowledge Growth: Network Analysis of US Patents,1975–1999*, PhD Thesis, Amsterdam: Amsterdam University Press/ Vossipeurs.

Castilla, E. J. 2003. *Venture Capital Firms and Entrepreneurship: An Empirical Analysis of Start-up Companies and Their Venture Capital Funding in the Silicon Valley and Route 128 regions*. Copenhagen: 19 EGOS Colloquium.

Chesbrough, H. 2004. *Open Innovation Cambridge*. Cambridge, Mass.: Harvard Business School Press.

Cohen, M. D. et al. 1996. 'Routines and Other Recurring Action Patterns of Organizations: Contemporary Research Issues,' *Industrial and Corporate Change* 5: 653–98.

Cohendet, P. et al. 2004. 'Matching communities and hierarchies within firms,' *Journal of Management and Governance* 8/1: 27–48.

Cowen, T. and D. Parker. 1997. *Markets in the Firm. A Market Process Approach to Management*. Institute of Economic Affairs.

Demsetz, H. 1991. 'The Theory of the Firm Revisited,' in O. Williamson and S. Winter (eds.) *The Nature of the Firm: Origins, Evolution and Development*. Oxford: Oxford University Press.

Foss, N. J. 2003. 'Selective Intervention and Internal Hybrids: Interpreting and Learning from the Rise and Decline of the Oticon Spaghetti Organization,' *Organization Science* 14: 341–9.

——2007. 'The Emerging Knowledge Governance Approach,' *Organization* 14: 29–52.

Furlotti, M. 2007. *Inter-Firm Contracts as an Organizational Phenomenon*, PhD Thesis, Milan: Bocconi University.

Galbraith, J. R. 1974. 'Organization Design: An Information Processing View,' *Interfaces* 4: 28–36.

Goldberg, V. 1976. 'Regulation and Administered Contracts,' *Bell Journal of Economics* 7: 426–48.

Grandori, A. 1984. 'A Prescriptive Contingency View of Organizational Decision Making,' *Administrative Science Quarterly* 29: 192–208.

——1997. 'Governance Structures, Coordination Mechanisms and Cognitive Models,' *Journal of Management and Governance* 1: 29–47.

——1999. *Organizzazione e comportamento economico*. Bologna: Il Mulino. (English version: *Organization and Economic Behaviour*. London: Routledge, 2001).

Grandori, A. 2001. 'Neither Hierarchy Nor Identity: Knowledge Governance Mechanisms and the Theory of the Firm,' *Journal of Management and Governance* 5: 3–4.

——2005. *Firm-Like Contracts: From Task Contingencies to Resource Commitments.* Milano: Università Bocconi, Crora working paper n. 10.

——2006. 'Innovation, Uncertainty and Relational Governance,' *Industry & Innovation* 13(2): 127–33.

——and B. Kogut. 2002. 'Dialogue on Knowledge and Organization,' *Organization Science* 13: 224–31.

——and M. Furlotti. 2006*a*. 'The Sustainable Lightness of Projects: Resource-Based and Procedural Contracting,' in A. Arino and J. J. Reuer (eds.) *Strategic Alliances: Governance and Contracts.* Palgrave.

————2006*b*. 'Facio ut facias: Associational Contracts for Innovation,' REF University of Pisa Conference; and EMNET Conference, Erasmus, 2007. Forthcoming in *International Studies of Management and Organization.*

————2007. 'From relational to associational contracting: The case of project-based strategic alliances,' Academy of Management Symposium 'Governance in temporary organization,' Philadelphia.

——and S. Furnari. 2006. 'Beyond Discrete Structural Alternatives: A Combinatory Model of Organization,' *Organization Studies.*

————2008. 'A chemistry of organization: Combinatory analysis and design,' *Organization Studies* 29: 315–41.

—— and L. Solari. 2006. 'The Governance of Knowledge-Intensive Human Capital Investments: Lessons from Emerging Industries,' Milano: Università Bocconi, Crora Research paper n. 20.

Grant, R. M. 1996. 'Toward a Knowledge-Based Theory of the Firm,' *Strategic Management Journal* 17: 109–22.

Hagedoorn, J. and G. Hesen. 2007. 'Contract Law and the Governance of Inter-Firm Technology Partnership: An Analysis of Different Modes of Partnering and Their Contractual Implications,' *Journal of Management Studies* 44: 3342–66.

Hansman, H. 1996. *The Ownership of Enterprise.* Cambridge: Harvard University Press.

Hanson, N. R. 1958. *Patterns of Discovery. An Enquiry into the Conceptual Foundation of Science.* Cambridge: Cambridge University Press.

Hart, O. and J. Moore. 1990. 'Property Rights and the Nature of the Firm,' *The Journal of Political Economy* 8: 1119–58.

Hayek, F., Von. 1945. 'The Use of Knowledge in Society,' *American Economic Review* 35: 519–30, September.

Hedlund, G. 1986. 'The Hypermodern Corporation: A Heterarchy?,' *Human Resource Management* 25: 9–35.

Hennart, J. F. 1988. 'A Transaction Costs Theory of Equity Joint Ventures,' *Strategic Management Journal* 9: 361–74.

Holmstrom. 1982. 'Moral Hazard in Teams,' *Bell Journal of Economics* 13: 324–40.

Ichniowski, C. and K. P. Shaw. 1997. 'The Effects of Human Resource Management Practices on Productivity: A Study of Steel Finishing Lines,' *American Economic Review* 87: 291–313.

Jensen, M. C. and W. H. Meckling. 1976. 'Theory of the Firm: Managerial Behavior, Agency Costs and Ownership Structure,' *Journal of Financial Economics* 3: 305–60.

Jensen, M. C. and W. H. Meckling. 1992. 'Specific and General Knowledge, and Organizational Structure,' in L. Werin and H. Wijkander (eds.) *Contract Economics*. Oxford: Blackwell.

Kaplan, S. N. and P. Stromberg. 2003. 'Financial Contracting Theory Meets the Real World: An Empirical Analysis of Venture Capital Contracts,' *The Review of Economic Studies* 70: 1–35.

Kogut, B. and U. Zander. 1996. 'What Firms Do? Coordination, Identity and Learning,' *Organization Science* 7(5): 502–18.

Lakatos, I. 1970. 'Falsification and the Methodology of Scientific Research Programmes,' in I. Lakatos and A. Musgrave (eds.) *Criticism and the Growth of Knowledge*. Cambridge: Cambridge University Press.

Lampel, J. 2004. 'The Benefit of Doubt: Shadow Norms and Governance in Trust-Based Organizations,' in A. Grandori (ed.) *Corporate Governance and Firm Organization*. Oxford: Oxford University Press.

Langlois, R. N. 1986. 'Rationality, Institutions and Explanation,' in R. N. Langlois (ed.) *Economics as a Process*. Cambridge: Cambridge University Press.

Laursen, K. and V. Manke. 2001. 'Knowledge Strategies, Firm Types and Complementarity in Human Resource Practices,' *Journal of Management and Governance* 5: 1–22. Lawrence, P. and D. Dyer. 1983. *Renewing American Industry*. Free Press.

Lawrence, P. and J. Lorsch. 1967. *Organization and environment*. Harvard Business School.

Lerner, J. and R. P. Merges. 1998. 'The Control of Technology Alliances: An Empirical Analysis of the Biotechnology Industry,' *Journal of Industrial Economics* 46(2): 125–56.

Lindkvist, L. 2004. 'Governing Project Based Firms: Promoting Market-Like Processes within Hierarchies,' *Journal of Management and Governance* 8: 3–25.

——2005. 'Knowledge Communities and Knowledge Collectivities: A Typology of Knowledge Work in Groups,' *Journal of Management Studies* 42(6): 1189–210.

Loasby, B. 1976. *Choice, complexity and ignorance*. Cambridge: Cambridge University Press.

Macauley, S. 1963. 'Non-Contractual Relations in Business: A Preliminary Study,' *American Sociological Review* 28(1): 55–67.

Macneil, I. R. 1978. 'Contracts: Adjustment of Long Term Economic Relationships under Classical, Neo-Classical and Relational Contract Law,' *Northwestern University Law Review* 72: 854–906.

Meyerson, D., K. E. Weick, and R. M. Kramer. 1996. 'Swift Trust and Temporary Teams,' in R. M. Kramer and T. R. Tyler (eds.) *Trust in Organizations*. Thousand Oaks: Sage Publications.

Miles, R. E. et al. 1997. 'Organizing in the Knowledge Age: Anticipating the Cellular Form,' *Academy of Management Executive* 11(4): 7–21.

Miller, G. J. 1992. *Managerial Dilemmas: The Political Economy of Hierarchy*. Cambridge: Cambridge University Press.

Nelson, R. 1993. *National Systems of Innovation*. Oxford: Oxford University Press.

Nonaka, I. and H. Takeuchi. 1995. *The Knowledge Creating Company*. Oxford: Oxford University Press.

Ouchi, W. G. 1979. 'A Conceptual Framework for Design of Organizational Control Mechanism,' *Management Science* 25: 833–48.

—— 1980. 'Markets, Bureaucracies and Clans,' *Administrative Science Quarterly* 25: 129–41.

—— and M. K. Bolton. 1988. 'The Logic of Joint Research and Development,' *California Management Review* 30: 9–33.

Perrow, C. 1967. 'A Framework for the Comparative Analysis of Organization,' *American Sociological Review* 32: 194–208.

Pisano, G. 1991. 'The Governance of Innovation. Vertical Integration and Collaborative Arrangements in the Biotechnology Industry,' *Research Policy* 20: 237–49.

Popper, K. R. 1935. *Der Logik der Forschung*. Vienna: Sperling. (English version: *The Logic of Scientific Discovery*. London: Hutchinson, 1959)

—— 1945. *The Open Society and Its Enemies*. London: Routledge.

—— 1989. 'The Critical Approach versus the Mystique of Leadership,' *Human Systems Management* 8: 259–65.

Powell, W. W. 1996. 'Interorganizational Collaborations in the Biotechnology Industry,' *Journal of Institutional and Theoretical Economics* 152(1): 197–215.

Richardson, G. B. 1972. 'The Organization of Industry,' *Economic Journal* 82: 883–96.

Roberts, J. 2004. *The Modern Firm. Organizational Design for Performance and Growth*. Oxford: Oxford University Press.

Sah, R. K. and J. E. Stiglitz. 1985. 'The Architecture of Economic Systems: Hierarchies and Poliarchies,' *Economic Growth Center paper 476*, New Haven, Connecticut.

Shackle, G. L. 1972. *Epistemics and Economics*. Cambridge: Cambridge University Press.

Simon, H. A. 1951. 'A Formal Theory of the Employment Relationship,' *Econometrica* 19: 293–305.

—— 1977. *Models of Discovery*. Boston: Reidel.

Teece, D. J. 1986. 'Profiting from Technological Innovation: Implication for Integration, Collaboration, Licensing and Public Policy,' *Research Policy* 15(6): 286–305.

Thompson, J. D. 1967. *Organization in Action*. New York: McGraw-Hill.

Vanberg, V. J. 1994. *Rules and Choice in Economics*. London: Routledge.

Volberda, H. V. 1998. *Building the Flexible Firm: How to Remain Competitive*. Oxford: Oxford University Press.

Weick, K. E. 1979. 'Cognitive Processes in Organizations,' *Research in Organizational Behavior* 1: 41–74.

Wilkins, A. L. and W. G. Ouchi. 1983. 'Efficient Cultures: Exploring the Relationship between Culture and Organizational Performance,' *Administrative Science Quarterly* 28(3): 468–81.

Williamson, O. E. 1975. *Markets and Hierarchies: Analysis and Antitrust Implications*. New York: Free Press.

——1980. 'The Organization of Work. A Comparative Institutional Assessment,' *Journal of Economics Behavior and Organization* 1: 5–38.

——1981. 'The Economics of Organization: The Transaction Cost Approach,' *American Journal of Sociology* 87: 548–77.

——2004. 'Herbert Simon and Organization Theory: Lessons for the Theory of the Firm,' in M. Augier and J. G. March (eds.) *Models of a Man*. Cambridge: MIT Press.

Zenger, T. R. and W. S. Hesterley. 1997. 'The Disaggregation of Corporations: Selective Intervention, High Powered Incentives and Molecular Units,' *Organization Science* 8(3): 209–22.

5

Managerial authority when knowledge is distributed: a knowledge governance perspective

Kirsten Foss and Nicolai J. Foss

5.1. Introduction

Much existing thinking on management and authority in organizations implicitly or explicitly makes strong assumptions about the knowledge held by managers. Thus, it is often assumed that managers are at least as knowledgeable about relevant tasks as employees; that they can instruct the latter to carry out the tasks, and that they can somehow ascertain whether employees are sufficiently skilled to adequately carry out specific tasks (Grandori 1997; Sharma 1997). It is, however, not clear what are the consequences for our understanding of management and authority if the knowledge that is essential in a work setting is partially *unknown* to the manager, *distributed* across several employees, and perhaps even—because of its tacit nature—must *remain* unknown? In particular, how can the manager rationally direct work under such conditions, that is, when he would seem to lack the knowledge required to instruct and monitor employees? Can the use of managerial authority give rise to an effective utilization of the knowledge held individually by employees?

These issues may have become increasingly important because of the knowledge conditions that accompany the emergence of the knowledge economy, specifically an increased need to source outside knowledge, rely on knowledge workers, and engage in distributed innovation processes. However, the issue of whether or to what extent authority can be deployed to efficiently govern activities in systems with distributed knowledge is a very general knowledge governance problem. It is hinted at, but not analyzed, by writers such as Cyert and March (1963) and Lawrence and Lorsch (1967) in the organization field, and Hayek (1973) in political economy. In spite of its apparent relevance (cf. Lessard and Zaheer 1996), the issue of the knowledge-based limits to management has attracted rather little interest from management theorists (for exceptions, see Mintzberg 1990; Sharma 1997; Brusoni 2005; Grandori 1997), emerging more indirectly under the guise of the knowledge-based boundaries to the firm (e.g., Kogut and Zander 1992). Indeed, as Lessard and Zaheer (1996: 513) indicate, the issue is usually sidetracked or at least black-boxed.[1]

The purpose of this chapter is to address a subset of the overall issue, namely, the implications of 'distributed knowledge' for the use in firms of the authority relation. The notion of distributed knowledge, coined in computer science about two decades ago (Halpern and Moses 1990), has fast become a household concept in various branches of management and organization studies (e.g., Cohen and Robert 1996; Coombs and Metcalfe 2000; Gherardi 1999; Larsen 2001; Lessard and Zaheer 1996; Marengo 1995; Potts 2001; Spangler and Peters 2001; Tsoukas 1996). For the moment, think of 'distributed knowledge' as knowledge that is not possessed by any single mind, but 'belongs to' a group of interacting agents, somehow emerges from the aggregation of the (possibly tacit) knowledge elements of the individual agents, and can be mobilized for productive purposes.

Many writers have argued that such distributed knowledge is becoming increasingly important in an innovation-rich, knowledge-based economy. This is because firms increasingly need to rely on a growing number of knowledge specialists, be they employees or outside knowledge agents, such as supplier firms or universities (e.g., Brusoni, Prencipe, and Pavitt 2001; Coombs and Metcalfe 2000; Granstrand, Patel, and Pavitt 1997; Hodgson 1998; Husted and Michailova this volume; Orlikowski 2002; Smith 2000; Wang and von Tunzelman 2000). This tendency is seen as having strong transformative implications for the boundaries of the firm (Coombs and Metcalfe 2000), as well as for internal organization

[1] They provide strategic management as an example: 'In strategy research, the issue of the expertise for strategic decision-making being spread across the firm is often assumed away by focusing exclusively on decision-making by the CEO or the top management team' (Lessard and Zaheer 1996: 513).

(Cowen and Parker 1997; Foss 1999)—including the use of authority as a mechanism of coordination (Grandori 1997, 2002).[2]

However, although the concept of distributed knowledge is often invoked, and rather far-reaching claims are made on its behalf, there is little systematic analysis of how distributed knowledge and economic organization relate. Thus, the concept is not clearly defined in the management literature, the causal links from distributed knowledge to economic organization are unclear, and an overall perspective that can frame the discussion is missing. In contrast, we proffer a definition and examine links, focusing on the relation between distributed knowledge and the use of authority in firms. We embed our arguments in the knowledge governance approach (Foss 2007; Foss, Husted, and Michailova 2008, see also the Introduction to this volume), that is, we examine the alignment between (the characteristics of) knowledge (i.e., distributed knowledge) and governance mechanisms (i.e., authority) in the context of an overall efficiency perspective.

Here is how we proceed: We begin by taking a closer look at the key constructs of 'authority' and 'distributed knowledge.' We then examine their interplay, focusing particularly on the role of authority as a mechanism of coordination when knowledge is distributed (see also Chapter 4 by Anna Grandori in this volume). An outcome of this discussion is that how well authority performs under these conditions depends on what we mean by authority. Thus, while the narrow notions of authority associated with Coase (1937) and Simon (1951) may indeed in certain cases (i.e., for certain specifications of distributed knowledge) be compromised by distributed knowledge, this does not imply that all manifestations of authority break down as mechanisms of coordination when knowledge is distributed. There is accordingly a need for a more fine-grained understanding of types of managerial authority, and we take steps in this direction. We end by exploring the conditions under which authority may be an efficient mechanism of coordination under distributed knowledge, relying on ideas on problem solving (Nickerson and Zenger 2004; Simon 1962, 1973 and their chapter in this volume) and on organizational economics. Thus, in addition to conceptual analysis, this chapter contributes

[2] By 'coordination,' we mean consistency of plans. By 'coordination mechanisms,' we refer to those mechanisms that may assure such plan-consistency, such as prices, authority, norms/rules/routines/standards/focal points (i.e., mechanisms that are based on behavioral regularities), consultation, and ratiocination (e.g., in games). For an excellent discussion of coordination mechanisms and their implications for organizational theory, see Grandori (2001).

the kind of 'feasibility' study recommended by Grandori (2002), that is, a relatively detailed, mainly theoretical, exploration of the working of a specific governance mechanism in the context of those knowledge conditions that are often taken to characterize our emerging knowledge economy.

5.2. Authority and Distribution Knowledge: Debate and Definitions

5.2.1. *Setting the Stage: Distributed Knowledge and Economic Organization*

Return to the question with which we began this chapter: how is it possible rationally to govern activities, such as work activities carried out by employees, by means of the authority mechanism when the holder of authority is partially ignorant about some, and potentially much, of the knowledge possessed by the employees, knowledge that may be vital for carrying out the relevant activities?

This question is a subset of a broader question on the role of centralized resource allocation in social systems where the central authority is, to a certain extent, ignorant of knowledge held by individual agents. In this broader formulation, the question harks back to debate on the viability and efficiency of planned resource allocation on the societal level (i.e., socialism) that raged among academic economists in (particularly) the interwar period (Lavoie 1985). Hayek (1945) famously argued that any economy-wide manager—a central planner—would be inherently constrained by the distributed (or 'dispersed') and tacit nature of knowledge in the economy. Planning confronted inherent knowledge-based constraints. In fact, Hayek argued, these constraints were binding at such a small scale of economic activity that comprehensive overall management/planning of economy-wide resource allocation would be deeply inefficient. However, he did not provide serious micro-foundations for this argument.

Though little systematic thinking exists on the issue in management, we can see the Hayekian idea popping up in many different contexts. For example, many of Mintzberg's (e.g., 1990) critiques of 'design' and 'planning' in the strategic management process invoked Hayek-like arguments, such as the notion that emergent strategies would be able to mobilize much more locally held knowledge than a centralized strategy process.

In a different context, Langlois (1995) explicitly links thinking on firm capabilities to Hayekian arguments: Since firms as planned entities are inherently limited in the extent to which they can absorb, process, and utilize knowledge—an idea that is reflected in the notion of 'capability'—there are knowledge-based limits to the size and scope of firms. Related reasoning can be found in Kogut and Zander (1992), Grant (1996), and other knowledge-based papers that link firm-level knowledge and economic organization. Again, this literature may be criticized for lacking micro-foundations: Because the argument is not systematically rooted in a theory of (individual-level) cognition, it remains unclear why exactly the size and scope of firms are constrained by capabilities.

As a final example consider the increasingly prevalent argument, forcefully put forward by Grandori (2002: 257), that '[d]istributed knowledge causes authority (as a centralized decision-making system) to fail in all its forms.' Similar statements can be found in, for example, Minkler (1993), Cowen and Parker (1997), Hodgson (1998), and Radner (2000). The reasoning behind the arguments seems to be as follows. First, it is argued that authority—that is, the right to make decisions which guide the decisions of another person (Coase 1937; Simon 1951, 1991)—presupposes considerable knowledge about the knowledge (and perhaps also the action set) that is available to those that are being directed. Second, the presence of distributed knowledge means that this condition cannot be fulfilled. Therefore, authority is an inefficient coordination mechanism, and alternative coordination mechanisms (Grandori 2001) emerge to handle the coordination task implied by distributed knowledge, such as prices (Cowen and Parker 1997; Hayek 1945), communication (Garicano 2000), and norms (Grandori 1997, 2002). These examples hopefully suffice to indicate what follows. First, scholars from different disciplines and fields put forward arguments that the distributed nature of knowledge in social systems is an independent constraint on the efficiency of planning/central management/authority. In particular, authority is argued to be an inefficient means of coordination under conditions of distributed knowledge. Second, the specific mechanisms through which the distributedness of knowledge constrains planning/central management/authority are not identified (the exception is Grandori, see Grandori 1997). Third, the arguments are implicitly critiques of those organizational theories that place emphasis on the authority relation as the mechanism of coordination that primarily characterizes firms, notably transaction cost theories (Coase 1937; Williamson 1985) and property rights theory (Hart 1995, 1996). Finally, it is fair to say that most of those writers who have argued that distributed knowledge is a force that impacts economic organization have generally failed to precisely define what is meant by knowledge being 'distributed.' Similarly, other key constructs, notably that of 'authority,' are seldom defined and implicitly taken to be unproblematic. They are not, as we shall see. Thus, in order to assess arguments relating distributed knowledge to authority, we therefore need to look at these two key constructs in some detail.

5.2.2. *Authority*

Organizational theories, drawing on sociology, economics, and psychology, present a huge number of interpretations of authority (e.g., Grandori 2001; Thompson 1956; Weber 1947). This is not the place to present a full review and critical evaluation of the multitude of definitions and ideas regarding the notion of authority. Rather, for the purpose of this chapter, the concepts of authority offered by Herbert Simon (1951, 1991) in two papers, separated by four decades, serve as useful starting points, because they are well known, precise, do not invite confusions with neighbor concepts (e.g., leadership), and are *different*. In fact, we shall them as springboards for developing notions of 'Type I' and 'Type II Authority.'

5.2.2.1. TYPE I AUTHORITY

Simon (1951) defines authority as obtaining when a 'boss' is permitted by a 'worker' to select actions, $\mathbf{A^0} \subset \mathbf{A}$, where $\mathbf{A}$ is the set of the worker's possible behaviors. More or less authority is then defined as making the set $\mathbf{A^0}$ larger or smaller. Simon develops a multi-period, incomplete contracts model with *ex post* governance. In the first period, the prospective worker decides whether to accept employment or not. Both parties know the possible set of actions and their associated expected and real costs and benefits, but none of the parties know which actions will be optimal, given circumstances. In the next period, the relevant circumstances are revealed to the boss. The boss then picks the action that he prefers and directs the worker to that action which—for the latter to accept the assignment—must lie within his or her 'zone of acceptance.'

A worker's zone of acceptance is defined in Simon as that set of actions where the worker's *expected* costs of carrying out these actions do not exceed the agreed upon on wage. An important feature of authority is that the authority of a superior is constrained by the acceptance of the subordinate of the authority. 'A subordinate may be said to accept authority,' Simon (1951: 22) explains, '...whenever he permits his behavior to be guided by a decision reached by another, irrespective of his own judgment as to the merits of that decision.'[3] That is, for some of the actions the costs to the worker may exceed the agreed on wage, but acceptance of authority implies that the worker carries out those actions *irrespectively* of his own cost of doing so.[4] The boss cannot commit to choose actions that maximize total surplus, and even if the worker is able to identify actions that yield a higher total surplus, he must carry out the action that is preferred by the boss. However, the boss never includes in the zone of acceptance those actions where the expected increase in wage to the worker exceeds his expected increase in benefits.

Simon's explanation of authority and the employment relation is quite akin to Coase's (1937). In the presence of uncertainty, Coase argues, contingencies are costly to anticipate and describe in advance, and rather than negotiating on a spot market basis over each contingency as they arise, an employment contract is concluded. The latter is defined as '... one whereby the factor, for a certain remuneration (which may be fixed or fluctuating) agrees to obey the directions of an entrepreneur *within certain limits*. The essence of the contract is that it should only state the limits to the powers of the entrepreneur. Within these limits, he can therefore direct the other factors of production' (idem. 242). Simon and Coase's understanding of authority is summarized in the following definition:

Definition (Type I Authority): *Authority is a decision right that an employer acquires, because he expects to obtain only ex post contracting the relevant information that will make it possible for him to pick his preferred actions within a specified subset of actions, which he will then direct the employee to carry out.*

In the Simon notion of authority symmetric knowledge/information is consistent with the authority relation. It is sufficient that one contracting party stands to gain more than the other from picking the actions once contingencies materialize, and that the contractors cannot make side-payments that enable them to agree on what is the best choice when contingencies arise. In the Coase notion of authority the employer picks well-defined actions from a set of discrete actions (about which the employer has perfect information). He does this on the basis of knowledge

[3] In contrast, in a market contract, the parties negotiate *ex ante* about the actions that the agent can take in response to various contingencies so as to fulfill the contract. Thus, the principal's flexibility under market contracting is limited compared to what it would be under authority.

[4] This is what makes the authority different from an agency relation. In the latter, the agent's participation constraint is never violated.

about contingencies that is superior to that of the employee. However, it is key that in either case the employer formally grants no discretion with respect to the choice of actions.

5.2.2.2. TYPE II AUTHORITY

In actuality it is hard to imagine an authority relation where absolutely no discretion is granted to the employee. Even for the most closely monitored and repetitive work, some employee discretion will remain (Knight 1921). Specifically, in the presence of costs of monitoring, the employer will grant de facto discretion to the employee. This already indicates that authority and employee discretion are not mutually exclusive. This was clearly recognized by Simon (1991), four decades after his paper on authority. Simon (1991: 31; our emphasis) argues that '[a]uthority in organizations is not used exclusively, or even mainly, to command specific actions.' Instead, he explains, it is a command that takes the form of a result to be produced, a principle to be applied, or goal constraints, so that '[o]nly the end goal has been supplied by the command, and not the method of reaching it.'[5]

5.2.2.3. DELEGATION AND AUTHORITY

Two crucial aspects of this understanding of authority should be noted. First, relative to Simon's earlier definition this notion of authority allows for the delegation of discretion. In a sense, this extension brings agency relations in hierarchies inside the orbit of authority relations, because it allows for the possibility that authority may (also) have the function of unilaterally changing the degree of delegation post contract agreement (see also Aghion and Tirole 1997, Baker, Gibbons, and Murphy 1999). Second, this second, more expansive notion of authority does not presuppose that the employer is at least as knowledgeable as the employee about how to best carry out a task. That is, an employer is able to direct or constrain employee actions in ways that benefit him, while allowing the existence of and possible use of knowledge held only by the employee. To see how delegation and authority connect, consider the benefits and costs of delegation.

[5] In fairness to Simon, it should be noted that the more expansive notion of authority in the 1991 paper can be found already in Simon (1947). Thus, Simon's views of authority did not change between 1951 and 1991. What arguably happened was that Simon in the 1951 paper developed a *formal* model of authority and that tractability of the formal analysis required that a relatively simple concept of authority be employed.

Employers grant discretion to employees for a number of reasons, including economizing with principals' opportunity costs (Salanié 1997), improving motivation through 'empowerment' (Conger and Kanungo 1988), fostering learning by providing more room for local explorative efforts, and improving collective decision-making by letting more employees have an influence on decisions (Miller 1992). Importantly, delegation is also granted in order to make efficient use of distributed knowledge in firms (Jensen and Meckling 1992).

There is also a cost side to delegation. In Simon (1951), the only restrictions in employment contracts are those that are defined by the agreed upon 'zone of acceptance' since actions are all well defined.... However, once delegation enters the employment relation the decision rights that are granted to employees are constrained in various ways. This brings a further function of authority into focus, namely, to constrain 'the method[s] of reaching' an end goal, in Simon's (1991) terminology. Also, top management keeps ultimate decision rights, so that it, if deemed necessary, can overrule decisions made on the basis of delegated decision rights (Baker, Gibbons, and Murphy 1999).

There are several reasons why an employer may want to constrain the discretion they delegate to employees. Employees are not full owners or residual claimants on the results of their decisions or do not share all relevant knowledge. Thus, delegation produces spillover effects (i.e., 'externalities') that may be harmful to the employer and to overall firm performance. The relevant externalities include, but are by no means limited to, morally hazardous behavior (Holmström 1979; Holmström and Milgrom 1991). They also include coordination failures, such as scheduling problems, duplicative efforts (e.g., of information gathering and R&D), cannibalization of product markets, and other instances of decentralized actions being inconsistent with the firm's overall aims. One way to reduce such harmful externalities is to constrain decision rights and monitor their use (Fama and Jensen 1983; Holmström and Milgrom 1991). Such monitoring may lead to overruling of decisions made on the basis of delegated rights.

This suggests a rationale for authority that is rather different from the one associated with Type I Authority but consistent with Simon (1991)—namely, to *delegate and constrain discretion*.[6] For example, the right to use

[6] The rather considerable literature on delegation in organizations (e.g., Fama and Jensen 1983; Galbraith 1974; Jensen and Meckling 1992) does not explain why delegation should be associated with the exercise of authority. Part of the reason may lie in the static nature of

an asset in certain ways may be delegated; however, it is understood that this right does not entail the right to use the asset in the service of a competitor firm, nor may the asset be used in a way that management perceives as being damaging to the firm. It is also understood that breaking this understanding will be sanctioned.[7] Defining constraints also implies the rights to veto decisions made on the basis of delegated rights, and to withdraw delegated decision rights (this may be seen as a special case of constraining rights). Employees may have different benefits and costs depending on the particular delegation and constraining of discretion. As in Type I Authority an agreed upon 'zone of acceptable delegation and constraining' limits the way in which authority can be exercised. As under Type I Authority the employer only includes actions where his expected benefits exceed his expected costs in terms of increased compensation to the employee. Given the above, we may put forward a second definition of authority:

Definition (Type II Authority): *Authority is a decision right that an employer acquires, because he expects to obtain only ex post contracting the relevant information that enables him to delegate discretion to employees and constraining such discretion in ways preferred by him and within a specified subset of actions.*

In this definition, the holder of authority makes choices from a set of alternative possibilities of delegation. He does not necessarily have complete information about the actions available to the employee given the level of delegation and constraints he chooses. As we shall argue, this directly means that Type II Authority can make efficient use of distributed knowledge. However, clarifying the latter notion still remains.

5.2.3. *Defining Distributed Knowledge*

During the last decade or so, the notion of distributed knowledge has been used with increasing frequency as a catchy description of the knowledge

the analysis: All costs and benefits associated with delegation are given (hence, optimum delegation is known immediately to decision-makers), and there is no role for authority, except than perhaps monitoring the use of delegated decision rights.

[7] Multitasking considerations (Holmström and Milgrom 1991) also suggest a basic reason why decision rights may be constrained; thus, agents' attempts to carry out activities that are easily measured and therefore directly rewarded at the expense of harder to measure, but necessary activities may lead to the former ones being curtailed.

conditions in which modern firms increasingly find themselves.[8] Thus, in the strategy field, Tsoukas (1996) conceptualized the firm as a distributed knowledge system; Granstrand, Patel, and Pavitt (1997) documented the increasing extent to which the knowledge bases controlled by major technology-intensive corporations are distributed; and Lessard and Zaheer (1996) discussed the implications of distributed knowledge for the strategy-making process. Hutchins (1995) and Gherardi (1999) discussed implications for organizational learning, Cohen and Robert (1996) applied the notion to technology management, Foss (1999) discussed implications for the modern economics of organization, and Larsen (2001) discussed the context in the context of knowledge-intensive service firms.

This scholarly activity may reflect reality. Thus, many writers argue that distributed knowledge conditions have become increasingly important in modern competitive conditions, as firms to a larger extent need to access an expanding set of external knowledge sources (Arora and Gambardella 1994; Coombs and Metcalfe 2000; Smith 2000), and increasingly need to rely on specialist knowledge controlled and accumulated by specialist employees (Miles et al. 1997). Of course, there is nothing new per se in the notion that knowledge for productive purposes may be distributed; indeed, it is a necessary consequence of the combination of the division of labor and bounded rationality (Arora and Gambardella 1994; Hayek 1945, 1973; March and Simon 1958). Rather, what is being asserted by a number of authors seems to be that there are significant discontinuities in the evolution of distributed knowledge, so that the distributed character of knowledge has strongly increased during the last decades. Thus, Granstrand, Patel, and Pavitt (1997) document the significantly increasing extent to which firms organize in-house distributed technological knowledge, drawn from a growing number of underlying technological disciplines. Wang and von Tunzelman (2000) emphasize that not only are the number of disciplines that firms draw on expanding, it is also the case that these disciplines themselves evolve in terms of their depth and specialization; firms' sourcing of technological knowledge reflects this. Although the construct thus seems to ring a bell in a number of contexts, the above contributions are not entirely forthcoming with respect to precise definitions.

[8] To our knowledge, the term originates with Halpern and Moses (1990). However, the basic idea has a much longer prehistory, not only in the logic of knowledge but also in economics and political philosophy (e.g., Hayek 1945, 1973).

Distributed knowledge is a member of a set of concepts that relate to the different ways in which knowledge may 'belong' to a group of agents. Two other examples of this kind of concepts are the game theory notion of 'common knowledge' and 'shared knowledge.' An event is common knowledge among a group of players if each player knows it, each one knows that the other players know it, each player knows that other players know that the other players know it, and so on (Aumann 1976).[9] Shared knowledge differs from common knowledge by not requiring that each agent knows that the other agents know, etc. Thus, there is shared knowledge of a fact if each agent knows this fact, but does not know that the other agents know it.

If common knowledge lies at one end of the spectrum, distributed knowledge lies at the other end. Loosely, knowledge is distributed when a set of agents knows something no single agent (completely) knows. Thus, the notions that firms (Tsoukas 1996) or whole economies (Hayek 1945, 1973) are distributed knowledge systems mean that the set of agents comprising these entities somehow can be said to collectively possess knowledge that no single agent possesses. Note that this does not amount to asserting the existence of mysterious supra-individual 'collective minds.' Knowledge still ultimately resides in the heads of individuals; however, when this knowledge is combined and 'aggregated' in certain ways, it means that considered as a system, a set of agents possesses knowledge that they do not possess if separated.

To add a slightly formal touch to this, consider the following definition based on epistemic logic (Hintikka 1962):

Definition (Distributed Knowledge): *If $K_i p_i$ means that agent i knows proposition i, a set of n agents has distributed knowledge of a proposition q (i.e., Dq) when:* $K_1 p_1 \wedge K_2 p_2 \wedge \ldots \wedge K_n p_n \Rightarrow Dq, q \neq p_i, \forall i$.[10]

For example, Jack knows that p is the case and Jill knows that p implies y, but neither know that y is the case. However, if Jack and Jill's knowledge states are 'added' there is a sense, which is more than metaphorical, in which they may know that y is the case (Gerbrandy 1998: 53). The information that y is the case is present in the system comprising Jack and Jill, but in a distributed form. The definition is clearly open to some interpretation. At one extreme, Jack and Jill may both be completely ignorant about

[9] Common knowledge is a core assumption in contract theory, including agency theory (Salanié 1997).

[10] p_i could be interpreted as a vector of propositions. Thus, we are not asserting that each agent only knows one thing.

the knowledge controlled by the other party.[11] At the other extreme, there is considerable, but not complete,[12] knowledge overlap (p_i may be close in some sense to p_j), but it is still the case that no single agent knows q. (An implication is that distributed knowledge is consistent with asymmetric information.) Between the extremes are different degrees of overlap between individual knowledge elements. Note that as a special, but very important, case, it is not inconsistent with the definition to have agent i knowing that if the various knowledge of all the other agents are 'added' in some activity, this will result in a beneficial outcome, even though he does not know any of these knowledge states, and may not even know the precise nature of the beneficial outcome.

5.2.4. *Distributed Knowledge as a Challenge to Authority?*

In a paper that is quite forthcoming about the relation between authority and distributed knowledge, Grandori (1997: 35) argued that

> ... whatever its basis, authority is a feasible governance mechanism only if information and competence relevant to solving economic action problems can be transferred to and handled by a single actor, a positive 'zone of acceptance' exists, the actions of other supervised actors are observable, and if the system is not as large as to incur an overwhelming communication channel overload and control losses.

Thus, Grandori nicely outlines the reasons why distributed knowledge may challenge authority. Specifically, authority is challenged as a 'feasible governance mechanism' for three reasons: Under distributed knowledge:

- the employer does not possess full knowledge of the employee's action set (i.e., the actions that he can take when uncertainty is resolved), so that the employee can take actions about which the manager has no knowledge;
- the employee is better informed than the employer with respect to how certain actions should (optimally) be carried out; and

[11] Sometimes such an interpretation is made of the 'competitive equilibrium' model in economics: although knowledge of technologies and preferences is private, all this knowledge is utilized in the best possible way, so that the knowledge of how to bring about an allocation of resources with superior welfare properties is distributed in the economy (Makowski and Ostroy 2001).

[12] If knowledge overlap is complete, the agents will also know or be able to infer q (if they have perfect rationality/perfect reasoning assumptions and/or the knowledge elements and how they connect is easy to comprehend).

- the employer does not know which actions should optimally be chosen from the action set in response to contingencies (because he lacks information on contingencies).

The ignorance on the part of the employer that is implied by (1) to (3) implies that authority cannot be employed as an efficient mechanism of coordination.

While intuitively appealing, this argument is problematic, and may be a *non sequitur*. The reasons are these: first, the scope conditions of the argument seem unclear clear. We have argued that there are (at least) two meaningful notions of managerial authority (Type I and Type II). Does the argument apply to both notions of authority, or only to one of them (and then which one?)? Second, the argument is based on an inference that seems flawed, namely, that because the holder of authority is ignorant about some of the knowledge held by employees, he just cannot rationally direct them. But in actuality managers are constantly engaged in directing employees whose knowledge in a number of dimensions is superior to theirs. Managers are often quite successful in this. The reason is that one can very well possess the knowledge that somebody else's knowledge may be productively used in a certain activity, even though one does not possess that knowledge oneself. Knight (1921) called this faculty 'judgement' and argued that management is first and foremost about exercising judgment over worker capabilities.

As we shall argue, the problem is therefore not that matching authority and distributed knowledge is always and inherently inefficient. It is not. Rather, what needs to be examined is *how* distributed knowledge constrains the efficient exercise of authority. The issue is, in other words, not one of whether a governance mechanism is inherently inefficient, but about choices between governance mechanisms.

5.3. Aligning Distributed Knowledge and Type I Authority

5.3.1. *An Example*

To focus things, consider a contract situation between Jack and Jill. Knowledge in this situation is distributed, because while Jill has knowledge of some of elements and Jack has knowledge of other elements that are relevant to their contractual relation, their respective knowledge is not overlapping.

Table 5.1. Contracting between Jack and Jill

Actions	Contingencies and their probabilities		
	Contingency p ($p = .2$)	Contingency b ($p = .6$)	Contingency q ($p = .2$)
y	Expected benefit: 6 Expected cost: 6	Expected benefit: 60 Expected cost: 12	Expected benefit: 32 Expected cost: 10
z	Expected benefit: 20 Expected cost: 10	Expected benefit: 48 Expected cost: 7	Expected benefit : 20 Expected cost: 2.2

Specifically, Jack can execute two different actions, y and z. Because of specialization only Jack is capable of carrying out the actions. The two actions can solve coordination problems in the contract situations. The costs and benefit of these actions depend on the contingencies (p, b, q) that arise with certain probabilities during the contractual relationship. See Table 5.1. The numbers in the cells show the expected benefit to the employer (Jill) from an action given a particular contingency and the expected costs to Jack of carrying out the actions under the three different contingencies.

The things that Jack and Jill can know and which are of relevance to their contractual relation (i.e., the 'knowledge elements') are (*a*) the actions available to Jack; (*b*) the costs and benefits of carrying out these actions (i.e., the implications of (p, b, q) on the choice between y and z); (*c*) the different ways in which the actions can be carried out; (*d*) their associated costs and benefits; (*e*) the type of contingencies that can arise (p, b, q); (*f*) the probability that these contingencies arise; and (*g*) the actual contingencies that have emerged. The coordination problem then consists of combining these knowledge elements in such a way that Jack chooses those actions that match the relevant contingencies in a value-maximizing manner (given the various constraints that may exist).

In a perfect world with symmetric information, complete contingent contracts and/or with costless renegotiation and contract enforcement, the problem would be easily solved, and all the value-maximizing actions would be chosen to match whatever contingency emerges. Recall that in Simon (1951), the assumption in a contracting situation as the one sketched above is that of symmetric information between the contracting parties on all relevant elements; however, the execution of the contract is characterized by uncertainty with respect to which one of the already identified contingencies arise during the contract execution phase. High contracting costs make it too costly to renegotiate as the contingencies emerge, and a third party cannot enforce a promise by the employer to choose only actions that maximize total surplus. Thus, the choice according to Simon is therefore between a market contract in which Jill and Jack contract on one of the known actions to be carried out independently of what contingency emerges, or an employment contract where the employer (Jill) choose actions as contingencies emerge, that is, exercise Type I Authority.

Given the specifications in Table 5.1, Jill will pick action y if contingency b emerges and action z if contingency p or q emerges. Given the assumed probabilities, the expected benefit to Jill of having authority is 112 and the expected cost to Jack 32, which is also the minimum flat wage he accepts for actions within this zone of acceptance (given that his opportunity costs are zero). The expected surplus from the authority relation is 80. In a market contract, Jack and Jill would contract on y and the surplus would be 70. Thus, in a situation of symmetric information Jack and Jill strike an employment contract in which Jack executes y or z depending on the benefit of these actions to Jill given the observed contingencies.

5.3.2. *Contracting Under Distributed Knowledge*

In the present context, knowledge is distributed when Jack and Jill have different sets of information on any of the above factors of importance to the contract. Will authority in the Type I sense be efficient under these conditions?

Consider first distributed knowledge about the actual or expected cost to the employee of the different actions under different contingencies (i.e., factor 2 above). If Jack is informed about his own cost of actions, but Jill is not, Jack can misrepresent the real costs in order to influence the sharing of the surplus. Such strategic misrepresenting can, of course, also happen in market contracts and there are no systematic differences in incentives to do so depending on the type of contract. Jack's misrepresentation of costs may influence what actions Jill wants to include in the zone of acceptance, if she is to assume the role of employer. For this reason, Jill may prefer a market contract rather than the employment contract she would have preferred in a setting of symmetric information.[13]

[13] The same conclusion can be drawn if employees (agents) can act in a morally hazardous manner and choose to exert less effort in the actions they choose or that are chosen by the employer. The employment law often grants employers more rights to monitor the employee

If there is distributed knowledge concerning the probability of a contingency, and Jill is the informed party, she can use this information strategically in both market and employment contract to extract a greater share of the surplus. Thus, Jill can misrepresent the probability of a contingency that makes her choose actions that are costly to Jack. However, she does not stand to gain from misrepresenting beyond what makes Jack accept the same zone of acceptance as he would have accepted in a setting of symmetric information.

The consequences of distributed knowledge for the choice between employment and market contracts are more difficult to track if there is asymmetric information about the actions (y and z) available to Jack and if this information is obtained by Jack *post* contracting. Consider the situation in which Jill does not know that y is a solution to the coordination problem when contingency b arises. If she enters an employment contract, she picks y if contingency q arises and z in all other cases. Her surplus from entering that contract compared to the market contract (i.e., choosing z in all cases) is the difference between the wage and the created value from choosing y if contingency q arises—which may not be sufficient to make her choose the employment contract. Jack may not have incentives to inform Jill of these actions *post* contracting, since he is not interested in revealing actions where his costs are higher than the agreed upon fixed wage. Jack will not inform Jill about y as a contract solution should contingency q arise, but would do so should contingency p arise. However, neither the 'employee' in a market contract has incentives to inform the 'employer' on actions that imply large costs relative to the payment for the job. Thus, if the employee obtains information about actions *post* contracting (and this is expected by the employer), it can positively influence the use of employment contracts and authority only if the employer is able to take advantage of emergent actions where the costs to the employee are less than the agreed upon wage without renegotiations.

Finally, the employment contract is always efficient compared to the market contract if there is symmetric information on the actions and factors that effect costs and benefits to the parties of entering the contract, but Jill is in a better position to observe what contingency materialize. A different situation obtains if Jill can observe the contingencies (p, b, q), but only Jack has the information on the actions available and on the

than is the case with a market contract. For that reason moral hazard may influence the choice of contract.

costs and benefits of these actions. In that case, Jack must be given discretion to make efficient use of the information.

From the above discussion, it may seem that the efficiency gain from using an employment contract compared to a market contract can be ascribed to the employer being more sensitive to the choice of actions compared to the employee when it is too costly for an employer to credibly enforce a promise to select only actions that maximize joint output. The latter situation arises in one-period games when some information about the actual contingencies and/or the actions and their associated costs and benefits are not available to third parties (e.g., courts) allowing them to enforce the promise. However, for the employment contract to be efficient, the employee must be able to commit to carry out actions that are not in his interest. How can that happen? For an employee to credibly commit to authority, a third party must refuse to interfere with the contract execution during execution stages. This noninterference from a third party supports the use of authority in contracting relations (Williamson 1996), and is efficient when contractual incompleteness arises because of asymmetrical information between an enforcing third party and the contracting parties. Moreover, courts allow employers to sanction employees who do not obey the authority of the employer. Courts can observe if an employee refuses to carry out any actions. In that case courts enforce authority by allowing the employer to cancel the contract and they may also sanction the breach of the promised acceptance of authority. Thus, accepting authority implies that the employee must carry out those actions that are preferred by the employer even when the costs exceed his payment for the particular action.

5.4. Aligning Distributed Knowledge and Type II Authority

5.4.1. *Delegation and Type II Authority*

Recall that Type II Authority implies that the employee has been delegated rights to make decisions that influence the contracting parties' welfare. Employees to whom such discretion has been granted may be remunerated by fixed wages or by some kind of incentive arrangement. However, as the vast body of agency theory shows, a well-designed incentive contract makes the agent act in the interest of the principal, even in the presence of asymmetric information concerning the agent's actions (Holmström 1979). In fact, incentive contracts can be used to allow the agent to choose actions including actions that may be unknown to the principal and based on knowledge that is not possessed by the agent.[14] Supplier contracts may exemplify this. For that reason we compare two incentive contracts, a market contract and an employment contract.

Continuing with the example, assume that *post* contracting, Jack becomes informed about high-yielding, low-cost actions that are available to him. Jill knows that such actions may emerge. In such a setting, consider a market contract in which a bonus payment is agreed upon, such that Jack signs the contract. Jack can now freely interpret what contingencies have emerged and choose actions in order to maximize his benefit from the contract. However, he has incentives to interpret contingencies in a manner that allow him to choose the least costly actions, and do so at the expense of Jill. For example, if (in Table 5.1) contingency q emerges, Jack can claim that it is really contingency p, and choose action z instead of Jill's preferred action y. The observed result will be 100. If there is asymmetric information between courts and the contracting parties regarding what contingencies have emerged, the promise may appear to be fulfilled according to legal standard, and Jack can get away with his cheating.

If instead Jill has the authority to interpret the contingencies, Jack has incentives to choose those actions that create the greatest surplus, given the contingency (and provided that the incentive compatibility constraint is met). The consequence of the asymmetric information between courts and contracting parties is that in the market contract setting there are more instances where incentive compatibility *cannot* be reached compared to an employment contract. For that reason the use of authority interpreted as the right to define the contingency may be more widespread with the use of incentive schemes.

5.4.2. *Type II Authority When Knowledge Becomes More Distributed*

As many writers have pointed out the distributed nature of knowledge in social systems (from economies to firms) is closely related to, and partly prompted by, specialization (Arora and Gambardella 1994; Hayek 1945). Specialization allows us to effectively handle more and more complex productive tasks of any kind, provided that individual actions are somehow aggregated to a coordinated set of actions. This coordination can take place through markets (negotiations among independent agents) or

[14] However, current formal models of agency do not allow for this.

through the use of Type I and Type II Authority. However, as economists have rediscovered (e.g., Romer 1986), specialization is an ongoing process. So far, we have argued that authority may be efficient in handling a certain level of specialization and distribution of knowledge within a well-defined problem; will it also be efficient if specialization and the attendant distribution of knowledge are increased (e.g., Arora and Gambardella 1994; Coombs and Metcalfe 2000; Smith 2000)?

Increasing specialization is likely to result in more *interdependencies* among the actions of different agents (Thompson 1967), and to some agents specializing in problem solving. For example, Jill knows that contingency b implies that Jack should carry out y and Will should carry out v, whereas contingency q implies that Will must never carry out v. Jane knows what contingencies emerge, but not the implications of these contingencies, and Jack and Will know the actions available to them. In such a setting, Jill acts as a problem solver or 'coordinator,' possessing the knowledge that *if* Jack, Will's and Jane's knowledge sets are somehow aggregated, this will result in their having, as a 'system,' a knowledge that none of them possess individually and that this system of knowledge is needed in order to make efficient choices. Thus, although Jill-the-coordinator may still be ignorant in an important sense about the knowledge controlled by Jack, Will, and Jane, she does not suffer from complete ignorance; there is some, possibly very modest, knowledge overlap. Jill may therefore be able to pass judgement on the overall abilities of Jack, Will, and Jane, and, in particular, about how actions based on their knowledge may be coordinated. In other words, it is quite possible to have knowledge of types of interdependencies between actions based on different knowledge elements without possessing much knowledge of the actual interdependencies or the actions themselves (see also Spangler and Peters 2001).[15]

[15] An illustration of the notion that 'systemic' knowledge can be had without necessarily having (much) knowledge of individual knowledge elements may be found in the theory and practice of software development. Thus, Parnas (1972) develops the notion of 'information hiding,' that is, the desirability in software development (particularly in big projects) of literally hiding information in decomposed modules and so bring interdependencies down to the absolute minimum. Individual programmers ideally (!) should have very little idea about what is going on in the other modules. The development effort is thus of a distributed nature. However, in order to coordinate the actions of individual programmers a system has to be designed. In the case of software development someone must create an architecture, interfaces, and standards that define the limits within which software programmers are allowed to choose among actions (i.e., types of code). An expert may possess knowledge of the structure of the software-programming problem that enables him to define a decomposition of the overall development problem without being cognizant about much of what goes on in individual modules.

5.4.3. *Problem Definitions and the Continuing Need for Authority*

The question then is whether there is a link between authority and such expert 'coordination knowledge.' If the expert has all the knowledge needed to create a perfect decomposition and there is no need to adapt his decision on how to decompose the problem, there is no need for the expert to hold authority. The expert may simply sell his knowledge on how problems should be decomposed or on what actions to choose given different types of contingencies (cf. Coase 1937).[16] However, in actual practice, the design of a problem architecture (Simon 1962), including interfaces and standards, is very much a trial-and-error learning process (e.g., Staudenmeyer and Cusumano 1998), a process of what Egidi (1992) aptly calls 'conjectural decomposition': A decomposition is tried out, whether 'online' or 'offline,' a response is received, feeding back into a new conjecture, etc. Major product development projects that involve the problem-solving efforts of highly interdependent teams with distributed knowledge are usually based on such recurrent conjectural decomposition. Recent examples include the Boeing 777 development effort as well as Microsoft Windows (Cusumano 1997).

Such recurrent conjectural decomposition appears to be an activity that predominantly takes place within firms rather than within market relations: firms formulate and change business plans and strategies; markets do not. Innovation, an iterative process if there is one, tends to take place in firms as interdependencies between the various resources and assets increase. The reason, we argue is that firm organization enables the use of the authority mechanism which is a low-cost way of governing recurrent conjectural decomposition.[17]

5.4.4. *Governing the Definition of Problems*

A first step in the creation of problem architectures is the decomposition of the problem (see Heimann, Nickerson, and Zenger this volume). This requires that the problem has been *made* well defined. For example, a

[16] Market exists for expert advice, although such advice as an economic good suffers from the well-known problems in connection with markets for information.

[17] For the expert on system creation to acquire authority in a setting of recurrent adaptation, the expert must be the part who is most sensitive to decisions such as choices among different way of decomposing the problem, identification of what contingencies (unexpected interdependencies between modules) has emerged and what action (new decompositions) to take. Moreover, the system creator must have more information on important aspects of these decisions compared to a third party (courts), such that authority of Type II becomes the efficient way of organizing the system designing (cf. Simon 1951).

strategic opportunity must be defined and made concrete by refining the business proposition and delineating its application. Authority is an efficient governance mechanism for promoting these processes (see also Nickerson and Zenger 2004). Moreover, the way in which problems gets defined and the kind of constraints that are chosen will to some extent influence whether problems can be fully decomposed, nearly decomposed, or not decomposed at all (Foss and Foss 2006). This has implications for the need for authority in managing residual interdependencies, specifically for the understanding of Type II Authority.

Simon (1973: 186) forcefully argues that virtually all problems presented to problem solvers are, from the outset, '... best regarded as ill structured problems. They become well structured problems only in the process of being prepared for the problem solvers. It is not exaggerating much to say that there are no well structured problems, only ill-structured problems that have been formalized for problem solvers.' Thus, well-structured problems are outcomes of deliberate problem-defining processes. Defining a problem requires that *constraints* are imposed on it. Simon (1973) provides several examples of problems (relating to ship-building and building a house) that are initially extremely ill structured, but which through the imposition of constraints *become* well structured. A key point in his discussion is that initial choices of constraints define the major interdependencies in the problem-solving effort; in the sense that these constraints define what are the (first levels of) subproblems and the relations between these. Not all constraints can be defined initially, and new constraints (around new subproblems) arise endogenously in the process. The necessity of iteration between subproblems and succeeding design changes, follow from the impossibility of getting the decomposition right initially (cf. Simon 1973: 191).[18] This provides a continued role for deliberate problem solving, and the use of authority in defining problem and creating architectures (Nickerson and Zenger 2004).[19]

[18] The following quotation from a software developer is illustrative: 'A lot of time people don't realize that they are dependent on something. It's just not obvious. For example, you don't realize that you have a dependency because you are not familiar with that part of the code. Or a dependency just sort of materializes out of thin air because of a need and is tracked informally. Or instances where the solution to one dependency creates problems for a third party. The real problems arise with the hidden interdependencies—the ones that no one thought about pop up at the last minute' (quoted by Staudenmeyer and Cusumano 1998: 18–19). The developer goes on to stress the need for carefully managing the process of iteration.

[19] Given the uncertain nature of the process, the process of decomposition will almost certainly be one of trial and error (Egidi 2002). Grandori (1997: 37) notes that it has been 'well-documented' in organization studies that '... authority is not very effective in managing uncertainty.' The arguments developed here imply rather the opposite.

5.4.5. *Governing Interdependencies by Means of Authority*

However, there may also be an ongoing role of authority once the problem is well defined and the corresponding architecture has emerged. Nickerson and Zenger (2004) assume that problems are *given*, and that the main problem is to organize the search for solutions. That is, a problem architecture has been identified which defines the patterns of interaction that are needed to resolve the remaining interdependencies between subproblems in order for the system to adapt to changes.

Consider the instance where the identification and gradual definition of a business opportunity has resulted in the creation of an organization that is designed to produce and sell various goods. Adaptations within the organization require that agents adapt their actions to newly discovered contingencies (Williamson 1996), implement actions not previously recognized as solutions to problems, or restructure the system as they learn more about the interdependencies involved in the ongoing problem solving. These are settings in which according to our previous discussion Type I or II Authority may be efficient, and the exercise of authority may take the form of orders, the creation of job descriptions (subdivisions of tasks), delegating and constraining rights to further subdivide subproblems, and establish information linkages and/or incentives that will allow actions taken on the bases of distributed knowledge to be aggregated in way that minimize negative externalities.

The constraining, planning, and direction that is needed—and therefore the need for authority—depend on *how* the business opportunity has been defined and decomposed, in particular what is the nature of the relevant interdependencies. If the problem has been defined and decomposed in a way such that only *sequential interdependencies* (Thompson 1967) remain between subproblems, adaptation to unexpected contingencies requires information to travel in one direction to ensure adaptation and agreements on adaptation only needs to be reached between agents engaged in adjacent activities, because that is where externalities emerge. Modular production systems exemplify this (Langlois 2002). The coordination may take place through, for example, prices, routines, standards, the use of kanban methods, or through the use of authority of Type I or II. What choice of governance mechanism (and structure) is made depends on the determinants that are highlighted in organizational economics, notably whether the parties have made complementary investments and the degree of enforceability of the incomplete contract governing the relationship.

If problem identification and decomposition create a system where the remaining interdependencies are *reciprocal* (Thompson 1967), these can be handled by means of communication between members of teams dealing with the relevant subproblems. Possible disagreements may be handled by outside arbitration or by the use of authority. However, when nearly decomposable problems contain very different kinds of reciprocal interdependencies between subproblems, the costs of mutual adaptation through consultation (i.e., lateral communication) and/or negotiations among agents may be very high. Increased specialization and the resulting distributed knowledge may lead to the choice of an authority-based governance of the adaptation process. A central agent who specializes in recognizing contingencies and in knowing the consequences can reduce renegotiation costs and will acquire authority depending on the specifics of the contracting situation (contractual incompleteness and enforceability, cf. Hart 1995 and Williamson 1996). As more interdependencies arise between knowledge elements of different kinds, the margin at which authority become costly in terms of increased mistakes may soon be reached. However, due to the nature of the numerous interdependencies market contracting may not be the efficient solution. In such instances, it may instead be efficient to redefine the problem and create an architecture, in which many of the complex interdependencies are transformed to sequential interdependencies and where market contracting becomes efficient. However, such a redefinition of the problem may require the use of authority. In product development, the redefinition of product development problems and the creation of modular or nearly modular systems exemplify the way in which system designers can reduce costs of market contracting for some transactions, thus reducing the scope of transactions for which authority must be applied. Thus, an important function of Type II Authority is to define problems and to redefine subproblems, such that at the margin the costs of making use of market contracts relative to authority is reduced (Langlois 2002).

5.5. Conclusions

Knowledge governance concerns the deployment of administrative machinery and other designable features of organization in order to steer processes of knowledge utilization, sharing, integration, and building in desired directions, that is, toward their efficient levels (Foss 2007;

Chapter 1 in this volume). This chapter has focused on the utilization of knowledge (Garicano 2000; Hayek 1945). Specifically, we have raised the issue of whether knowledge that is distributed is misaligned with the governance mechanism of authority in terms of efficiently utilizing that knowledge (this is how we interpret those management writers who claim that authority relations become strained under the impact of knowledge for productive purposes becoming increasingly distributed).

Overall, the conclusion of this chapter is that there is no apparent contradiction between the use of authority and the existence of distributed knowledge. This conclusion seems to be at odds with Hayek's famous claim that distributed knowledge puts binding constraints on the size of an economic system for which central planning is feasible (Hayek 1935, 1945). However, two observations seem important to the argument. First, the introduction of Type II Authority allows for some degree of decentralization in the use of distributed knowledge and thus expands the binding constraints on 'central planning' as a feasible mode. Second, Hayek's argument refers to the decline in the quality of planning and direction as more economic activities are subsumed under a central planner. Thus, it is not a matter of whether authority can be used at all, but at what *scale* it becomes inefficient *relative* to market contracting; that is, the issue is comparative-institutional (Williamson 1985). The strong emphasis on the marginal limitation to the use of authority is also present in Coase's (1937) analysis of the boundaries of the firm. At some point, he argues, the costs of managerial mistakes offset the costs of using markets as means of coordinating. Accordingly, we should also examine the influence of increasingly distributed knowledge on the effective scale at which authority of Type I and II can be applied. However, this goes beyond the present work, the aim of which has been to contribute conceptually to the discussion of important notions that characterize much contemporary discussion of governance in the emerging knowledge economy, and to specifically argue that authority may very well be consistent with efficient governance under distributed knowledge conditions.

References

Aghion, P. and J. Tirole. 1997. 'Formal and Real Authority in Organizations,' *Journal of Political Economy* 105: 1–29.

Arora, A. and A. Gambardella. 1994. 'The Changing Technology of Technical Change: General and Abstract Knowledge and the Division of Innovative Labour,' *Research Policy* 23: 523–32.

Aumann, R. 1976. 'Agreeing to Disagree,' *The Annals of Statistics* 4: 1236–9.

Baker, G., R. Gibbons, and K. J. Murphy. 1999. 'Informal Authority in Organizations,' *Journal of Law, Economics and Organization* 15: 56–73.

Bolton, P. and J. Farrell. 1990. 'Decentralization, Duplication, and Delay,' *Journal of Political Economy* 98: 803–26.

Brusoni, S. 2005. 'The Limits to Specialization: Problem Solving and Coordination in Modular Networks,' *Organization Studies* 26: 1885–1907.

——A. Prencipe, and K. Pavitt. 2001. 'Knowledge Specialization, Organizational Coupling, and the Boundaries of the Firm: Why Do Firms Know More Than They Make?,' *Administrative Science Quarterly* 46: 597–621.

Casson, M. 1994. 'Why Are Firms Hierarchical?,' *International Journal of the Economics of Business* 1: 47–76.

Coase, R. H. 1937. 'The Nature of the Firm,' in Nicolai J. Foss (ed.) *The Theory of the Firm: Critical Perspectives in Business and Management*, Vol II. London: Routledge.

Cohen, M. and R. A. Robert. 1996. 'Managing Internal Consistency in Technology Intensive Design Projects,' *Competitiveness Review* 6: 42–59.

Conger, J. and R. Kanungo. 1988. 'The Empowerment Process: Integrating Theory and Practice,' *Academy of Management Review* 13: 471–82.

Cowen, T. and D. Parker. 1997. *Markets in the Firm*. London: Institute for Economic Affairs.

Cremer, J. 1990. 'Common Knowledge and the Coordination of Economic Activities,' in M. Aoki, B. Gustafsson, and O. Williamson (eds.) *The Firm as a Nexus of Treaties*, London: Sage.

——1993. 'Corporate Culture: Cognitive Aspects,' *Industrial and Corporate Change* 3: 351–86.

Cusumano, M. 1997. 'How Microsoft Makes Large Teams Work Like Small Teams,' *Sloan Management Review* 39: 9–20.

Cyert, R. M. and J. G. March. 1963. *A Behavioral Theory of the Firm*. Englewood Cliffs: Prentice-Hall.

Demsetz, H. 1991. 'The Nature of the Firm Revisited,' in O. E. Williamson and S. G. Winter (eds.) *The Nature of the Firm*. Oxford: Blackwell.

Egidi, M. 1992. 'Organizational Learning, Problem-Solving, and the Division of Labor,' in H. A. Simon (ed.) *Economics, Bounded Rationality, and the Cognitive Revolution*. Aldershot: Edward Elgar.

Fama, E. and M. C. Jensen. 1983. 'Separation of Ownership and Control,' *Journal of Law and Economics* 26: 301–25.

Foss, K. and N. J. Foss. 2006. 'Simon on Problem-Solving,' *International Journal of Learning and Intellectual Capital* 3: 339–56.

Foss, N. J. 1999. 'The Use of Knowledge in Firms,' *Journal of Institutional and Theoretical Economics* 155: 458–86.

——2005. *Strategy and Organization in the Knowledge Economy*. Oxford University Press.

Foss, N. J. 2007. 'The Emerging Knowledge Governance Approach,' *Organization* 14: 29–52.

——K. Husted, and S. Michailova. 2008. 'Governing Knowledge Sharing in Organizations: A Research Agenda,' Working Paper.

Galbraith, J. R. 1974. 'Organization Design: An Information Processing View,' *Interfaces* 4: 28–36.

Garicano, L. 2000. 'Hierarchies and the Organization of Knowledge in Production,' *Journal of Political Economy* 108: 874–904.

Gerbrandy, J. D. 1998. *Bisimulations on Planet Kripke*. Ph.D. dissertation, Institute for Logic, Language and Computing, Amsterdam University.

Granstrand, O., P. Patel, and K. Pavitt. 1997. 'Multitechnology Corporations: Why They Have Distributed" Rather Than "Distinctive Core" Capabilities,' *California Management Review* 39 (4): 8–25.

Grant, R. 1996. 'Toward a Knowledge-Based Theory of the Firm,' *Strategic Management Journal* 17: 109–22.

Gherardi, S. 1999. 'Learning as Problem-Driven or Learning in the Face of Mystery?,' *Organization Studies* 20: 101–24.

Grandori, A. 1997. 'Governance Structures, Coordination Mechanisms and Cognitive Models,' *Journal of Management and Governance* 1: 29–42.

——2001. *Organizations and Economic Behavior*. London: Routledge.

——2002. 'Cognitive Failures' and Combinative Failures,' *Journal of Management and Governance* 6: 252–60.

Halpern, J. Y. and Y. Moses. 1990. 'Knowledge and Common Knowledge in a Distributed Environment', *Journal of the Association for Computing Machinery* 37: 549–87.

Hammond, T. H. and G. J. Miller. 1985. 'A Social Choice Perspective on Expertise and Authority in Bureaucracy,' *American Journal of Political Science* 29: 611–38.

Hart, O. 1995. *Firms, Contracts, and Financial Structure*. Oxford: Oxford University Press.

——1996. 'An Economist's View of Authority,' *Rationality and Society* 8: 371–86.

Hayek, F. A. von. 1935. 'Socialist Calculation: The State of the Debate,' in idem. 1948. *Individualism and Economic Order*. Chicago: University of Chicago Press.

——1945. 'The Use of Knowledge in Society,' in idem. 1948. *Individualism and Economic Order*. Chicago: University of Chicago Press.

——1973. *Law, Legislation and Liberty. Vol.1: Rules and Order*. Chicago: University of Chicago Press.

Hintikka, J. 1962. *Knowledge and Belief*. Ithaca, NY: Cornell University Press.

Hodgson, G. 1998. *Economics and Utopia*. London: Routledge.

Holmström, B. 1979. 'Moral Hazard and Observability,' *Bell Journal of Economics* 10: 74–91.

——1999. 'The Firm as a Subeconomy,' *Journal of Law, Economics, and Organization* 15: 74–102.

——and P. Milgrom. 1991. 'Multitask Principal-Agent Analysis: Incentive Contracts, Asset Ownership and Job Design,' *Journal of Law, Economics and Organization* 7: 24–54.

Hutchins, E. 1995. *Cognition in the Wild*. Cambridge: MIT Press.

Jensen, M. C. and W. H. Meckling. 1992. 'Specific and General Knowledge and Organizational Structure,' in L. Werin and H. Wijkander (eds.) *Contract Economics*. Oxford: Blackwell.

Knight, F. H. 1921. *Risk, Uncertainty, and Profit*. Reprint 1965. New York: A. M. Kelley.

Kogut, B. and U. Zander. 1992. 'Knowledge at the Firm, Combinative Capabilities, and the Replication of Technology,' *Organizational Science* 3: 383–97.

Kreps, D. 1990. 'Corporate Culture and Economic Theory,' in J. E. Alt and K. Shepsle (eds.) *Perspectives on Positive Political Economy*. Cambridge: Cambridge University Press.

Langlois, R. N. 1995. 'Do Firms Plan?,' *Constitutional Political Economy* 6: 247–61.

——2002. 'Modularity and Organizations,' in N. J. Foss and P. G. Klein (eds.) *Entrepreneurship and the Firm: Austrian Perspectives on Economic Organization*. Aldershot: Edward Elgar.

Larsen, J. N. 2001. 'Knowledge, Human Resources and Social Practice: The Knowledge-Intensive Business Service Firm as a Distributed Knowledge System,' *The Service Industries Journal* 21: 81–103.

Lavoie, D. 1985. *Rivalry and Central Planning*. Cambridge: Cambridge University Press.

Lawrence, P. R. and J. W. Lorsch. 1967. 'Differentiation and Integration in Complex Organizations,' *Administrative Science Quarterly* 12: 1–47.

Lessard, D. R. and S. Zaheer. 1996. 'Breaking the Silos: Distributed Knowledge and Strategic Responses to Volatile Exchange Rates,' *Strategic Management Journal* 17: 513–34.

Levinthal, D. A. 1997. 'Adaptation on Rugged Landscapes,' *Management Science* 43: 934–50.

Liebeskind, J. P., A. L. Oliver, L. Zucker, and M. Brewer. 1995. 'Social Networks, Learning, and Flexibility: Sourcing Scientific Knowledge in New Biotechnology Firms,' *Organization Science* 7: 428–43.

Loasby, B. 1976. *Choice, Complexity and Ignorance*. Cambridge: Cambridge University Press.

Makowski, L. and J. M. Ostroy. 2001. 'Perfect Competition and the Creativity of the Market,' *Journal of Economic Literature* 39: 479–535.

March, J. G. and H. A. Simon. 1958. *Organizations*. New York: Wiley.

Marengo, L. 1995. 'Structure, Competence, and Learning in Organizations,' *Wirtschaftspolitische Blätter* 6: 454–64.

Miles, R. E., C. C. Snow, J. A. Mathews, G. Miles, and H. J. Coleman, Jr. 1997. 'Organizing in the Knowledge Age: Anticipating the Cellular Form,' *Academy of Management Executive* 11: 7–20.

Milgrom, P. and J. Roberts. 1992. *Economics, Organization, and Management.* Prentice-Hall.

Miller, G. 1992. *Managerial Dilemmas*. Cambridge: Cambridge University Press.

Minkler, A. P. 1993. 'Knowledge and Internal Organization,' *Journal of Economic Behavior and Organization* 21: 17–30.

Mintzberg, H. 1990. 'The Design School: Reconsidering the Basic Premises of Strategic Management,' *Strategic Management Journal* 11: 171–95.

—— D. Raisinghani, and A. Théorêt. 1976. 'The Structure of "Unstructured" Decision Processes,' *Administrative Science Quarterly* 21: 246–75.

Nickerson, J. and T. Zenger. 2004. 'A Knowledge-based Theory of the Firm—The Problem-solving Perspective,' *Organization Science* 15: 617–32.

Orlikowski, W. J. 2002. 'Knowing in Practice: Enacting a Collective Capability in Distributed Organizing,' *Organization Science* 13: 249–73.

Osterloh, M. and B. Frey. 2000. 'Motivation, Knowledge Transfer and Organizational Form,' *Organization Science* 11: 538–50.

Parnas, D. L. 1972. 'On the Criteria for Decomposing Systems Into Modules,' *Communications of the ACM* 15: 1053–8.

Potts, J. 2001. 'Knowledge and Markets,' *Journal of Evolutionary Economics* 11: 413–31.

Radner, R. 2000. 'Costly and Bounded Rationality in Individual and Team Decision Making,' *Industrial and Corporate Change* 9: 623–58.

Richardson, G. B. 1972. 'The Organisation of Industry,' *Economic Journal* 82: 883–96.

Romer, P. 1986. 'Increasing Returns and Long-Run Growth,' *Journal of Political Economy* 94: 1002–38.

Salanié, B. 1997. *The Economics of Contracts*. Cambridge: MIT Press.

Sharma, A. 1997. 'Professional as Agent: Knowledge Asymmetry in Agency Exchange,' *Academy of Management Review* 22: 758–98.

Simon, H. A. 1947. *Administrative Behavior.* New York: Macmillan.

—— 1951. 'A Formal Theory of the Employment Relationship,' in idem. 1982. *Models of Bounded Rationality*. Cambridge: MIT Press.

—— 1962. 'The Architecture of Complexity,' *Proceedings of the American Philosophical Society* 156: 467–82.

—— 1973. 'The Structure of Ill-Structured Problems,' *Artificial Intelligence* 4: 181–201.

—— 1991. 'Organizations and Markets,' *Journal of Economic Perspectives* 5: 25–44.

Smith, K. 2000. 'What is the "Knowledge Economy"? Knowledge-Intensive Industries and Distributed Knowledge Bases,' *Working Paper,* STEP group, Oslo.

Staudenmayer, N. and M. A. Cusumano. 1998. 'Alternative Designs for Product Component Integration,' *Working Paper,* MIT.

Spangler, W. E. and J. M. Peters. 2001. 'A Model of Distributed Knowledge and Action in Complex Systems,' *Decision Support Systems* 31: 103

Thompson, J. D. 1956. 'Authority and Power in "Identical" Organizations,' *American Journal of Sociology* 62.

—— 1967. *Organizations in Action*. New York: McGraw-Hill.

Tsoukas, H. 1996. 'The Firm as a Distributed Knowledge System: A Constructionist Approach,' *Strategic Management Journal* 17: 11–25.

Wang, Q. and G. N. von Tunzelman. 2000. 'Complexity and the Functions of the Firm: Breadth and Depth,' *Research Policy* 29: 805–18.

Weber, M. 1947. *The Theory of Economic and Social Organization*. New York: Oxford University Press.

Williamson, O. E. 1985. *The Economic Institutions of Capitalism*. New York: Free Press.

——. 1996. *The Mechanisms of Governance*. Oxford: Oxford University Press.

Zenger, T. 2002. 'Crafting Internal Hybrids,' *International Journal of the Economics of Business* 9: 79–96.

Zucker, L. 1991. 'Markets for Bureaucratic Authority and Control: Information Quality in Professions and Services,' *Research in the Sociology of Organizations* 8: 157–90.

6

The governance of explorative knowledge production

Margit Osterloh and Antoinette Weibel

6.1. Introduction

Firms' competitive advantage is increasingly seen to accrue from the particular capabilities organizations have for creating and sharing knowledge (e.g., Kogut and Zander 1996; Nahapiet and Ghoshal 1998). How organizational knowledge is handled, however, is dependent on the type of knowledge production focused on (Grant and Baden-Fuller 2004). The knowledge management literature distinguishes two types of knowledge production: knowledge exploration and knowledge exploitation (March 1991). Knowledge exploration refers to activities that lead to new knowledge, for example activities such as knowledge search, experimentation, and discovery (Holmqvist 2004; Spender 1992). Knowledge exploitation refers to activities that deploy existing knowledge to create value, for example activities such as routinization and implementation of knowledge (Holmqvist 2004).

Explorative and exploitative knowledge production differ in both their cognitive and their motivational underpinnings. In a recent article, Grant and Baden-Fuller (2004) have carefully explained the differing *cognitive underpinnings* and the consequences of these different underpinnings for knowledge management: during the *exploration* phase, knowledge bases should differ sufficiently, that is, the actors should have some degree of cognitive distance (Nooteboom 2000*b*). This is the case for two reasons. First, the variety of cognition is a prerequisite to create novelty and to explore the potential of a new technology. Second, creative approaches often lie dispersed across distinct technological trajectories (Spencer 2003). Careful observation of other approaches reduces the risk of getting stuck on a trajectory that ends up not being selected as the dominant design. As a consequence to be efficient in knowledge generation participants of a knowledge-creating team have to be specialized to a high degree. In contrast, during the *exploitation* phase *a certain overlap of knowledge is crucial* (McEvily, Eisenhardt, and Prescott 2004). It increases efficiency of cooperation, because a greater alignment of mental categories facilitates communication and understanding. The whole knowledge production process of a firm is composed of both types of knowledge production—exploration and exploitation—and in each type there exists an optimal trade-off between specialization and overlap of knowledge (Postrel 2002). However, specialization and differentiation of knowledge is more efficient for exploration and a high degree of knowledge overlap facilitates exploitation (Postrel 2002: 307).

What is lacking so far, however, is an elaboration on how the *motivational underpinnings* of both types of knowledge production differ and what the consequences of these different underpinnings are for knowledge management. Vining (2003) characterizes knowledge production—exploration or exploitation—as an internal public good: Employees have strong incentives to withhold their knowledge or to underinvest in collective knowledge sharing. Similarly, according to Cabrera and Cabrera (2002) knowledge production can be conceptualized as a particular case of a social dilemma in which individual rationality—trying to maximize individual payoff—leads to collective irrationality. However, as we will argue in this chapter, the solutions offered by Vining (2003) and by Cabrera and Cabrera (2002) are better suited to handle social dilemmas in the exploitation phase. During exploitation, *transactional solutions*, that is, solutions which change the rules of the game to make cooperation more attractive even for selfish actors, are sufficient. During exploration, transactional solutions will not suffice. Exploration is better handled through *transformational solutions*, which focus on the change of preferences of economic actors. More precisely we will argue that organizational measures to foster intrinsic motivation are best equipped to overcome social dilemmas in explorative knowledge work. Thus we review evidence from psychological economics and organizational behavior to redress this apparent imbalance in the knowledge management literature and discuss the transformational solutions for social dilemmas in the exploration phase.

6.2. Cooperation as a Social Dilemma

Cooperation in organization is often characterized by social dilemmas (Miller 1992). Cooperation takes place when the economic actors together can produce a higher output than the sum of the separate outputs of each economic actor working independently. Cooperation thus creates what is commonly known as synergy (Foss and Iversen 1997). The more effort exerted by one economic actor, the more productive other economic actors become. As a result, activities are characterized in firms and networks by a high degree of complex interdependencies. Simon (1991: 33) makes this point clear in his important paper on organizations and markets:

> In general, the greater the interdependence among various members of the organization, the more difficult it is to measure their separate contributions to the achievement of organizational goals. But of course, intense interdependence is precisely what makes it advantageous to organize people instead of depending wholly on market transactions.

However, interdependencies also make team members more vulnerable to each other. By exploiting interdependencies a collective good is generated. A collective good (in contrast to a private good) is a good that can be used by people who have not contributed their share to its production. This is the case in interdependent cooperation. It is hard to determine exactly what input each of the economic actors has contributed to the joint output. Some actors could free ride at the cost of others. This was found to be true in a great number of situations: when people realize that their contribution cannot be measured, individual effort declines (Messick and Brewer 1983). More generally, this situation is referred to as a 'social dilemma.' It characterizes situations in which the actions of self-interested and rational individuals lead to situations of collective irrationality in which everyone is worse off (Dawes 1980). A 'tragedy of the commons' (Hardin 1968) may arise, which exemplifies the true meaning of a tragedy: each team member is fully aware of the situation and realizes that their action leads to a negative outcome and 'every team member would prefer a team in which no one, not even himself, shirked' (Alchian and Demsetz

1972: 790). However, rational selfish single actors are unable to solve such dilemmas on their own. If all or most of the team members' free ride, the collective good will not be achieved, or will at least be undersupplied. As a consequence, all cooperation is undertaken to raise productivity by leading to a joint output that exceeds the sum of the individual outputs. At the same time, all cooperation is faced with the problem of social dilemmas.

The traditional solution to social dilemmas is giving a central agency (principal) the right to supervise the other actors (agents) and to reward effort or punish shirking (Alchian and Demsetz 1972). The principal is assigned the role of supervisor. Her main job is to monitor the agents and to make sure that nobody shirks. This task includes selection, instruction, observation of individual effort, sanctioning, and rewarding, as well as (re)negotiation of the contracts. As an incentive to doing her job well, the principal gets the net earnings of the joint production. Such supervision, or the 'visible hand' of the owner, is characteristic of firms, in contrast to the 'invisible hand' of markets (Chandler 1977). With rational selfish actors, markets will not provide collective goods. This is the reason why social dilemmas are at the heart of management in firms and other forms of cooperation (Miller 1992; Vining 2003).

6.2.1. *Cooperation in Knowledge Teams as a Special Kind of Social Dilemma*

The convincing explanation by Alchian and Demsetz (1972) of how cooperation can be managed is flawed if we take into account knowledge work. This solution does not work if there are information asymmetries between the principal and the agents. While this is a problem in all knowledge work (Cabrera and Cabrera 2002), in the exploitation phase to overcome this problem is mainly a question of transaction costs, concerning the costs of collecting, evaluating, and applying existent knowledge. Social dilemmas during this phase can be solved—as we will show—mainly with transactional solutions based on monetary incentives. This is not the case in the exploration phase, because the arising problems of free riding, spillover, and holdup (Nooteboom 2000*a*) have different origins and cannot be solved in the same way.

The *problem of free riding* in (explorative and exploitative) knowledge work arises, because knowledge work in contrast to manual teamwork enhances productivity of joint production only if different knowledge is dispersed among different people (Foss and Foss 2000; Grant 1996). If all knowledge workers in a group have the same knowledge, one person could do the whole job almost entirely alone. If the principal knows what the agents know, then she also could do the knowledge work for herself. However, if she does not know what the agents know, then she can monitor neither whether the agents have chosen the most productive activities nor whether they shirk. The only thing she can do is (*a*) to evaluate whether certain professional standards are met and (*b*) to benchmark the output without understanding exactly how the output was obtained, just as you can benchmark certain machines or software programs without knowing exactly how they work. But this does not help to prevent shirking by individual agents producing a team output. As a result, self-interested knowledge workers in teams are in a good position to hide their expertise vis-à-vis their superiors (Davenport and Prusak 1998).

The *problem of spillover* consists in the danger that sharing of knowledge can lead to a competitive disadvantage (Bogenrieder and Nooteboom 2004). Sharing or publishing new individual knowledge means changing a private good into a public good. Once published, nobody can be excluded from this good. The access to this knowledge—for example knowledge that is collected in an electronic database—is unrestricted to members of the firm or a network which have access to this database. Why should an agent do that? By sharing his knowledge, he enables the principal to monitor him. He may gain some reputation, but at the same time lose his competitive edge. Sharing knowledge with others may negatively affect an economic actor's ability to outperform them. As a result, self-interested knowledge workers in teams are not only in a better position but also have an incentive to hide their expertise vis-à-vis their principals as well as vis-à-vis their coworkers.

The *problem of holdup* consists in the necessity to make firm- or network-specific investments in order to raise the joint productivity. Such investments may not be recoverable for the individual economic actor, except by successfully carrying out the project and sharing the joint output. Thus the members of a knowledge team make themselves vulnerable to the principal and to each other. In such cases, the danger of underinvestment in such resources arises among self-interested team members without the principal being able to control this underinvestment efficiently. As a consequence, the competitive advantage of the firm or the network will suffer. Again, a social dilemma arises.

6.3. Can Social Dilemmas in Explorative Knowledge Work be Solved by Transactional or Transformational Solutions?

The suggestions discussed for solving social dilemmas can be divided into transactional and transformational solutions (Kollock 1998).[1] Transactional solutions change the rules of the game to make cooperation more attractive for selfish employees. Transformational solutions focus mainly on the change of preferences of the economic actors.

6.3.1. *Transactional Solutions*

6.3.1.1. ACTIVATING THE 'SHADOW OF THE FUTURE'

The most influential proposal for solving social dilemmas is to extend the shadow of the future by long-term, reciprocal relationships (Axelrod 1984). There are *two* conditions for a shadow of the future to promote cooperation: the relationship must have a long-term outlook and the partners employ a 'tit for tat' strategy. Organizational careers with a high longevity which cover a wide range of employees may create such *a long-term outlook* (e.g., Whitley 2003). Under such circumstances, employees are more willing to share their knowledge. Such a *'tit for tat' strategy* is easier adopted in the exploitation phase. However, it is often disregarded that, among self-interested economic actors, this strategy only works on condition that individuals have perfect information as to how the other persons behaved in the past (Kollock 1998). In the exploitation phase this condition is better fulfilled than in the exploration phase. Although also in the exploitation case there is room for misperceptions and mistakes, due to the greater knowledge overlap between partners it is easier to evaluate past cooperative behavior. In contrast, in the exploration case one can simply not evaluate how much cooperative behavior in sharing knowledge was exerted in the past, irrespective of transaction costs.

6.3.1.2. SELECTIVE INCENTIVES

A selective incentive is a private good (e.g., a bonus) given to individuals as an inducement to contribute to a public or common good

[1] Kollock (1998) differentiates between strategic (in our terminology transactional) solutions and motivational (in our terminology transformational) solutions. We have chosen a different terminology because strategic solutions include (extrinsic) motivation.

(Olson 1965). All firm or network members may have access to the electronic database, but only contributors receive a reward. If selective incentives exist, a social dilemma can be transformed into a coordination game where several equilibria exist (Sen 1974). However, selective incentives raise two problems. First, they increase costs, and second, some kind of performance-contingent measure must be applied, which raises the so-called multitask problem (Holmström and Milgrom 1991). Take the case of a reward for contributions made to an electronic database. As a result, you might get a high number of contributions with little value. If you do not count the contributions as such, but the actual downloads, the incentive to enhance the value of the contribution might work. However, it might also happen that the contributors induce their colleagues to download their contributions. As a result, you have become the victim of 'the folly of rewarding A while hoping for B' (Kerr 1975). This multitask problem is the consequence of a pay for performance system that calls for a clear link between actions and results that can be easily measured. Thus, high-powered selective incentives in firms undermine the provision of firm-specific common goods (Vining 2003). This is the reason why even orthodox economists reach the conclusion: 'The use of low-powered incentives within the firm, although sometimes lamented as one of the major disadvantages of internal organization, is also an important vehicle for inspiring cooperation and coordination' (Frey and Osterloh 2005; Holmström and Milgrom 1994: 989). This is true in particular for knowledge work. This work contains some easy to measure components (e.g., pages of written text) and some hard to measure components (e.g., the importance of a text). Selective incentives have to concentrate on few criteria that are clear-cut. As a consequence, rational economic actors will focus on the easily measurable components and leave aside the components that are not so easy to measure. While this problem in the exploitation phase can be mitigated by evaluation by expert peer groups, this solution often fails in the exploration phase (Frey and Osterloh 2006). Even peers mostly do not know what might be the characteristics of a future dominant trajectory design or dominant design. Peers often disregard that path-breaking explorative innovations demand for new criteria of evaluation. There exists for example empirical evidence that in academic research expert peer groups often reject creative and unorthodox contributions and reward the mainstream (Frey 2003). Many rejections in highly ranked journals are documented regarding papers that later were awarded high prizes, even the Nobel Prize (Campanario 1996; Gans and Shepherd 1994; Weingart 2005). Many path-breaking radical innovations could only be appreciated after decades (Gillies 2006). As a consequence explorative knowledge work often cannot be evaluated adequately even by expert peers.

6.3.1.3. PROFIT CENTERS AND MODULARIZATION

One frequently discussed suggestion is to decentralize decision authority into profit centers or modules or outsource activities so that market forces can do their work via (transfer-) prices. This suggestion refers to the traditional solutions of common good problems by internalization of external effects through privatization of gains and losses. The leader of the profit centers or modularized groups could be remunerated according to measurable criteria.

However, there are some problems with knowledge work organized as profit centers. *First,* the leader of the profit centers has no incentive to share knowledge voluntarily with other profit centers, because then she would be giving away transactional opportunities for free. This is especially true for tacit knowledge. The transfer of tacit knowledge cannot be monitored or contracted as long as it is not embodied in a tradable product (Osterloh and Frey 2000). *Second,* the sources of hard to imitate competitive advantages will be undermined. In order to be able to bargain over (transfer-) prices and service-level agreements across the boundaries of profit centers, some tacit knowledge must be made explicit. As a consequence, the knowledge incorporated in the profit centers may become more tradable and imitable (Chesbrough and Teece 1996). As a consequence, there are no incentives to produce synergies or common knowledge goods across the boundaries of profit centers. During the exploitation phase this problem is less relevant than during the exploration phase. In the exploitation phase when a dominant design or a dominant trajectory exists, most relevant knowledge is made explicit, while in the exploration case this is not the case.

During exploration, another problem arises. A precondition for profit centers is modularization. However, little attention has been paid to the problem of identifying what constitutes an appropriate modularization and what risks are involved with incorrect partitioning. Inappropriate modularization can take two forms: (*a*) undermodularization and (*b*) overmodularization, in particular modularization cutting through strong interdependencies. An example for overmodularization is Intel's Itanium chip design process (Hamilton 2001). In a well-designed chip, signals flit from module to module, with the speed of the chip determined by the slowest signals. The engineers found ways to speed up the slowpokes via slight changes within single modules. However, it became clear that many of these changes disrupted the whole choreography, forcing engineers of other modules to rework their designs. As a result, several hundred engineers found themselves in a nightmare situation, because a change in one module ripples through the whole design process. As a consequence, inappropriate modularization carries the risk of destroying possible synergies. Whenever knowledge integration with complex tasks is crucial, it is better to 'undermodularize' than to 'overmodularize' (Ethiraj and Levinthal 2004). A low degree of modularizing increases the amount of information exchanged between all relevant actors, which is important in situations of high uncertainty as it is the case during the exploration phase.

To *summarize,* transactional solutions might mitigate the social dilemma, but have serious flaws in the case of explorative knowledge work. *First,* the transactional solutions do not work if there are few overlaps of knowledge between the knowledge workers. *Second,* splitting knowledge work into modules to make it easier for supervisors to monitor the quality often carries with it the risk of inappropriate modularization. *Third,* transactional solutions only work if the criteria for monetary incentives are clear-cut. With complex tasks, as it is the case with explorative knowledge work, the risk of multitasking and of rewarding according to conventional criteria arises. As a consequence, social dilemmas in explorative knowledge teamwork cannot sufficiently be solved by transactional solutions.

6.3.2. *Transformational Solutions*

As Simon (1991: 31–2) stated, 'in most organizations, employees contribute much more to goal achievement than the minimum that could be extracted from them by supervisory enforcement.' The incomplete contract literature emphasizes that in complex environments complete contracts cannot be written or enforced (Milgrom and Roberts 1992). Therefore honesty and intrinsic job satisfaction lead to better results for contracting parties than reliance on monetary incentives (Gintis and Khurana 2006; Jensen 2006). This makes clear that motivation is a main factor in cooperations. As far as explorative knowledge work is concerned, 'management by motivation' (Frey and Osterloh 2002; Osterloh et al. 2002) might even become the most important factor in sustaining a competitive advantage. As the capability to produce new knowledge is the main source of inimitability, and its creation and transfer cannot be monitored and remunerated accordingly, motivation and, in particular, intrinsic motivation are the keys to dynamic capabilities as a foundation of long-term strategy. By introducing transformational solutions to social dilemmas, we contradict traditional economics which assume that motivations or preferences should be treated as given. In contrast, we consider preferences as plastic and changeable by institutional measures such as job design, feedback mechanisms, procedural fairness, and communication opportunities.

6.4. Extrinsic and Intrinsic Motivation

Two kinds of motivation can be distinguished: extrinsic and intrinsic motivation. In reality, pure extrinsic motivation and pure intrinsic motivation are extremes on a continuum (Deci and Ryan 2000).

Extrinsic motivation serves to satisfy indirect or instrumental needs, for example money or reputation. As such, money is almost always the means to an end—for example, paying for a vacation or buying a car—and not an end in itself. Extrinsic motivation stems from the desire to satisfy one's nonwork-related needs. In this instance, a job is simply a tool with which to satisfy one's needs by means of the salary it pays. Transactional solutions focus mainly on extrinsic motivation.

Intrinsic motivation works through immediate need satisfaction. An activity is valued for its own sake and is undertaken without any reward except the activity itself (Deci 1985). Intrinsic motivation is fostered by commitment to the work, which is satisfactory in an immediate way for the individuals. If one is motivated intrinsically, then shirking is not a preferable action, because the activity causes a benefit instead of a cost. The social dilemma disappears and cooperation becomes a possible solution. There are two kinds of intrinsic motivation: enjoyment-based motivation and obligation-based or pro-social motivation (Lindenberg 2001).

Enjoyment-based intrinsic motivation refers to a satisfying flow of activity without an external reward. Examples are skiing, reading a good novel, or solving an interesting puzzle. In each case, pleasure is derived from the activity itself and not just by arriving at the destination, that is, with reading, reaching the last page of the novel would be the goal. During whatever activity, people often report a 'flow experience' (Csikzentmihalyi 1975) that makes them lose track of time. During explorative work it is often reported that people feel this kind of motivation, for example in research (Amabile 1996) or during innovative software programming (Torvalds and Diamond 2001).

Pro-social motivation takes the well-being of others into account without expecting a reward. The good of the community enters into the preferences of the individuals. These may be ethical standards, professional codes of practice, norms of fairness, or reciprocity, group identity, or team spirit. A wealth of empirical evidence demonstrates that many people are indeed prepared to contribute to the common good of their company or community (Frey 1997). Empirical work shows that substantial differences exist in shirking between branches of a company, despite identical monetary incentives due to different group norms (Ichino and Maggi 2000). Two major instances have been discussed, which both include sacrificing individual interests for the sake of the community:

- *Voluntary rule following*. People are prepared to follow rules and regulations that limit their self-interests without sanctions, as long as they accept their legitimacy (Tyler and Blader 2000).
- *Extra-role behavior*. Individuals do not only observe rules voluntarily, but also exert 'organizational citizenship behavior' (Organ and Ryan 1995). They provide voluntary inputs, going far beyond the duties stipulated in their contracts. 'Extra-role behavior' is thought of as a 'willingness to cooperate.'

Laboratory experiments also reveal that a large number of people voluntarily contribute to common goods (see the survey by Rabin 1998). The most extensively discussed experiments are the public good game and the ultimatum game:

- *Public good game*. According to standard economics, people do not contribute to public goods; rational actors free ride on the contributions of others (Fehr and Gächter 2000). However, when people trust others to contribute to a common good, they are also prepared to do the same. Suppose that subjects A and B are endowed with a certain amount of money, for example $10. They have to decide how much they want to donate to a common pool. They are also told that any money donated will be doubled and then redistributed equally among the subjects. If both keep what they got, each earns $10. If both transfer their whole endowment, each earns $20. This setting resembles team production, where cooperation leads to a surplus. If both actors are selfish, they donate nothing, regardless of how much they expect the other subject to give. Despite the incentive to cheat in experiments, people typically contribute about 50 percent of their initial stake (Sally 1995).

- *Ultimatum game*. This game reveals that a sizeable number of people are willing to punish unfair behavior at a cost to them (Güth, Schmittberger, and Schwarze 1982). Two persons have to agree on the division of a fixed sum of money. The proposer can make a proposal how to divide the money. If the responder rejects, both receive nothing. In the case of the responder accepting, the proposal is implemented. Rejection can be viewed as punishment for the violation of a social norm of fairness, which comes at a price for the responder. In experiments, responders typically reject amounts below 40 percent (Fehr, Falk, and Fischbacher 2003; Fehr and Fischbacher 2003).

With both games, considerable variation across different cultures has been found (Henrich et al. 2001). This indicates that pro-social preferences are not 'hardwired.' They can be changed by institutional measures. As argued, transactional solutions which concentrate on extrinsic motivation fail in the case of explorative knowledge work; however, social psychology and psychological economics indicate that intrinsic motivation can be fostered by adequate institutional arrangements.

6.4.1. *How to Foster Intrinsic Motivation*

It is more difficult to guide intrinsically motivated persons to work according to the particular goals than to guide persons who work mainly for monetary compensation. First, intrinsic motivation cannot be enforced. It can only be enabled. Second, it is difficult to govern intrinsic motivation precisely. Firms are not interested to enhance intrinsic motivation per se, for example to further employee's pleasure of reading a novel during business hours. Rather firms aim to influence intrinsic motivation for work and contextual performance. As transactional measures fail to work with explorative knowledge work the question arises how the kind of intrinsic motivation can be induced that is required for this kind of activity. In the remainder of this chapter we will review empirical evidence from psychological economics and organizational behavior on conditions which facilitate intrinsic motivation. Where applicable we will also cite evidence, which investigates the interplay of intrinsic incentives and knowledge work. However, empirical evidence which reviews this interplay is still rather rare as the knowledge management literature in general has only recently turned to study the motivational underpinnings of knowledge work and to intrinsic motivation as a facilitator in particular (Argote and Ophir 2002; Kelloway and Barling 2000). Even less research exists on motivation and exploration due to the inherent measurement problems when it comes to explorative knowledge production.

Crowding theory (Frey 1997) and self-determination theory (Deci 1980; Deci and Ryan 2000) demonstrate how specific intrinsic motivation can be enabled. More precisely both theories analyze the effect of external interventions—such as rewards, organizational processes, and communication—on intrinsic motivation. The so-called *crowding-out effect* states that external interventions which are primarily perceived as controlling undermine intrinsic motivation for an activity. External interventions which are perceived as supportive and competence-enhancing enhance intrinsic motivation, and lead to the *crowding-in effect*.

6.4.2. *Crowding-Out of Intrinsic Motivation*

Under certain conditions external interventions can reduce intrinsic motivation for an activity. A first condition for crowding-out to occur is that the individuals concerned have intrinsic motivation in the first place, which can then be undermined. In contrast, in situations where no intrinsic motivation exists, monetary rewards can increase performance, like simple manual work on an assembly line.[2] Second, the crowding-out of intrinsic motivation occurs if people perceive an external intervention as reducing their self-determination, when doing an intrinsically interesting activity. In this case people feel that they are not the origins of their behavior. Their attention shifts from the activity itself to the external circumstances. The content of the activity loses its importance.

[2] Lazear (1999) provides an empirical example. He found that, in a large auto glass company, productivity increased from 20% to 36% when the firm switched from paying hourly wages to piece rates.

The crowding-out effect has been observed for two types of external interventions: incentives and managerial controls. It has shown to be relevant for both types of intrinsic motivation, that is, for enjoyment-based intrinsic motivation as well as for pro-social motivation.

6.4.3. *Crowding-out by Setting Incentives*

Several meta-analyses of (field) experiments in both psychology and economics have shown that task-contingent rewards undermine intrinsic motivation. Examples are paying someone for volunteering, or paying performance-contingent rewards for innovative ideas (for an overview compare Deci, Koestner, and Ryan 1999; Frey and Jegen 2001). In a recent meta-study of experiments, Weibel, Rost, and Osterloh (2007) have shown that performance-contingent rewards also hurt work performance in the case of complex and/or interesting tasks. In the field of knowledge management, Bock and Kim (2002) as well as Bock et al. (2005) show that expected rewards for sharing one's knowledge impact negatively on intentions to share knowledge.

The effects of performance-contingent rewards can best be illustrated by an field experiment of Gneezy and Rustichini (2000*b*). It analyzes the behavior of school children collecting money voluntarily, that is, without monetary compensation (e.g., for cancer research or disabled children). The children reduced their efforts by about 36 percent when they were promised a bonus of 1 percent of the money collected. Their effort to collect for a good cause could be raised when the bonus was increased from 1 to 10 percent of the money collected. But they did not reach the initial collection level again. This field experiment shows clearly that there are two countervailing forces affecting behavior: a crowding-out effect of rewards and an effect of motivating the children extrinsically after the intrinsic motivation has been decreased. It also shows that a 'hidden cost of rewards' (Lepper and Greene 1978) exists: the money collected after having been given a bonus comes at a high price compared to strengthening intrinsic motivation. On average, monetary incentives explain only 10 percent of the variance in performance, compared to 30 percent, which are explained by obligation-based intrinsic norms (Tyler and Blader 2000).

Burks and coauthors (Burks, Carpenter, and Goette 2006) demonstrate another aspect of the crowding-out effect caused by performance-contingent rewards: among bicycle messengers, they find that employees in firms that pay for performance are significantly less cooperative than those who are paid hourly or are members of cooperatives. Performance pay appears to make messengers between 12 and 15 percent more likely to behave egoistically toward their coworkers (Burks, Carpenter, and Goette 2006: 9). These bicycle messengers when asked to play a sequential prisoners dilemma were more likely to defect than those bicycle messengers paid by the hour or working in a cooperative. The authors suggest that in practice this could mean that performance-contingently rewarded messengers are more likely to 'cherry pick' the best appointments, regardless of whether they are the best suited from the firm's perspective to make the delivery.

6.4.4. *Crowding-out by Managerial Control*

Managerial control too can undermine intrinsic motivation and performance. Managerial control, that is, the process of standard setting, monitoring, evaluation, and providing feedback undermines intrinsic motivation if employees perceive control predominantly as a signal of distrust and autonomy thwarting (Weibel 2007). Intrinsic motivation is strengthened, however, if the informative content of managerial control such as the feedback component and/or the supportive content of managerial control such as employee development perspective prevail (see Section 6.5).

Falk and Kosfeld (2006) test the negative effect of managerial control in a two-stage principal–agent game. The principal can choose whether he wants to control the effort of his agent lightly, moderately, severely, or not at all. Those principals who choose to trust, that is not to monitor their agents at all, fare best. For example agents who are trusted show twice the effort of agents who are lightly controlled. In an effort to understand the underlying reason for the performance reduction the authors design two games with different types of control: in the first case control is chosen by the principal, in the second case control is exogenously given. As a result agents reduce their efforts only in the first case, that is, they react negatively to the controlling intention of the principal and not to control per se.

The downside of the emphasis of a distrust-signaling managerial control system is also vividly illustrated by Gittell's research on American Airlines (Gittell 2000*a*, 2000*b*). American Airlines' then-CEO Robert Crandall insisted that delays come to his attention and get assigned to individuals and departments, so they would be accountable for their results and, moreover, would compete with each other to avoid creating problems.

One field manager told Gittell that when a plane making a connection was late, 'Crandall wants to see the corpse.' Thus the characteristics of American Airlines control system were extensive monitoring, brief feedback, and a focus on the 'bad apples.' The post-monitoring phase consisted almost exclusively of sanctioning 'the culprit.' The result of this approach was to create a culture of fear and infighting as people and units tried to pin the blame for problems on others. As a consequence performance faltered and pro-social motivation was greatly reduced.

6.5. Crowding-In of Intrinsic Motivation

Under certain conditions external interventions can enlarge intrinsic motivation for an activity. External interventions have a positive impact on intrinsic motivation if they are (*a*) targeted to create an intrinsically rewarding job environment and/or (*b*) support employees' feelings of competence and relatedness.

6.5.1. *Crowding-In by Job Design*

Research in job characteristics theory shows that intrinsic motivation can be enhanced through altering job characteristics along five dimensions (Hackman and Oldham 1974, 1980). These are:

- variety (the degree to which a job requires the use of a number of different skills and talents);
- identity (the degree to which the job requires completion of a 'whole' piece of work, or doing a task from beginning to end with a visible outcome);
- significance (the degree to which the job has a substantial impact on the lives of other people);
- autonomy (the degree to which the job provides substantial freedom); and
- feedback (the degree to which the job provides clear information about performance levels).

Such an intrinsically involving job is shown to augment intrinsic motivation (Gagne, Senecal, and Koestner 1997), contextual performance (Podsakoff et al. 2000), and cooperative learning (Janz and Prasarnphanich 2003).

Finally Brickner, Harkins, and Ostrom (1986) show that an intrinsically motivating job reduces free riding and thus is instrumental in helping to overcome the social dilemma of knowledge management.

6.5.2. *Crowding-In by Setting Incentives*

Frey and Osterloh (2002) propose that incentives can crowd-in intrinsic motivation either (*a*) in a situation where incentives induce individuals to try new tasks whereby they might develop a taste for these tasks and/or (*b*) if these incentives signal support, generosity, and high esteem for the individual. Evidence for both types of crowding-in situation is rare.

Charness and Gneezy (2006) conducted a field experiment on the effect of incentives on physical exercise and thereby provide evidence on how incentives can help do develop a new taste. One group of participants is offered $125 under the condition that they would visit the gym once a week for five weeks. This intervention leads to an attendance level that is twice as high as the level when people have not been paid. In addition attendance level remains high even after the end of the intervention. However, the effect only holds for those participants who had not been regular attendees to the gym. These are presumably those individuals who did not enjoy exercising before the intervention but developed a taste for it while being paid to do it for some time.

Two studies show that non-controlling generosity-signaling incentives can foster intrinsic motivation. Experiments show that if labor contracts are regarded primarily as a 'gift exchange' (Akerlof 1982) rather than as a disciplining tool, then employees exert more effort. In a telling experiment, two different settings were compared (Irlenbusch and Sliwka 2003). In the first setting, the 'principals' offered a fixed amount of money and the 'agents' chose an effort level. In the second setting, the principals had to make a choice between a fixed wage and an incentive scheme and then the agents chose their effort level. Efforts were higher in the first setting than in the case when piece rates were paid. Also, in the first setting, agents mentioned the well-being of the principal significantly more often than in the second setting. Autonomy, which was higher in the first setting, was reduced in the second setting (Irlenbusch and Sliwka 2003). This provides a strong argument for fixed wages whenever intrinsic motivation is crucial. Bard Kuvaas (2006) demonstrates in a field setting, a knowledge-intensive industry, the positive effect of a generous fixed wage. He shows a strong and positive effect of a generous fixed wage on work performance. Furthermore this effect can be partially explained by the fact that a generous fixed wage has a positive effect on intrinsic motivation and on affective commitment. Interestingly, bonus schemes (a mixture of group and individual performance contingent pay) had no effects on the work performance of the knowledge workers studied.

6.5.3. *Crowding-In by Feedback*

Managerial feedback supports intrinsic motivation if the informational and supportive component of feedback is strengthened. Empirical support to this proposition is, however, mixed.

In a meta-analysis, Kluger and DeNisi (1996) conclude that feedback has on average a moderately positive effect on job outcomes. However, more than 38 percent of the effects found in the literature were negative. The authors conclude that only constructive feedback can have positive effects. Baron (1993) characterizes constructive feedback as feedback that is specific in content, timely, delivered in an appropriate setting, and not containing threats and attributions concerning causes of poor performance. Oldham and Cummings (1996) find constructive feedback particularly relevant for creativity: manufacturing employees produced the most creative outcomes when they worked on complex, challenging jobs and were provided positive and mainly informational feedback.

6.5.4. *Crowding-In by Fair Processes*

Fair processes are proposed to raise perceived social relatedness and thereby to strengthen pro-social motivation (Tyler and Blader 2000, 2001). Empirical evidence shows that procedural fairness impacts the willingness to contribute to common goods and to follow rules. This is true even in situations that are not favorable to one's own self-interest (Tyler and Blader 2003). A first indication that procedural fairness also helps to overcome social dilemmas in knowledge production is the study of Lin (2007) who shows that procedural and distributive justice perceptions are positively related to tacit knowledge-sharing behavior. The characteristics that lead to perceived procedural fairness can be summarized as participation, neutrality, and being treated with dignity and respect.

Participation gives individuals a process control or the use of voice. It has been found that the use of voice is not just dependent on controlling outcomes; people value the mere opportunity of expressing their views (Folger 1977). A precondition of *neutrality* is the belief of individuals that decisions are made in an objective way and that rules forestall favoritism.

In laboratory experiments, it was shown that sanctions that served the punisher's self-interests crowded out cooperative behavior, whereas sanctions perceived as pro-socially motivated enhanced self-interests (Fehr and Rockenbach 2003). It follows that persons, who lay down the rules and regulations, should not be given an incentive to manipulate the corresponding criteria in their own favor. *Being treated with dignity and respect* has proved to be of high importance for organizational citizenship behavior, including helping behavior, altruism, and extra role behavior (Niehoff and Moorman 1993). Note that all three characteristics of procedural fairness (participation, neutrality, and being treated with dignity and respect) are essentially unrelated to outcomes. Therefore, procedural fairness is crucial in situations which might lead to unfortunate results for the employees, for example, in conflict resolution or making decisions concerning promotions.

6.5.5. *Crowding-In by Communication*

Communication, or other conditions reducing social distance between persons, increases contribution in public good games (Dawes, van de Kragt, and Orbell 1988). Communication has two important effects.

First, experiments show that most people, after some minutes of talking to each other, have higher expectations of the other's cooperative behavior. If they believe that others do not free ride, their willingness to contribute increases (Fischbacher, Fehr, and Gächter 2001). This effect is even stronger when communicating face to face than when communicating via the computer. Second, communication provides an opportunity to invite other individuals to cooperate. It has been shown that being personally asked enhances contributions to collective goods greatly (Meier 2006: 65).

The growing role that 'communities of practice' and 'epistemic communities' play in knowledge-based industries underpins the significance of personal contacts and communication (Lave and Wenger 1991). These communities that are based on communication and personal contacts foster not only creativity but also social relatedness and identification within the group. Also the literature on psychological contracts emphasizes that relational contracts (including the necessity for interaction), long-time frames, and many socio-emotional elements elicit greater commitment to the firm than transactional contracts, short-time frames, and no socio-emotional elements (Rousseau 1995).

6.5.6. *Crowding-In by Instructions*

People seem to be inclined to do what they are asked to do, especially when the request comes from someone who is perceived as a legitimate authority. Instructions to cooperate in public good games raise the cooperation rate as much as 40 percent (Sally 1995). In real-life settings, it is shown that people adhere to rules and accept the decisions of authorities they believe to be legitimate, even if it is not in their own self-interest to do so (Tyler 1990; Tyler and Huo 2002).

Unfortunately in the last decade, standard economics instructs people to act otherwise (Osterloh and Frost 2007). As standard economics had become dominant in social science, people overestimate the power of self-interest to affect the behavior of others, even when their own behavior was not primarily self-interested (Miller and Ratner 1998). As a result, more people behave in a selfish way: economics have to some extent become a self-fulfilling prophecy (Ferraro, Pfeffer, and Sutton 2005). Management can stop this self-fulfilling prophecy by providing employees with information about existing social norms and social behavior in their company and in their community.

6.5.7. *Crowding-In by Framing*

People are highly sensitive to signals about socially appropriate behavior. This became evident in a public good game. Players were divided into two groups. Each group played exactly the same game. The first group was told they were going to play 'the Wall Street Game.' One third of the group cooperated. The second group was told that they were playing 'the Community Game.' More than two thirds cooperated (Liberman, Samuels, and Ross 2003).

A strong framing effect was also shown in a field study, with parents being fined for picking up their children late from a childcare center. The fine had an adverse effect: it led to a significantly lower level of punctuality. When the fine was discontinued, punctuality remained at the lower level (Gneezy and Rustichini 2000*a*). Fining switched the frame from a 'normative frame' to a 'gain frame' (Lindenberg 2003). The fine indicated that in the gain frame, it was socially acceptable that parents arrive too late. A similar affect can be assumed with pay for performance. It signals that doing one's duty without extra pay is not socially appropriate. This signal could become a self-fulfilling prophecy. Fixed pay, based on fair overall procedural evaluations, avoids framing the teamwork into the 'Wall Street Game.'

These results might be *summarized* in such a way that the less the situation approximates to a competitive market or to an iron cage bureaucracy, the more enjoyment-based and pro-social intrinsic motivated behavior is likely to be observed. Anthropological field studies also provide examples for such changing behavior (Bowles 1998: 899). Although the empirical evidence cited mostly shows this effect with physical work (because it is easier to measure), there is no reason to suspect that with knowledge work there would be different evidence. As a consequence, the conditions for solving social dilemmas in explorative knowledge work are the better the less transactional solutions to solve it are applied.

6.6. Conclusions

The ideas presented in this chapter are based on five ideas. *First,* cooperation in firms or in networks is undertaken to create synergies. All such cooperation causes interdependencies between the contributing economic actors. We, *second,* analyzed these interdependencies with the theoretical framework provided by the social dilemma literature. We compared the solutions to social dilemmas for exploitative and for explorative knowledge work. *Third,* we introduced the idea that explorative knowledge work differs from exploitative knowledge work mainly with respect to cognitive distance or cognitive overlap. This difference is crucial for the solutions that can be applied to overcome social dilemmas. We showed that transactional solutions, based on extrinsic incentives, cannot solve the social dilemma arising in explorative knowledge work entirely. *Fourth,* we applied empirical evidence of social psychology and psychological economics to show how this special kind of social dilemma is to be solved by raising intrinsic motivation. *Fifth,* we showed that there exist convincing proposals for organizational design to strengthen intrinsic motivation. These proposals clash with conventional wisdom of standard economics while they confer with the insights of psychological economics.

As a next step the proposals to strengthen intrinsic motivation should be tested empirically. The effect of intrinsic motivation and intrinsic incentives could be tested in the fields of the academic commons (Hellstrom 2003), epistemic communities (Cowan, David, and Foray 2000), knowledge alliances (Weibel 2002), or the open source software community (Osterloh and Rota 2007). Because of the inherent measurement difficulties pertaining to explorative knowledge production a new research agenda is needed. We propose a triangulation of different methods, for example a combination of qualitative studies and quantitative vignette surveys or field experiments combined with longitudinal survey data.

To enhance productivity of knowledge work, in particular productivity of explorative knowledge, is the biggest challenge of the twenty-first century. Peter Drucker (1999: 83) states that less than one fifth of the workforce nowadays are blue-collar workers doing manual work, while white-collar workers doing knowledge work make up two fifths of the workforce. Yet, when it comes to our understanding of a knowledge worker's productivity, we are in the year 2000 roughly where we were in the year 1900 in terms of productivity of the manual worker. If companies could enhance productivity of knowledge workers in the twenty-first century as much as they did of manual workers in the twentieth century, the payoffs would be astronomical.

References

Akerlof, G. A. 1982. 'Labor Contracts as Partial Gift Exchange,' *Quarterly Journal of Economics* 97: 543–69.

Alchian, A. A. and H. Demsetz. 1972. 'Production, Information Costs and Economic Organization,' *American Economic Review* 62: 777–95.

Amabile, T. 1996. *Creativity in context.* Boulder: Westview Press.

Argote, L. and R. Ophir. 2002. 'Interorganizational Learning,' in J. A. C. Baum (ed.) *The Blackwell Companion to Organizations.* Oxford: Blackwell Publishers.

Axelrod, R. 1984. *The Evolution of Cooperation.* New York: Basic Books.

Baron, J. N. 1993. 'Criticism (Informal Negative Feedback) as a Source of Perceived Unfairness in Organizations: Effects, Mechanisms, and Countermeasures,' in R. Cropanzano (ed.) New Jersey: L. Erlbaum Associates, Hillsdale.

Bock, G. W. and Y. G. Kim. 2002. 'Breaking the Myths of Rewards: An Exploratory Study of Attitudes about Knowledge Sharing,' *Information Resources Management Journal* 15: 14–21.

——R. W. Zmud, Y. G. Kim, and J. N. Lee. 2005. 'Behavioral Intention Formation in Knowledge Sharing: Examining the Roles of Extrinsic Motivators, Social-Psychological Forces, and Organizational Climate,' *MIS Quarterly* 29: 87–111.

Bogenrieder, I. and B. Nooteboom. 2004. 'Learning Groups: What Types Are There? A Theoretical Analysis and an Empirical Study in a Consultancy Firm,' *Organization Studies* 25: 287–313.

Bowles, S. 1998. 'Endogenous Preferences: The Cultural Consequences of Markets and Other Economic Institutions,' *Journal of Economic Literature* 36: 75–111.

Brickner, M. A., S. G. Harkins, and T. M. Ostrom. 1986. 'Effects of Personal Involvement—Thought-Provoking Implications for Social Loafing,' *Journal of Personality and Social Psychology* 51: 763–9.

Burks, S., J. Carpenter, and L. Goette. 2006. *Performance Pay and the Erosion of Worker Cooperation Field Experimental Evidence*. Bonn: IZA.

Cabrera, A. and E. F. Cabrera. 2002. 'Knowledge-Sharing Dilemmas,' *Organization Studies* 23: 687–710.

Campanario, J. M. 1996. 'Using Citation Classics to Study the Incidence of Serendipity in Scientific Discovery,' *Scientometrics* 37: 3–24.

Chandler, A. D. J. 1977. *The Visible Hand. The Managerial Revolution in American Business*. Massachusetts: Cambridge.

Charness, G. and U. Greezy. 2006. 'Incentives to Exercise,' *SSRN Working Paper.*

Chesbrough, H. W. and D. J. Teece. 1996. 'When Is Virtual Virtuous?: Organizing for Innovation,' *Harvard Business Review* 74: 65–73.

Cowan, R., P. A. David, and D. Foray. 2000. 'The Explicit Economics of Knowledge Codification and Tacitness,' *Industrial and Corporate Change* 9: 211–53.

Csikzentmihalyi, M. 1975. *Beyond Boredom and Anxiety: The Experience of Play in Work and Games*. San Francisco: Jossey Bass.

Davenport, T. and L. Prusak. 1998. *Working Knowledge*. Massachusetts, Cambridge: Business School Press.

Dawes, R. M. 1980. 'Social Dilemmas,' *Annual Review of Psychology* 31: 169–93.

——A. J. C. van de Kragt, and J. M. Orbell. 1988. 'Not Me or Thee but We: The Importance of Group Identity in Eliciting Cooperating in Dilemma Situations—Experimental Manipulation,' *Acta Psychologica* 68: 83–97.

Deci, E. L. 1980. *The Psychology of Self-Determination*. Lexington, Mass: D.C. Heath Lexington Books.

——1985. *Intrinsic Motivation and Self-Determination in Human Behavior*. New York: Plenum Press.

——and R. M. Ryan. 2000. 'The "What" and "Why" of Goal Pursuits: Human Needs and the Self-Determination of Behavior,' *Psychological Inquiry* 11: 227–68.

——R. Koestner, and R. M. Ryan. 1999. 'A Meta-Analytic Review of Experiments Examining the Effects of Extrinsic Rewards on Intrinsic Motivation,' *Psychological Bulletin* 125: 627–68.

Ethiraj, S. K. and D. A. Levinthal. 2004. 'Modality and Innovation in Complex Systems,' *Management Science* 50(2): 159–73.

Falk, A. and M. Kosfeld. 2006. 'The Hidden Costs of Control,' *American Economic Review* 96: 1611–30.

Fehr, E. and U. Fischbacher. 2003. 'The Nature of Human Altruism,' *Nature* 425: 785–91.

——and S. Gächter. 2000. 'Cooperation and Punishment in Public Goods Experiments,' *American Economic Review* 90: 980–94.

——and B. Rockenbach. 2003. 'Detrimental Effects of Sanctions on Human Altruism,' *Nature* 422: 137–40.

——A. Falk, and U. Fischbacher. 2003. 'On the Nature of Fair Behavior,' *Economic Inquiry* 41: 20–6.

Ferraro, F., J. Pfeffer, and R. Sutton. 2005. 'Economics Language and Assumptions: How Theories Can Become Self-Fullfilling,' *Academy of Management Review* 30(1): 8–24.

Fischbacher, U., E. Fehr, and S. Gächter. 2001. 'Are People Conditionally Cooperative? Evidence from Public Good Experiments,' *Economic Letters* 71: 397–404.

Folger, R. 1977. 'Distributive and Procedural Justice—Combined Impact of Voice and Improvement on Experienced Inequity,' *Journal of Personality and Social Psychology* 35: 108–19.

Foss, N. and M. Iversen. 1997. 'Promoting Synergies in Multiproduct Firms: Toward a Resource-Based View,' *IVS/CBS Working Paper* 97–12.

Foss, N. J. and K. Foss. 2000. 'The Knowledge-Based Approach and Organizational Economics: How much Do They Really Differ? And Does It Matter?,' in N. J. Foss and V. Mahnke (eds.) Oxford: Oxford University Press.

Frey, B. S. 1997. *Not just for the Money: An Economic Theory of Personal Motivation.* Cheltenham, UK/Brookfield, USA: Edward Elgar.

——2003. 'Publishing as Prostitution?—Choosing between One's Own Ideas and Academic Success,' *Public Choice* 116: 205–23.

——and R. Jegen. 2001. 'Motivation Crowding Theory: A Survey of Empirical Evidence,' *Journal of Economic Surveys* 15: 589–611.

——and M. Osterloh. 2002. *Successful Management by Motivation. Balancing Intrinsic and Extrinsic Incentives*. Berlin/Heidelberg/New York: Springer.

——2005. 'Yes, Managers Should Be Paid like Bureaucrats,' *Journal of Management Inquiry* 14: 96–111.

————2006. 'Evaluation: Hidden Costs, Questionable Benefits, and Superior Alternatives,' *IEW Working Paper* No. 302.

Gagne, M., C. B. Senecal, and R. Koestner. 1997. 'Proximal Job Characteristics, Feelings of Empowerment, and Intrinsic Motivation: A Multidimensional Model,' *Journal of Applied Social Psychology* 27: 1222–40.

Gans, J. S. and G. B. Shepherd. 1994. 'How Are the Mighty Fallen—Rejected Classic Articles by Leading Economists,' *Journal of Economic Perspectives* 8: 165–79.

Gillies, D. 2006. 'Why Research Assessment Exercises Are a Bad Thing,' *Post-Autistic Economics Review* 37: 2–9.

Gittell, J. H. 2000*a*. 'Paradox of Coordination and Control,' *California Management Review* 42: 101–17.

——2000*b*. 'Organizing Work to Support Relational Co-Ordination,' *International Journal of Human Resource Management* 11: 517–39.

Gneezy, U. and A. Rustichini. 2000*a*. 'A Fine Is a Price,' *Journal of Legal Studies* 29: 1–17.

————2000*b*. 'Pay Enough or Don't Pay at all,' *Quarterly Journal of Economics* 115: 791–810.

Grant, R. 1996. 'Prospering in Dynamically Competitive Environments: Organizational Capability as Knowledge Integration,' *Organization Science* 7: 375–87.

Grant, R. M. and C. Baden-Fuller. 2004. 'A Knowledge Accessing Theory of Strategic Alliances,' *Journal of Management Studies* 41: 61–84.

Güth, W., R. Schmittberger, and B. Schwarze. 1982. 'An Experimental-Analysis of Ultimatum Bargaining,' *Journal of Economic Behavior & Organization* 3: 367–88.

Hackman, J. R. and G. R. Oldham. 1974. *The Job Diagnostic Survey: An instrument for the Diagnosis of Jobs and the Evaluation of Job Redesign Projects*. Massachusetts, New Haven: Yale University.

—— —— 1980. *Work Redesign*. Massachusetts, Reading: Addison-Wesley.

Hamilton, D. P. 2001. 'Intel Gambles It Can Move Beyond the PC with New Microprocessors,' *The Wall Street Journal* 29: 1.

Hardin, G. 1968. 'The Tragedy of the Commons,' *Science* 1243–8.

Hellstrom, T. 2003. 'Governing the Virtual Academic Commons,' *Research Policy* 32: 391–401.

Henrich, J., R. Boyd, S. Bowles, C. Camerer, E. Fehr, H. Gintis, and R. McElreath. 2001. 'In Search of Homo Economicus: Behavioral Experiments in 15 Small-Scale Societies,' *American Economic Review* 91: 73–8.

Holmqvist, M. 2004. 'Experiential Learning Processes of Exploitation and Exploration within and between Organizations: An Empirical Study of Product Development 10.1287/orsc.1030.0056,' *Organization Science* 15: 70–81.

Holmström, B. and P. Milgrom. 1991. 'Multitask Principal-Agent Analyses: Incentive Contracts, Asset Ownership, and Job Design,' *Journal of Law, Economics and Organization* 7: 24–52.

Holmström, B. R. and Milgram. 1994. 'The Firm as an Incentive System,' *American Economic Review* 84: 972–91.

Ichino, A. and G. Maggi. 2000. 'Work Environment and Individual Background: Explaining Regional Shirking Differentials in a Large Italian Firm,' *Quarterly Journal of Economics* 115: 1057–90.

Irlenbusch, B. and D. Sliwka. 2003. *Incentives, Decision Frames and Motivation Crowding Out—An Experimental Investigation*. Bonn: IZA.

Janz, B. D. and P. Prasarnphanich. 2003. 'Understanding the Antecedents of Effective Knowledge Management: The Importance of a Knowledge-Centered Culture,' *Decision Sciences* 34: 351–84.

Kelloway, E. K. and J. Barling. 2000. 'Knowledge Work as Organizational Behavior,' *International Journal of Management Reviews* 2: 287–304.

Kerr, S. 1975. 'On the Folly of Rewarding A, while Hoping for B,' *Academy of Management Journal* 18: 769–83.

Kluger, A. N. and A. DeNisi. 1996. 'The Effects of Feedback Interventions on Performance: A Historical Review, a Meta-Analysis, and a Preliminary Feedback Intervention Theory,' *Psychological Bulletin* 119: 254–84.

Kogut, B. and U. Zander. 1996. 'What Firms Do? Coordination, Identity and Learning,' *Organization Science* 7: 502–18.

Kollock, P. 1998. 'Social Dilemmas: The Anatomy of Cooperation,' *Annual Review of Sociology* 22: 183–205.

Kuvaas, B. 2006. 'Work Performance, Affective Commitment, and Work Motivation: The Roles of Pay Administration and Pay Level,' *Journal of Organizational Behavior* 27: 365–85.

Lave, J. and E. Wenger. 1991. *Situated Learning: Legitimate Peripheral Participation*. New York, Cambridge: Cambridge University Press.

Lazear, E. P. 1999. 'Personnel Economics. Past Lessons and Future Directions,' *Journal of Labor Economics* 17: 199–236.

Liberman, V., S. Samuels, and L. Ross. 2003. *The Name of the Game: Predictive Power or Reputation vs. Situational Labels in Determining Prisoners' Dilemma Game Moves*. Palo Alto, Calif.: Stanford University Press.

Lin, C. P. 2007. 'To Share or Not To Share: Modeling Tacit Knowledge Sharing, Its Mediators and Antecedents,' *Journal of Business Ethics* 70: 411–28.

Lindenberg, S. 2001. 'Intrinsic Motivation in a New Light,' *Kyklos* 54: 317–43.

——2003. 'The Cognitive Side of Governance,' in V. Buskens, W. Raub, and C. Snijders (eds.) Oxford: JAI Press.

March, J. G. 1991. 'Exploration and Exploitation in Organizational Learning,' *Organization Science* 2: 71–87.

McEvily, S. K., K. M. Eisenhardt, and J. E. Prescott. 2004. 'The Global Acquisition, Leverage, and Protection of Technological Competencies,' *Strategic Management Journal* 25: 713–22.

Messick, D. M. and M. B. Brewer. 1983. 'Solving Social Dilemmas: A Review,' in L. Wheeler, (ed.) Beverly Hills: Sage.

Meier, S. 2006. *The Economics of Non-Selfish Behavior: Decisions to Contribute Money to Public Goods*. Cheltenham, Glos./Brookfield, Mass.: Edward Elgar.

Milgrom, P. and J. Roberts. 1992. *Economics, Organization, and Management*. New Jersey Englewood Cliffs: Prentice-Hall.

Miller, D. T. and R. K. Ratner. 1998. 'The Disparity between the Actual and Assumed Power of Self-Interest,' *Journal of Personality and Social Psychology* 74: 53–62.

Miller, G. 1992. *Managerial Dilemmas. The Political Economy of Hierarchy*. Cambridge: Cambridge University Press.

Nahapiet, J. and S. Ghoshal. 1998. 'Social Capital, Intellectual Capital and the Organizational Advantage,' *Academy of Management Review* 23: 242–66.

Niehoff, B. P. and R. H. Moorman. 1993. 'Justice as a Mediator of the Relationship between Methods of Monitoring and Organizational Citizenship Behavior,' *Academy of Management Journal* 36: 527–56.

Nooteboom, B. 2000*a*. *Learning and Innovation in Organizations and Economies*. Oxford: Oxford University Press.

——2000*b*. 'Learning by Interaction: Absorptive Capacity, Cognitive Distance and Governance,' *Journal of Management and Governance* 4: 69–92.

Oldham, G. R. and A. Cummings. 1996. 'Employee Creativity: Personal and Contextual Factors at Work,' *Academy of Management Journal* 39: 607–34.

Olson, M. 1965. *The Logic of Collective Action*. Massachusetts, Cambridge: Harvard University Press.

Organ, D. W. and K. Ryan. 1995. 'A Meta-Analytic Review of Attitudinal a Dispositional Predictors of Organizational Citizenship Behavior,' *Personnel Psychology* 48: 775–82.

Osterloh, M. and B. S. Frey. 2000. 'Motivation, Knowledge Transfer, and Organizational Forms,' *Organization Science* 11: 538–50.

——and S. Rota. 2007. 'Open Source Software Development—Just Another Case of Collective Invention?,' *Research Policy* 36: 157–71.

Podsakoff, P. M., S. B. MacKenzie, J. B. Paine, and D. G. Bachrach. 2000. 'Organizational Citizenship Behaviors: A Critical Review of the Theoretical and Empirical Literature and Suggestions for Future Research,' *Journal of Management* 26: 513–63.

Postrel, S. 2002. 'Islands of Shared Knowledge: Specialization and Mutual Understanding in Problem-Solving Teams,' *Organization Science* 13: 303–20.

Rabin, M. 1998. 'Psychology and Economics,' *Journal of Economic Literature* 36: 11–46.

Rousseau, D. M. 1995. *Psychological Contracts in Organizations: Understanding Written and Unwritten Agreements*. California, Thousand Oaks: Sage Publications.

Sally, D. 1995. 'Conversation and Cooperation in Social Dilemmas—a Metaanalysis of Experiments from 1958 to 1992,' *Rationality and Society* 7: 58–92.

Sen, A. K. 1974. 'Choice, Orderings and Morality,' in S. Körner (ed.) Oxford: Blackwell.

Simon, H. A. 1991. 'Organization and Markets,' *Journal of Economic Perspectives* 5: 25–44.

Spencer, J. W. 2003. 'Firms' Knowledge-Sharing Strategies in the Global Innovation System: Empirical Evidence from the Flat Panel Display Industry,' *Strategic Management Journal* 24: 217–33.

Spender, J. C. 1992. 'Strategy Theorizing: Expanding the Agenda,' in P. Shrivastava, A. Huff, and J. Dutton (eds.) Greenwich.

Torvalds, L. and D. Diamond. 2001. *Just for Fun: The Story of an Accidental Revolutionary*. New York: HarperBusiness.

Tyler, T. and S. Blader. 2001. 'Identity and Cooperative Behavior in Groups,' *Group Processes and Intergroup Relations* 4: 207–26.

Tyler, T. R. 1990. *Why People Obey the Law*. New Haven: Yale University Press.

——and S. L. Blader. 2000. *Cooperation in Groups: Procedural Justice, Social Identity, and Behavioral Engagement*. Philadelphia: Psychology Press.

————2003. 'The Group Engagement Model: Procedural Justice, Social Identity, and cooperative Behavior,' *Personality and Social Psychology Review* 7: 349–61.

——and Y. J. Huo. 2002. *Trust in the Law: Encouraging Public Cooperation with the Police and Courts*. New York Russell: Sage Foundation.

Vining, A. R. 2003. 'Internal Market Failure: A Framework for Diagnosing Firm Inefficiency,' *Journal of Management Studies* 40: 431–57.

Weibel, A. 2002. *Kooperation in strategischen Wissensnetzwerken: Vertrauen und Kontrolle zur Lösung des sozialen Dilemmas*. Dissertation Universität Zürich: Zürich.

Weibel, A. 2007. 'Formal Control and Trustworthiness—Never the Twain Shall Meet?,' *Group & Organization Management* 32: 500–17.

Weingart, P. 2005. 'Impact of Bibliometrics upon the Science System: Inadvertent Consequences?,' *Scientometrics* 62: 117–31.

Whitley, R. 2003. 'The Institutional Structuring of Organizational Capabilities: The Role of Authority Sharing and Organizational Careers,' *Organization Studies* 24: 667–95.

7

Superordinate identity and knowledge creation and transfer in organizations

Linda Argote and Aimée A. Kane

7.1. Introduction

Knowledge management has become increasingly important to organizations. Advances in transportation, communication, and information technologies have contributed to the rise of geographically distributed, multiunit organizations. The creation and transfer of knowledge is critical to survival in competitive business environments (McGregor 2006; Nussbaum 2006). Both knowledge creation and transfer bolster innovation, which occurs when a firm or its units develop, implement, and commercialize beneficial new ideas, processes, or products (Van De Ven et al., 1999).

Although sparks may ignite into a luminescent innovation within the confines of an organizational unit, they tend to smoulder without the oxygenating force of diverse ideas and perspectives. Indeed scholars have recognized that knowledge creation increases with the number of possible ways of recombining and building on existing knowledge (Kogut and Zander 1992; Nickerson and Zenger 2004; Schumpeter 1934). Knowledge transfer across diverse units bolsters these recombinative possibilities. Although units that learn from the experience of others (Huber 1991; Levitt and March 1988) are more likely to survive and are more productive than their counterparts (Argote and Ingram 2000), knowledge often remains obfuscated in its unit of origin and fails to transfer to other units (Katz and Allen 1982; Rogers 2003).

There are memorable industrial examples of innovations that have spent time in obscurity. Engineers in Sony's tape recorder unit worked to develop a smaller version of a recorder sold in the late 1970s. Difficulties in minimizing the Pressman, while preserving its recording function, halted the project at the prototype stage. Although the engineers had created new knowledge in the form of a small, high-quality prototype, it remained a silhouette of what it was to become until the company's cofounder and honorary chairman, Masara Ibuka, suggested combining the prototype with the portable headphones under development in another unit of Sony. Accounts suggest that psychological barriers inhibited the transfer and recombination of the knowledge across units that were ultimately responsible for creating the company's flagship product, the Walkman. According to chroniclers of the development of the Walkman, a member of the tape recorder unit explained, 'We're not very interested in what they do in the Headphone Division' (Nayak and Ketteringham 1986: 135).

In another example, salient national identities were blamed for hindering the transfer and recombination of knowledge across globally distributed units of Airbus working in parallel on the development of the A380, superjumbo jet (Clark 2007). When sections of the A380 built in Germany arrived in France without the appropriate electrical wiring, it became painfully apparent that the software used by the company's German site was incompatible with that used at the French location. This major mistake delayed the A380 two years and cost about 5 billion euros of profit. Louis Gallois, the chief executive of Airbus, was quoted in the *New York Times*: 'It is because of national pride that we have the problem of the A380.... I don't want to see any flags on slides, because when you have a flag you have always an issue of national identity.' Thus, Mr. Gallois banned the use of national symbols on PowerPoint presentations because they reinforced identity at the level of the country (France, Germany, Great Britain, and Spain) rather than at the level of the overall firm (Airbus).

In contrast to these examples, there are also cases when innovations diffuse, knowledge transfers from innovators to recipients, and organizations learn from the experience of others (Argote 1999; Rogers 2003; Szulanski 2000). Several empirical field studies have shown that organizations can learn from the experience of other organizations (Argote, Beckman, and Epple 1990). Organizational units have been found to be affected by the experience of other units in the same franchise (Darr, Argote, and Epple 1995), chain (Baum and Ingram 1998), or federation (Ingram and Simons 2002). For example, Darr, Argote, and Epple (1995) showed that knowledge of innovative processes was more likely to transfer across units owned by the same franchisee than across units owned by different franchisees. Knott (2001) also demonstrated the benefits of being part of a franchise for knowledge transfer and innovation.

We contend that a certain type of relationship between units contributes to the transfer of knowledge and innovations across them. This relationship exists when the employees in the units share a sense of belonging to a higher-order unit—a superordinate social identity. Consistent with work in the social identity tradition (e.g., Brewer 2000, Gaertner and Dovidio 2000), this collective identity derives from employees' awareness that they belong to a superordinate group from which they derive a portion of their own identity. This conceptualization differs from research in the organizational identity tradition that conceptualized organizational identity as those features of the organization that are central, distinctive, and enduring (Albert and Whetten 1985). Thus, while Albert and Whetten (1985) took a content-based approach to defining identity, we take a relational approach. A superordinate social identity is a psychological state that derives from members of multiple units feeling a sense of belonging to or identification with a higher-order organizational aggregate. When shared by organizational members, a superordinate social identity provides a metaphorical kindling that facilitates knowledge transfer and enables innovations to reach their full potential. Thus, we see a superordinate identity as a governance and coordination mechanism that influences the processes of knowledge transfer and creation in organizations (Foss 2007; Foss and Michailova in preparation).

The chapter is organized as follows. First, we discuss the concept of a superordinate social identity and argue that it facilitates knowledge transfer. Second, we present evidence from both the field and the laboratory that a superordinate identity facilitates receptivity to innovations. Third, we discuss how a superordinate social identity has the potential to lead to the creation of new knowledge, in addition to facilitating knowledge transfer. Fourth, we describe the conditions under which a superordinate social identity is most likely to enhance knowledge transfer. Fifth, we argue that promoting a superordinate identity across the units of an organization is an effective strategy for increasing competitive advantage. Sixth, we discuss how to build a superordinate identity in organizations. The chapter concludes with a discussion of promising future research directions on superordinate identity and knowledge creation and transfer.

7.1.1. *A Theory of Superordinate Social Identity and Knowledge Transfer*

Social identity can be defined as a sense of belonging to a social aggregate, such as a group, organization, or association (Ashforth and Mael 1989; Tajfel and Turner 1979). Social identity consists of an individual's 'knowledge that he or she belongs to certain groups together with some emotional and value significance to him [or her] of that group membership' (Tajfel 1972: 31). Researchers agree social identity has significant and consistent effects on opinions, attitudes, and behaviors toward members of one's own group compared to other group members. For example, a review of nearly one hundred empirical studies (Dasgupta 2004) confirms earlier findings (Brewer 1979) that individuals view those with whom they share a social identity more positively than those with whom they do not share such an identity—as more valuable, trustworthy, honest, loyal, and cooperative. There is considerable evidence of this 'own-group' favoritism in behaviors ranging from the allocation of rewards (Brewer 1979) to cooperation (Bartel 2001; Tyler and Blader 2000) from studies in both laboratory and field settings (for a review, see Hewstone, Rubin, and Willis 2002).

Individuals have also been found to be more influenced by the opinions of those with whom they share a social identity compared to those with whom they do not share such an identity (for a review, see Wood 2000). The consistent differences in evaluations of those with whom one shares or does not share a social identity contribute to significant differences in recipients' willingness to consider knowledge, ideas, and innovations from other sources. For example, the positive evaluation of those with whom one shares a social identity is likely to increase receptivity to their ideas.

Evidence from the attitude change literatures suggests that the social identity of a source of a persuasive message affects the extent to which a recipient thoroughly considers the source's ideas (for related discussions, see Fleming and Petty 2000; Van Knippenberg 1999). Individuals who shared a social identity with the source of a message concerning an issue relevant to them were more likely to be affected by the persuasiveness of the argument and to adopt attitudes consistent with high- but not low-quality messages (Mackie, Worth, and Asuncion 1990; Mackie, Gastardo-Conaco, and Skelly 1992: study 1; Van Knippenberg and Wilke 1991). This pattern of adoption provides evidence of thorough consideration of the source's ideas. In contrast, individuals who did not share a social identity with the source of a message were not affected by the persuasiveness of the source's arguments, which suggests a lack of consideration of the source's ideas. Additional evidence was found in arguments that recipients generated in response to messages. Individuals generated more arguments about a source's persuasive message when they shared compared to when they did not share a social identity with the source (Van Knippenberg and Wilke 1991).

When the source and recipient do not share an identity, the recipient is more likely to be threatened by new ideas or approaches proposed by the source. This experience of threat can lead to a reduction in information processing or a lack of thoughtful consideration of the sources' ideas and arguments (Staw, Sandelands, and Dutton 1981). Further, because individuals view others with whom they do not share an identity negatively, individuals are likely to reject ideas proposed by a source with whom they do not share an identity.

A common social identity could be created by dismantling subgroups and merging them into a new group that performs a collective task (Gaertner and Dovidio 2000; Sherif et al. 1961). For example, two product development groups could be merged into one. This approach, however, may not be feasible in many organizational contexts where there are geographic, strategic, or expertise-based reasons for keeping groups separate. Firms operate establishments in different countries in order to access markets, raw materials, and expertise around the world ('A Survey of Manufacturing: Meet the Global Factory' 1998). It is not feasible to dismantle these groups and merge them into one group. Furthermore, doing so would reduce diversity of experience, perspectives, and ideas that is valuable for innovation. In addition, the increased size of merged groups would engender greater agency costs to monitor the performance of group members (Alchian and Demsetz 1972; Holmstrom 1982).

Instead of merging groups, researchers have posited and shown that one can create an overarching superordinate identity that encompasses existing groups and includes them in a higher-level categorization (Dovidio et al. 2006; Gaertner et al. 2000; Gonzalez and Brown 2003). Separate groups or units share a common social identity when their members derive a sense of belonging or social identity from a common, superordinate entity. Field research indicates that employees can develop a psychological sense of belonging to a superordinate entity (the organization), even though they are distributed across different groups because of geographic distance (Hinds and Mortensen 2005), disciplinary expertise (Van der Vegt and Bunderson 2005), or organizational functions (Sethi 2000). The

Airbus mandate to purge national symbols from presentations represents an effort by management to increase the psychological salience of member's sense of superordinate social identity with Airbus, while maintaining the firm's multiunit structure that is distributed across countries.

The strength of a superordinate identity describes the extent to which employees in different subunits derive a psychological sense of belonging to a superordinate group. The strength of superordinate identity is not a discrete (yes, no) variable but rather a continuous variable that can range from zero to very high. Because identity is something individuals experience, it is generally measured through questionnaires (e.g., Doosje, Ellemers, and Spears 1995; Gaertner et al. 1989; Mael and Ashforth 1992). A low level of social identity reflects members' weak identification with a superordinate entity, while a high level of superordinate identity reflects members' strong identification. Identification with a superordinate entity might also be measured by observing interactions and counting the number of collective references to the superordinate identity (we, us) relative to references to subunits (e.g., see Liang, Moreland, and Argote 1995).

A strong superordinate identity is distinct from a strong, cohesive social network. Whereas the former refers to employees' psychological attachment to a social aggregate, the latter refers to their sociological embeddedness in a web of interpersonal relationships. People psychologically identify themselves and others as members of social aggregates, such as departments, organizations, cities, and nations, based on a sense of attachment rather than as a result of interpersonal relationships. Simon (1991) highlights the many levels at which this psychological mechanism operates.

Although a strong superordinate identity may predispose members to form interpersonal relationships on the basis of positive regard and mutual trust, neither the formation nor the continuation of a superordinate social identity depends on interpersonal relationships. For example, members of geographically distributed groups with few or no ties linking them can develop a strong superordinate identity with the organization (e.g., Hinds and Mortensen 2005). Moreover, because the likelihood that a set of employees forms a cohesive social network characterized by many third party ties decreases as a function of the size of the set (Reagans and McEvily 2003), superordinate identities that span work groups, units, and divisions are not likely to be characterized by cohesive social networks. Thus, our theory complements previous theories highlighting the importance of social network connections and social network structures to knowledge sharing (e.g., Hansen 1999; Reagans and McEvily 2003) by offering a distinct social facilitator—superordinate social identity—that impacts knowledge transfer.

We predict that a superordinate social identity renders organizational units more receptive to knowledge generated by other units with whom they share the identity. Thus, we argue that knowledge transfer is likely to be greater across units that share a superordinate identity than across units not part of such a superordinate relationship. We are not predicting that recipients blindly adopt knowledge from sources with whom they share a superordinate identity but rather predicting that recipients thoughtfully consider knowledge from sources with whom they share an identity. If recipients perceive the knowledge as likely to improve their outcomes, they will adopt it. Conversely, if recipients do not perceive the knowledge as beneficial, they will not adopt it. By contrast, recipients are more likely to reject knowledge from sources with whom they do not share a superordinate identity, without full consideration of the sources' knowledge. Thus, recipients are likely to reject knowledge, even knowledge that would have improved their performance, if the knowledge were contributed by a source with whom they did not share an identity. We now turn to a discussion of evidence from the field and the laboratory on the contribution of a superordinate social identity to knowledge transfer.

7.2. Evidence from the Field and Laboratory

Evidence from the field suggests that a superordinate social identity increases receptivity to innovations. The innovation that we study is a fuel, cellulosic ethanol, that is produced biologically from sugars found in the earth's most abundant carbohydrate—biomass (i.e., switch grass, hybrid trees, and agricultural wastes). Although the fuel is still in development, cellulosic ethanol is fairly well understood because it is similar to the more expensive ethanol, currently produced in the United States from corn and in Brazil from sugarcane. Cellulosic ethanol is known to be superior to gasoline in terms of carbon emissions, sustainability, life-cycle environmental impact, and energy security (MacLean et al. 2000) and is functionally comparable to gasoline in terms of energy density, octane value, and compatibility with vehicle engines (Bailey 1996). With increasing concerns about carbon emissions, environmental sustainability, energy security, fuel costs, and the supply of petroleum, cellulosic ethanol seems to warrant greater consideration as an alternative fuel.

Consideration of cellulosic ethanol by firms in the fuel and automobile industries appears related to the extent to which the firms see themselves as belonging to a superordinate category. For example, employees of oil companies could see their firms as producing oil or they could see themselves as producing fuel. The former firm would not share a superordinate identity with producers of other types of fuel, while the latter would. Similarly, employees of automotive firms could see themselves primarily as producers of gasoline-powered cars and trucks or as producers of cars and trucks powered by any fuel. Again the former firm would not share a superordinate identity with producers of cars and trucks powered by fuels other than gasoline, while the latter firm would.

We explored the relationship between superordinate social identity and the anticipated adoption of ethanol in interviews with 10 employees who were based at 3 fuel and 2 automobile firms. The interviews were part of a larger study investigating facilitators and obstacles to the introduction of cellulosic ethanol as an alternative fuel for the motor vehicle fleet of automobiles and light trucks in the United States. To assess the strength of superordinate social identity, we asked informants from fuel firms to assess on a five-point scale the extent to which they saw themselves as belonging to either a subgroup of producers of petroleum or a superordinate group of producers of fuel. Similarly, we asked informants from automotive firms to report the extent to which they belonged to either a subgroup that produced gasoline-powered cars and trucks or a superordinate group that produced cars and trucks regardless of fuel. We examined how responses to this question related to responses to another question, also measured on a five-point scale, about the likelihood that their firm would produce ethanol (or cars and trucks that run on ethanol) in three years.

We found an association between the strength of respondent's superordinate identities and the likelihood they reported that their firms would introduce ethanol within a three-year period. More specifically, we examined participants' responses about whether their organization was likely to start producing ethanol (or cars and trucks that run on ethanol) as a function of their company type (fuel vs. automotive) and the extent to which they saw themselves as belonging to a superordinate group. The relationship between the strength of superordinate identification and the expectation of adopting ethanol was positive and significant ($B = .86$), ($SE = .20$), and ($p < .05$). Company type was not significant. Automotive manufacturers who saw themselves as belonging to a superordinate group that produced cars and trucks regardless of fuel were more likely to report that they would produce cars and trucks that run on ethanol in the next three years than manufacturers reporting that they saw themselves as belonging to a group that produced gasoline-powered cars and trucks. Similarly, energy firms whose members reported that they belonged to a superordinate group of firms that produced fuel were more likely to report that they would produce cellulosic ethanol in the future than firms that saw themselves as belonging to a group that produced petroleum.

Although these data suggest an association between a superordinate identity and receptivity to new ideas and innovations, the data are exploratory. They do not permit us to establish causality or to examine whether superordinate identity affects the actual adoption of innovation. To overcome these limitations and to examine whether a superordinate social identity improves receptivity to innovations from other groups, we brought the phenomenon of knowledge transfer into the controlled setting of the laboratory (Kane, Argote, and Levine 2005). We created an opportunity for the transfer of task-relevant knowledge from a source to a recipient group via personnel rotation and varied whether the work groups shared a superordinate social identity. Participants were randomly assigned to condition, which removed the possibility that they selected into the condition they preferred.

Using perceptual, linguistic, and common fate manipulations from previous research (Gaertner and Dovidio 2000), we induced participants to think of themselves as belonging to either a larger group composed of two work groups (superordinate identity) or one of two work groups (no superordinate identity). We separated the work groups and trained them to assemble products using slightly different production routines. Midway through production, one member from each work group rotated into the other group for the remainder of the study. Work groups were not aware that they possessed knowledge of different production routines until the rotating member began working in their group's assembly line. The group's production output and conversations during the subsequent production trials provided objective, behavioral measures of the extent to which recipient groups considered and adopted the rotator's production routine.

In the Kane, Argote, and Levine (2005) study, we systematically varied the quality of a rotating member's knowledge to be either superior or inferior to that of the recipient group so that we could differentiate between blind acceptance/rejection of the rotator's knowledge and thorough consideration of his or her knowledge. Adoption patterns characterized by greater adoption of higher compared to lower quality knowledge would indicate consideration of the innovation. By contrast, adoption patterns not affected by the quality of the innovation would indicate a lack of consideration.

As we predicted, recipient groups were more likely to adopt the rotator's production routine when both groups shared a superordinate identity compared to when they did not. Recipient groups were also more likely to adopt a rotator's routine when it was superior rather than inferior to their own. The interaction we predicted between superordinate identity and knowledge quality was also significant. Groups that shared a superordinate identity with the rotating member were more likely to adopt the rotator's routine when it was superior rather than inferior to their own. By contrast, groups that did not share a superordinate identity with the rotating member were not likely to adopt the rotator's routine, regardless of its quality. Results from mediation analyses also indicated that the reported strength of superordinate identity accounted for the effect of the manipulations on knowledge transfer.

Building on this work, Kane (2005) proposed that superordinate social identity impacts transfer through the extent that recipients consider a source's knowledge. To test this proposition and further investigate the effect of superordinate social identity on receptivity and adoption of knowledge, the study examined whether knowledge demonstrability, or the extent that the merits of knowledge are recognizable, affects its adoption. Social psychological research on task and solution demonstrability (Laughlin 1980; Laughlin and Ellis 1986) suggests that distinct forms of knowledge can be similar in their positive effect on performance; yet, they can be quite different in terms of how much consideration is needed to recognize those merits. Because demonstrability affects the degree to which thorough consideration is needed to recognize the merits of knowledge and superordinate social identity is expected to increase knowledge consideration, a superordinate social identity was expected to be a more important predictor of knowledge adoption when knowledge was less rather than more demonstrable.

The data from this study provide additional support for our theory of superordinate social identity and knowledge transfer. Process data obtained from coding recipient groups' conversations support the superordinate social identity increases knowledge consideration hypothesis. Moreover, behavioral evidence confirms the predicted interaction between superordinate social identity and knowledge demonstrability:

superordinate identity was a more important predictor of knowledge adoption when knowledge was less rather than more demonstrable. When knowledge demonstrability was low, recipient groups that shared a superordinate identity with the rotating member were more likely to adopt the rotator's routine than were recipient groups that did not share such an identity with the rotator. By contrast, when knowledge demonstrability was high, recipient groups that shared a superordinate identity with the rotator were as likely to adopt the rotator's routine as were recipient groups that did not share such an identity with the rotator.

Data from these studies indicate that superordinate social identity promotes consideration of knowledge, ideas, and innovations from others within the superordinate boundary. A superordinate identity does not lead group members to blindly adopt knowledge from groups with whom they share an identity. Rather it leads to thoughtful consideration of knowledge and adoption of performance-enhancing ideas. This consideration is especially valuable when knowledge is not easily demonstrable.

7.3. A Superordinate Identity and Knowledge Creation

The process of transferring knowledge across organizational units can lead to knowledge being transformed (Carlile 2004; Leonard-Barton 1995). Thus, new knowledge can be created through attempts to transfer knowledge across units. Because units that are embedded in a superordinate relationship are exposed to more knowledge, they have more opportunities to combine knowledge in new ways than their independent counterparts. Further, because units that are involved in a superordinate relationship consider knowledge thoroughly, they are more adept at developing new knowledge than units lacking such a relationship. Thus, we argue that a superordinate social identity leads to more knowledge creation among units sharing the relationship. The diversity of groups within the superordinate category affects the range of knowledge that members are exposed to and the likelihood of knowledge transfer (Reagans and McEvily 2003). Increases in the diversity and inclusiveness of the set of subgroups constituting the superordinate group are likely to be associated with exposure to a larger and more diverse set of innovations. Knott's results (2001) are consistent with our theory: units that departed from a franchise were less innovative than those that remained and therefore had access to larger and more diverse pools of knowledge.

Could a shared superordinate identity among subgroups combined with subgroup diversity facilitate the generation of new innovations? There is some evidence suggestive of the effects of shared relationships on creativity. Pairs of individuals who shared a more inclusive relational category were more likely to build on and refine one another's ideas in Hollywood pitch meetings than were pairs who were separated by differentiating relational categories (Elsbach and Kramer 2003). A survey of managers of cross-functional product development teams revealed a positive association between team-level identity and the performance of the team's new products, suggesting that superordinate social identity facilitates the creation of knowledge across members with different functional expertise (Sethi 2000). Research on minority dissent in groups indicates that exposure to diverse ideas also stimulates more divergent and creative thinking in groups (Nemeth 1992). A similar process may occur in subgroups that share a superordinate relationship with other subgroups. Along related lines, field research indicates that a team-level superordinate social identity is associated with spontaneous communication (Hinds and Mortensen 2005) and team learning behaviors, such as challenging members' ideas and perspectives (Van der Vegt and Bunderson 2005). Thus, the theory and evidence suggest that superordinate social identity may spark behavioral, as well as cognitive, facilitators of knowledge creation.

7.4. Conditions under which a Superordinate Identity Enhances Knowledge Creation and Transfer

When is a superordinate identity most likely to increase knowledge creation and transfer? We use the Argote, McEvily, and Reagans (2003) framework to illustrate how characteristics of knowledge, characteristics of the context, and characteristics of units in a superordinate relationship can affect the extent to which a shared superordinate identity promotes knowledge creation and transfer in firms. As noted previously, Kane (2005) demonstrated that a superordinate social identity was more beneficial for transferring knowledge that is low in demonstrability than for transferring knowledge that is high in demonstrability. Knowledge that is low in demonstrability requires more consideration to recognize its merits than easier-to-recognize, more demonstrable knowledge. For similar reasons, the transfer of knowledge that is tacit (Nonaka 1991; Polyani 1966), complex (Galbraith 1990), or causally ambiguous (Szulanski 1996) is more likely to benefit from a shared superordinate relationship than knowledge that is explicit, simple, or easily understood.

Characteristics of the context in which groups are embedded are also likely to moderate the relationship between a superordinate identity and knowledge transfer. One important contextual characteristic is the extent to which groups are geographically distributed. A superordinate identity may be especially valuable when groups are geographically dispersed. For example, Hinds and Mortensen (2005) compared geographically collocated and distributed groups in a multinational firm. The researchers found that conflict was greater in distributed than in collocated groups and further that a shared identity moderated the effect of location on interpersonal conflict. The relationship between geographical distance and conflict was weaker when group members shared an identity. Building on this work, we predict an interaction between geographic distance and superordinate identity in promoting knowledge transfer: a strong superordinate identity will mitigate the negative effect of geographic distance on knowledge transfer. A superordinate identity is likely to be especially important in multinational firms where units are geographically distributed around the globe.

Characteristics of the units involved in the superordinate relationship may also moderate the relationship between superordinate identity and knowledge transfer. For example, the diversity of participants in the relationship is likely to be an important predictor of its value. Although diverse groups benefit from more information and a greater number of perspectives than their more homogeneous counterparts, diverse groups also generally have more conflict and more trouble communicating than groups composed of similar members (Williams and O'Reilly 1998). A superordinate identity can help groups overcome the costs of diversity while realizing its benefits. Van der Vegt and Bunderson (2005) found that when collective team identification was stronger, expertise diversity contributed positively to team learning and performance while when collective identification was weaker, diversity was negatively related to learning and performance. The greater consideration afforded members in the superordinate category may help groups realize the informational benefits of diversity while overcoming the communication difficulties associated with it. Thus, we expect that diversity and superordinate identity will interact to predict knowledge creation and transfer. Diversity will be more positively related to knowledge creation and transfer when superordinate identity is stronger than when it is weaker.

7.5. Superordinate Identity and Competitive Advantage

Researchers have argued that the ability to create and transfer knowledge is a source of competitive advance for firms (Spender and Grant 1996; Teece, Pisano, and Shuen 1997). In this chapter, we have shown that a shared superordinate identity promotes knowledge creation and transfer. In this section, we argue that a superordinate identity can contribute to competitive advantage in firms. Our arguments, which are based on a relational view of identity, complement Fiol's focus on the content of identity as a source of competitive advantage (e.g., see Fiol 2001).

Promoting the internal transfer of knowledge while minimizing its external transfer, or spillover, to competitors is central to competitive advantage. Strategies that promote the transfer of knowledge within the firm can also make it easier for knowledge to transfer or spillover to competitors. For example, embedding knowledge in technology is effective for increasing internal knowledge transfer (Zander and Kogut 1995). Yet knowledge embedded in technology leaks out very quickly to other firms (Mansfield 1985).

Argote and Ingram (2000) developed a theory that predicts how organizations can manage this tension of promoting internal knowledge transfer while minimizing external knowledge spillover. Their theory builds on a theoretical framework of knowledge reservoirs or repositories developed in McGrath and Argote (2001). According to the framework, knowledge is embedded in an organization's members, tools, and tasks and the networks formed by crossing members, tools, and tasks. For example, knowledge can be embedded in the organization's social or member–member network. Knowledge can also be embedded in the member–task (who performs which task) or the member–tool (who uses which tool) network. These latter networks comprise the organization's transactive memory network (Brandon and Hollingshead 1999; Lewis et al. 2007; Liang, Moreland, and Argote 1995; Wegner 1986). Finally knowledge can also be embedded in the task–tool (which tasks are performed with which tools), and the member–task–tool networks (who performs which tasks with which tools).

Knowledge transfer occurs through modifying or moving the basic organizational components of members, tasks, and tools and the networks formed by crossing them. For example, knowledge transfer can occur by moving members from one group to another (Almeida and Kogut 1999; Kane, Argote, and Levine 2005). Knowledge transfer can also occur by embedding knowledge in task sequences or routines (Argote and Darr 2000; Winter and Szulanski 2001) or tools and technology (Zander and Kogut 1995) and making the routines or tools available to other units. Similarly, knowledge can be embedded in transactive memory networks (Lewis, Lange, and Gillis 2005) and transferred to other contexts.

Argote and Ingram (2000) argued that it is more difficult to transfer the networks to new contexts than to transfer the basic elements of members, tools, and tasks. The networks have more components that must fit the new context or be adapted to it in order for transfer to be successful. For example, a division of labor developed in one context may not fit another where members have different capabilities (Rao and Argote 2006). By contrast, knowledge embedded in tools transfers quickly to other contexts (Mansfield 1985). Further, because of selection and training processes within firms that increase member homogeneity (Jackson et al. 1991), it is easier to transfer the networks involving people successfully *within* than *between* organizations. In addition, the common language and communication codes that develop within organizations (Weber and Camerer 2003) make it easier to share knowledge within their boundaries rather than across organizations in market transactions (Monteverde 1995). Embedding knowledge in the networks involving people is an effective strategy for promoting its internal transfer while minimizing its external spillover.

A strong superordinate identity in organizations amplifies the speed and success of transfer of knowledge through networks involving people. As noted previously, when members share a superordinate social identity, they are more receptive to knowledge contributed by a member of the superordinate group. Thus, in organizations where a strong superordinate identity exists, knowledge transfer through moving the networks involving people is likely to be more effective than in organizations that lack a strong superordinate social identity. Further, the benefits of a strong superordinate social identity are present only within the boundaries of the superordinate category, which in this case is the organization. Thus, a strong superordinate identity improves the speed and success of internal knowledge transfer while having a negligible effect on or even decreasing external knowledge spillover.

7.6. Building a Superordinate Identity

Researchers debate individuals' motivations for social identification (Hewstone et al. 2002) and the conditions needed to create the experience of a shared superordinate identity. The debate hinges on whether perceptual and linguistic cues are sufficient to create the perception of shared identity or whether common fate or reward interdependence is also needed (Gaertner and Insko 2000). Perceptual and linguistic cues include whether units are given common (superordinate) or different (subordinate) names, symbols, and artifacts. For example, in the Airbus example, Louis Gallois banned the use of national flags on PowerPoint presentations because they reinforced identity at the level of the subgroup rather than the superordinate entity (Airbus). The experience of common fate occurs when individuals feel that their outcomes are related. The experience of common fate can be created by offering a reward for performance that is distributed at the level of the superordinate entity.

In the laboratory studies we reported here, we varied both perceptual/linguistic cues and common fate to create the experience of identity. Participants in the superordinate identity condition were given a common name, had nametags with the same color and symbol, and were seated in an integrated fashion around the table for the introduction to the experiment. In addition, the six participants in the superordinate identity condition were informed that the best-performing group would win a $60 prize. By contrast, participants in the subordinate identity condition were given two different names and received nametags with two different colors and symbols corresponding to their particular subgroup. The three members of each subgroup sat on the same side of the table, opposite the members of the other subgroup. Further, the prize was offered at the level of the subgroup: Participants were told that the best-performing three-member subgroup would win a $30 prize.

Choosing which of various governance mechanisms, such as identity to build and to use involves assessing their relative costs and benefits. The financial costs of creating an identity, through perceptual and linguistic cues, such as names and symbols, are not great. The prize or reward given to reinforce the identity through the experience of a common fate could be modest. For example, an organization could give a bonus based on how well the superordinate entity performed. There are also the costs of managerial attention to use the names and symbols and disburse the rewards. On balance though, the direct costs of a creating a superordinate identity are not great.

As reported here, the benefits of developing a superordinate identity for promoting knowledge creation and transfer can be large. These benefits accrue to units within the superordinate boundary. These benefits must be weighed against a decrease in knowledge creation and transfer with units not included within the superordinate boundary. Creating a superordinate identity that includes one set of subunits may decrease knowledge creation and transfer outside the superordinate boundary. Thus, it is important to include the most critical knowledge transactions within the superordinate boundary.

7.7. Future Directions

We have argued and presented evidence that sharing a superordinate social identity leads to more thorough consideration of ideas. We have also argued and shown in the laboratory that the benefits of sharing a superordinate social identity are more pronounced when knowledge is not demonstrable or easily recognized. A similar effect seems to occur in the field. It was not easy to demonstrate the superiority of the alternative fuel, cellulosic ethanol, because its merits can be measured on multiple dimensions whose value depends on a range of factors, including market demand, governmental regulations, and international relations. Organizations that saw themselves as belonging to a superordinate group were more likely to consider adopting ethanol, an innovation low in demonstrability.

Future work should consider how characteristics of knowledge, units in the superordinate relationship, and their contexts either increase or decrease the strength of the effects of sharing a superordinate social identity on the creation and transfer of knowledge. For example, characteristics that might limit the importance of greater consideration afforded by a strong superordinate identity on transfer of knowledge include inertia and commitment to accepted and legitimate courses of action (Choi and Levine 2004; DiMaggio and Powell 1983). Groups might reject promising innovations that have been afforded through consideration when adopting them is outside of the group's set of appropriate or legitimate behaviors (Akerlof and Kranton 2000; Dutton and Dukerich 1991; Kogut and Zander 1996). For example, Dutton and Dukerich (1991) documented that the New York Port Authority initially rejected potentially innovative actions, such as providing social services, for dealing with the homeless in their terminals because doing so was not considered appropriate behavior.

Future work should also explore what leads to the experience of a strong superordinate social identity and what determines the optimal size of a superordinate entity. As noted previously, researchers debate the minimal conditions necessary to create a sense of belonging to or identification with a social entity (Gaertner and Insko 2000). Much of the current debate centers around whether a sense of common fate, such as what is derived from reward interdependence, is necessary to create a superordinate social identity. As Brewer's (1991) optimal distinctiveness theory illustrates, a group's viability as a source of social identity depends on it providing both inclusiveness and exclusiveness. Thus, a superordinate group can become too large and inclusive for it to be a viable source of social identity. Because the optimal size and level of inclusiveness depends on the context and group, future research is needed to understand the determinants of when organizational groups of different sizes (e.g., business units, divisions, organizations, and industry groups) provide a source of superordinate social identity to their members.

An important issue for future research centers on whether superordinate identity is a complement or substitute for other knowledge governance mechanisms such as organizational structures, reward systems, and accounting systems. That is, does a superordinate identity amplify the effect of other knowledge governance mechanisms or does it substitute for those mechanisms? The question is complicated because identity can be shaped by these other governance mechanisms. For example, rewarding employees at the level of the overall organization increases the likelihood that they identify with a superordinate entity—the organization.

We build on work by Gulati and Nickerson (in press) that differentiates between the choice and effectiveness of governance mechanisms in predicting whether they will be complements or substitutes. Concerning choice of knowledge governance mechanisms, we predict that a strong superordinate identity would serve as a substitute for mechanisms whose main function is monitoring (e.g., close supervision). A strong superordinate identity motivates members to act in the interest of the superordinate entity (Tyler and Blader 2000). Therefore, less monitoring is required in systems where superordinate identity is strong than when it is weak.

Concerning the effectiveness of knowledge governance mechanisms, we predict that superordinate identity will generally function as a complement. Because superordinate identity leads to greater consideration of knowledge, it reinforces or complements governance mechanisms that surface knowledge. For example, information brought to light through an information or accounting system would get greater consideration when superordinate identity was strong than when it was weak Further research is needed to determine when a superordinate identity is a complement or a substitute for various knowledge governance mechanisms.

In sum, we have shown that a superordinate identity can increase consideration of and receptivity to knowledge. We have argued that a superordinate identity is likely to be a powerful mechanism for increasing consideration of ideas from other groups within the superordinate boundary. Thus, knowledge is more likely to transfer across groups that share than across those that lack a superordinate identity. We have highlighted how superordinate social identity, through promoting the consideration of knowledge from others within the superordinate boundary, can increase a firm's recombinative and generative capabilities. Further research on factors promoting the development of superordinate identities in organizations as well as on the conditions under which superordinate identities promote knowledge creation and transfer seems worthwhile.

References

A Survey of Manufacturing: Meet the Global Factory. June 20, 1998. *The Economist* M1-M18.

Akerlof, G. A. and R. E. Kranton. 2000. 'Economics and Identity,' *Quarterly Journal of Economics* 115: 715–53.

Albert, S. and D. A. Whetten. 1985. 'Organizational Identity,' in L. L. Cummings and B. M. Staw (eds.) *Research in Organizational Behavior*. Connecticut, Greenwich: JAI.

Alchian, A. A. and H. Demsetz. 1972. 'Production, Information Costs and Economic Organization,' *The American Economic Review* 62: 777–92.

Almeida, P. and B. Kogut. 1999. 'Localization of Knowledge and the Mobility of Engineers in Regional Networks,' *Management Science* 45: 905–17.

Argote, L. 1999. *Organizational Learning: Creating, Retaining and Transferring Knowledge*. Massachusetts, Norwell: Kluwer Academic Publishers.

Argote, L. and E. Darr. 2000. 'Repositories of Knowledge about Productivity and Timeliness in Franchise Organizations: Individual Structural and Technological,' in G. Dosi, R. Nelson, and S. Winter (eds.) *Nature and Dynamics of Organizational Capabilities*. Oxford: Oxford University Press.

——and P. Ingram. 2000. 'Knowledge Transfer: A Basis for Competitive Advantage in Firms,' *Organizational Behavior and Human Decision Processes* 82: 150–69.

——S. Beckman, and D. Epple. 1990. 'The Persistence and Transfer of Learning in Industrial Settings,' *Management Science* 36: 140–54.

——B. McEvily, and R. Reagans. 2003. 'Managing Knowledge in Organizations: An Integrative Framework and Review of Emerging Themes,' *Management Science* 49: 571–82.

Ashforth, B. E. and F. Mael. 1989. 'Social Identity Theory and the Organization,' *Academy of Management Review* 14: 20–39.

Bailey, B. K. 1996. 'Performance of Ethanol as a Transportation Fuel,' in C. E. Wyman (ed.) *Handbook on Bioethanol: Production and Utilization*. Washington: Taylor & Francis.

Bartel, C. A. 2001. 'Social Comparisons in Boundary-Spanning Work: Effects of Community Outreach on Members' Organizational Identity and Identification,' *Administrative Science Quarterly* 46: 379–413.

Baum, J. A. C. and P. Ingram. 1998. 'Survival-Enhancing Learning in the Manhattan Hotel Industry, 1898–1980,' *Management Science* 44: 996–1016.

Brandon, D. P. and A. B. Hollingshead. 1999. 'Collaborative Learning and Computer-Supported Groups,' *Communication Education* 48: 109–26.

Brewer, M. B. 1979. 'In-Group Bias in the Minimal Intergroup Situation: A Cognitive Motivational Analysis,' *Psychological Bulletin* 86: 237–43.

——1991. 'The Social Self: On Being the Same and Different at the Same Time,' *Personality and Social Psychology Bulletin* 17: 475–82.

——2000. 'Superordinate Goals versus Superordinate Identity as Bases of Intergroup Cooperation,' in D. Capozza and R. Brown (eds.) *Social Identity Processes*. London: Sage.

Carlile, P. R. 2004. 'Transferring, Translating, and Transforming: An Integrative Framework for Managing Knowledge Across Boundaries,' *Organization Science* 15: 555–68.

Choi, H. S. and J. M. Levine. 2004. 'Minority Influence in Work Teams: The Impact of Newcomers,' *Journal of Experimental Social Psychology* 40, 273–80.

Clark, N. 2007. 'Turnaround Effort Is Challenging at Airbus, a Stew of European Culture,' *New York Times*, May 17, 2007.

Darr, E. D., L. Argote, and D. Epple. 1995. 'The Acquisition, Transfer, and Depreciation of Knowledge in Service Organizations: Productivity in Franchises,' *Management Science* 41: 1750–62.

Dasgupta, N. 2004. 'Implicit Group Favoritism, Outgroup Favoritism, and Their Behavioral Manifestations,' *Social Justice Research* 17: 143–70.

DiMaggio, P. J. and W. W. Powell. 1983. 'The Iron Cage Revisited: Institutional Isomorphism and Collective Rationality in Organizational Fields,' *American Sociological Review* 48: 147–60.

Doosje, B., N. Ellemers, and R. Spears. 1995. 'Perceived Intragroup Variability as a Function of Group Status and Identification,' *Journal of Experimental Social Psychology* 31: 410–36.

Dovidio, J. F., et al. 2006. 'Recategorization and Crossed Categorization: The Implications of Group Salience and Representations for Reducing Bias,' in R. J. Crisp and M. Hewstone (eds.) *Multiple Social Categorization: Processes, Models and Applications*. New York: Psychology Press.

Dutton, J. E. and J. M. Dukerich 1991. 'Keeping an Eye on the Mirror: Image and Identity in Organizational Adaptation,' *Academy of Management Journal* 34: 517–54.

Elsbach, K. D. and R. M. Kramer. 2003. 'Assessing Creativity in Hollywood Pitch Meetings: Evidence for a Dual-Process Model of Creativity Judgments,' *Academy of Management Journal* 46: 283–301.

Fiol, C. M. 2001. 'Revisiting an Identity-Based View of Sustainable Competitive Advantage,' *Journal of Management* 27: 691–9.

Fleming, M. A. and R. E. Petty. 2000. 'Identity and Persuasion: An Elaboration Likelihood Approach,' in D. J. Terry and M. A. Hogg (eds.) *Attitudes, Behaviors, and Social Context: The Role of Group Norms and Group Membership*. New Jersey, Mahwah: Erlbaum.

Foss, N. J. 2007. 'The Emerging Knowledge Governance Approach: Challenges and Characteristics,' *Organization* 14: 29–52.

—— and S. Michailova (eds.) in preparation. In *Knowledge Governance: Processes and Perspectives*. Oxford: Oxford University Press.

Gaertner, L. and C. A. Insko. 2000. 'Intergroup Discrimination in the Minimal Group Paradigm: Categorization, Reciprocation, or Fear?,' *Journal of Personality and Social Psychology* 79: 77–94.

Gaertner, S. L. and J. F. Dovidio (eds.) 2000. In *Reducing Intergroup Bias—The Common Ingroup Identity Model*. Philadelphia: Psychology Press.

—— et al. 1989. 'Reducing Intergroup Bias: The Benefits of Recategorization,' *Journal of Personality and Social Psychology* 57: 239–49.

—— et al. 2000. 'The Common Ingroup Identity Model for Reducing Intergroup Bias: Progress and Challenges,' in D. Capozza and R. Brown (eds.) *Social Identity Processes: Trends in Theory and Research*. London: SAGE.

Galbraith, C. S. 1990. 'Transferring Core Manufacturing Technologies in High-Technology Firms,' *California Management Review* 32: 56–70.

Gonzalez, R. and R. Brown. 2003. 'Generalization of Positive Attitude as a Function of Subgroup and Superordinate Group Identifications in Intergroup Contact,' *European Journal of Social Psychology* 33: 195–214.

Gulati, R. and J. A. Nickerson. In press. 'Interorganizational Trust, Governance Choice and Exchange Performance,' *Organization Science*.

Hansen, M. T. 1999. 'The Search-Transfer Problem: The Role of Weak Ties in Sharing Knowledge Across Organizational Units,' *Administrative Science Quarterly* 44: 82–111.

Hewstone, M., M. Rubin, and H. Willis. 2002. 'Intergroup Bias,' *Annual Review of Psychology* 53: 575–604.

Hinds, P. J. and M. Mortensen. 2005. 'Understanding Conflict in Geographically Distributed Teams: The Moderating Effects of Shared Identity, Shared Context, and Spontaneous Communication,' *Organization Science* 16: 290–307.

Holmstrom, B. 1982. 'Moral Hazard in Teams,' *The Bell Journal of Economics* 13: 324–40.

Huber, G. P. 1991. 'Organizational Learning: The Contributing Processes and the Literatures,' *Organizational Science* 2: 88–115.

Ingram, P. and T. Simons. 2002. 'The Transfer of Experience in Groups of Organizations: Implications for Performance and Competition,' *Management Science* 48: 1517–33.

Jackson, S. E., et al. 1991. 'Some Differences Make a Difference: Individual Dissimilarity and Group Heterogeneity as Correlates of Recruitment, Promotions, and Turnover,' *Journal of Applied Psychology* 76: 675–89.

Kane, A. A. 2005. 'Superordinate Social Identity, Knowledge Demonstrability, and Knowledge Transfer across Groups,' *Dissertation Abstracts International* 66(04), 2339. (UMI No. 3171949).

——L. Argote, and J. M. Levine. 2005. 'Knowledge Transfer between Groups via Personnel Rotation: Effects of Social Identity and Knowledge Quality,' *Organizational Behavior and Human Decision Processes* 96: 56–71.

Katz, R. and T. J. Allen. 1982. 'Investigating the Not Invented Here (NIH) Syndrome: A Look at the Performance, Tenure, and Communication Patters of 50 R & D Project Groups,' *R & D Management* 12: 7–19.

Knott, A. M. 2001. 'The Dynamic Value of Hierarchy,' *Management Science* 47: 430–48.

Kogut, B. and U. Zander. 1992. 'Knowledge of the Firm, Combinative Capabilities, and the Replication of Technology,' *Organization Science* 3: 383–97.

————1996. 'What Firms Do? Coordination, Identity, and Learning,' *Organization Science* 7: 502–18.

Laughlin, P. R. 1980. 'Social Combination Processes of Cooperative Problem-Solving Groups on Verbal Intellective Tasks,' in M. Fishbein (ed.) *Progress in Social Psychology*. New Jersey, Hillsdale: Erlbaum.

——and A. L. Ellis. 1986. 'Demonstrability and Social Combination Processes on Mathematical Intellective Tasks,' *Journal of Experimental Social Psychology* 22: 177–89.

Leonard-Barton, D. 1995. *Well Springs of Knowledge Building and Sustaining the Sources of Innovation*. Massachusetts, Boston: Harvard Business School Press.

Levitt, B. and J. G. March. 1988. 'Organizational Learning,' *Annual Review of Sociology* 14: 319–40.

Lewis, K., D. Lange, and L. Gillis. 2005. 'Transactive Memory Systems, Learning, and Learning Transfer,' *Organization Science* 16: 581–98.

—— et al. 2007. 'Group Cognition, Membership Change, and Performance: Investigating the Benefits and Detriments of Collective Knowledge,' *Organizational Behavior and Human Decision Processes* 103: 159–78.

Liang, D. W., R. Moreland, and L. Argote. 1995. 'Group versus Individual Training and Group-Performance—the Mediating Role of Transactive Memory,' *Personality and Social Psychology Bulletin* 21: 384–93.

Mackie, D. M., L. T. Worth, and A. G. Asuncion. 1990. 'Processing of Persuasive In-Group Messages,' *Journal of Personality and Social Psychology* 58: 812–22.

—— M. C. Gastardo-Conaco, and J. J. Skelly. 1992. 'Knowledge of the Advocated Position and the Processing of In-Group and Out-Group Persuasive Messages,' *Personality and Social Psychology Bulletin* 18: 145–51.

MacLean, H., et al. 2000. 'A Life-Cycle Comparison of Alternative Automobile Fuels,' *Journal of the Air & Waste Management Association* 50: 1769–79.

Mael, F. and B. E. Ashforth. 1992. 'Alumni and Their Alma Mater: A Partial Test of the Reformulated Model of Organizational Identification,' *Journal of Organizational Behavior* 13: 103–23.

Mansfield, E. 1985. 'How Rapidly Does Industrial Technology Leak Out?,' *The Journal of Industrial Economics* 34: 217–24.

McGrath, J. E. and L. Argote. 2001. 'Group Processes in Organizational Contexts,' in M. A. Hogg and R. S. Tindale (eds.) *Blackwell Handbook of Social Psychology*. UK, Oxford: Blackwell.

McGregor, J. 2006. 'Special Report—Innovation,' *Business Week*, April 24, 2006.

Monteverde, K. 1995. 'Technical Dialog as an Incentive for Vertical Integration in the Semiconductor Industry,' *Management Science* 41: 1624–38.

Nayak, P. and J. Ketteringham. 1986. *Breakthroughs*. New York: Rawson Associates.

Nemeth, C. J. 1992. 'Minority Dissent as a Stimulant to Group Performance,' in S. Worchel, W. Wood, and J. A. Sampson (eds.) *Group Process and Productivity*. California, Newbury Park: Sage Publications.

Nickerson, J. and T. Zenger. 2004. 'A Knowledge-Based Theory of the Firm: The Problem-Solving Perspective,' *Organization Science* 15: 617–32.

Nonaka, I. 1991. 'The Knowledge-Creating Company,' *Harvard Business Review* 69: 96–104.

Nussbaum, B. 2006. 'Business: Innovation and Its Enemies,' *The Economist*, Jan 14, 2006, 64.

Polyani, M. 1966. *The Tacit Dimension*. New York: Anchor Day Books.

Rao, R. D. and L. Argote. 2006. 'Organizational Learning and Forgetting: The Effects of Turnover and Structure,' *European Management Review* 3: 77–85.

Reagans, R. and B. McEvily. 2003. 'Network Structure and Knowledge Transfer: The Effects of Cohesion and Range,' *Administrative Science Quarterly* 48: 240–67.

Rogers, E. M. 2003. *Diffusion of Innovations*. New York: Free Press.

Schumpeter, J. A. 1934. *The Theory of Economic Development: An Inquiry into Profits, Capital, Credit, Interest, and the Business Cycle*. R. Opie Translation. New Jersey, New Brunswick: Transaction Books.

Sethi, R. 2000. 'Superordinate Identity in Cross-Functional Product Development Teams: Its Antecedents and Effect on New Product Performance,' *Journal of the Academy of Marketing Science* 28: 330–44.

Sherif, M., et al. 1961. *Intergroup Conflict and Cooperation: The Robbers Cave Experiment*. Oklahoma, Norman: Institute of Group Relations.

Simon, H. A. 1991. 'Organizations and Markets,' *Journal of Economic Perspectives* 5(2): 25–44.

Spender, J. C. and R. M. Grant. 1996. 'Knowledge and the Firm: Overview,' *Strategic Management Journal* 17: 5–9.

Staw, B. M., L. E. Sandelands, and J. E. Dutton. 1981. 'Threat-Rigidity Effects in Organizational-Behavior—A Multilevel Analysis,' *Administrative Science Quarterly* 26: 501–24.

Szulanski, G. 1996. 'Exploring Internal Stickiness: Impediments to the Transfer of Best Practice within the Firm,' *Strategic Management Journal* 17, 27–43.

——2000. 'The Process of Knowledge Transfer: A Diachronic Analysis of Stickiness,' *Organizational Behavior and Human Decision Processes* 82: 9–27.

Tajfel, H. 1972. 'La Categorisation Sociale,' (English translation) in S. Moscovici (ed.) *Introduction a la Psychologie Sociale*. Paris: Larouse.

——and J. C. Turner. 1979. 'An Integrative Theory of Group Conflict,' in W. G. Austin and S. Worchel (eds.) *The Social Psychology of Intergroup Relations*. California, Monterey: Brooks/Cole.

Teece, D. J., G. Pisano, and A. Shuen. 1997. 'Dynamic Capabilities and Strategic Management,' *Strategic Management Journal* 18: 509–33.

Tyler, T. R. and S. L. Blader. 2000. *Cooperation in Groups: Procedural Justice, Social Identity, and Behavioral Engagement*. Pennsylvania, Philadelphia: Psychology Press/Taylor & Francis.

Van De Ven, A. H., et al. (eds.) 1999. *The Innovation Journey*. New York: Oxford University Press.

Van der Vegt, G. S. and J. S. Bunderson. 2005. 'Learning and Performance in Multidisciplinary Teams: The Importance of Collective Team Identification,' *Academy Of Management Journal* 48: 532–47.

Van Knippenberg, D. 1999. 'Social Identity and Persuasion: Reconsidering the Role of Group Membership,' in D. Abrams and M. A. Hogg (eds.) *Social Identity and Social Cognition*. Massachusetts, Malden: Blackwell Publishers.

——and H. Wilke (eds.) 1991. *Sociale categoristaie, verwerking van argumenten en attitudeverandering*. Tilburg: Tilburg University Press.

Weber, R. A. and C. F. Camerer. 2003. 'Cultural Conflict and Merger Failure: An Experimental Approach,' *Management Science* 49: 400–15.

Wegner, D. M. 1986. 'Transactive Memory: A Contemporary Analysis of the Group Mind,' in B. Mullen and G. R. Goethals (eds.) *Theories of Group Behavior*. New York: Springer-Verlag.

Williams, K. Y. and C. A. O'Reilly. 1998. 'Demography and Diversity in Organizations: A Review of 40 Years of Research,' *Research in Organizational Behavior* 20: 77–140.

Winter, S. G. and G. Szulanski. 2001. 'Replication as Strategy,' *Organization Science* 12: 730–43.

Wood, W. 2000. 'Attitude Change: Persuasion and Social Influence,' *Annual Review of Psychology* 51: 529–70.

Zander, U. and B. Kogut. 1995. 'Knowledge and the Speed of the Transfer and Imitation of Organizational Capabilities: An Empirical Test,' *Organization Science* 6: 76–92.

8

Socialization tactics as a governance mechanism in R&D collaborations

Kenneth Husted and Snejina Michailova

8.1. Introduction

Firms increasingly rely on knowledge acquired from other firms to facilitate the development of their own knowledge and capabilities. Engaging in interorganizational research and development (R&D) collaborations could be an efficient way for firms to get access to, and appropriate, knowledge that otherwise appears remote and arcane, and (Carson et al. 2003; Cowan et al. 2006; Feller et al. 2006; Hagedoorn 2002; Oxley and Sampson 2004) to build innovativeness from the absorption and utilization of such external knowledge (Chesbrough 2003*a*, 2003*b*).

Employees in R&D collaborations are under pressure to be loyal and committed simultaneously to their own organization *and* to the collaboration. In other words, they experience dual allegiance which puts them in a situation of constantly making decisions about what knowledge to share, how much, with whom, and when, so that they are allegiant to their own organization while, at the same time, playing a meaningful role in, and adding value to, the collaboration.

In this chapter, we examine how managers in collaborating companies can govern the individual employees' knowledge-sharing decisions and behavior in the collaborations in an efficient and cost-effective way. Managers face a serious challenge: they want their companies to achieve the intended benefits from the R&D collaboration without risking unintended knowledge sharing that can potentially damage their companies' competitive advantages and distinctive (or unique) knowledge stocks. We argue that socialization tactics are a highly efficient and relatively low-cost mechanism for governing individual knowledge-sharing behavior. In our framework socialization tactics are an informal intrafirm governance mechanism that can be utilized to influence employees' dual allegiance, and, in this way, shape knowledge-sharing behaviors and firm-level outcomes from interorganizational relationships. While this governance mechanism deserves attention in general, it is particularly relevant to complex settings where it is very difficult and often impossible to codify all important issues in formal contracts. As such, socialization tactics are an attractive alternative to more resource-demanding governance mechanisms.

Although knowledge sharing appears to receive an important emphasis in the literature dealing with R&D alliances, the microlevel/behavioral foundation of knowledge sharing has not received much detailed attention in the context of R&D collaborations. Since most of the valuable knowledge resides with individuals, the actual individual knowledge-sharing behavior deserves in-depth understanding and competent governance. While this is true in general, it holds even more for knowledge-intensive settings and contexts like R&D collaborations: first, R&D-intensive environments are inherently uncertain and complex (Fleming and Sorenson 2004), and second, much of the value in R&D projects is not realized until the collaborative effort is finalized.

We borrow insights from the socialization literature and apply them to knowledge-sharing processes in R&D collaborations. R&D projects are complex, dynamic, and often temporary. This implies that R&D collaborators are constantly in the role of newcomers, that is, they are in the state of being socialized into new assumptions, values, norms, and practices. We assert, and argue more carefully below, that there are some conditions in terms of socialization context, socialization content, and social aspects of socialization that are more fertile than others for managing employees' dual allegiance.

The reminder of this chapter is organized as follows: first we introduce some of the core literature on R&D collaboration and knowledge sharing in R&D alliances. We then develop a typology of R&D employees' dual allegiance along two dimensions—their loyalty to their own organization and to the collaboration. This is followed by our theoretical proposition development centered on the link between socialization tactics (context, content, and social aspects), dual allegiance, knowledge-sharing behavior, and firm-level outcomes from R&D collaboration. We conclude with a discussion of potential extensions of our research, implications, and limitations.

8.2. R&D Collaborations and Why Firms Engage in Them

R&D collaborations[1] are 'specific sets of different modes of inter-firm collaboration where two or more firms, that remain independent economic agents and organizations, share some of their R&D activities' (Hagedoorn 2002: 478). The use of R&D collaboration has changed from being of peripheral relevance to being fundamental to many firms' R&D strategy (Duysters, Kok, and Vaandrager 1999). Firms frequently collaborate on R&D to create advantages that can help them outperform others through risk and resource sharing, spreading development costs, learning from partners (Huber 1991; Khanna, Gulati, and Nohria 1998; Lane and Lubatkin 1998), shortening development times, and innovating (Powell, Koput, and Smith-Doerr 1996). Other important factors are innovation-based competition and the speed of technological change, combined with increased globalization (Miotti and Sachwald 2003), larger than before dependence on diversified knowledge bases (Granstrand et al. 1997), multidisciplinarity in research (Nowotny, Gibbons, and Scott 2001), innovation ability of networks (Powell, Koput, and Smith-Doerr 1996), and open innovation (Chesbrough 2003*a*, 2003*b*). This has led to a significant increase in the use of both formal (Hagedoorn 2002) and informal R&D collaboration (Bouty 2000) by R&D-active firms of all sizes (Hagedoorn 2002).

The various motives for collaborating on R&D tend to be intertwined (Hagedoorn 2002) and may change over time due to changes in the firm itself, the environment, and/or the collaboration (Harrigan 1988). Part of the economics literature, for instance, suggests that corporate motives for participating in R&D collaboration are sharing of costs, seeking economy of scale, and avoiding wasting resources on duplicating already achieved results (Sakakibara 1997, 2003). Transaction cost influences the mode of cooperation in terms of resource allocation to transaction-specific or relation-specific assets, uncertainties about the character of the outcome, and cost related to execution of the contractual agreement (Pisano 1991). Transaction cost also includes the cost of monitoring and keeping parties to the agreement. Collaborative research is also considered to be a useful

[1] For the rest of the chapter, we use R&D 'collaboration,' 'partnership,' 'alliance,' 'network,' and 'project' interchangeably.

cost-sharing strategy to deal with spillover from research (Stolpe 2002; von Hippel 1987). R&D consortia with complementary knowledge bases result in higher spillover rates among participants and more dedicated resources allocation to learn from other members in the consortia (Sakakibara 2003).

The cost rationale seems to be especially relevant in capital- and R&D-intensive industries, where the cost from initiation until successful commercialization of a single R&D project often is beyond the reach of a single firm (Hagedoorn 2002). Clear definitions of responsibilities, objectives and tasks of the participating partners, individually and for the collaboration as a whole, contribute to the success of the R&D partnership (Davenport, Davies, and Grimes 1999; Mora-Valentin, Motoro-Sanchez, and Guerras-Martin 2004). Firms try to assess the cost and benefits by sharing knowledge in various ways. For instance, they may consider whether the receiver can use the shared knowledge in an unrestricted manner or the receiver will be restricted through agreements or similar instruments. Another consideration could be whether access to new knowledge are public (e.g., through journals, patents, conference presentations) or private (e.g., through e-mail, telephone, or face-to-face meetings) (Appleyard 1996).

From a resource-based point of view, access to external knowledge is a central motive for participation in R&D consortia: particularly risky and/or complex research will be conducted in collaboration, and preferably among partners holding complementary (knowledge) resources (Miotti and Sachwald 2003). Appropriability conditions in the specific industry may influence firms' general willingness to enter R&D collaborative projects and how these are governed. Firms in industries with high spillover may see an opportunity for internalizing R&D externalities by taking part in R&D collaborations (Sakakibara 2003). The heterogeneity in the participating firms' capabilities fits well with the increasing need in many industries for a multidisciplinary approach which spans the boundaries between various distinctive scientific and technological disciplines.

Yet another motive for participating in R&D partnerships is access to markets and to public research funds (Davenport, Davies, and Grimes 1999). From a strategy perspective, collaborative research is used to deal with high uncertainty about the relevance of the output for the participating firms (Hagedoorn 2002). Companies seeking knowledge advantages rather than cost advantages from their participation in R&D collaboration tend to invest dedicated resources (additionally to the resources allocated to activities in the R&D consortia) for accessing and capturing knowledge from other consortia members (Sakakibara 1997). Knowledge advantage seeking firms tend to find it easier to start R&D partnerships without predefined and clearly specified goals than firms with dominant cost motives (Sakakibara 1997).

8.3. Knowledge Sharing in R&D Alliances

The transformation of potential benefits into real ones relies on the ability to share knowledge across organizational boundaries[2] as well as internally in the organization.[3] In other words, knowledge sharing is an imperative for gaining advantages from R&D collaborations (Bouty 2000). While knowledge sharing is challenging to manage within a single firm, its management across firm boundaries poses even bigger challenges. We discuss these challenges at an organizational and individual level.

8.3.1. *Organizational Issues*

The nature of collaborative work is complex: two or more separate organizations, with different, often competing expectations, objectives, interests, and with their own way of doing things, face the challenge of coordination across their own boundaries. When making strategic-level decisions about collaborations, the collaborating firms not only need to build consensus internally but also with their partners' organizations (Sampson 2005). These two types of consensus are not necessarily aligned and this poses multiple challenges to the R&D alliance partners.

To start with, partner companies need to balance their desire to protect the outcome of their internal knowledge production with the ambition to access external knowledge through the collaboration (Oxley and Sampson 2004; Rappa and Debackere 1992). They also need to balance knowledge sharing and knowledge expropriation (Heiman and Nickerson 2004). Some studies emphasize the choice of appropriate governance structures and organizational forms as a mechanism to promote knowledge sharing while at the same time protecting against unintended knowledge

[2] We do not engage in a discussion of types of boundaries. For such a discussion, please refer to, amongst others, the *Long Range Planning* 2004 special issue (37) on boundaries and innovation.

[3] Cohen and Levinthal (1990: 131) observed that '(...) an organization's absorptive capacity does not simply depend on the organization's direct interface with the external environment. It also depends on transfers of knowledge across and within subunits.'

spillover in alliances (e.g., Kale, Singh, and Perlmutter 2000; Mowery, Oxley, and Silverman 1996; Pisano 1989; Sampson 2004). Other studies propose co-location of partners as a mean to facilitate knowledge sharing (von Hippel 1994), and reducing the alliance scope as a way to control the threat of knowledge leakage while engaging in knowledge sharing in R&D cooperation (Oxley and Sampson 2004). Yet other authors point out the role of trust as an effective means for coordinating economic exchange, especially in asymmetric R&D collaborative projects (e.g., Blomqvist et al. 2005; Carson et al. 2003; Duysters, Kok, and Vaandrager 1999; Forrest and Martin 1992; Jeffries and Reed 2000; Littler and Leverick 1995; Whipple and Frankel 2000). Recently, the use of legal clauses has been suggested as a governance mechanism in the initiation of knowledge sharing in R&D relationships (Faems, Janssenns, and van Looy 2007).

Since individuals on each side of the exchange are unlikely to possess highly overlapping knowledge, the likelihood of spanning different bodies of knowledge is high (Reagans and McEvily 2003). In this situation successful knowledge sharing is dependent on individual knowledge-sharing efforts and behavior (Reagans and McEvily 2003). Efficient knowledge sharing involves complex social processes that demand collaborative effort (Tsai 2002). Firms can increase their ability to capture knowledge in return for shared knowledge or in accessing knowledge from their partners in the R&D consortia by dedicating human resources to the task. By appointing people to be 'knowledge trackers' within specific strategically important areas, firms enhance their ability to internalize knowledge that employees acquire intentionally, or stumble across, in their knowledge-sharing activities (Appleyard 1996).

The difficulties of sharing idiosyncratic, context-bound knowledge between partners in R&D projects are eased in cases where the partners have overlapping knowledge bases (Hansen 2003), strong social relations (Tsai 2002), past collaboration-based relations (Heide and Miner 1992), information-processing abilities in terms of 'reading' their counterparts (Carson et al. 2003), and trust (Gambetta 1988). The more complex the knowledge, the more advantageous strong ties are for knowledge sharing (Hansen 1999). Additionally, the organizational benefits from participating in R&D alliances tend to be distributed asymmetrically. The partners may have different levels of absorptive capacity, and hence, different abilities for assessing, assimilating, and applying knowledge generated in the R&D network for their own ends. The partners may also differ in terms of their integrative competences: some firms are better than others at combining new knowledge with existing knowledge resources in a constructive and efficient way (Teece 2000). The firm's network position matters as well (Clarysse, Debackere, and Rappa 1996)—in R&D collaborations the more centrally located parties usually get an earlier warning of upcoming promising new results as compared to the more periphery-located partners.

There are also flip sides of knowledge sharing in R&D alliances. The knowledge shared among similarly minded units in well-established networks tends to be of narrower scope and variety (Hansen 2003; Uzzi 1997). Another potential negative effect of sharing knowledge across organizational boundaries is the possibility of increased competition among participants. Also, cross-organizational knowledge sharing is marked by different interpretations of the same idea, false starts, and disruptions (Zellmer-Bruhn 2003). As a consequence, sharing across boundaries is often resource demanding and dependent on iterations and patience. The cost of establishing and maintaining a network needs to be considered along with the positive effects of networks on knowledge sharing (Hansen 2003). Approximately 50 percent of all R&D alliances fail (Narula 2004) as they are marked by difficulties in exercising control, by complexity of joint activities, and by different preconditions and abilities to benefit from the interaction. All these (and other) potentially negative consequences of knowledge sharing increase the importance of examining specific mechanisms that can efficiently govern R&D workers' individual behavior, so that their firms can achieve the intended benefits from the collaboration activities.

8.3.2. *Individual Issues*

At a fundamental level collaboration takes place through people, not through institutions (Katz and Martin 1997). Much of the exchange of resources across organizational boundaries is based on decisions by individuals (Bouty 2000). Some authors suggest that the individual decision is based on a judgment of the value of the shared knowledge to the organization (von Hippel 1987). Basing the decision about sharing knowledge with an external person on a judgment of the economic interest of the company does, however, not account for the inherent difficulties of assessing the economic interest from using particular knowledge (Rosenberg 1990). Additionally, it does not consider the possibility of goal tensions/conflict between the company and the individual. Finally, the exchange often takes place in informal networks (Kreiner and Schultz

1993) where social norms and social relations play a major role in guiding the individual decision about whether to share knowledge or not (Bouty 2000).

Research analyzing knowledge sharing at the individual level has mostly concentrated on the antecedents of individual knowledge-sharing behavior (e.g., Ardichvili et al. 2003; Bartol and Srivastava 2002; Bock et al. 2005, 2006; Burgess 2005; Cabrera et al. 2006; Chiu et al. 2006; Hsu 2006; Husted and Michailova 2002; Kankanhalli et al. 2005; King and Marks, Jr, 2008; Ko et al. 2005; Kwok and Gao 2004, 2005–6; Lin 2007; Osterloh and Frey 2000; Quigley et al. 2007; Wasko and Faraj 2005). Most of these studies focus predominantly on what motivates people to share knowledge and what are the outcomes of knowledge sharing. At the same time, there is less of a nuanced examination of the mechanisms that govern individual knowledge-sharing behavior and how these mechanisms interact with one another.

In general, individuals tend to be aware that the decisions they make about sharing knowledge should not clash with the interests of their company. In many settings, confidentiality agreements are used in connection with the employment of individuals, and these agreements, naturally, intensify the individuals' attention to the issue. At the same time, the agreements are often too general to be able to address all types of confidentiality-related problems. The decision about sharing knowledge with members of other organizations relies on multiple criteria (Bouty 2000). The first one is the individual's judgment of the confidentiality of the knowledge: if he or she believes it will harm the interest of the firm, the knowledge will not be shared. The second criterion is the level of acquaintance and direct competition with the partner who requests the sharing of the knowledge. The third important consideration is that where an individual is ready to exchange certain knowledge with a partner, this does not necessarily mean he or she will do it. The final decision usually depends on whether the interaction is perceived as fair and/or profitable.

8.4. R&D Employees' Dual Allegiance and Its Governance

Employees' dual loyalty toward the company that employs them, on the one hand, and to the partner organization(s), on the other hand, has been studied in various contexts, for example union association (Gordon and Ladd 1990), expatriation (Black and Gregersen 1992; Gregersen and

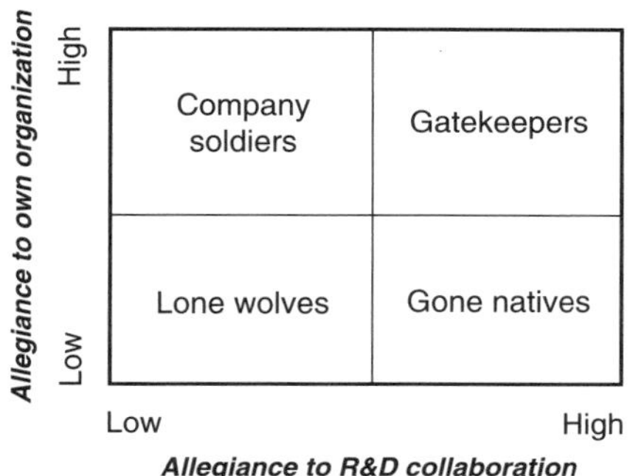

Figure 8.1. Types of R&D employee allegiance

Black 1992), and profession (Husted 1998, 2002). A core common issue is how employees deal with the objectives, norms, values, and regulations of both the focal organization and another organization, such as union, subsidiary, or, as in our case, an R&D collaboration.

The question of allegiance in our context is, in essence, to whom is the R&D employee most committed—the company or the R&D collaboration. Facing the challenge of 'serving two masters,' some R&D employees may deliberately or unconsciously end up directing an asymmetrically large level or their allegiance toward *either* the R&D collaboration *or* their company. Both types of imbalance might have significant negative impact on the company's ability to manage strategically its participation in the R&D partnership. If R&D employees feel more loyal toward the collaboration, they would be inclined to share more (intensively) knowledge than would probably be in the company's best interest. In contrast, if R&D employees fail to engage in the R&D collaboration in a constructive manner, their company will be prevented from accessing the benefits the collaboration was intended to create access to. In Figure 8.1, we present a matrix positioning R&D employees along two dimensions: their allegiance to their own firm and to the R&D collaboration. Along these dimensions we identify four types of R&D employees which we label respectively 'lone wolves,' 'company soldiers,' 'gone native,' and 'gatekeepers.'

8.4.1. *Lone Wolves*

Especially in knowledge-intensive professions one finds a relatively large number of individuals who have a low level of genuine commitment to both the company employing them and the R&D project they take part in. They perceive both their company employment and their participation in R&D collaborations as enablers of their own individual career and their performance in the wider professional community to which they belong. Their personal objectives might be different from those of their firm and the collaboration and in such cases they are focused on their own interests and reputation in the broader professional circles.

As compared to the other three types of R&D individual collaborators, *Lone Wolves* are more likely to reject requests for knowledge sharing. Rejected requests for knowledge sharing are rather common in some disciplines. A large survey among geneticists showed that in a period of three years 47 percent of geneticists who made a request for additional knowledge and input regarding a published research result were rejected (Campbell et al. 2002). The withheld information concerned additional information about laboratory techniques, findings not included, and biomaterial mentioned in the publication (Campbell et al. 2002). It is not surprising that especially very productive and more senior people report that they have hidden knowledge from their colleagues. They do so for several reasons. Their higher performance level means they are more exposed to frequent requests which can really pose a burden. Another reason is the effort involved in producing the requested knowledge (Husted and Michailova 2002), and resistance toward providing this in an easily-used form to others. In order to protect commercial interests it is a rather widespread phenomenon to delay academic publication until the relevant property rights are secured. Around one out of five scientists in life science delay publication of research results for more than six months primarily to protect commercial interests (Blumenthal et al. 1997).

Campbell et al. (2002) found that as a consequence of not receiving the knowledge then requested, 28 percent of the rejected scientists reported that they had failed to replicate the published result. This also had a significant impact on the research agendas of the scientist making the request, since approximately 20 percent of the rejected scientists reported they were forced to change, or even abandon, an otherwise promising line of research as a result of the unwillingness of another researcher to share additional knowledge about published research results. In more than 1/4 of the incidents studied, the refusal to respond to a request to share information, research material, or data resulted in the termination of the ongoing collaboration, and a refusal to share knowledge in the future (Campbell et al. 2002).

8.4.2. *Company Soldiers*

R&D workers with a strong sense of loyalty primarily to their own firm often find it difficult, and even disturbing, to engage in external R&D collaborations. Even more so if the collaboration involves cross-institutional and multidisciplinary work. When these individuals participate in R&D alliances, they are, more than others, inclined to be particularly careful not to hurt their company's interest by sharing too much knowledge with external participants. Also, being strongly attached to their own organization, *Company Soldiers* might not be able to see exciting new opportunities in the collaboration, many of which tend to emerge by chance rather than by design. Their careful calculations about how new ideas and their results can affect their company might prevent them from engaging in exploration and effective knowledge sharing with the external partners in the R&D alliance. Ironically, in this way *Company Soldiers* may act against their organization's interest.

8.4.3. *Gone Natives*

These R&D employees tend to be fully absorbed into the R&D collaboration and tend to prioritize the objectives of the collaboration above the interests and the objectives of their firm. They engage in too extensive knowledge sharing, and invest time and effort in activities which might further the objective of the collaboration at the cost of achieving the objectives of the firm. Due to their dominant allegiance to the collaboration, *Gone Natives* are most exposed to the risk of unintended knowledge sharing with collaboration partners. In other words, their company would associate them with elevated leakage concerns. These concerns are intensified in the case of the collaborators being direct competitors because the hazards of knowledge sharing are most salient in such a context (Oxley and Sampson 2004). Foreign-based researchers are more inclined to 'go native' due to the lack of physical proximity with their own organizations. Having their company out of sight is also likely to result in having it out of mind.

8.4.4. *Gatekeepers*

The behavior of knowledge workers tends to be strategic. They use the credibility they gain through dissemination of results and other similar sources to recruit and organize new allies in the pursuit of personal scientific objectives (Latour and Woolgar 1988). It is not unusual that researchers are strategically selective about what data or/and results to share with other researchers both inside and outside the organization as well as when to share them (Eisenberg 1987). One aspect of this strategic behavior is that researchers do not have any incentive to share more knowledge in one publication than needed in order to get the result published in the desired journal. Researchers can also hold back results and information if they believe that this will put them in a better position for winning the next scientific race they take part in. Finally, access to resources also plays a role here. By holding back crucial information, for example, about research methods and results individual researchers and research groups may believe that they have a competitive advantage in the competition for research resources. As observed by Stephan (1996: 1208), in many instances agents can have their cake and eat it too, selectively publishing research findings while monopolizing other elements with the hope of realizing future returns.

The four types of allegiance pose different challenges to knowledge governance. Even if *Lone Wolves* are consistently high performing and excell in their individual careers, their low level of allegiance to both the company and the collaboration tends to lessen the potential influence the firm has on them. Consequently, governance of strategic knowledge sharing on behalf of the company will also be limited in terms of the effects it will have on the individual employee. In this case objectives and priorities are often set by the professional community at large through the definition of which problems are more important than others, which contributions are more valuable than others, etc. Decisions regarding which knowledge to share with whom and when would be directed by individual self-interest and/or broader professional norms, rather than by the firm's strategic interests.

In the case of *Company Soldiers*, appropriate governance mechanisms will be those that provide adequate instruments for protecting the interests of the firm. Such governance mechanisms may include providing R&D workers with legal counseling and easy-to-use standardized nondisclosure agreements or license agreements. Otherwise, *Company Soldiers* will tend to choose a low-transaction cost mode of sharing knowledge.

R&D workers who conform with the pattern of *Gone Natives* invite a different way of governing their knowledge-sharing behavior. Because they tend to identify strongly with the collaboration at the cost of subscribing to the norms and values of their own organization, a company mentor who would act as an anchor to keep the R&D participant attached to the company would be one possible efficient mechanism. Other possible mechanisms would be intensified communication channels with the company and legal clauses and contracts. Also, it would be worth considering engaging *Gone Natives* in alliances of a more narrow scope and shorter time frame. Finally, since they are, like *Lone Wolves*, more likely to leave the company, resocialization after the R&D project is finalized would be a mechanism to consider.

As compared to the other categories, *Gatekeepers'* dual focus makes them least challenging in terms of governing their knowledge-sharing behavior. This is because they are, as a rule, more capable of managing efficiently the role conflicts and role ambiguity inherently associated with dual allegiance. And yet, there can be challenges posed by this category when role conflicts and role ambiguity are beyond the usually tolerable level. Stricter coordination between the firm and the collaboration and more explicit communication related to this coordination would be appropriate mechanisms in this context.

Prior research has identified several organizational mechanisms to deal with the issue of balancing knowledge sharing and knowledge leakage in collaborations. Among those mechanisms are choosing an appropriate governance structure (e.g., Kale, Singh, and Perlmutter 2000; Mowery, Oxley, and Silverman 1996; Oxley 1997; Pisano 1989; Sampson 2004), nurturing trust between partners (e.g., Bailey et al. 1998; Bruce et al. 1995; Carson et al. 2003; Duysters, Kok, and Vaandrager 1999; Forrest and Martin 1992; Jeffries and Reed 2000; Littler and Leverick 1995; Whipple- and Frankel 2000), and applying legal clauses (Faems, Janssenns, and van Looy 2007). However, none of these studies have examined in detail the individual knowledge-sharing behavior as being positioned between these workers' dual allegiance on the one hand and the firm-level outcomes from the R&D partnership. We employ socialization theory to investigate exactly this.

8.5. Governance of Knowledge-Sharing Behavior in R&D Collaborations: Socialization Tactics

We now unfold our central argument, namely, that socialization tactics can be employed as an efficient mechanism to govern R&D workers' dual allegiance. We start by briefly outlining the key arguments for the value of socialization of R&D workers, as they are proposed in the existing literature.

8.5.1. *The Importance of Socialization of R&D Workers*

Socialization is a process through which newcomers learn the appropriate behaviors to become effective members (Louis 1980). It focuses on how new members learn the values, norms, beliefs, and behaviors of societies, organizations, or groups (Schein 1988). Consequently, an important component of the socialization process is learning what is 'customary and desirable' (Van Maanen and Schein 1979: 212) in the new environment, as well as what is not. The individual is faced with confusing environmental cues that must be interpreted in order to make sense of the surroundings, so he or she must engage in a process of social learning to determine the expectations of others. In the literature, the six institutionalized socialization tactics (collective < = > individual, formal < = > nonformal, sequential < = > random, fixed < = > variable, serial < = > disjunctive, investiture < = > divestiture) have been examined to study, among others, information technology professionals' role adjustment and organizational attachment variables (King et al. 2005), the success of expatriates (Lueke and Svyantek 2000), and the effectiveness of organizational socialization (Anakwe and Greenhaus 1999). The common element in those contexts is the need for adjustment to a new environment, which requires substantial social learning.

Most collaborations begin through informal contact and exchange of information (Kreiner and Schultz 1993), and these are used to identify the potential of collaboration and to establish trust. Trust is an important ingredient in interfirm collaboration in general (McEvily et al. 2003), and in R&D collaborations in particular (Davenport, Davies, and Grimes 1999; Gulati and Singh 1998). An integrative aspect of organizational trust is benevolence, that is, the extent to which one partner believes that the other part will not deliberately behave in a way that harms the interest of or otherwise damage the first part even if conditions change in unanticipated directions (Zaheer et al. 1998).

Interfirm partnering is to some extent related to the firm's past experience in partnering and collaboration. More experienced firms tend to be better at judging with whom they should collaborate (Dyer and Singh 1998; Powell et al. 1996). They also appear to be more attractive to others, partly due to the expectation that they are able to shape and design the partnership in a way that increases the mutual benefits (Lorenzoni and Lipparini 1999). Their attractiveness tends to attract more desirable partners (Powell et al. 1997).

An increasing share of the more critical areas of R&D are performed outside the focal company's home country (Birkinshaw 2002). Globalization of business requires the management of geographically and culturally dispersed knowledge repositories and processes in an effective manner (Simonin 1999). By collaborating internationally, firms get access to country-specific advantages through their foreign partners' embeddedness in their national innovation systems (Miotti and Sachwald 2003). It seems that technological access counts as much as, or more than, market access in deciding with whom to collaborate (Miotti and Sachwald 2003).

In strong, well-established networks, organizational as well as individual behavior are guided by cooperative norms that define what is considered appropriate and inappropriate behavior. Individuals are more willing to put a serious effort into sharing knowledge with persons with whom they have a close personal relationship (Reagans and McEvily 2003). Individuals share knowledge when this is considered a shared value in the network, even if it is not in their short-term interest to do so (Uzzi 1997). Socially connected people tend to focus more on maintaining their social relation by sharing the knowledge they have in common rather than sharing knowledge they uniquely possess (Thomas-Hunt, Ogden, and Neale 2003). People surrounded by a diverse network develop a stronger ability to communicate their knowledge in different ways and are, as a consequence, better at sharing their knowledge (Reagans and McEvily 2003).

8.5.2. *Socialization Tactics as a Governance Mechanism*

The learning processes associated with socialization can be similarly extended to R&D collaborations to explain the adjustment that occurs upon entering into R&D collaborative ties (Black, Mendenhall, and Oddou 1991). Entering an R&D collaboration, formal or informal, requires individual adjustment to a new organizational context, with new members coming together and working on a shared project. Immersion in an unfamiliar environment, for example meeting new people, working on the same project with members from other organizations or even direct competitors, involves uncertainty concerning the role the individual is expected to play (Black, Mendenhall, and Oddou 1991). Hence, the individuals who are involved must engage in a process of social learning to

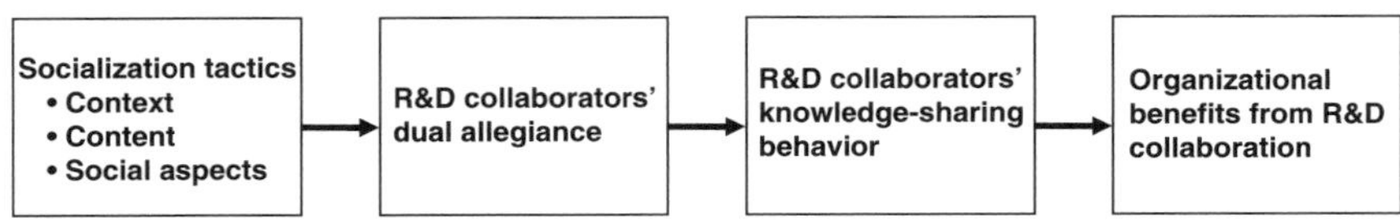

Figure 8.2. Research model

determine the expectations of both their own organization and the R&D collaboration.

Knowledge-sharing behavior is highly embedded in the socialization process. The way individuals interact and share knowledge with each other varies when they engage in different socialization contexts, deal with different socialization content, and establish a different sense of identity and belonging in the new setting. We argue that socialization tactics influences R&D employees' dual allegiance, which, in turn, has an impact on their individual knowledge-sharing behavior, and consequently on firm-level outcomes. We develop propositions which focus on the conditions under which the knowledge-sharing behavior of individuals will be aligned with their dual allegiance. We are not concerned with the performance of the R&D collaboration, instead we focus on what the company can do in order to deal with the dual allegiance of its employees who participate in the collaboration so that the company objectives are achieved. We explicate these relationships in the research model in Figure 8.2.

We have argued that *Gatekeepers* pose least challenges in terms of governance of their knowledge-sharing behavior. We therefore focus on the other three types: *Lone Wolves*, *Company Soldiers*, and *Gone Natives*. We develop our core ideas in more detail below, and propose how context, content, and social aspects of socialization will influence R&D collaborators' dual allegiance and their individual knowledge-sharing behavior.

8.6. Context of Knowledge Sharing in R&D Collaborations

The context of the socialization process can affect the learning outcomes of individuals (Jones 1986; Van Maanen and Schein 1979). Whether the socialization experience occurs in a collective or individual and in a formal or nonformal context will influence the role orientation of organizational entrants. A collective socialization tactic is one in which all organizational entrants face common learning experiences designed to produce standardized responses to situations (Jones 1986). In contrast, an individual context is one in which each entrant faces unique experiences, allowing the individual to develop his or her own unique definitions and responses. A formal context is one in which the individual receives information and training about his or her role while being kept separate from other organizational members (Jones 1986; Van Maanen and Schein 1979). A nonformal context, in which the individual enters the new environment immediately, provides newcomers with great latitude to make differentiated responses, and innovative responses are a likely result (Jones 1986).

When considering the collective < = > individual context of knowledge sharing in R&D collaborations, it is the individuals themselves who could correctly determine how they are supposed to respond to situations and exchange knowledge with others, according to their own unique knowledge stock and definitions of what complementary knowledge other members might possess from personal interaction. An individual context which offers new entrants opportunities to have unique experiences with each other, for example through coffee talk or after-hours socialization events, will certainly provide them sufficient room to personalize the collaborative ties, which could make the later actual R&D collaboration on specific projects functional. On the contrary, a collective context, which makes all new members face common learning experience regardless of their personal knowledge stock and learning needs, will be likely to make the acquaintance of members in terms of personality, technological background, potential to contribute knowledge etc. stop at the surface level instead. Without a deep understanding of each other's knowledge background and strengths and weaknesses, and in what way the exchange and initialization of knowledge will work out, the corporate benefits from the participation in the R&D collaboration will be neutralized despite the value of shared knowledge.

We relate the formal < = > nonformal context distinction to the issue of formal contracting and informal cooperation between participating organizations. However, the context of sharing knowledge does not necessarily correspond to the organizational form of R&D collaborations. Formal arrangements, such as introducing and transferring new members, organizing welcome seminars, handing out information packs, explaining the collaboration objectives, and conducting regular meetings may be all present in an informal collaboration, while in formal R&D collaborations new members may be immediately brought onto the functional task and left to pick everything up on their own. In relation to the corporate benefits of the R&D collaboration that result from knowledge-sharing behavior, a formal context seems to be more fertile than a nonformal one. Although a nonformal context may stimulate one's innovative ideas after personal probing into the problems and situations (Jones 1986), it may also divert the individual's attention and focus from the primary objective of her or his organization's participation in the collaboration. For example, knowledge that might be supposed to be shared and utilized for a particular new product launch might actually not be shared and utilized during the collaboration, due to which the losses may occur associated with efforts of other functional areas like, for instance, marketing research. By contrast, a formal context of knowledge sharing in R&D collaborations could clearly bring all relevant people and the knowledge they possess together to focus on a desirable, achievable, and purposeful aim and fulfill the primary objective of the collaboration. It is also very likely that some innovative ideas are generated as by-products during the process—they are a bonus of R&D collaboration rather than an expense. On the basis of the above observations we propose the following:

- *Proposition 1a: Socialization which takes place in a collective and nonformal context is optimal for governing Lone Wolves' dual allegiance and, consequently, their individual knowledge-sharing behaviors.*
- *Proposition 1b: Socialization which takes place in an individual and formal context is optimal for governing Gone Natives' dual allegiance and, consequently, their individual knowledge-sharing behaviors.*
- *Proposition 1c: Socialization which takes place in an individual and nonformal context is optimal for governing Company Soldiers' dual allegiance and, consequently, their individual knowledge-sharing behaviors.*

8.7. Content of Knowledge Sharing in R&D Collaborations

The socialization content concerns the information given to organizational newcomers and determines the degree of ambiguity and task conflict they perceive (McMillan and Lopez 2001). At the institutional end of the continuum are sequential and fixed socialization tactics, where organizational entrants are provided with information on the order and timing of the socialization process (Griffin, Colella, and Goparaju 2000) or, more broadly, reward systems and career advancement in the organization (McMillan and Lopez 2001). Random and variable tactics reside at the individualized end of the continuum and involve no pre-set events or timings (Griffin, Colella, and Goparaju 2000; McMillan and Lopez 2001). Thus, institutionalized content provides individuals with greater certainty about the socialization process and the work setting.

The content of knowledge sharing in R&D collaborations will have different implications for the organizational benefits of the collaboration. For example, sequential and fixed tactics give new entrants necessary information in a systematic manner, which helps them establish a relatively comprehensive overview of what is expected to happen and be achieved in the collaboration in what period of time. This gives individuals the sense of a high degree of control and they engage in knowledge sharing in a purposeful way as the socialization process proceeds through different stages. Having the necessary information on the socialization process, on the work setting, and on the expected outcome of the collaboration, individuals can better gauge what knowledge he or she may have to share, what knowledge needs to be acquired from others, and what he or she and her or his organization could benefit from the sharing process, and so forth. This will help achieve the objective of the focal organization.

In contrast, if the socialization tactics is random and variable, it would be difficult for individuals to determine what is going to take place and what is expected as time goes on. They will also be uncertain about what knowledge to share with collaborators and what knowledge to seek from them in the socialization process. This is likely to result in a high level of ambiguity: it will be hard to predict the expectations of other members and of the organization if there is no concern with sequence of events and timing. All in all, there is too much uncertainty associated with random and variable tactics. Consequently, the R&D collaboration is not well prepared due to the ambiguous perceptions of the individuals, and the benefits from it will also be reduced. This logic leads to the following proposition:

- *Proposition 2a: Socialization which involves sequential and fixed content is optimal for governing Lone Wolves' and Gone Natives' dual allegiance and, consequently, their individual knowledge-sharing behaviors.*
- *Proposition 2b: Socialization which involves either random and fixed or sequential and variable content is optimal for governing Company Soldiers' dual allegiance and, consequently, their individual knowledge-sharing behaviors.*

8.8. Social Aspects of Knowledge Sharing in R&D Collaborations

The social (interpersonal) aspects are a third major element of the socialization environment for learning and comprise serial versus disjunctive tactics and investiture versus divestiture tactics (Van Maanen and Schein 1979). Serial and investiture tactics have been found to significantly increase the newcomer's perception of fit with the organization (Cable and Parsons 2001). In a serial experience, the individual is helped through the socialization process by an experienced organizational member acting as a mentor or role model (Griffin, Colella, and Goparaju 2000). The presence of a supportive mentor will lead to individuals accepting the definitions offered by the mentor. Observation and interaction with coworkers and supervisors is a highly important learning source for newcomers in terms of learning about their new roles, tasks, work groups, and organizations (Ostroff and Kozlowski 1992). Absorptive capacity at an organizational unit level has been found to be significantly related to serial socialization tactics (Jansen et al. 2005). Experienced colleagues play the most prominent role in predicting effective socialization as they represent an important source of information regarding job knowledge, the group norms, the organizational culture, and role expectations (Anakwe and Greenhaus 1999). Investiture reinforces the identity of the newcomer (Griffin, Colella, and Goparaju 2000) and focuses on providing social support (McMillan and Lopez 2001). In contrast, disjunctive tactics means organizational entrants are left to form their own opinions and views of the organization in the absence of a mentor or role model (McMillan and Lopez 2001). Divestiture encourages the individual to adopt the organizational identity over self-identity (Griffin, Colella, and Goparaju 2000).

The social aspects of socialization can be extended to the context of R&D collaborations. Serial and investiture tactics in this case will most likely be associated with the repeated collaborations between participating organizations. In repeated collaborations there is likely to be an experienced member, who could guide new members from the same organization on the subsequent collaboration in terms of getting to know other new members, adapting to the new environment quickly, providing existing information about the other party's background, and way of doing things, and, most importantly, about knowledge sharing issues in the particular R&D collaboration. Besides, the experienced coworkers from the other party could also help with general background information, even if it might not be that specific and in the interest of the organization which the new member comes from. Having a supportive mentor who can help with various matters, new members could conveniently continue the virtuous cycle of previous collaborations and achieve desirable performance. Obviously, disjunctive tactics without a role model would make new members more likely to meet with difficulties, discomfort, and uncertainty when entering a new collaboration. This will reduce the organizational benefits from eventual knowledge sharing.

A similar pattern holds true for the investiture < = > divestiture aspect. Investiture tactics that reinforce the identity of newcomers over that of the organization are beneficial for the newcomer establishing a clear mission for the R&D collaboration. More specifically, emphasizing the individual's own identity is about personalizing the collaborative ties, being clear about in whose interest he or she is working, what knowledge he or she must (not) share with others, and what knowledge needs to be acquired, for the good of her or his own knowledge gains, her or his own organization, and the R&D collaboration. In other words, investiture tactics provides a good way for individuals to reconcile and mediate the interest of all parties involved in the collaboration, which would help achieve optimal knowledge sharing and the organizational benefits from the R&D collaboration. The divestiture tactics, in contrast, encourages newcomers to adopt the R&D alliance identity over their self-identity and their organizational identity, and so, it may reduce the individuals' intrinsic motivation to perform. This may also produce inconsistency of making efforts in knowledge sharing as the individuals seem to be tied up too closely with the R&D collaboration so that they cannot make personal adaptation when needed for the good of their company. Thus, we propose the following:

- *Proposition 3a: Socialization which involves serial and investiture social aspects is optimal for governing Lone Wolves' dual allegiance and, consequently, their individual knowledge-sharing behaviors.*
- *Proposition 3b: Socialization which involves serial and investiture social aspects is optimal for governing Gone Natives' dual allegiance and, consequently, their individual knowledge-sharing behaviors.*
- *Proposition 3c: Socialization which involves disjunctive and investiture social aspects is optimal for governing Company Soldiers' dual allegiance and, consequently, their individual knowledge-sharing behaviors.*

We summarize the theoretical propositions in Table 8.1.

Table 8.1. Dual allegiance and socialization

Dual allegiance Type	Socialization tactics Context	Content	Social aspects
Lone Wolves	Collective and nonformal	Sequential and fixed	Serial and investiture
Gone Native	Individual and formal		Serial and divestiture
Company Soldiers	Individual and nonformal	Random and fixed or Sequential and variable	Disjunctive and investiture

8.9. Conclusion, Implications, and Limitations

In this chapter, we have focused on socialization tactics as a mechanism that can be used to govern R&D workers' dual allegiance and, through this, their knowledge-sharing behavior so that the company can harvest the benefits from participating in a R&D collaboration. Our focus on socialization tactics is sensible because R&D workers usually go through intensive socialization when they engage in interfirm collaborations on behalf of their organization. We argued that socialization tactics are a desirable governance mechanism because it is cost-effective, and hence, an attractive alternative to more resource-demanding governance mechanisms.

We also developed a classification of four distinct types of R&D individual collaborators' dual allegiance. We argued that *Lone Wolves, Gone Natives, Company Soldiers*, and *Gatekeepers* differ on several dimensions, and hence, require different governance. We proposed that these different types of allegiance predispose the employment of different context, content, and social aspects of socialization.

The actions we suggest are observable and controllable and hence, relatively easy to implement in order to accomplish the organizational goals and how these can be achieved through influencing individual knowledge-sharing behavior. It is not extremely demanding to design a socialization context which, under particular circumstances, will be more fertile than others. Socialization contexts can be either individual or collective and either formal or nonformal and a combination of these dichotomies. Obviously, different combinations will predispose different ways for individuals to share knowledge. Knowing that the content of socialization tactics stretches on a continuum between random and sequential and between variable and fixed allows managers to design a combination which will be more appropriate in relation to achieving the desired individual organizational behavior. Finally, there is a variety of social aspects mangers can choose from, from serial to disjunctive and from investiture to divestiture. Knowing their specificity is a necessary condition for executives to make an informed decision about when to design what social aspects so that the individual shares knowledge in an aligned way with the organizational goals.

From the standpoint of future research, our study is, to a great extent, a response to the call to investigate questions of governance choice (Carson et al. 2003). Our chapter is an important step in this regard and contributes to the growing literature on knowledge governance. A promising avenue for future research is to analyze how socialization tactics as a particular knowledge governance mechanism interacts with other possible mechanisms. For instance, are socialization tactics a substitute for formalized contracts which attempt to specify in detail issues related to R&D employees' participation in collaborations? Or are socialization tactics a mechanism that is optimally employed along with written contracts? Along the same line, and as outlined by Heiman and Nickerson (2001), it is important to examine which governance alternatives become more attractive under what conditions and what efforts are invested in order to initiate and apply a particular mechanism. For instance, are there any particular circumstances under which socialization tactics are more attractive than other governance mechanisms?

The discussion above suggests that further work is necessary to link the application of socialization tactics with certain organizational features. For example, do socialization efforts and socialization knowledge benefit all firms equally, or more so those firms that engage in R&D collaborations more frequently? Additionally, one might expect that socialization would play a more important role for firms involved in complex R&D alliances as compared to more simple ones.

The ramifications of our study for management practice are that executives should try to eliminate undesirable spillover and/or leakage of valuable knowledge while at the same time ensuring open knowledge sharing to achieve the goals of the collaboration. The typology of R&D collaborators we have developed can be used by managers to decide whom to employ in what collaboration depending on the desired benefits from these collaborations. If the nature of a collaboration invites unintended knowledge sharing, it would be advisable to opt for *Company Soldiers*. If, in contrast, the firm can foresee that it will benefit from intensive knowledge sharing in the alliance, *Gone Natives* will be more suitable to be employed to achieve this objective.

Companies should keep a careful eye on the *Gone Natives* category. Besides the specificities of this pattern already discussed, these are the R&D employees who might have difficulties transferring back to the company the new knowledge they have acquired in the R&D project, and are most likely to leave the company once the R&D project with which they have identified strongly is finalized. From that perspective, the company loses potentially relevant knowledge in the acquisition of which it has invested by its very participation in the R&D project. Socialization tactics can be highly efficient in governing the behavior of these employees.

Often companies participate in R&D alliances through teams of knowledge workers rather than single individuals. Depending on the company objectives, the company managers are advised to opt for teams that involve employees belonging to different patterns of dual allegiance. It would not be advisable, for instance, to have a team consisting of only *Gone Natives* or of only *Company Soldiers*. Instead, a more balanced team constitution should be considered which does not exclude the option of a dominant pattern but is not exclusive to that pattern.

Although we have specifically focused on R&D collaborations, our arguments apply to other types of knowledge-intensive interfirm ties between independent firms. While our propositions apply to 'pure' R&D collaborations, they also seem to be important to alliances that encompass broader activities. This is so because the extent of knowledge sharing rises when the collaboration scope is broader (Reuer, Zollo, and Singh 2002).

There are some important limitations in our study. First, we have not discussed the issue of the location of R&D collaborators. R&D collaboration participants would be governed differently depending on whether they are located at their organization or at the R&D collaboration site. It will be relatively easier for company executives to monitor and govern the individual employees' behavior and their socialization into new settings (e.g., the R&D collaboration) if the individuals can be directly observed and if face-to-face interaction within the company can frequently take place.

Another limitation of our study is the lack of specification about whether the R&D collaboration is relatively symmetric (in terms of the size of the collaborating firms) or heavily asymmetric. Large firms will be able to invest more resources in designing the appropriate socialization tactics whereas smaller firms might not have the designated resources and knowledge in relation to activating this mechanism. On the other hand, a small firm might invest a more serious effort into ensuring that both it gains the intended benefits and the collaboration works well simply because it is in a more vulnerable position—big firms will be more able to identify alternative partners to collaborate with.

References

Anakwe, U. P. and J. H. Greenhaus. 1999. 'Effective Socialization of Employees: Socialization Content Perspective,' *Journal of Managerial Issues* 11(3): 315–29.

Appleyard, M. M. 1996. 'How Does Knowledge Flow? Interfirm Patterns in the Semiconductor Industry,' *Strategic Management Journal* 17: 137–54.

Birkinshaw, J. 2002. 'Managing Internal R&D Networks in Global Firms—What Sort of Knowledge Is Involved?,' *Long Range Planning* 35: 245–67.

Black, J. S., M. Mendenhall, and G. Oddou. 1991. 'Toward a Comprehensive Model of International Adjustment: An Integration of Multiple Theoretical Perspectives,' *Academy of Management Review* 16(2): 291–317.

Black, S. J. and H. B. Gregersen. 1992. 'Serving Two Masters: Managing the Dual Allegiance of Expatriate Employees,' *Sloan Management Review* 33(4): 61–71.

Blomqvist, K., P. Hurmelinna, and R. Seppänen. 2005. 'Playing the Collaboration Game Right—Balancing Trust and Contracting,' *Technovation* 25: 497–504.

Blumenthal, D., E. C. Campbell, M. S. Anderson, et al. 1997. 'Withholding Research Results in Academic Life Science,' *JAMA* 277(15): 1224–8.

Bouty, I. 2000. 'Interpersonal and Interaction Influences on Informal Resource Exchange between R&D Researchers across Organizational Boundaries,' *Academy of Management Journal* 43(1): 50–65.

Cable, D. M. and C. K. Parsons. 2001. 'Socialization Tactics and Person-Organization Fit,' *Personnel Psychology* 54(1): 1–23.

Carson, S. J., A. Madhok, R. Varman, et al. 2003. 'Information Processing Moderators of the Effectiveness of Trust-Based Governance in Interfirm R&D Collaboration,' *Organization Science* 14(1): 45–56.

Chesbrough, H. 2003*a*. 'The Era of Open Innovation,' *Sloan Management Review* Summer: 35–41.

—— 2003*b*. *Open Innovation*. Massachusetts, Cambridge: Harvard University Press.

Clarysse, B., K. Debackere, and M. A. Rappa. 1996. 'Modeling the Persistence of Organizations in an Emerging Field: The Case of Hepatitis C,' *Research Policy* 25(5): 671–87.

Cohen, W. M. and D. A. Levinthal. 1990. 'Absorptive Capacity: A New Perspective on Learning and Innovation,' *Administrative Science Quarterly* 35(1): 128–52.

Cowan, R., N. Jonard and J. B. Zimmermann. 2006. 'Evolving Networks of Inventors,' *Journal of Evolutionary Economics* 16(1–2): 155–76.

Davenport, S., J. Davies, and C. Grimes. 1999. 'Collaborative Research Programmes: Building Trust from Difference,' *Technovation* 19: 31–40.

Duysters, G., G. Kok, and M. Vaandrager. 1999. 'Crafting Successful Strategic Partnerships,' *R&D Management* 29: 343–51.

Dyer, J. H. and H. Singh. 1998. 'The Relational View: Cooperative Strategy and Sources of Interorganizational Competitive Advantage,' *Academy of Management Review* 23: 660–79.

Faems, D., M. Janssenns, and B. van Looy. 2007. 'The Initiation and Evolution of Interfirm Knowledge Transfer in R&D Relationships,' *Organization Studies* 28(11): 1669–728.

Feller, J., A. Farhankangas and R. Smeds. 2006. 'Process Learning in Alliances Developing Radical versus Incremental Innovations: Evidence from the Telecommunications Industry,' *Knowledge and Process Management* 13(3): 175–91.

Fleming, L. and O. Sorenson. 2004. 'Science as a Map in Technological Search,' *Strategic Management Journal* 25(8): 909–28.

Gambetta, D. 1988. 'Can We Trust Trust?,' in D. Gambetta (ed.) *Trust: Making and Breaking of Cooperative Relations*. New York: Basil Blackwell.

Gordon, M. E. and R. T. Ladd. 1990. 'Dual Allegiance: Renewal, Reconsideration, and Recantation,' *Personnel Psychology* 43(1): 37–69.

Granstrand, O., P. Patel and K. Pavitt. 1997. 'Multi-Technology Corporations: Why They Have "Distributed" Rather than "Distinctive Core" Competencies,' *California Management Review* 39(4): 8–25.

Gregersen, H. B. and J. S. Black. 1992. 'Antecedents to Dual Commitment during International Assignments,' *Academy of Management Journal* 35: 65–90.

Griffin, A. E. C., A. Colella, and S. Goparaju. 2000. 'Newcomer and Organizational Socialization Tactics: An Interactionist Perspective,' *Human Resource Management Review* 10(4): 453–74.

Hagedoorn, J. 2002. 'Interfirm R&D Partnerships: An Overview of Major Trends and Patterns since 1960,' *Research Policy* 31: 477–92.

Hansen, M. T. 1999. 'The Search-Transfer Problem: The Role of Weak Ties in Sharing Knowledge across Organizational Sub-Units,' *Administrative Science Quarterly* 44: 82–111.

——2003. 'Knowledge Networks: Explaining Effective Knowledge Sharing in Multiunit Companies,' *Organization Science* 13(3): 232–48.

Harrigan, K. R. 1988. 'Joint Ventures and Competitive Strategy,' *Strategic Management Journal* 9: 141–58.

Heide, J. B. and A. S. Miner. 1992. 'The Shadow of the Future: Effects of Anticipated Interaction and Frequency of Contact on Buyer-Seller Cooperation,' *Academy of Management Journal* 35(2): 265–91.

Heiman, B. and J. A. Nickerson. 2001. 'Towards Reconciling Transaction Cost Economics and the Knowledge Based View of the Firm: The Context of Interfirm Collaborations,' *Working Paper*, Missouri, St; Lous, Washington University, Olin School of Business.

————2004. 'Empirical Evidence Regarding the Tension between Knowledge Sharing and Knowledge Expropriation in Collaborations,' *Managerial and Decisions Economics* 25: 401–20.

Huber, G. P. 1991. 'Organizational Learning: The Contributing Processes and the Literature,' *Organization Science* 2: 88–115.

Husted, K. 1998. PhD dissertation, Copenhagen Business School.

——2002. 'Industrial Researchers as Decision Makers: Balancing Autonomy and Control,' *Journal for Science and Technology Studies* 15(1): 33–53.

——and S. Michailova. 2002. 'Diagnosing and Fighting Knowledge Sharing Hostility,' *Organizational Dynamics* 31(1): 60–73.

Jones, G. 1986. 'Socialization Tactics, Self Efficacy, and Newcomer's Adjustments to Organizations,' *Academy of Management Journal* 29(2): 262–79.

Kale, P., H. Singh, and H. Perlmutter. 2000. 'Learning and Protection of Proprietary Assets in Strategic Alliances: Building Relational Capital,' *Strategic Management Journal* 21: 217–37.

Khanna, T., R. Gulati, and N. Nohria. 1998. 'The Dynamics of Learning Alliances: Competition, Cooperation, and Relative Scope,' *Strategic Management Journal* 19: 193–210.

Kreiner, K. and M. Schultz. 1993. 'Informal Collaboration in R&D—The Formation of Networks Across Organizations,' *Organization Studies* 14(2): 189–209.

Lane, P. J. and M. Lubatkin. 1998. 'Relative Absorptive Capacity and Interorganizational Learning,' *Strategic Management Journal* 19: 461–77.

Larysse, B., K. Debackere, and M. A. Rappa. 1996. 'Modeling the Persistence of Organizations in an Emerging Field: The Case of Hepatitis C,' *Research Policy* 25(5): 671–88.

Louis, M. R. 1980. 'Surprise and Sense Making: What Newcomers Experience in Entering Unfamiliar Organizational Settings,' *Administrative Science Quarterly* 25: 226–51.

Lueke, S. B. and D. J. Svyantek. 2000. 'Organizational Socialization in the Host Country: The Missing Link in Reducing Expatriate Turnover,' *International Journal of Organizational Analysis* 8(4): 380–400.

McMillan, A. and T. B. Lopez. 2001. 'Socialization and Acculturation: Organizational and Individual Strategies toward Achieving P-O Fit in a Culturally Diverse Society,' *The Mid-Atlantic Journal of Business* 37(1): 19–34.

Miotti, L. and F. Sachwald. 2003. 'Co-operative R&D: Why and with Whom? An Integrated Framework of Analysis,' *Research Policy* 32: 1481–99.

Mora-Valentin, E. M., A. Motoro-Sanchez, and L. A. Guerras-Martin. 2004. 'Determining Factors in the Success of R&D Cooperative Agreements between Firms and Research Organisations,' *Research Policy* 33: 17–44.

Mowery, D. C., J. E. Oxley, and B. S. Silverman. 1996. 'Strategic Alliances and Interfirm Knowledge Transfer,' *Strategic Management Journal* 17: 77–91.

Narula, R. 2004. 'R&D Collaboration by SMEs: New Opportunities and Limitations in the Face of Globalization,' *Technovation* 24: 153–61.

Nowotny, H., M. Gibbons, and P. Scott. 2001. *Re-thinking Science—Knowledge and the Public in the Age of Uncertainty.* Oxford: Polity Press.

Osterloh, M. and B. S. Frey. 2000. 'Motivation, Knowledge Transfer, and Organizational Forms,' *Organization Science* 11(5): 538–50.

Ostroff, C. and S. W. J. Kozlowski. 1992. 'Organizational Socialization as a Learning Process: The Role of Information Acquisition,' *Personnel Psychology* 45: 849–74.

Oxley, J. E. and R. C. Sampson. 2004. 'The Scope and Governance of International R&D Alliances,' *Strategic Management Journal* 25: 723–49.

Pisano, G. P. 1989. 'Using Equity Participation to Support Exchange: Evidence from the Biotechnology Industry,' *Journal of Law, Economics, and Organization* 5: 109–26.

—— 1991. 'The Governance of Innovation: Vertical Integration and Collaborative Arrangements in the Biotechnology Industry,' *Research Policy* 20(3): 237–49.

Powell, W. W., K. W. Koput, and L. Smith-Doerr. 1996. 'Interorganizational Collaboration and the Locus of Innovation: Networks of Learning in Biotechnology,' *Administrative Science Quarterly* 41(1): 116.

Rappa, M. A. and K. Debackere. 1992. 'Technological Communities and the Diffusion of Knowledge,' *R&D Management* 22(3): 209–20.

Reagans, R. and B. McEvily. 2003. 'Network Structure and Knowledge Transfer: The Effects of Cohesion and Range,' *Administrative Science Quarterly* 48: 240–67.

Reuer, J. R., M. Zollo, and H. Singh. 2002. 'Post-Formation Dynamics in Strategic Alliances,' *Strategic Management Journal* 23(2): 135–51.

Rosenberg, N. 1990. 'Why Do Firms Do Basic Research with Their Own Money?,' *Research Policy* 19: 165–74.

Sakakibara, M. 1997. 'Heterogeneity of Firm Capabilities and Cooperative Research and Development: An Empirical Examination of Motives,' *Strategic Management Journal* 18: 143–64.

—— 2003. 'Knowledge Sharing in Cooperative Research and Development,' *Managerial and Decisions Economics* 24: 117–32.

Sampson, R. C. 2004. 'Organizational Choice in R&D Alliances: Knowledge-Based and Transaction Cost Perspectives,' *Managerial and Decision Economics* 25: 421–36.

—— 2005. 'Experience Effects and Collaborative Returns in R&D Alliances,' *Strategic Management Journal* 26: 1009–31.

Stephan, P. E. 1996. 'The Economics of Science,' *Journal of Economic Literature* 34: 1199–235.

Stolpe, M. 2002. 'Determinants of Knowledge Diffusion as Evidenced in Patent Data: The Case of Liquid Crystal Display Technology,' *Research Policy* 31(7): 1181.

Teece, D. J. 2000. *Managing Intellectual Capital*. Oxford: Oxford University Press.

Thomas-Hunt, M. C., T. Y. Ogden, and M. A. Neale. 2003. 'Who's Really Sharing? Effects of Social and Expert Status on Knowledge Exchange within Groups,' *Management Science* 49(4): 464–77.

Tsai, W. 2002. 'Social Structure of "Coopetition" within a Multiunit Organization: Coordination, and Intraorganizational Knowledge Sharing,' *Organization Science* 13(2): 179–90.

Uzzi, B. 1997. 'Social Structure and Competition in Interfirm Networks: The Paradox of Embeddedness,' *Administrative Science Quarterly* 42: 35–67.
Van Maanen, J. and E. Schein. 1979. 'Toward a Theory of Organizational Socialization,' *Research in Organizational Behaviour* 1: 209–64.
Von Hippel, E. 1987. 'Cooperation between rivals: Informal know-how trading,' *Research Policy* 16(4): 291–302.
—— 1994. 'Sticky Information and the Locus of Problem Solving: Implications for Innovation,' *Management Science* 40(4): 429–38.

9

Knowledge governance for open innovation: evidence from an EU R&D collaboration

Harry Scarbrough and Kenneth Amaeshi

9.1. Introduction

This chapter highlights a particularly challenging arena for knowledge governance, by focusing on the governance issues associated with large-scale programs of what has been termed 'open innovation.' As outlined in more detail below, open innovation—also sometimes labeled synonymously as 'networked' or 'distributed' innovation—is an increasingly important component of the wider patterns of innovation in advanced economies. It can be seen in large part as a response to firms' increasing needs to draw on external sources of knowledge in order to remain competitive in a global economy.

Issues of knowledge governance are at the heart of open innovation inasmuch as such innovation is acutely dependent on the organization of knowledge flows between and within firms. The ability of firms to acquire externally sourced knowledge has been a major subject of academic debate since the pioneering work of Cohen and Levinthal on 'absorptive capacity,' and Von Hippel's studies of user-driven innovation (Cohen and Levinthal 1990; von Hippel 1988). However, the distinctive challenges posed by an avowedly open approach to innovation processes are still being digested by researchers. These challenges go some way beyond the problem of absorbing knowledge. According to its proponents, open innovation involves a qualitative shift in the way the firm creates, exploits, and organizes knowledge. This has wide-ranging implications for the way the focal firm manages itself and its knowledge base. At the very least, open innovation implies a reduced dependence on internal R&D functions and a greater willingness to trade knowledge with external collaborators. More broadly, though, the serious pursuit of open innovation is likely to extend to radical changes in the structure and management practices of the firm to foster greater interactivity with the expanding ecology of knowledge providers.

It is not within the scope of this chapter to address all of the many challenges which open innovation creates for established governance arrangements. Rather, our aim is to provide an initial exploration of some of these challenges by analyzing a case study of a more open form of innovation. This is an important but also especially complex case because it has to do with MOZART,[1] one of the major collaborative research programs sponsored by the European Union (EU). This program represents a unique institutional response to the needs of the aerospace industry in Europe, reflecting not only the diverse needs of the participating companies but also the strategic interests formulated by the EU as a political body. As such it raises the challenges of knowledge governance to a new level, since it encompasses not only questions of effective governance for an innovation process, and the interfirm collaboration underpinning it, but also the wider challenge of linking private enterprise with the strategic objectives of multistate bodies.

The remainder of this chapter then proceeds as follows. We begin, in the following section, by identifying the major governance challenges arising from open innovation. This is followed by our case study of the MOZART program, and subsequently our analysis of that case in terms of the governance challenges highlighted previously. The chapter concludes with a brief discussion of the implications of the case and an outline of areas for further research in the future.

9.2. Context for the Study

At least since the 1980s (Pisano 2006), there has been a trend for firms to pursue innovation through collaborations reaching beyond firm boundaries. Such collaborations range from greater reliance on external networks for accessing knowledge, through to formal alliances and joint ventures. One of the principal motives for this trend is the need to

[1] MOZART is a pseudonym, adopted here to protect confidentiality.

access and integrate those distributed sources of knowledge which provide the raw material for innovation processes (Gulati and Gargiulo 1999). Most recently this increasing reliance on external collaborations has been highlighted by Chesbrough's notion of 'open innovation.' This is said to describe a paradigm shift in how companies commercialize industrial knowledge (Chesbrough 2003), and it is contrasted with the 'closed innovation' model in which companies are largely self-reliant in their innovation efforts. Chesbrough argues that a number of factors have undermined the logic of closed innovation. These include the dispersion of scientific and technological knowledge due to the mobility of highly skilled workers; the growing presence of venture capital (VC) in funding innovation; the increasing role of user groups; the role of universities and technological service centers; and the shortening of technology life cycles. These factors are seen as encouraging open innovation by placing much greater emphasis on the acquisition of external knowledge, a greater role for user groups, and a more collaborative approach to the management of intellectual property.

As Chesbrough's account indicates, the increasing importance of more open forms of innovation encompasses a wide variety of interactions between firms, suppliers, customers, and users. The particular focus of our study, however, is upon the development of more open approaches to the R&D component of the innovation process. The drivers for such R&D-centered collaborations have been widely discussed in the literature (Hagedoorn 2002). They are seen as enabling the exchange of knowledge and competencies (Borgatti and Cross 2003), so as to accelerate innovation processes, reap economies of scale in R&D, share risks and costs (Nakamura, Vertinsky, and Zietsma 1997), and enhance access to the market (Acha and Cusmano 2005). Such collaborations have been variously described under the headings of R&D consortia (Nakamura, Vertinsky, and Zietsma 1997), R&D alliances (Oxley and Sampson 2004), R&D joint ventures (equity and non-equity), communities of creation (Sawhney and Prandelli 2000), R&D cooperation (Acha and Cusmano 2005), and R&D partnerships (Hagedoorn 2002).

Despite the growth in the number of R&D collaborations and the interest they have generated, they are also seen as presenting significant governance challenges (Dyer and Nobeoka 2000; Simon and Kotler 2003). Many of these challenges center on the fundamental transactional problems affecting any traffic in knowledge between parties, as highlighted by Williamson and other economists. These challenges include, for example, the problem of information asymmetry between parties, the dilemma of disclosure involved in valuing knowledge, and the risk of appropriation (Teece 1986). However, as described in more detail below, these transactional problems also need to be placed in the wider governance context where the forms of knowledge involved, and the evolving relationships between parties, may exert a crucial influence on actual outcomes.

It is certainly true that in practical terms, the failure to overcome these governance challenges has resulted in many collaborations falling short of expectations (Bleeke and Ernst 1993; Ritter and Gemünden 2003). This suggests that the advantages which open innovation creates in relation to accessing external sources of knowledge also need to be balanced against the difficulties of collaboration in circumstances where exchanges are subject to neither the explicit criteria of the market nor the authority structure of the hierarchy. As Powell points out, in such circumstances, 'Collaboration can be fraught with other risks. Parties may bring hidden agendas to the venture. There is an ever-present threat that one party will capture the lion's share of the benefits, or defect with the other party's knowledge and expertise' (Powell 1990: 318). These governance challenges create some profound dilemmas for firms, who, as Oxley and Sampson (2004) put it, 'must... find the right balance between maintaining open knowledge exchange to further the technological development goals of the alliance, and controlling knowledge flows to avoid unintended leakage of valuable technology' (p. 723).

In the subsequent section, we aim to outline a theoretical framework capable of addressing the governance challenges posed by open innovation, and their associated dilemmas of openness and closure.

9.3. Theory Review and Development

The framework outlined here is based on a review of the wide and diverse literature pertaining to open innovation. We have viewed this literature through the lens of 'knowledge governance' which we interpret broadly in terms of a concern with the interplay between knowledge processes (Argote 1999) and the deployment of governance mechanisms (Foss 2007), within a context of exchange hazards created by appropriability risk and opportunism. Applying this approach to open innovation highlights, first, the distinctive knowledge processes associated with such innovation. One strand of the literature here has focused on the transformations of knowledge encompassed by the innovation process. This strand has been highly influenced by Nonaka's account of a 'spiral of knowledge creation.' Thus, Nonaka describes the innovation process in terms of four stages of knowledge creation which he terms 'internalization' (explicit to tacit knowledge), 'socialization' (tacit to tacit knowledge), 'externalization' (tacit to explicit), and 'combination' (explicit to explicit) (Nonaka 1994). Although subsequent work has tended to focus on the conversion of tacit to explicit knowledge as a key feature of this account, an equally important contribution is the way Nonaka highlights the episodic character of the innovation process, showing the transformation of knowledge into different intermediate states prior to its final realization as an innovative offering in the marketplace.

While the transformation of knowledge is one important dimension of open innovation, reliance on wider external networks of collaborators also places an emphasis on the need to integrate knowledge across organizational boundaries. Although the concept of knowledge integration is sometimes used broadly to denote the coordination of different knowledge-based activities (Grant 1996), in the context of innovation it is seen as closely linked to the quality of relationships between individuals and groups. One study, for instance, concludes that 'while the factual content of information is important to knowledge integration ... the way in which that knowledge is accessed and the point of view from which it is considered ... also influences how individual knowledge is combined' (Okhuysen and Eisenhardt 2002: 384). Relationships are important here, because as Carlile puts it, knowledge integration involves overcoming the 'knowledge boundaries' between groups (Carlile 2002). Overcoming such boundaries is critical to enabling the transformations in knowledge required by the innovation process.

Given these characteristic features of open innovation—the dynamic nature of the process, combined with the importance of the relationships between groups—it is not surprising to discover widespread agreement that governance structures or organizational forms play a crucial role in enabling knowledge sharing and protection within interorganizational collaborations (Kale, Singh, and Perlmutter 2000; Pisano 1990). Where there is much less agreement, however, is on the role played by specific governance mechanisms in different settings. Here, we find studies diverging between those which emphasize formal mechanisms of governance, on one hand, and those emphasizing what are termed 'relational' mechanisms, on the other. Formal mechanisms here refer to defined organizational and legal features such as corporate ownership, structural design, and legally binding contracts. Joint ventures and strategic alliances, for instance, represent different formal mechanisms of governance. Relational mechanisms, however, refer to forms of governance which rely upon the social ties created by prior experience and trust between partners.

Despite the tendency to view them as alternatives or substitutes, there is increasing evidence to suggest that formal and relational mechanisms operate in a complementary fashion (Poppo and Zenger 2002). For example, studies of formal organizational networks frequently depict them as being reinforced by informal, or interpersonal, networks (Grandori and Soda 1995; Kreiner and Schultz 1993). Indeed, Gulati and Singh (1998) concluded that the social networks underpinning strategic alliances not only influenced the creation of new ties but also affected the design, evolutionary path, and ultimate success of such alliances.

Existing work has identified a number of possible interaction effects between formal and relational governance mechanisms (Ouchi 1980). Relational mechanisms are identified in a number of instances as exerting a moderating effect upon the scope and complexity of formal mechanisms. Thus, the relational influence of prior ties on partner selection may affect the use of formal mechanisms for interorganizational collaboration (Gulati 1995). Linked to this is the idea that relational governance moderates formal governance through the learning process created by repeated interactions between partners (Uzzi 1997). This is seen as providing greater information on the partner's intentions and competence (Gulati and Gargiulo 1999).

Others see the interaction between formal and relational mechanisms more in terms of one substituting for the other. Thus, some writers argue that trust between partners reduces the need for formal governance mechanisms since social ties help to reduce goal conflict and weaken the risk of opportunistic behavior (Dekker 2004; Poppo and Zenger 2002). This substitution effect, though positive in terms of partnership costs, may not always be functional for the organizations concerned. As recent studies have suggested, overreliance on socially embedded relationships as a proxy for formal governance may also be detrimental to interorganizational collaboration. Thus, studies have found that overreliance on interpersonal trust may undermine effective partner selection (Newell and Swan 2000), and that embedded social networks may limit the exchange of knowledge and information (Edelman et al. 2004).

Another area where existing studies diverge is in the way they characterize the object of governance mechanisms (Dekker 2007). A great number of studies highlight the importance of such mechanisms in relation to exchange hazards (Geyskens, Steenkamp, and Kumar 2006). Here, the extent and complexity of governance—that is, the organizational elaboration and effort involved (Gulati and Singh 1998)—is related to the severity of the exchange hazards involved in a particular interorganizational collaboration. Others, however, link to the wider literature on organization design by focusing on the role of governance as a means of coordinating interdependent tasks (Grant 1996; Gulati and Singh 1998; Thompson 1967). The emphasis in these studies is on the implications of complex and distributed divisions of knowledge and labor for task coordination (Grant 1996). A higher level of task interdependence is seen as associated with more complex governance structures (Gulati and Singh 1998).

Again, as with formal and relational mechanisms, we note that exchange hazards and coordination requirements frequently interact. From the existing literature, there seems to be a strong reinforcing effect between the level of coordination requirements and the level of exchange hazards. As Oxley and Sampson put it, 'The more extensive, interdependent, complex, and uncertain are the activities performed in the alliance, the greater is the potential risk of opportunism. This is because the extent of coordination and more intimate face-to-face contact necessary to achieve success increases along these dimensions... and uncertainty raises the costs of monitoring and assessing partner behavior' (Oxley and Sampson 2004: 726). This uncertainty has implications also for appropriability, since greater interdependence makes it more difficult to identify and enforce claims to the knowledge produced through interorganizational collaboration.

9.3.1. *Developing Propositions*

The above discussion of the existing literature in this field highlights features of the knowledge processes, interfirm relationships, and governance mechanisms encompassed by open innovation. We have noted that open innovation creates distinctive challenges for governance, due to the transformative and episodic nature of the innovation process itself, combined with the need to integrate knowledge across organizational boundaries. The aim of this section is to further extend this account by focusing more closely upon the interplay between knowledge process and governance mechanisms. This leads us to outline some indicative propositions on that interplay, which will subsequently inform our case analysis and discussion.

One important aspect of the knowledge process for open innovation is the forms of knowledge involved. As noted previously, the work of

Nonaka highlighted the importance of tacit knowledge within innovation processes. The problems of contracting and monitoring such knowledge (as compared to explicit knowledge), and its asset specificity, are generally seen as an argument for hierarchical or joint venture-based forms of governance to minimize the problem of opportunism, free riding, and misappropriation (Oxley and Sampson 2004; Williamson 1985). In addition, (but often related to the tacit dimension of knowledge) is its 'system embeddedness.' This is contrasted with modularity, where knowledge can be acquired and transferred in a more discrete way (Winter 1987). Knowledge may be modularized by specialism or episodically, as with precompetitive R&D collaboration (Oxley and Sampson 2004; Sanchez and Heene 1997). Greater modularity can be seen as reducing the need for complex forms of governance, and as enabling more transparent and arms-length relationships between the partners involved.

Consideration of these governance implications of tacitness and system embeddedness for open innovation leads to the following proposition: *open innovation will occur most readily when it involves the integration of more modular and explicit forms of knowledge*. Conversely, *dependence on tacit and embedded forms of knowledge will be more difficult to accommodate within an open innovation process due to the complexity of governance mechanisms required*.

Further propositions can be derived when we consider the implications of knowledge form for relational mechanisms of governance. Thus, interpersonal networks, involving deep, trust-based relationships, have been seen as more appropriate for the integration of tacit forms of knowledge (Oliver and Liebeskind 1998). Conversely, inter- and intraorganizational networks based on weak/shallow ties are found to be more effective for the integration of explicit forms of knowledge (Hansen 1999). This leads to the following proposition: *where open innovation processes do require the integration of tacit knowledge, this will only be possible through relational mechanisms involving strong ties between network participants*.

In turn, we also need to address the temporal and episodic nature of the innovation process and its implications for governance. In much of the existing literature, governance mechanisms are viewed as a function of the characteristics of the knowledge process or interorganizational relationships. However, this emphasis on the structural solutions to the governance challenge may also be neglecting the recursive relationships that operate between knowledge processes, interfirm relationships, and governance mechanisms. Such recursiveness is an important issue for innovation processes which, as we have noted, unfold episodically over time. This suggests that governance mechanisms may well react back upon the relationships between partners or the scope of knowledge processes—that is, the extent and forms of knowledge which are shared under a particular form of governance. This may occur, for instance, through the relationship building effects of particular governance choices. Thus, Oxley and Sampson found that in some instances 'the choice of an equity joint venture encourages alliance partners to engage in joint activities that go beyond "pure" R&D' (Oxley and Sampson 2004: 724). Equally, governance arrangements may also have relationship-inhibiting or even damaging effects, as where formal governance mechanisms are taken to signal distrust between parties (Das and Teng 1998). Similar considerations may arguably apply also to the influence of governance mechanisms upon knowledge processes. Delimiting the scope of joint activities, for instance, is likely to emphasize the modularization of knowledge within the innovation process (Brusoni, Prencipe, and Pavitt 2001).

Summarizing the implications of these recursive and unfolding aspects of the innovation process suggests the following overarching proposition: *the governance mechanisms adopted for open innovation are likely to evolve over time, with some path dependency in the course of their evolution—that is, initial governance conditions are likely to exert an enduring influence*. Specifying the possible governance paths involved is inherently problematic given the above comments. However, two contrasting propositions help to highlight the possible variance. First, *the initial adoption of formal mechanisms with positive relational effects, such as the joint venture form, is likely to encourage stronger ties and hence greater ability to integrate tacit and embedded forms of knowledge*. Second, *the adoption of formal mechanisms with negative relational effects (as with legalistic forms of contract) is likely to encourage weaker ties between firms, and hence greater ability to integrate explicit and modularized forms of knowledge*.

Finally, one issue which we have not focused on explicitly in our review of the literature is the appropriability of the knowledge created within the innovation process. This may clearly be an important consideration, and, as noted above, is linked to other issues such as the degree of task interdependence within the knowledge process, and the embeddedness of relationships between firms. What makes it difficult to specify this feature any further, however, is the importance of the wider appropriability regime as an exogenous influence on open innovation. Thus, we can note that where the appropriation regime is weak, there is a strong likelihood that innovators would likely exploit innovation internally, either by using internal resources or by creating a spin-off, rather than through external

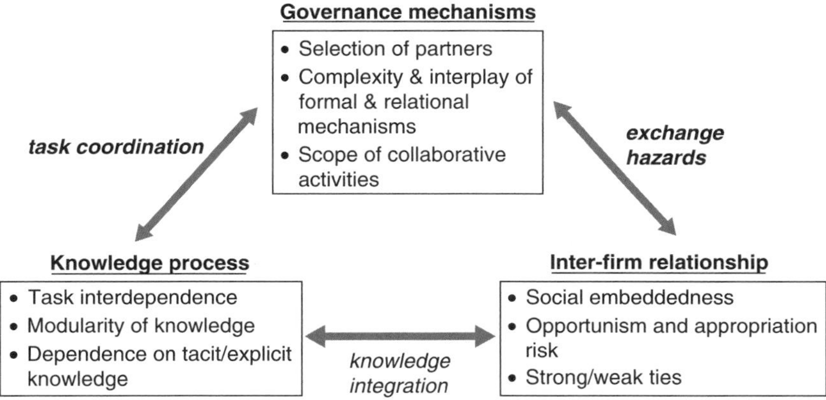

Figure 9.1. The governance challenge of open innovation

means like patents and licenses (Shane 2002). However, while the conventional view has suggested that 'strong' appropriation regimes are the most conducive to interorganizational collaboration, Pisano notes that there may also be occasions on which strong intellectual property protection may not be most advantageous to innovating firms (Pisano 2006). As he notes, weak regimes for the R&D component of open innovation may sometimes be preferred even by established firms because they provide a more effective way of leveraging their advantages in complementary capabilities such as marketing and manufacturing.

In Figure 9.1, we have sought to bring together and summarize these interactions as a propositional framework to be applied to our empirical study. In Section 9.4, we will provide a brief description of our case study of the MOZART program, allowing us to ground our subsequent analysis and discussion in the comparison between the propositional framework outlined here and the actual conduct of this large-scale, highly complex example of open innovation.

9.4. MOZART and ITNET[2]: A Case Study of R&D Collaboration in the Aerospace Sector

This case study is provided here primarily as a means of illuminating the theoretical propositions outlined above. Data for the case was elicited through multiple means, including participant observation, and

[2] As with MOZART, 'ITNET' is a pseudonym adopted to protect confidentiality.

hands-on involvement in project delivery, together with interviews with some key actors in the program, and analysis of documents.

9.4.1. *MOZART—An Overview*

To explore our propositions about knowledge governance within an open innovation context, we turn now to our case study. MOZART is one of the FP6 research projects of the European Commission. MOZART was officially launched in January 2004 to run till December 2007. However, it has a longer 'informal' lifespan dating back to the days of a previous FP5 project—that is, the ENHANCE program. The MOZART integrated research and technology project, which is coordinated by Airbus, was set up by the European Union with a budget of around 74 million euros, as one of its objectives to addressing its aerospace Vision 2020 objectives. To foster collaboration in the sector, the budget is shared between 63 companies and institutions that are cooperating in the program.

MOZART can be seen as reflecting a distinctively European approach to open innovation, in that it involves the application of public funding to the development of a wide network of organizations. As we will describe in more detail below, this is an open approach to innovation only in the minimal sense that it involves multiple firms and a requirement to integrate multiple, distributed sources of knowledge. The relative openness of the interfirm networks engaged by MOZART—that is, their willingness to access and share knowledge with outside groups—varied significantly over time and across different work packages.

The formal goal of MOZART is to achieve a 5 percent cost reduction in aircraft development and a 5 percent reduction in the development phase of a new aircraft design, combined with a contribution to a 30 percent reduction in the lead time and 50 percent reduction in development costs respectively for a new or derivative gas turbine. It is expected that MOZART will deliver a virtual product design and validation platform, based on a distributed concurrent engineering methodology supporting the virtual enterprise. The main result of MOZART will be an innovative Aeronautical Collaborative Design Environment and associated processes, models, and methods. This environment, validated through concrete Use Cases (i.e., real-life cases on industrial sites), will help to design an aircraft and its engines, providing virtual products to the aeronautics supply chain operating in an extended enterprise, which has all the requested functionality and components for each phase of the product-engineering life cycle. It is also expected that the new approach of working developed by MOZART would be made available to the aerospace supply chain via existing networks, information dissemination, training, and technology transfer actions.

9.4.2. *MOZART and the Innovation Process*

The MOZART program is based on a 'concurrent engineering' approach to innovation (Clark and Fujimoto 1991). Concurrent engineering (CE) is an engineering practice that came into prominence in the auto industry in the late 1980s in relation to the increasing competitiveness of the economic landscape. It was a radical break with the sequential engineering (over-the-wall) approach that had dominated new product introduction for decades. It was seen as a way to respond faster to market needs, reduce time to market, and minimize cost. CE subsequently diffused into other sectors, including aerospace. One of the means of this diffusion was through recruitment of people with experience of CE in automotive in the mid-1990s. Currently, CE is widely adopted in the aerospace sector as an important approach to open innovation.

One of the key characteristics of CE is its emphasis on collaboration and teamwork among stakeholders—especially in the design phase of new products. However, collaboration within and across firms brings with it challenges, which include difficulty in data exchange, knowledge boundaries, knowledge leakages, transaction costs, and other governance and coordination problems. The practice of CE has been sustained, however, despite these challenges as firms seek new ways of mitigating the challenges. An example of how CE is coping with these challenges is the use of information technology, and especially the Internet, to minimize knowledge leakages and reduce transaction costs through standardized security systems and web-based processes.

At a policy level, the MOZART program was predicated on the EU's goal of pursuing 'sustained competitiveness of the EU aerospace sector.' This goal was manifest in different strategy and vision texts produced by the EU, as well as national governments (e.g., SBAC, UK), and aerospace firms (e.g., through MOZART vehicle). In addition, exploiting these new IT-based opportunities for CE was also in line with the EU's strategic objective of developing new ways of working in Europe based on opportunities offered by ICT: MOZART was funded 50 percent by the aerospace and 50 percent by ICT units of the European Commission. The overall rationale for the program came from the policymakers' belief that the aerospace sector needed to change its design and development practices as well as work more closely with its supply chain. Structural changes in the industry (e.g., privatization) and the global economy had already ushered in outsourcing, which in turn necessitated migration of competences from OEMs to supply chains. Large companies had become focused on their core competencies, becoming system integrators or builders, rather than manufacturers (Bhattacharya, Coleman, and Brace 1995). Against this backdrop, collaborative approaches to innovation were trumpeted as a way to cope with the challenges of competition (mainly coming from the USA and lately Asia–Japan) and to retain the EU aerospace sector as the crown jewel of Europe's industrial base. It was also expected that developments in ICT could contribute significantly to achieving these changes in product design and development as well as enhancing supply chain relationships.

The aerospace sector has historically not been very enthusiastic about promoting collaborative work in new product development. One of the reasons for this could be the military antecedents of the sector which rather promoted an attitude of 'keeping your cards close to your chest' and protecting national interests, which militated against collaborating and sharing expertise. The second reason is that the major OEMs (original equipment manufacturers) in the sector originally had all the required expertise in-house and did not see the need to collaborate. The preference for in-house development and the hoarding of knowledge persisted with some firms even as the MOZART program was being developed. This clashed with the program imperative to share knowledge within European networks. A good example of this was the situation where one of the initial partners was forced to withdraw because other partners feared the results of MOZART would be applied outside the European networks through operations in North America.

9.4.3. *MOZART Governance Structure*

MOZART was deeply embedded in both formal and informal networks. The EU aerospace sector is a close-knit network of OEMs, first- and second-tier suppliers, and so on. However, the tentacles of these networks are not limited to Europe. For instance, a good number of the OEMs are multinational firms that have offices outside Europe. Given that the primary goal of MOZART was to enhance the EU aerospace expertise, the selection of project members reflected this intention. As a result, the network evolved mainly through informal networks or existing relationships, reflecting the existing structure of the EU aerospace sector.

Most of the members of the network were invited to join through prior working relationships with one another in the past or at the time of organizing the network. A good number of them were involved in the FP5 project ENHANCE. In fact, the MOZART project was originally conceived as two separate projects—one focusing on engine design and development, led by Rolls Royce, and the other focusing on airframe design and development, led by Airbus. Both Rolls Royce and Airbus had their own networks. But because the projects were closely related, the European Commission decided to merge the two—in effect, a forced marriage—which meant that the two hitherto separate networks needed to fashion new ways of working together. The overlapping informal networks between engine manufacturers and airframe manufacturers helped to foster some links within the resulting network. For example, both Rolls Royce and Volvo Aero are first tier suppliers to Airbus, which required them to work closely with each other. This previous relationship helped in building a new network of partners through what could be termed 'a cross-fertilization of social capital' among existing innovation networks.

Alongside the relational mechanisms based on prior experience, the development of MOZART also involved the development of some complex formal mechanisms of governance. In particular, the requirements from each partner and the anticipated working procedure of the network were explicitly specified in a detailed 200-page contract. This also required each of the participating firms to declare and document, ab initio, the know-how and expertise they were bringing to the collaboration. Despite this level of bureaucratic detail, however, these contracts were not seriously applied as mechanisms for the governance of interfirm collaboration. They were rather artifacts designed to meet the requirements of the funding body. In terms of day-to-day activities, governance at the interfirm level was much more reliant on the relational mechanisms created by trust and prior experience.

MOZART itself was divided into work packages according to areas of specialization—that is, engine, airframe, and information technology—with different firms acting as work package team leaders. Each of these work packages had its own selection and governance mechanisms. However, there were situations where participating firms straddled work packages. In such instances, the partners were bound by the governance mechanisms of each of the work packages they belonged to. This involved some adaptation of internal organizational practices to harmonize or cope with the demands of the various contracting regimes.

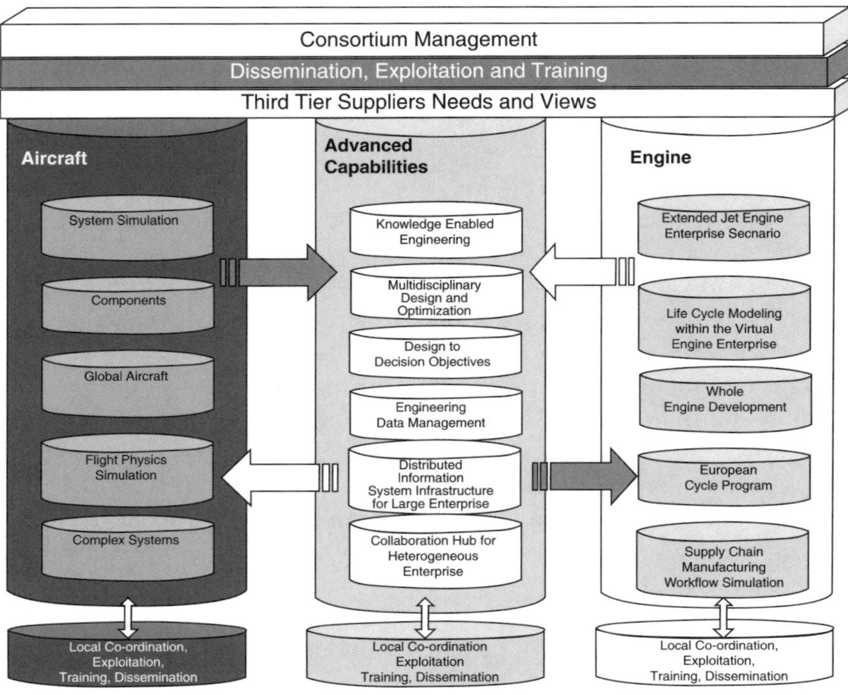

Figure 9.2. Work breakdown structure for the MOZART program

Overall, and in addition to the common contract, MOZART had a formal work breakdown structure as illustrated in Figure 9.2 above. The work packages decided for themselves on how and who to share their results with. In some cases, these work packages reflected preexisting collaborations, while in some others, such as firms in the forced marriage network, they did not.

This distribution of authority between program and work packages was also linked to the fears among some firms that the MOZART network did not provide a reliable context to minimize knowledge spillover. It could also have arisen from the fact that the different specializations had different collaborative work cultures and histories. For instance, firms on the engine side of the program were well versed in collaborating with each other. In contrast, the airframe side was heavily linked to defense and military interests that constrained collaboration.

A significant finding from the study, however, was the degree of variation which took place in the knowledge sharing and exploitation practices of these work groups over time. Some work groups started with the explicit intention of being open in terms of sharing knowledge with other groups within the wider MOZART network, only to adopt a more closed policy later. Some groups followed the opposite path. These variations in governance and policy reflected, in part, the shifting relationships between firms, within the MOZART network. In some instances, however, they reflected the transformative and episodic character of the early-stage innovation process itself. Thus, some work groups shifted toward a closed network posture when they believed they had created original and valuable knowledge in their early-stage work, only to relax toward a more open stance when that work was reassessed as having little intellectual property potential. Again, other work groups followed the opposite trajectory. Both of these trajectories were facilitated by renegotiations of contracting regimes at the work package and project levels. The ITNET work package presented below offers a good case of a movement from closed to open innovation.

9.4.4. *ITNET Work Package*

MOZART was made up of three core components—engine, airframe, and information technology. The information technology part (called Advanced Capabilities) was there essentially as an enabler to both engine and airframe design and development. This element was advanced principally through the ITNET work package (outlined in Figure 9.3) which was given the responsibility of developing tools and methodologies to enhance data interoperability via the web. It was the anticipated technology on which the virtual enterprise architecture would be built. The project was made up of information technologies companies that supplied to both the airframe and engine sides of the consortium. Their main role was to provide an enabling information technology infrastructure that would facilitate effective virtual new product development collaboration without compromising on intellectual property or company know-how.

Initially, one of these work packages (i.e., Collaboration Hub) started by agreeing to limit the exploitation of results of the research to work package members. This may have been because the firms in the information technology subgroup were not necessarily tied to the aerospace sector. They came with generic skills and expertise, and the technologies they developed could have had applications outside aerospace. Information from our interviews suggested that ITNET members did not wish to restrict

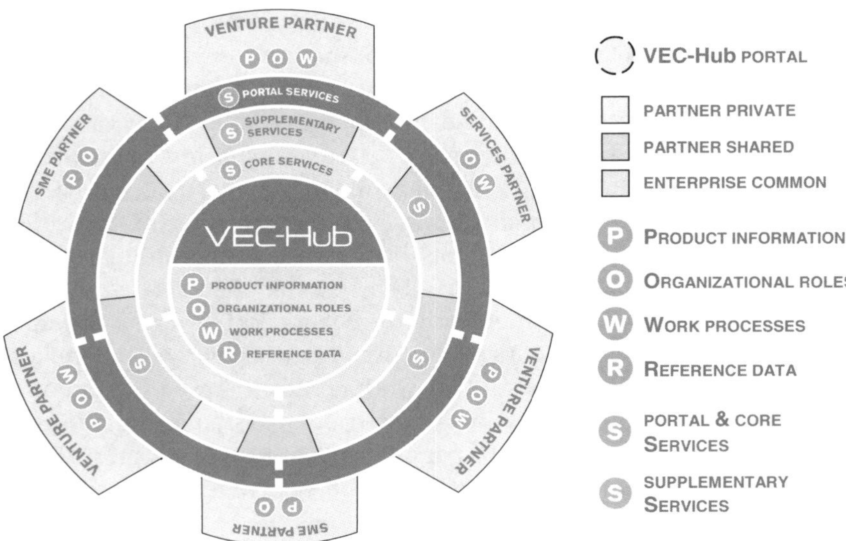

Figure 9.3. ITNET interconnectedness with other work packages

themselves to aerospace intellectual property in the first instance, but rather wanted findings they could commercialize in the broader IT market. Given this, the work package members decided initially to limit its exploitation within familiar networks of information technology partners in the same subgroup, the broader formal contract governing MOZART notwithstanding.

Despite this initially closed and relatively marginal position, with the passage of time the ITNET work package migrated from being a fringe player in the network to being a dominant one, at least in the sense that it became perceived as one of the key result providers (classed as one of the five 'wonders' achieved by MOZART). This transition could be attributed to a number of things, including the pioneering role of the leader and his firm, but also a change in its governance structure toward an 'open-source' model. To begin with the leader's role, this individual was employed by the subsidiary of a major engine collaborator in the project. He was able to leverage his network influence and access to powerful resources (e.g., the influence of the engine side of his corporation in the MOZART network) to reposition the ITNET work package to the fore. The ITNET also built a network around itself by creating links to other work packages, which created interconnectedness to other work packages (Engine and Aircraft); see Figure 9.3. To do this, it had to position itself as a 'commonly available tool having no particular allegiance,' which could be of value to the different projects without threats.

This work package started canvassing for people in other work packages who championed their cause, through such means as training programs, presentations at conferences, and provision of e-learning demos. It also positioned itself as a solution that went beyond the current demands of the R&D network and sold its value post the duration of the research project. At the same time, it was involved in standardization of its content through such bodies as ISO14001 and other standardization bodies. This gave the project a visibility that was quickly noticed by the consortium management.

A final strategy in this gaining of center stage position and interconnectedness involved making the ITNET research outcomes accessible to others in order to maximize its usefulness and centrality. The ITNET thus became an open resource to members of MOZART. All its documents became available on the MOZART portal. Originally, the ITNET was meant to support only the integration of the engine and airframe components of the MOZART project. It later positioned itself as a form of open source in order to attract significant interest that could lead to possible standardization of the hub both within and without MOZART. One could argue that with time, the ITNET learned to adapt to both the airframe and engine sides of the consortium and leveraged its expertise to gain a centrality that made it indispensable in the program. This indispensability also meant that the ITNET needed to shift from its original position of exploiting its results among its core members to an open-source approach within the broader governance of the MOZART R&D network.

9.5. Analysis and Discussion

Before analyzing what the MOZART case has to tell us about the relationships outlined in our theory framework, it is worth noting that one of the most striking features of this case is the sheer complexity of governance and the overall scale of transaction costs involved. Given the uncertain benefits of the R&D collaboration advanced here, as well as the difficulties of appropriation for quasi-public goods, it seems reasonable to argue that MOZART could only have been developed with the institutional and financial support of the EU and its member states. The involvement of the EU is not only important in providing the necessary resources for complex governance structures but also a major contributor to their complexity as the vertical relationship between the EU and the program creates additional needs for coordination, oversight, and transparency. The resulting complexity of the governance structure for MOZART also brings into sharp relief the crucial role which new internet-based technologies played in absorbing complexity and reducing transaction costs to a feasible level (Child and McGrath 2001). As was noted in the case, and as we will explore in more detail below, the influence of IT on governance, indeed its role as a mode of governance alongside organizational form (Weick 1990), was not only a feature of the program as a whole but also important in shaping the paths taken by different work packages within that program.

If the complex governance of MOZART reflects the potential impact of strategic state intervention when allied with new IT systems, we must not forget also that the overall scope of the program was restricted to precompetitive R&D, which arguably tells us something about the limits of what is achievable by such intervention. The willingness of companies to engage in collective programs is obviously greater where such programs are broadly aligned with their strategic objectives—something which MOZART sought to achieve by linking EU interests to the goals of established EU-based firms—but also for arenas, such as precompetitive R&D, which are not subject to the same risks of knowledge spillover and appropriability as would apply to later episodes of the innovation process.

These considerations may help to account for the relative complexity of governance in the MOZART case. This level of complexity would certainly caution against generalizing too far from this special case to other instances of open innovation. On the other hand, in many other respects the interactions between the members of the MOZART program reflected many of the relationships which our theory framework derived from previous work in this field. To begin with the relationship between knowledge process and interfirm relationships, we can readily see the implications of MOZART's emphasis on 'concurrent engineering' for the level of task interdependence within the knowledge process. Concurrent engineering specifies much higher levels of cross-functional interaction in developing new products. In other words, it creates a greater requirement for the integration of tacit and embedded forms of knowledge. This is difficult enough to achieve within the focal firm, but for open innovation it also involves overcoming interorganizational boundaries. One consequence, as seen in the MOZART program, seems to have been a reduced emphasis on the modularization of knowledge in favor of greater reliance on strong ties and the socially embedded relationships capable of supporting high levels of knowledge integration that continuously developed during the program. In this sense, the importance of prior ties in the selection of partners seems to have not only mitigated against the risks of appropriation and opportunism but also aided the level of knowledge integration required by this more interactive approach to innovation.

These factors also help to make sense of the important role which work packages played within the program as a whole. Caught between the need to integrate knowledge across boundaries, yet alert to the exchange hazards thereof, companies were best able accommodate their concerns at the work package level of governance since the latter's domain scope fitted best both the required extent of knowledge integration and the pattern of prior network ties that would contain unwanted knowledge spillovers. Governance mechanisms at the program level were more problematic from this point of view, because they were driven more by EU goals than by the dynamics of the open innovation process.

To turn now to the governance mechanisms developed within the MOZART program, it is clear from the account above that these mechanisms had to address the demands posed both by task coordination and by exchange hazards. Doing this involved fully exploiting the complementarity between relational and formal mechanisms. Thus, the detailed strictures of the 200-page formal contract were complemented by a selection of partners based to a large extent on prior ties (Dekker 2007). Similarly, as noted above, the scope of collaborative activities was also carefully designed to meet the task coordination of the work packages while aligning with established networks within the sector.

9.5.1. *Reflections on Propositions*

This is an appropriate juncture to reflect back on the indicative propositions outlined earlier. The first proposition suggested that *open innovation will occur most readily when it involves the integration of more modular and explicit forms of knowledge*. We further suggested that *dependence on tacit and embedded forms of knowledge will be more difficult to accommodate within an open innovation process due to the complexity of governance mechanisms required*.

As noted above, modularization was reflected to some degree in the work breakdown and packages defined by the MOZART program. However, the role of modularization was limited by the interdependence between partners created by the concurrent engineering methods adopted in the innovation process. The resulting reliance on the networks created by prior collaboration—effectively underpinning the allocation of work packages—gives some support to the following proposition: *where open innovation processes do require the integration of tacit knowledge, this will only be possible through relational mechanisms involving strong ties between network participants*

Another important factor highlighted by the case study is the dynamic and transformative character of the innovation process. We noted previously that governance mechanisms, especially their relationship-building or -inhibiting effects, were likely to exert some influence on the innovation process. As stated: *the governance mechanisms adopted for open innovation are likely to evolve over time, with some path dependency in the course of their evolution—that is, initial governance conditions are likely to exert an enduring influence.* Based on this, we speculated, first, that *the initial adoption of formal mechanisms with positive relational effects, such as the joint venture form, is likely to encourage stronger ties and hence greater ability to integrate tacit and embedded forms of knowledge.* Second, we suggested that *the adoption of formal mechanisms with negative relational effects (as with legalistic forms of contract) is likely to encourage weaker ties between firms, and hence greater ability to integrate explicit and modularized forms of knowledge.*

Interestingly, the evidence from our case suggests that initially adopted governance mechanisms may be less influential than this suggests. Rather such mechanisms seem themselves to be adapted to shifting expectations attaching to the outcomes of the innovation process. Thus, concerns over appropriability seem to have prompted the adoption of closed networks as a relational mechanism enabling and encouraging greater reciprocity among partner firms. The strategy of limiting exploitation to closed groups of firms helped to alleviate concerns over appropriability—concerns which likewise ebbed and flowed with changing perceptions of the intellectual property potential of innovation outcomes. We can note, though, that this strategy is not without its own problems; closer dependence among partners, as noted by Oxley and Sampson (2004), being potentially confounding for any attempts to stake IP claims for one firm over another.

9.5.2. *Theoretical and Practical Implications*

Up to this point, we can say that the governance of MOZART reflects many of the insights derived from the existing literature on knowledge governance. Where it begins to part company with those existing views, however, is in relation to the stability of governance and the role which it plays within an open innovation process. Here it departs from an important strand in the existing literature which has sought to specify knowledge as a contingency variable in the design of organizational forms (e.g., Birkinshaw, Nobel, and Ridderstrale 2002). This strand of work has certainly illuminated those characteristics of knowledge processes which have important implications for governance. At the same time, however, this strand implies a static analysis of the relationship between knowledge process and governance mechanisms. This seems less relevant to the open innovation process discussed here for a number of reasons. First, such innovation processes are inherently dynamic. As noted in Nonaka's account (1994), they involve the episodic transformation of existing knowledge into new forms. As a result they create an almost continually shifting set of challenges for governance. The needs for openness to allow knowledge integration across boundaries may quickly be overturned should the new ideas thus created be seen as possessing significant value. At this point, concerns for appropriability may outweigh the need for openness resulting in a more exclusionary governance structure and closed, not open, networks. This pattern of initially open forms of governance giving way to more closed forms is certainly apparent in some of the work packages within the MOZART program.

A second feature of the MOZART program, which is not amenable to the contingency approach to governance, is exemplified by the ITNET work package. This is actually one of those parts of the program which moved from an initial position of sharing findings within the work package toward a more open approach to governance. It did so, however, as part of a strategy to increase its centrality within the program as a whole. This involved eliciting the involvement of an expanding network of users from MOZART member organizations through an 'open-source' approach to knowledge governance. 'Open source' has been widely discussed elsewhere (Pisano 2006; von Hippel and von Krogh 2003) and is seen as recasting old questions on the role of intellectual property protection in innovation. It does so by enabling the creation of a new source of value through the network externalities (Arthur 1989) arising from the widespread adoption of common systems and standards. This source of value is especially applicable to the development of IT systems. This helps to explain why the ITNET changed its governance toward a more open-source model since it sought to develop and diffuse common systems and standards as widely as possible among MOZART members. In this sense, therefore, we would argue that this shift highlights the limitations of a stable structure when more open governance can be a critical part of a consciously destabilizing innovation. In this sense, ITNET's approach to governance is compatible with Pisano's analysis of the appropriability benefits of more open innovation for established players in certain fields. By adopting an open standards approach, ITNET succeeded in leveraging its complementary capabilities (training, integration, development) much more effectively across the whole program.

A further thought on the success of the ITNET project are its implications for the management of projects within an open innovation context. Such a context demands new strategies and skills from managers. As noted in the ITNET case, the ability of individual managers to champion their project across a wider network of organizations may be critical, and may involve a different set of skills to those required within a focal organization. Chesbrough (2004), for example, has likened the change in skills required between closed and open innovation to the difference between playing chess and playing poker. The open innovation 'game' with its multiple players and shifting stakes demands the poker-player's attention to the strategies of others, and the ability to use scarce information effectively. In the ITNET project, for example, we see the project leader's agency and skill in playing the counter-card of openness in an environment where many other groups were developing closed networks.

9.6. Conclusions

As noted above, the complex governance structure of the MOZART program and its sponsorship by the EU makes us cautious about overgeneralizing its implications to other cases of open innovation. MOZART is partly a product of a unique institutional context and would not be replicable in other regional economies. On the other hand, as an extreme case, MOZART usefully illuminated many of the most acute governance challenges posed by open innovation. Thus, it underlined the extent to which such innovation poses genuine dilemmas for governance. These included the challenge of addressing the task coordination needs of open innovation—requiring more open networks at certain points—while at the same time mitigating exchange hazards which leads toward closed networks. Since these challenges are linked by the knowledge integration requirement of open innovation, effective governance solutions are difficult to achieve.

A further dilemma, which has been highlighted in our discussion above, is between stability and change in the form of governance adopted. Because innovation proceeds sporadically and sometimes erratically from existing knowledge to new knowledge, it is difficult to sustain a particular governance solution over the course of the whole process. We also noted how, in the case of MOZART, this dilemma is exacerbated by the scope and complexity of the work involved. Speaking of other such 'mega-projects' as they term them, Miller and Hobbs argue that 'there is a sharp contrast between the binary, hierarchical and static nature of corporate principal-agent governance relations, and the time-dependent co-determination found in the network relations typical of the governance of mega-projects . . . ' (Miller and Hobbs 2005: 47).

The implication of this kind of analysis is that the pursuit of stability in governance structures may be unrealistic and even undesirable in the development of more open forms of innovation. It may be more important that such structures are able to change and adapt to the shifting needs of knowledge integration than pursue a best fit with circumstances prevailing at a single point in time. This has important consequences for companies pursuing strategies of open innovation in particular. It would be simplistic to conclude that such strategies merely require more open forms of governance. Rather, the dynamics of the open innovation process make knowledge governance an even more critical and explicit question for the organizations involved, precisely because stable institutional arrangements become somewhat less sustainable.

References

Acha, V. and L. Cusmano. 2005. 'Governance and Co-Ordination of Distributed Innovation Processes: Patterns of R&D Co-Operation in the Upstream Petroleum Industry,' *Economics of Innovation and New Technology* 14(1): 1–21.

Argote, L. 1999. *Organizational Learning: Creating, Retaining, and Transferring Knowledge*. Kluwer Academic Pub.

Arthur, W. B. 1989. 'Competing Technologies, Increasing Returns, and Lock-In by Historical Events,' *The Economic Journal* 99(394): 116–31.

Bhattacharya, A. K., J. L. Coleman, and G. Brace. 1995. 'Re Positioning the Supplier: An SME Perspective,' *Production, Planning and Control* 6(3): 218–26.

Birkinshaw, J., R. Nobel, and J. Ridderstrale. 2002. *Organization Science* 13(3): 274–89.

Bleeke, J. and D. Ernst. 1993. *Collaborating to Compete: Using Strategic Alliances and Acquisitions in the Global Marketplace*. Wiley.

Borgatti, S. P. and R. Cross. 2003. 'A Relational View of Information Seeking and Learning in Social Networks,' *Management Science* 49(4): 432.

Brusoni, S., A. Prencipe, and K. Pavitt. 2001. 'Knowledge Specialization, Organizational Coupling, and the Boundaries of the Firm: Why Do Firms Know more than They Make?,' *Administrative Science Quarterly* 46(4): 597–621.

Carlile, P. R. 2002. 'A Pragmatic View of Knowledge and Boundaries: Boundary Objects in New Product Development,' *Organization Science* 13(4): 442–55.

Chesbrough, H. 2004. 'Managing Open Innovation,' *Research Technology Management* 47: 23–6.

Chesbrough, H. W. 2003. 'The Era of Open Innovation,' *MIT Sloan Management Review* 44(3): 35.

Child, J. and R. G. McGrath. 2001. 'Organizations Unfettered: Organizational Form in an Information-Intensive Economy,' *The Academy of Management Journal* 446: 1135–48.

Clark, K. B. and T. Fujimoto. 1991. *Product Development Performance: Strategy, Organization, and Management in the World Auto Industry*. Harvard Business School Press.

Cohen, W. M. and D. A. Levinthal. 1990. 'Absorptive-Capacity—A New Perspective on Learning and Innovation,' *Administrative Science Quarterly* 35(1): 128–52.

Das, T. K. and B. S. Teng. 1998. 'Between Trust and Control: Developing Confidence in Partner Cooperation in Alliances,' *The Academy of Management Review* 23(3): 491–512.

Dekker, H. C. 2004. 'Control of Inter-Organizational Relationships: Evidence on Appropriation Concerns and Coordination Requirements,' *Accounting, Organizations and Society* 29(1): 27–49.

—— 2007. 'Partner Selection and Governance Design in Inter-Firm Relationships,' *Accounting, Organizations and Society* forthcoming.

Dyer, J. H. and K. Nobeoka. 2000. 'Creating and Managing a High-Performance Knowledge-Sharing Network: The Toyota Case,' *Strategic Management Journal* 21(3): 345–67.

Edelman, L. F., et al. 2004. 'The Benefits and Pitfalls of Social Capital: Empirical Evidence from Two Organizations in the United Kingdom,' *British Journal of Management* 15: S59–S69.

Foss, N. J. 2007. 'The Emerging Knowledge Governance Approach: Challenges and Characteristics,' *Organization* 14(1): 29.

Geyskens, I., J. Steenkamp, and N. Kumar. 2006. 'Make, Buy, or Ally: A Meta-analysis of Transaction Cost Theory,' *Academy of Management Journal* 49(3): 519–43.

Grandori, A. and G. Soda. 1995. 'Inter-Firm Networks: Antecedents, Mechanisms and Forms,' *Organization Studies* 16: 184–214.

Grant, R. 1996. 'Towards a Knowledge Based Theory of the Firm,' *Strategic Management Journal* 17: 109–22.

Gulati, R. 1995. 'Does Familiarity Breed Trust? The Implications of Repeated Ties for Contractual Choice in Alliances,' *The Academy of Management Journal* 38(1): 85–112.

——and M. Gargiulo. 1999. 'Where Do Interorganizational Networks Come from?,' *American Journal of Sociology* 104(5): 1439–93.

——and H. Singh. 1998. 'The Architecture of Cooperation: Managing Coordination Costs and Appropriation Concerns in Strategic Alliances,' *Administrative Science Quarterly* 43(4): 781–4.

Hagedoorn, J. 2002. 'Inter-Firm R&D Partnerships: An Overview of Major Trends and Patterns since 1960,' *Research Policy* 31(4): 477–92.

Hansen, M. T. 1999. 'The Search Transfer Problem: The Role of Weak Ties in Sharing Knowledge across Organizational Sub-Units,' *Administrative Science Quarterly* 44: 82–111.

Kale, P., H. Singh, and H. Perlmutter. 2000. 'Learning and Protection of Proprietary Assets in Strategic Alliances: Building Relational Capital,' *Strategic Management Journal* 21(3): 217–37.

Kreiner, K. and M. Schultz. 1993. 'Informal Collaboration in R & D. The Formation of Networks across Organizations,' *Organization Studies* 14(2): 189–209.

Miller, R. and B. Hobbs. 2005. 'Governance Regimes for Large Complex Projects,' *Project Management Journal* 36(3): 42–50.

Nakamura, M., I. Vertinsky, and C. Zietsma. 1997. 'Does Culture Matter in Inter-Firm Cooperation? Research Consortia in Japan and the USA,' *Managerial and Decision Economics* 18(2): 153–75.

Newell, S. and J. Swan. 2000. 'Trust and Inter-Organizational Networking,' *Human Relations,* 53(10): 1287–1328.

Nonaka, I. 1994. 'A Dynamic Theory of Organizational Knowledge Creation,' *Organization Science* 5(1): 14–37.

Okhuysen, G. A. and K. M. Eisenhardt. 2002. 'Integrating Knowledge in Groups: How Formal Interventions Enable Flexibility,' *Organization Science* 13(4): 370–86.

Oliver, A. L. and J. P. Liebeskind. 1998. 'Three Levels of Networking for Sourcing Intellectual Capital in Biotechnology,' *International Studies of Management and Organization* 27(4): 76–103.

Ouchi, W. G. 1980. 'Markets, Bureaucracies, and Clans,' *Administrative Science Quarterly* 25(1): 129–41.

Oxley, J. E. and R. C. Sampson. 2004. 'The Scope and Governance of International R & D Alliances,' *Strategic Management Journal* 25(89): 723–49.

Pisano, G. P. 1990. 'The R&D Boundaries of the Firm: An Empirical Analysis,' *Administrative Science Quarterly* 35: 153–76.

——2006. 'Profiting from Innovation and the Intellectual Property Revolution,' *Research Policy* 35(8): 1122–30.

Poppo, L. and T. Zenger. 2002. 'Do Formal Contracts and Relational Governance Function as Substitutes or Complements?,' *Strategic Management Journal* 23(8): 707–25.

Powell, W. W. 1990. 'Neither Market Nor Hierarchy: Network Forms of Organization,' *Research in Organizational Behavior* 12(295): 336.

Ritter, T. and H. G. Gemünden. 2003. 'Network Competence: Its Impact on Innovation Success and Its Antecedents,' *Journal of Business Research* 56(9): 745–55.

Sanchez, R. and A. Heene (eds.) 1997. In *Strategic Learning and Knowledge Management*. New York: John Wiley.

Sawhney, M. and E. E. Prandelli. 2000. 'Communities of Creation: Managing Distributed Innovation in Turbulent Markets,' *California Management Review* 42(4): 24.

Shane, S. 2002. 'Selling University Technology: Patterns from MIT,' *Management Science* 48(1): 122–38.

Simon, F. and P. Kotler. 2003. *Building Global Biobrands: Taking Biotechnology to Market*. Free Press.

Teece, D. J. 1986. 'Profiting from Technological Innovation—Implications for Integration, Collaboration, Licensing and Public-Policy,' *Research Policy* 15(6): 285–305.

Thompson, J. D. 1967. *Organizations in Action*. New York: Wiley.

Uzzi, B. 1997. 'Social Structure and Competition in Interfirm Networks: The Paradox of Embeddedness,' *Administrative Science Quarterly* 42: 35–67.

von Hippel, E. 1988. *The Sources of Innovation*. Oxford: Oxford University Press.

——and G. von Krogh. 2003. 'Open Source Software and the "Private-Collective" Innovation Model: Issues for Organization Science,' *Organization Science* 14(2): 209–23.

Weick, K. E. 1990. 'Technology as Equivoque: Sensemaking in New Technologies,' in P. S. Goodman, L. S. Sproull, and Associates (eds.) *Technology and Organizations*. Oxford: Jossey-Bass.

Williamson, O. E. 1985. *The Economic Institutions of Capitalism*. New York: Free Press.

Winter, S. 1987. 'Knowledge and Competence as Strategic Assets,' in D. J. Teece (ed.) *The Competitive Challenge: Strategies for Industrial Innovation and Renewal*. Massachusetts, Cambridge: Ballinger.

10

An exchange of ideas about knowledge governance: seeking first principles and microfoundations

Teppo Felin and J.C. Spender

10.1. Teppo Felin (Henceforth Teppo):

First, let me thank the Oxford University Press and the editors, Nicolai Foss and Snejina Michailova, for allowing us to engage in this informal, unusual, and we hope, informative interaction and exchange of ideas.

To get us going, let me propose a few points and positions that might be worth pursuing. These are informed by what Nicolai labels the 'knowledge governance approach' (KGA) (Foss 2007)—which I see as an attempt to focus on some fundamental issues in the area of knowledge management (KM); that is, issues which have heretofore received relatively little attention. So let me start with three 'first principles' that might anchor our discussion in KM more generally and the KGA in particular. These three points in essence represent areas of research that deserve more attention in knowledge-based arguments of the firm, and, the KGA may indeed provide a vehicle for addressing them.

First, 'microfoundations' are needed for knowledge-related arguments pertaining to organizations. By microfoundations I mean there is a need to understand various individual-level factors in knowledge creation and production: abilities, decision-making, actions, beliefs, expectations, interests, imagination, preferences, and so forth. Thus, rather than assume individuals are simply heavily socialized toward perceiving their environments in a certain way, the KM literature would benefit from starting out from lower-level notions and systematically building theory upwards to understand how macro, knowledge-related outcomes emerge and form from these microlevel antecedents. This microfoundations program and intuition shares much with the social theory pioneered by James Coleman (1990, cf. Felin and Foss 2006).

Second, building on the above, the key microfoundations of organization and organizing—and KM—are individuals. That said, I recognize that JC has helped pioneer a version of KM that focuses quite heavily on collective issues, perhaps at the expense of individual-level factors or microfoundations (Spender 1996). The analysis that builds on JC's work, such as his widely used matrix of knowledge types (Spender 1993), seems to have continued along this heavily collectivist route (Felin and Hesterly 2007). But, it would seem that a natural, next step is to explicate the underlying microfoundations of KM. In other words, the natural progression of the KM field requires that it move toward understanding *the origins and sources* of where knowledge resides as well as toward an understanding of how knowledge develops and transfers. All this implies a renewed focus on the relevant microelements, of how these micro-, individual-level elements create and aggregate up to the macro-, organizational-level. It might be worth noting a similar progression in theoretical understanding, from the macro- to more microelements—generally seen as a shift from macro-explanatory variables to micro-explanatory variables—has also occurred in numerous other disciplines where progress has been made. Elster in fact argues that 'science progresses through reduction' (Elster 1989). I should note that the shift toward the microlevel is less a critique of the work that JC and others have pioneered, rather it is more of a natural and necessary next step in helping us understand the origins of the collective knowledge structures that have been posited.

The third point is that a focus on microfoundations scarcely precludes or denies the importance and existence of the social environment in which individuals are embedded. In other words, microfoundations ought also to be highly sensitive to the fact that individual-level activities (or preferences, interests, and so forth) are often necessarily pursued in collective settings, via collective action. That is, while individuals may have preferences, interests, and dreams that they hope to realize, the actualization or realization of these interests often can only happen via collective action, via an organization. In modern society, collective action and organization provide the key vehicles through which many meaningful, large-scale, innovative, and valuable activities are accomplished. A key point then is that individuals need to negotiate and interact with others to ensure that interests are aligned, that interests and preference cohere.

This type of 'political' negotiating and coalition building was important to the early Carnegie school (March 1962), but that intuition seems to have been lost in more recent theories of organization.

10.2. JC Spender (Henceforth JC):

OK Teppo, let's see if we are headed in the same direction here. You offer us three principles—first, a focus on microfoundations; second, the assumption that these are where individuals are, and third, that we need not leave the macrolevel behind. I cannot help but agree with these principles, but perhaps not in the way you want me to; so let me start in by responding to your first two points.

In the long tradition of methodological individualism (MI), for example, the Hayekian argument that economic and social theorizing needs to be grounded in the observable characteristics of human beings, there is much debate. It reflects a reductionist mode of explanation that goes back to Heraclitus and beyond. You, others, and Nicolai too, have written to this (Arrow 1994; Elster 1989; Felin and Foss 2005). The problem, of course, is that the supposedly universal characteristics of the individual are far from self-evident or undisputed. Most of the time those now appealing to MI are actually doing a 'bait and switch,' citing Hayek but actually suggesting the individual they have in mind is the familiar fully rational *homo economicus*. Since Hayek's time we have two substantial attacks on this poor chap, Simon's 'bounded rationality' (Foss 2003) and, more recently, 'behavioral economics' (Camerer 2003). So I need to know more about the putative individual underpinning your MI and why invoking her or him is going to clarify things.

Second, I am concerned about KGA's problematic. What question is it targeting and hoping to answer? My assumption, based largely on my reading of Nicolai's considerable contribution, is that it heralds a new round in his wrestling match with formal economics as he attempts to develop a nontrivial theory of the firm—and here I would cite Demsetz's critical assessment of the discipline's situation (Demsetz 1991; Gibbons 2005). I am guessing Foss's interest in the KGA starts, first, from the Coasian intuition that organizations exist because they are home to or congenial to some knowledge phenomena untypical of markets, such as the exercise of hierarchical power, and, second, if we think about the various modes of organizational governance, accepting power as opposed to letting individuals pursue their self-interest rationally, these seem more appropriate to managing such nonmarket phenomena.

This kind of distinction between free choice and power has long been present in Williamson's work (Williamson 1975, 1986) so it might be clarifying to talk about the differences between TCE and KGA. Are the KGA's alternative modes of governance not focused on cost? Does poor governance not lead to economic inefficiency? On the other hand, if cost is actually determinable, why the exercise of power, why not let actors choose, applying their rationality? Williamson would say that power is necessary because we see uncertainty colliding with guile—an assumed dimension of individuals, supplementing their rationality. So if the KGA sees there is more to it than optimizing cost, I suspect we need some clarification. I raise this point because I suspect the new theory of the firm we all have in mind here may well address the question last seriously framed, as far as I am aware, by Cyert and March. On page 16 of their classic (Cyert and March 1963), they suggest a viable theory of the firm—defined as one useful to practicing managers—would also bring microeconomics together with organization theory (OT). Hence, I hope the KGA's agenda is a move toward such a theory for I see OT today as an endangered discipline. On one flank the RBV advances its neo-economic reasoning against the ancient art of strategy, on the other, the survivors' retreat into organizational psychology and OB is cut off by economics's new behavioral analysis. Where are we to look for a defensible basis for OT?

To search in the knowledge management (KM) literature for some insight into how economic reasoning might explain the existence or clarify the operations of organizations may strike many as hopeless. After all, the KM discipline itself is also in parlous condition, increasingly unsure of its foundations and its objectives (Spender and Scherer 2007; Tsoukas 2005). As Nicolai's citation of Argote's work indicates (Argote 1999), the bulk of those working within KM treat knowledge as unproblematic; an objectifiable commodity, sometimes valuable but often costly to produce, that can be collected, stored, redistributed, and applied to produce value in the future. This defines organizational knowledge as a form of capital (Dean and Kretschmer 2007) and there is no obvious reason why it cannot then be handled by market-typical modes of choice and governance. If, on the other hand, knowledge is too sticky or slippery for markets to handle, 'tacit' perhaps or more a process of knowing, then other issues open up which may call for other ways of managing actors' choices. So I would ask about your notions of organizational knowledge and your confidence that what economists mean by governance can actually impact its creation, flow, or application.

10.3. Teppo:

First, I do not see the attempt at microfoundations, nor the knowledge governance approach more specifically, as an attempt to smuggle in the old *homo economicus*. Scarcely so. Rather, a better conceptualization might be what Baker and Pollock recently label '*homo-multifacetus*' (2007). That is, it is evident that individuals seldom have all the answers given uncertainty, limited time, information processing capabilities, and local knowledge (cf. Hayek 1945), *but*, it is important to note individuals also have heterogeneous preferences, interests, expectations, and understandings about the types of actions that they consider valuable rather than assume these preferences emerge simply from social interaction, or socialization more broadly. So, the goal of a microfoundational approach is to specify the individual's nature and decision-making capabilities appropriately, and to understand how heterogeneous interests—thus, perhaps taking the existence of individual interests for granted—are negotiated and aggregated. And, importantly, evidence suggests that we can move forward with the presumption that individuals not only have their own independent preferences and interests, but also that human capabilities exist somewhere between the highly idealized, perfectly rational, agent of economics and the heavily bounded and socially determined agent of sociology. The attempt, in terms of microfoundations, is to expand the bounds of rationality, to recognize and theoretically account for, not only heterogeneous interests, preferences, and so forth, but more importantly to account for (or, be able to explain) the many correct and imaginative decisions that individuals make, something that Grandori has recently called 'epistemic rationality' (Grandori 2006).

Thus, as has been recently noted in social psychology as well (see Krueger and Funder 2005), there has been much too heavy a focus on incorrect, poor, and biased decision-making. While poor decision-making undoubtedly exists, as do biases, the social sciences, management science included, have not accounted adequately for much of the progress of the past century, and the associated *correct* and imaginative decision-making. This type of intuition is emerging in psychology (e.g., Gigerenzer et al. 1999; see McKenzie 2005 for an overview), so perhaps its diffusion into management science will take a while. That said, the organization sciences should be at the forefront of understanding decision-making and associated actions and outcomes, as much of human activity and accomplishment and decision-making happens in collective, organizational settings.

Second, what is being advocated here can be construed as a need to understand some of the forgotten behavioral and social foundations of human and organizational action; these foundations indeed were originally embodied in the work of the Carnegie tradition (see Felin and Foss 2005, cf. Gavetti et al. 2007). That is, a need to focus on how individual preferences get negotiated in collective settings (March 1962), how organizational goals aggregate from individuals preferences and interests (Simon 1964), and so forth. This intuition has been lost as extant behavioral approaches focus heavily on the environmental aspects of organizational behavior (for a summary, see Greve 2005). So, rather than begin the analysis with a taken-for-granted environment, or taken-for-granted organization (cf. Coleman 1990), or taken-for-granted routine for that matter, all these collective constructs require further explanation, which microfoundations can indeed provide.

Third, you are reacting fairly negatively toward economic reasoning, wondering whether it can contribute anything to organization theory and the knowledge literature specifically. Economics absolutely has, and continues to, contributed to our understanding of organizations and knowledge. It is not that we need to import the full theoretical apparatus and assumptions of economics to understand organizations and knowledge; rather, I would suggest that a selective use of the logical and methodological intuition from economics can provide tremendous insights for organization theory and strategy. The logical and methodological intuition I am advocating here is not only embodied in economics, but an equally persuasive source of intuition comes from rational choice theory in sociology (cf. Boudon 2003; Coleman 1990). Both of these literatures assume—commensurate with recent evidence from psychology (cf. Stanovich 1999)—that individuals are rational and 'prone' to *correct* human decision-making and this intuition naturally lends itself to opening up the bounds of rationality, even warranting an assumption of a (more) rational agent (McKenzie 2004). Humans are not perfectly rational of course, but agents who do an admirable job of making decisions correctly with little information, little time, much uncertainty, and natural constraints to computation. Rationality for some reason appears to be a dirty word in management—thus the heavy emphasis on boundedness rather than rationality—but, I believe a rational choice model provides a promising future path for management science (Felin and Foss 2006).

Economic and rational choice reasoning and intuition will also help us unpack (open up the black box of) many of the collective constructs that are so readily taken for granted so in the organizational literature: whether it is the organization itself, or networks, culture, the environment, and so forth. Thus, methodological individualism adds some helpful analytical rigor and leads to a much-needed unpacking of various collective constructs. I should restate that my call for a rational choice program—and, I see KGA as one potential embodiment of it—should not be seen as a critique of extant work, rather, again, I see it as a natural progression for the field to begin to explicate underlying microfoundations, to make progress via reduction (Elster 1989).

10.4. JC:

Well, Teppo, I agree with you completely that the overarching project is to 'specify human nature and decision-making capabilities appropriately' hence I do not see what you find helpful in the work of Stanovich or Baker and Pollock or, indeed, in that of Krueger and Funder. As I read them, these authors seem to stand on some fundamental misunderstandings about the notion of rationality and what it means to attempt to modify or add to it. Frankly, I am not familiar with this literature or with their kind of psychologizing but I sense they are confusing some observational impressions—that people seem to exhibit characteristics they find difficult to capture using the notion of logicality—with some epistemological notions of rationality. So they feel driven to seek alternative forms of thought and/or explanation, unsure about whether these are empirically based or conceptual. In particular, Baker and Pollock's notion of *homo-multifacetus*, which I presume means 'multifaceted man,' is neither defined nor developed and seems more like a throwaway observation than a real theoretical proposition (Baker and Pollock 2007: 301). My immediate problem is that we are not told whether the 'multi' here is of the multiple goals which a fully rational person might pursue, or whether it implies something like a 'tolerance for ambiguity,' often associated with leadership, which finds some unspecified way of dealing with a truly heterogeneous goal-set. My reading is that 'the facets' are the different goals a single rational mind might be able to hold onto rather than some conceptually distinct mode of thought or action like intuition. Likewise you speak of 'heterogeneous preferences, interests, expectations and understandings' so I guess you see the facets as multiple goals, each pursued 'mind*fully*' as Weick might say, which seems a reasonable enough observation of our fellows and ourselves perhaps.

But how do you see this kind of heterogeneity being resolved, so moving us on from mere description toward a coherent theory-based explanation? Likewise I am not sure what it means to position the individual's operating goals somewhere between being the freely chosen and the negotiated or enforced. Do you have some algorithm for netting out the psychological and sociological determinants? Even then there would surely be residual heterogeneity since neither offers any coherent theory of the person. Perhaps you see some form of meta-preference against which all your heterogeneous goals can be ranked, so moving us on from the mere observation? Absent this Archimedean place of full rationality, such as the economists' rational self-interest, the heterogeneity you raise seems to push us irrevocably toward a relativism of 'it all depends' or 'anything goes,' as Feyerabend so famously remarked (Feyerabend 1993).

While not at all suggesting goal heterogeneity, Krueger and Funder's piece seems to be an expansive critique of the methodological dispositions of a particular research community, again with little consideration of what it might mean to move away from rationality as the basis for explanation and theory. Their avowed target is the 'negativity' of focusing on how people are sometimes less than fully rational, a parallel to medical research's evident focus on people who are sick. They correctly point out the ideal of total rationality is their null hypothesis, just as medics take wellness as the null to which they are trying to restore their patients. But their call for a 'more balanced' research program, one that lauds their assumption that people sometimes act rationally, or maybe even always try to be (intendedly) rational, seems a misunderstanding of how empirical research actually works. We can invoke Popperian falsification and argue that theoretical progress is about the empirical falsification of the reasonable conjecture that we thinking rationally about what we see around us. So the balanced program they call for could either be a careful recording of every observation of people acting rationally, the kind of everlasting verificationist project that drove Popper nuts, or, more interestingly, an attempt to explain our rationality itself. By this I mean to go behind the mere assumption of Rational Man typical of economics to some kind of explanation for the occurrence of this characteristic of our minds—psychological, neurological, or evolutionary perhaps. This searching behind the assumption seems to be what interests you about Krueger and Funder's work. But they are not, in fact, proposing any modes of thought as alternative to full rationality, nor do they seem interested in plotting the empirically discovered boundaries to practical reason—a task they would presumably see as 'negative.' Equally many neurobiologists search behind the assumption of rationality without pausing to consider the implications of trying to use the notion of rationality—as embedded in the notion of cause and effect—to construct an explanation of rationality as an neurobiological effect. Perhaps they are searching for some overarching biologically determined characteristic of which rationality is simply one manifestation, contingent perhaps on the excitation particularities of the different domains of the brain or on the quantum issues explored by Penrose (Penrose 1989). Likewise most of our fellow commentators seem happy enough with rationality as the principal explanatory characteristic of human thought, that is, to explain is to propose a logical and falsifiable cause and effect relationship. Most rational choice theorists simply presume the dominance of rationality as their null, entertaining illustrated in Harford's new book (Harford 2007), and you certainly seem sympathetic to this position.

I am not sympathetic, so we clearly differ on this. For me the challenge is to find a way of moving beyond the limits to rationality which Simon reminded us of. I think one way to do this is to define and adopt as axiomatic some contrasting characteristic of mind that can stand *pari passu* with rationality, so I am especially interested in what you call the 'forgotten behavioral and social foundations of human and organizational action' and the issues explored in the Carnegie Tech program. But how do you see these? Do you mean the politics of power, as interested March, or some Durkheimian collective consciousness, or some blind nonthinking herd instinct? It is clear that three or four centuries ago rationality was not as fetishized as it is today, so you might have in mind something like the Model of Man adopted by the Enlightenment philosophers. From Locke's position, for he saw judgement as a complement to reason, we can see our task is not to reject rationality, after all we are often logical and goal oriented. Rather the project is to complement the narrow and astringent rationality of *homo economicus* with some of the other modes of human thought and behavior that embrace more of what we know about ourselves and presume about others. Smith, you recall, spun his whole thinking from the notion of 'sympathy,' which interaction generated the social and human space within which rationality was sometimes appropriate. Thus I see the 'behavioral economic' (BE) thrust, in which 'bias' is proposed as a universal characteristic, as an attempt to replace a logically defined rationality with an empirically established behavioral one, so preserving the idea of rationality without either dismissing or complementing it. That is clearly professionally important for economics and might help explain why Kahneman won his Nobel. Personally, having tried out 'prospect theory' on my students, a homogeneous enough population, and found it rather wanting, so I see no compelling reason to think the BE biases are any more universal than are people themselves. And without this asserted universality we slip into the chasm of relativism noted above, in which each person's rationality—or systematic bias—is whatever it is and generalized theorizing is impossible.

At issue is whether we can say anything meaningful about any mode of human thought other than rational reasoning, where the meaning of this phrase is grounded externally in the abstractions of logic and our computer-likeness rather than subjectively in our uniqueness. What sense can it make to talk of reasoning 'illogically'? Is this not a contradiction? As Krueger and Funder note, we often describe emotion as that which disturbs rational reasoning. But does that do more than describe it? It tells us neither what emotion is, nor explicates its causes (if there are any), nor how we might theorize it. The fact that some neurobiologists, such as Damasio or Ledoux, observe 'different parts of the brain lighting up' under circumstances in which they say 'the subject' is experiencing emotion, might well tell us something about the neurophysiology of what they call the emotions but does not tell an epistemologist much about how emotion interferes with rationality. In fact, absent a theory of the individual as an integrated mind/body system, there seems no compelling reason to think these two concepts of emotion—the one epistemological, the other empirical, are even related, let alone interfere with each other. As Nussbaum shows in her fine analysis, the urban myth of this interference is an epistemological overhang from the Greek Stoics, one that cannot be sustained in the light of current philosophy or biology (Nussbaum 2001).

But, to get back to the central topic of our discussion, organizations and the degree to which economic thought (i.e., that based on an MI itself standing on the shoulders of *homo economicus*) can illuminate them. You are quite right I am questioning this. I am more than happy to agree with you that individuals, because they are human beings, often appear to be rational, and as they go about their everyday organizational work frequently apply their rationality. But what is this to do with the nature of organizations? Yes, employees may be pursuing goals that are organizational rather than personal, but is the organization no more than a system for broadcasting the goal of the day? Organizations may be 'made up' of people—though that seems to neglect the role of capital and land in Smith's model—but does that mean organizations can be given the same attributes of rationality that we simply assume in people? Just as an organization is made up of people so is the line at the checkout. Following the rational choice theorists, we might be able to create a tolerably good explanation for why people line up. But can we do the same for their collaboration into organizations? Under what universal, as opposed to socially or politically contingent, circumstance does it make sense for me to labor at less that statutory minimum wage to keep Wal-Mart's shareholders comfortable? With a 60 percent annual turnover, or thereabouts, clearly even the most needy get the message soon enough. So does this selection from a narrow range of feasible alternatives really be what we mean by economic rationality?

At the same time you talk of economic thought illuminating the 'knowledge literature.' I find this curious and wonder if it should not be the other way around. The knowledge management literature, standing as it does on the notion of 'tacit knowledge' to take it beyond the reach of *homo economicus*, certainly embraces a notion of rationality but is, by definition, not limited to it. Were it so limited the 'knowledge literature' would embrace the entirety of all 'scientific' theorizing and the term knowledge would be entirely redundant. Being interested in knowledge management as Polanyi shaped it with the notion of 'tacit knowing,' what I find absent from the economic discourse is something that complements our logicality. The impulse to look for this is not simply the evident poverty of economic reasoning and its inability to explain either why organizations exist or how they work, a situation which many great economists have remarked. Even more it is a result of occasionally recognizing ourselves as something other than mere theorists, cold-blooded (that emotion thing again) and interested only in the pursuit of Truth. On those occasions we struggle to recognize more of what goes on within ourselves and, we suspect, in others as we try to 'get along' with those we love or hate or otherwise share the human condition. I consider economics the lesser for having narrowed itself away from political economy in the pursuit of abstract rigor. I would argue the knowledge management literature rejects this narrowness and kicks open a door to an arational discourse, well illustrated by March's examination of Don Quixote (March and Augier 2004), a discourse that, like novels and plays, embraces politics, love, judgment, morality and, our fallibility in ways that economic reasoning clearly cannot. My hope, therefore, is that by searching beyond rationality alone, as the great economist Simon indicated we should, we might find something intrinsically human about our organizations, that is, that they only exist because of our arational dimensions. If we can indeed 'specify human nature and decision-making capabilities appropriately' we shall also find organization as an aspect of both.

10.5. Teppo:

First, let me defend economic *reasoning* (though, not all of economics), specifically as I think you overreach by pointing to 'the evident poverty of economic reasoning and its inability to explain why organizations exist or how they work, a situation which many great economists have remarked.' This goes too far. Economics remains central to organization science and strategy in particular (cf. Mahoney 2006), even though some would have us 'avoid the dangerous liaison with economics' (Pfeffer 1997: 192, cf. Ferraro et al. 2005). For example, transaction costs economics has said much—much of it seminal—about the origins of firms and their boundaries (Williamson 1975). And, the 'markets-in-hierarchy' type of intuition (Zenger and Hesterly 1997) is central and increasingly relevant to our understanding of organizations (particularly given increasing moves toward professional services which are knowledge intensive—see Greenwood and Empson 2001; Teece 2003). In other words, I think you are throwing the baby out with the bathwater, specifically as economic reasoning provides some of our most central insights about organizations and organizing. This of course is not to say that economics as a whole represents some capital-T truth (e.g., hyperrationality is obviously erroneous), of course not. The point more simply is that the more general ethos and approach of economics has much to commend it, including its focus on parsimony and tendency toward microfoundations, reduction, and so forth.

Second, I think you create an unnecessary chasm between economics and behavioral approaches. That is, while the Carnegie School was explicitly reacting to matters that they disagreed with in mainstream economics, nonetheless the Carnegie School also importantly *retained* much of the underlying intuition of economics, and, rightly so. For example, March and Simon's (1958) classic book *Organizations* is replete with economic reasoning. Note the heavy emphasis they put on 'inducements and contributions' and 'payments'; in other words, individual incentives were critical to understanding organizations (Barnard 1938 made similar points), and still are (Zenger and Hesterly 1997; Zenger and Marshall 2000). And, note that March and Simon's approach is significantly more methodologically individualist compared to where behavioral approaches of organizations have ended up of late, that is, heavily focused on the environment (Greve 2003). Others have also noted that we may have in part lost our way, highlighting the need to understand the micro-foundations of interaction and decision-making (Gavetti et al. 2007). For example, the focus on routines may have unnecessarily masked important dynamics related to where routines come from in the first place, and more importantly the routines 'hegemony' has unnecessarily tied the hands (=rationality) of managers (Felin and Foss 2005). It may be that routines are simply an *epi*-phenomenon. Furthermore, the focus on various *extra*-organizational, environmental factors as *the* locus of knowledge—such as networks or alliances (Kogut 2000; Powell et al. 1996)—has left many underlying, individual-level questions unanswered. So, in sum, I think you create an unnecessary chasm between economics and knowledge-based approaches of organization. I think economic reasoning can deeply and meaningfully help us to understand organizations (just as organization theory itself can also influence economics), as suggested by Nicolai's (2007*a*) efforts to advocate a 'knowledge governance approach.'

Third, what then are the meaningful questions that might be addressed from a behavioral perspective, perhaps with economic reasoning as an analytical tool? I think many of these questions were anticipated by early organizational scholars, and thus in part I think we need to return to these roots. So, for example, you bring up the issue of organizational goals. Goals are exactly the types of matters that I believe need significantly more focus; other closely related matters that deserve emphasis include: beliefs, preferences, expectations, values, interests, and so forth. Specifically, one of *the* key questions is the emergence of collective goals and expectations (or, interests for that matter); where do these come from, how do individual goals aggregate? Note for example that Simon's (1964) early work in this area was explicitly an effort to understand how individual goals aggregate and how new collective goals might emerge. Furthermore, in a key piece in the *Journal of Politics* (1962), titled 'The Business Firm as a Political Coalition,' March wrestles with questions about how coalitions emerge, and specifically how individual interests are in essence negotiated and aggregated (cf. Cohen et al. 2001). The intuition heavily relies on economic reasoning, and in both papers the underlying intuition is almost game theoretic (see similar game-theoretic intuition in Foss 2007*b*). In short, I think there is much here at the nexus of individuals and organizations that deserves significantly more attention.

10.6. JC:

Well Teppo, we seem to be talking past each other, as organization theorists and economists normally do. Why is this? How can I make my point to someone already committed (emotionally perhaps?) to the notion that economic reasoning illuminates our behavior at the microfoundational level, though I see you are now using the term 'intuition' a great deal? Is this intuition, evidently so important to the advance of theory, rational in the sense we have used this term previously? Anyway, I have no problem with macroeconomic (i.e., loose) assertions about, say, supply and demand, or even with the make-or-buy decisions that inform TCE. Although these tend to ignore the evident fact of power and its place in our lives, they are important ways of talking about human behavior that are blessedly free of religious and cultural idiosyncrasy. Yes, it is useful to think through the larger consequences of giving individuals the freedom to pursue their own interests (de Tocqueville 2000). It is simply that when you try to move, as I agree we should, to the microlevel to build a rigorous theory of human behavior, you have to invoke some model of the individual that differs from *homo economicus* if one is to say anything relevant. I am certainly open to the charge of overreaching but, with respect, I think it is you who does this as you glide blithely from the abstract assumption of *homo economicus* into making assertions about real human behavior.

Let me illustrate. It is clear that disciplines in general, and economists in particular, develop sophisticated ways of protecting their discourses from those who, like hecklers, would upset them. The crux of *sprachethik* is to know the distinction between the discourse's axioms and its reasoned deductions. Disciplines remain open to criticism of their deductions, indeed that is much of what research and theoretical debate is about, but they are immunized *ex definitio* against having their axioms replaced. There is a tautology here, for new axioms mean a new paradigm, in a Kuhnian sense, or more specifically, a new theory and discourse. For example, commenting on peoples' marriages we would normally use language that cannot be related to Becker's analyses of why people have children. Do our comments then critique Becker's work? No, they are part of a different language game. In this same vein I have given various economists occasion to remark 'Well that's interesting JC, but it isn't economics.' So you and I are using different languages. This is why all of us should study McCloskey's work closely, especially her wonderfully tart summary of economics as a rhetorical pastime (McCloskey 1998).

At a more specific level let me rebut your suggestion that Williamson's work or indeed the TCE has illuminated the origins of organizations, that is why they exist. I'll give you that they might provide insights into the movement of an existing organization's boundaries. But what they have really done is given economists the smug feeling that they know something about firms, and this is far from being the same thing as addressing managers' questions. If you tell the average entrepreneur that her or his firm came into existence because its transaction costs were lower than those in the market for those same transactions you'll likely get a terse and not-too-friendly response about ivory towers and economists not understanding anything about innovation and the travails of making it happen.

As I have written elsewhere, the idea of comparing transaction costs within and without the firm seems obvious enough to managers, among whom I would include myself, while considering a make or buy decision. Indeed it was Coase's conversations in 1934 with real American corporate executives, rather than with economists, that precipitated his 1937 'intuition.' But such managers are not making the comparison economists suggest—about an isolated transaction, as Williamson insists was Commons's assertion. Commons's argument was actually quite different, but let us skip that for today; rather his point is that every transaction is embedded in a complex situation (Commons 1924) and it is from their grasp of that managers bring a substantial amount of tacit knowledge to bear—all of which is effectively disallowed by your *homo economicus*. But let's stick with your characterization. Let's take the notion of the internal cost of a transaction. Even assuming we could get our cost-and-works accountant to estimate this—which is why they are known as 'estimators'—what about the allocation of overheads, that is, the classic managerial accountant's problem? How much of the unique, historically contingent, and ongoing costs of setting up the firm and maintaining its infrastructure should be allocated to this particular transaction? Here the abstract and not very demanding idea of determining this cost collides with the reality of a firm which cannot ever calculate, as opposed to estimate, such costs. The possibility of doing this, even if one had a complete record of every cost incurred going back to the foundation of the firm, is finally completely undercut by the uncertainty on which Penrose's work (Edith's that is, though Roger's would do as well) pivots.

What is the value to the business of its recorded resources and other inventory? We cannot tell—that's the point. The only thing we know for certain is that it cannot be 'at cost,' for if its value is really that then we are denying the possibility of profit, and with that, survival in an imperfect nonzero transactions cost environment. Thus, managers estimate rather than calculate when considering their make-or-buy decisions and these processes are (*a*) historically and subjectively contingent and thus cannot be illuminated by the abstraction of *homo economicus* and (*b*) can never be pinned down enough as basis to provide a 'theory of the firm.' I leave on one side the complementary issue that organizations are composed of more than managers and the question of how managers communicate their make or buy decisions to those managed, given that they too are less than fully rational. Thus your assertion that economic reasoning underpins organization theorizing is precisely incorrect. On the contrary, economics deploys its rhetoric, unsuccessfully from the organizational or management theorist's point of view, to hide the very arational intuitive aspects of human beings that must be brought into view if we are ever to understand why organizations exist rather than simply taking them for granted—as economists do when applying a TCE approach to the location of their boundaries (yet another contentious concept). To presume we can bypass these issues of uncertainty and bounded rationality with some a-cognitive behavioral notions seems quite bizarre to me, denying as it does the whole notion of human agency. Thus, while the Carnegie Tech group's work is extremely interesting and provocative it ultimately fails because of its horror of abandoning *homo economicus*.

You go on to cite Barnard and the 'inducement/contributions schema.' This is especially curious for you are appealing to a critic of MI rather than its supporter (I think you really mean to cite March and Simon). I have long regarded Barnard as one of less than a handful of people who have said something fundamentally revealing about organizations. Taylor, Veblen, Coase, and Penrose would be others. But it has taken me 35 years to grasp where I part company from Barnard. It is a bit peripheral to our discussion but at issue is whether the organization is a closed and thereby calculable system. This bears on our discussion in the same way that I try and distinguish estimation and calculation above—estimation being our intuitive way of abbreviating or 'closing off' an open system to render it calculable. There is a wonderfully evocative paper by Klapp about the 'opening and closing' of systems (Klapp 1975). Thus managerial estimates depend on heuristics (routines?) rather than on theory or calculation, and these are inevitably specific to the firm and its operations and history. In all probability, they are all that can be known of the firm. This is why Penrose's theory requires one to consider not only the difficult-to-estimate costs of learning how to generate services from resources in a first period but also the reduced costs of reapplying the resulting knowledge in a second period. It is this second and subsequent period reduction, and the resulting dynamism, which drives the growth of the firm, not the costs incurred in the first period. At the same time the knowledge generated is hostage to unforecastable changes of circumstance that might render it worthless. Penrose's firm is open, closed only by the management team's intuitions and actions, and their learning as a result of their experience of applying that knowledge. Likewise the richness in Barnard is that he positions 'the executive' as the one whose intuition and creativity 'closes off' the epistemological openness that he defines into his analysis with his trinity of subsystems 'incommensurate between themselves.' Thus, the inducements/contributions schema is the very antithesis of rational calculation. No one can calculate the ultimate benefits of participating in a firm. Nor can the inducing firm do this, since much of what it requires of its participants is to innovate in the face of the inevitable uncertainty of business. Nor can the firm ever know the entire set of inducements acting on any one individual—it may all be due to his mother or sibling jealousy. Thus the Benthamite calculus fails and both Penrose and Barnard see managers and all others as having arational capabilities which go far beyond those implied by *homo economicus*.

Let me wrap up my case. Yes, I completely agree with you that it would be good to surface and clarify the microfoundations to our theorizing about organizations (and markets too perhaps, but that is for another day). I also agree with the general thrust of your comments, along with Nicolai's, that the way we see collective level notions deployed often indicates no more than sloppy thinking. In my defense, I originally intended to use the contrast of individual and collective levels to mutually define and so illuminate some KM issues rather than, as you presumed, proposing we could talk usefully about collective knowledge on its own. But as we probe for some microfoundations we differ widely in our views of the consequences of doing this. I suspect you and Nicolai both want to hang onto *homo economicus* because it is the mother lode of and justification for economic discourse, for example, you see bright prospects for rational choice theory. You know that if you move to another model of man, one that embraces intuition and emotion, perhaps, you depart the discipline itself—interesting perhaps, but it's not economics.

For my part, I am narrowly interested in managers and their organizations and believe we face stark conceptual choices, that is, either we believe that economic theory can give us a managerially useful theory of the organization or we do not. Likewise we might assume and take organizations as axiomatic and unproblematic, self-evident socioeconomic entities that have boundaries and exist, and are separable from their managers. This is the main attraction of systems theory, for the popularity of which Barnard must clearly take some blame. From this assumption we probe for the organizational system's inherent nature and characteristics—feedback, double-loop learning, environmental sensing, and autopoietic perhaps. I see such theorizing about human organizations as a blind alley simply because it pushes people and their arational characteristics out of the analysis. Organizations are made up of people, we say. The alternative is to see organization as the problematic and place our modest conceptual chips on an axiomatic model of the individual, which is the MI impulse.

But here comes the hook. We have to adopt a model of man that makes being organized, as opposed to operating self-interestedly in a market, explicable. *Homo economicus* is actually Nonorganizable Man, by assumption, for there can never be a decontextualized rational reason for him to collaborate with others in the pursuit of a nonpersonal goal, so goals and goal-setting are central, as you suggest. The explanation for an individual's adopting an organizational goal as opposed to a personal goal lies in the particularities of the context of that choice, and the resulting theory is thus about that context rather than a universal theory of organization. The *apologia*, the idea that a participant's goal can be perfectly aligned with that of an organization is just the kind of rhetorical stuff which McCloskey exposes. *Homo economicus* is a creature of self-interest alone. There can never be a theory of human organization which makes such an inhuman axiom its basis.

I applaud your drive to the microfoundations for it forces these questions to the surface and in so doing brings nearer the time when we go beyond *homo economicus* and adopt a richer more contextualized and realistic model of man—such as might appear in any of great novel. So I believe you have yet to come to terms with the fact that our project will ultimately render mainstream microeconomic discourse a curiosity of the past, as McCloskey suggests. As we probe the governance characteristics of real organizations and extend the KGA we confront the core issue for our theorizing, of managing the intuition and agency of human others. *Homo economicus* is not a good place to start for he, alas, has neither.

10.7. Teppo:

JC, I agree. Transactions are complex and hard to calculate. Power is important, so are social dynamics. Disciplines have their norms; perhaps we are engaged in 'language games.' *But,* the underlying ethos that informs my approach to management science is more analytical in nature and more realist in perspective. That is, in the end we have to explain something theoretically, in parsimonious fashion. We cannot include everything in the model. Or, we cannot simply say that everything is mutually instantiated (cf. Giddens 1984). Rather, we have to focus on key elements and drivers and assume away the rest: idealization and abstraction is the essence of science, its power and beauty. So, it is not sufficient to simply point to complexity, or some other x-factor (whether environment or power) and say that an approach is somehow wrong. Rather, we need to come up with alternative or complementary or expansive explanations to the ones already proffered, to offer better idealizations and models. Now, economics is certainly not a panacea, I have simply advocated economic *reasoning* and intuition given its analytical nature and tendency toward reduction. I might note that—despite your pronouncements to the contrary—Barnard (1938) and March and Simon (1958) certainly appeared to share this intuition. For example, Barnard was fairly clear not only in his emphasis on inducements and contributions, but more generally his approach was explicitly driven by methodological individualism: 'The individual is always the basic strategic factor of organization' (1938: 139).

Now, where does this leave us? Let me offer two concluding thoughts: an epistemological point and then hopefully some key points oriented toward 'first principles'-type of research questions.

First, I do not think that caricatures of economics help us advance discussions about understanding organizations, knowledge, and organizing. In short, I really do not buy into the language game intuition of epistemology introduced by Kuhn, Wittgenstein, and others. I would rather like to think, naively perhaps, that we are all engaged in an effort to truly understand organizations: their nature, origins, advantage, and so forth. Microfoundations are central to this. I do not see disciplinary boundaries as being relevant to the effort to understand organizations. There is excellent work on organizations being done in economics (e.g., Garicano 2000), much of it formal and analytical, and there is excellent work being done in strategy and organization theory (e.g., Nickerson and Zenger 2004). I see 'transdisciplinarity' as offering an important future for organization science, the boundaries simply are unnecessary and the disappearance of disciplinary boundaries will ought to give way to a better understanding about organizational phenomena. Thus, programmatic efforts, such as Nicolai's 'knowledge-governance approach,' appear to be highly conducive to the integration of insights from numerous disciplines, to help us understand specific questions surrounding knowledge and collective effort, organizing, and organizations.

Now, I am not completely naïve. Theoretical insights from different disciplines can be, and often are, contradictory, sometimes wildly so, as illustrated by the reemergence of the neoclassical economics versus organization theory clash (cf. Ferraro et al. 2005; Pfeffer 1997). But, being the naïve realist that I am, I believe that these clashes can and ought to be settled via the merits of the respective arguments rather than merely referring to 'language games.' In other words, we must realize that reasoning and science relies (at least in part) on that 'massive central core of human thinking which has no history' (Strawson 1959: 10). Thus, referencing language games is simply an act of academic cowardice—an effort to avoid engaging with the issues, logic, and arguments at stake. Furthermore, citing language games inherently does not recognize that some theories and arguments and facts simply are false period. Thus, vetting the 'true' and 'false' of arguments, proposed facts, and theories is at the very heart of science.

Second, back to the matter of 'first principles'—what are the key foundational research questions that relate to knowledge and organizations? From my perspective, many of these revolve around the need for a microfoundations 'program'; again, I see the knowledge governance approach (Foss 2007*a*) as one vehicle for carrying this out. So, let me try to articulate some key areas that deserve further consideration. A key issue implicated by microfoundations is our model of human rationality and human nature. Specifically, given recent changes in our conception of human rationality and decision-making capabilities (e.g., Gigerenzer et al. 1999; Krueger and Funder 2000; McKenzie 2004), our models of rationality in management also need to evolve and reflect these changing conceptions. Thus, some key questions include: How do we specify rationality appropriately in organization science? How do our specifications of rationality relate to strategy and organizational contexts? Human nature also is central to our understanding of decision-making, learning, and so forth, and thus extant 'blank slate-like,' heavily behavioral, models also need to be updated. And, in general, our conceptions of bounded rationality need to place more emphasis on rationality and less on boundedness.

A second key issue is the matter of how various social effects emerge and originate from individual action and interaction. Specifically two things need to be recognized. First, that various social effects (whether the organization itself or matters such as networks) necessarily have individual-level origins and antecedents. Second, it must be recognized that individual action is taken within social context, which in essence requires the negotiation of heterogeneous preferences and interests. Key questions then include the following: How do various social effects—whether networks, organizations themselves, structure, etc.—emerge from individual interaction? How does collective action emerge from heterogeneous interests or beliefs? How do heterogeneous preferences and interests get aggregated or negotiated?

Another interesting micro–macro issue is the relationship between individual judgment and various organizational forms. Scholars have recently raised these issues (see Knudsen and Levinthal 2007), but numerous important questions remain. The questions are particularly interesting and important in a knowledge economy (cf. Foss 2006; Teece 2003): What are key organizational forms that best tap into knowledge housed in specialized experts? How is an individual's judgment best optimized in collective settings and what implications does this have for governance and new organizational forms? This area of investigation, at the nexus of judgment and organizational forms, appears to be particularly promising, and practically highly relevant given the demands of knowledge work. There are also important and daunting issues to be investigated at the nexus of individual and collective judgment. Extant theories often assume that social interaction somehow optimizes judgment and decision-making, but, there is plenty of psychological literature that suggests that this simply is not the case. Thus, the following type of questions seems to be critical: How does judgment get aggregated? What forms best optimize individual decision-making capabilities and what situations might benefit from forms that privilege collective judgment?

Overall, we've covered much ground here, in part perhaps talking past each other, but nonetheless the exercise has been engaging and, we hope, interesting for the reader.

10.8. JC:

Thanks Teppo, this has been fun and makes for another step in the ongoing conversation we have been having for several years now. We are certainly as one in our interest in organizations and management—and in economics too. They are important frames for the steps we take to try and better the human condition. I think economists are inclined, like Williamson, to argue that 'in the beginning there were markets' (Williamson 1975: 20). I would want to resist this and argue that perhaps in the beginning there were organizations, hierarchies perhaps, which established the title that property owners might then exchange. Irrespective of any historical claims, it seems obvious that in a property-owning democracy such as ours there is something of a conceptual divide between socioeconomic relations in which people pursue their own interests, a system of free exchange that appealed to Hayek and his colleagues, and those in which some individuals are obliged to pursue another's interest within a system of power. If this is accepted we can try to understand our situation from at least two bases in the hope that we might eventually bring them together in the way that physics advanced substantially when mass and energy were equated. Until that time, of course, we risk talking past each other.

But maybe it is only the conversation that is important, for to deny the relevance or usefulness of language games is itself no more than another language game. Thus the implication is that we must continue to interact across our disciplinary boundaries (language games), and resist the temptation to talk only to the members of our own community, thereby separating what we do and whatever intelligence we produce from the really important questions that concern those whose life is not lived in the ivory tower, the people who create real value, and the real conditions of life.

References

Argote, L. 1999. *Organizational Learning: Creating, Retaining and Transferring Knowledge*. Massachusetts, Boston: Kluwer.

Arrow, K. J. 1994. 'Methodological Individualism and Social Knowledge,' *American Economic Review* 84(2): 1–9.

Baker, T. and T. G. Pollock. 2007. 'Making the Marriage Work: The Benefits of Strategy's Takeover of Entrepreneurship for Strategic Organization,' *Strategic Organization* 5(3): 297–312.

Barnard, C. 1938. *The Functions of the Executive*. Harvard University Press.

Boudon, R. 2003. 'Beyond Rational Choice Theory,' *Annual Review of Sociology* 29: 1–21.

Camerer, C. F. (ed.) 2003. In *Advances in Behavioral Economics*. New Jersey: Princeton University Press.

Coase, H. 1937. 'Nature of the Firm,' *Economica* 16: 386–405.

Coleman, J. 1990. *Foundations of Social Theory*. Cambridge, Mass.: Harvard University Press.

Commons, J. R. 1924. *The Legal Foundations of Capitalism*. New York: Macmillan.

Cyert, R. M. and J. G. March. 1963. *A Behavioral Theory of the Firm*. New Jersey, Englewood Cliffs: Prentice-Hall.

de Tocqueville, A. 2000. *Democracy in America* (H. C. Mansfield and D. Winthrop, Translation). Illinois, Chicago: University of Chicago Press.

Dean, A. and M. Kretschmer. 2007. 'Can Ideas Be Capital? Factors of Production in the Postindustrial Economy: A Review and Critique,' *Academy of Management Review* 32(2): 573–94.

Demsetz, H. 1991. 'The Theory of the Firm Revisited,' in O. E. Williamson and S. G. Winter (eds.) *The Nature of the Firm: Origins, Evolution, and Development*. Oxford: Oxford University Press.

Elster, J. 1989. *Nuts and Bolts for the Social Sciences*. Cambridge: Cambridge University Press.

Felin, T. and N. J. Foss. 2005. 'Strategic Organization: A Field in Search of Micro-Foundations,' *Strategic Organization* 3: 441–55.

—— —— 2006. 'Individuals and Organizations: Further Thoughts on a Microfoundations Project,' *Research Methodology in Strategy and Management* 3: 253–88.

—— and W. S. Hesterly. 2007. 'The knowledge-based view, nested heterogeneity, and new value creation: Philosophical considerations on the locus of knowledge,' *Academy of Management Review* 32: 195–218.

Ferraro, F., J. Pfeffer, and R. Sutton. 2005. 'Economics Language and Assumptions: How Theories can become Self-Fulfilling,' *Academy of Management Review* 30: 8–24.

Feyerabend, P. 1993. *Against Method*. London: Verso.

Foss, N. J. 2003. 'Bounded Rationality and Tacit Knowledge in the Organizational Capabilities Approach: An Assessment and a Re-Evaluation,' *Industrial and Corporate Change* 12(2): 185–201.

—— 2006. *Strategy, Economic Organization, and the Knowledge Economy*. Oxford: Oxford University Press.

—— 2007. 'The emerging knowledge governance approach: challenges and characteristics,' *Organization* 14: 29–52.

—— 2007. 'The Emerging Knowledge Governance Approach: Challenges and Characteristics,' *Organization* 14(1): 29–52.

Garicano, L. 2000. Hierarchies and the Organization of Knowledge in Production. *Journal of Political Economy* 108: 874–904.

Giddens, A. 1984. *The Constitution of Society: Outline of the Theory of Structuration*. Berkeley, CA: University of California Press.

Gibbons, R. 2005. 'Four Formal(izable) Theories of the Firm?,' *Journal of Economic Behavior and Organization* 58: 200–45.

Gigerenzer, G. and the ABC Reasearch Group. 1999. *Simple Heuristics That Make Us Smart*. Oxford University Press.

Grandori, A. 2006. 'Form Bounded to Epistemic Rationality: Toward a Theory of Rational Discovery,' Bocconi University working paper.

Greenwood, R. and L. Empson. 2003. 'The professional partnership: Relic or exemplary form of governance,' *Organisation Studies* 24: 909–33.

Greve, H. 2005. *Organizational Learning from Performance Feedback: A Behavioral Perspective on Innovation and Change*. Cambridge: Cambridge University Press.

Harford, T. 2007. *The Logic of Life: The Rational Economics of an Irrational World*. New York: Random House.

Hayek, F. A. 1945. 'The Use of Knowledge in Society,' *American Economic Review* 35: 519–30.

Klapp, O. 1975. 'Opening and Closing of Systems,' *Behavioral Science* 20: 251–7.

Knudsen, T. and D. Levinthal. 2007. 'Two faces of search: alternative generation and alternative evaluation,' *Organization Science* 18: 39–54.

Kogut, B. 2000. 'The Network as Knowledge: Generative Rules and the Emergence of Structure,' *Strategic Management Journal*, 21: 405–25.

Krueger, J. I. and D. C. Funder. 2004. 'Towards a Balanced Social Psychology: Causes, Consequences and Cures for the Problem-Seeking Approach to Social Behavior and Cognition,' *Behavioral and Brain Sciences* 27: 313–27.

Mahoney, J. 2006. *Economic Foundations of Strategy*. Sage: New York.

March, J. G. 1962. 'The Business Firm as a Political Coalition,' *Journal of Politics* 24(4): 662–78.

March, J. and H. Simon. 1958. *Organizations*. New York: John Wiley.

——and M. Augier. 2004. 'James March on Education, Leadership, and Don Quixote: Introduction and Interview,' *Academy of Management Learning & Education* 3: 169.

McCloskey, D. N. 1998. *The Rhetoric of Economics*. Winconsin, Madison: University of Wisconsin Press.

McKenzie, C. R. M. 2003. 'Rational Models as Theories – Not Standards – of Behavior,' *Trends Cognitive Science* 7: 403–6.

——2005. Judgment and Decision Making. K. Lamberts, R. L. Goldstone eds. *Handbook of Cognition*. Sage, London, 321–38.

——and L. A. Mikkelsen. 2007. 'A Bayesian View of Covariation Assessment,' *Cognitive Psychology* 54: 33–61.

Nickerson, J. A. and T. R. Zenger. 2004. 'A Knowledge-Based Theory of the Firm: The Problem-Solving Perspective,' *Organization Science* 15: 617–32.

Nussbaum, M. C. 2001. *Upheavals of Thought: The Intelligence of Emotions*. Cambridge: Cambridge University Press.

Penrose, R. 1989. *The Emperor's New Mind*. New York: Oxford University Press.

Pfeffer, J. 1997. *New Directions for Organization Theory: Problems and Prospects*. New York: Oxford University Press.

Powell, W. W., K. W., Koput, and L. Smith-Doerr. 1996. 'Interorganizational collaboration and the locus of innovation: Networks of learning in biotechnology,' *Administrative Science Quarterly* 41: 116–45.

Spender, J. C. 1993. 'Competitive Advantage from Tacit Knowledge? Unpacking the Concept and Its Strategic Implications,' *Academy of Management Best Paper Proceedings* 37–41.

Spender, J. C. 1996. 'Making Knowledge the Basis of a Dynamic Theory of the Firm,' *Strategic Management Journal* 17: 45–62.

——and A. G. Scherer. 2007. 'The Philosophical Foundations of Knowledge Management: Editors' Introduction,' *Organization* 14(1): 5–28.

Stanovich, K. E. 1999. *Who is Rational? Studies in Individual Differences in Reasoning*. New York: Laurence Erlbaum.

Strawson, P. F. 1959. *Individuals*. London.

Tsoukas, H. 2005. *Complex Knowledge: Studies in Organizational Epistemology*. Oxford: Oxford University Press.

Williamson, O. E. 1975. *Markets and Hierarchies: Analysis and Antitrust Implications*. New York: Free Press.

——1986. *Economic Organization: Firms, Markets and Policy Control*. Sussex, Brighton: Wheatsheaf Books.

Zenger, T. R. and W. S. Hesterly. 1997. The Disaggregation of Corporations: Selective Intervention, High-Powered Incentives, and Molecular Units. *Organization Science* 8: 209–22.

——and C. R. Marshall. 2000. 'Determinants of incentive intensity in group-based rewards.' *Academy of Management Journal* 43: 149–63.

11

Knowledge governance: what have we learned? and where are we heading?

Nicolai J. Foss and Snejina Michailova

11.1. Introduction

Pondering some years ago the issue of what 'knowledge approaches can contribute to organizational theory,' Anna Grandori (in Grandori and Kogut 2002: 225) observed that these approaches had contributed '...a new "contingency" factor for understanding organizational arrangements.... Knowledge complexity, differentiation, and specialization, complementarity and interdependence are emerging as important contingencies affecting effective organization and governance solutions.'

However, we submit that an overall implication of the chapters in this book is that one can go further than saying that 'knowledge approaches' have merely added a '"contingency" factor for understanding organizational arrangements': it is, in fact, more ambitious and increasingly meaningful to claim the emergence of a knowledge governance approach (a notion coined by Grandori 1997). A pertinent question is, however, *how* distinctive and coherent the knowledge governance approach is. In other words, where are we in terms of shared ideas, insights, research strategies, and so on—and where are we likely to head in the future? We address these questions in this concluding chapter.

The purpose is not to ambitiously argue that immediately ahead of us is something akin to a 'research program' in the sense of Lakatos (1970) with 'hard core,' 'protective belt,' 'positive heuristics,' etc. Such an argument would not be viable. To exemplify, there do not seem to be any shared heuristics between the highly abstract treatment by Christensen and Knudsen (Chapter 3) on the one hand and the empirically based argument by Scarbrough and Amaeshi (Chapter 9), or between Grandori's (Chapter 4) discussion of polyarchic governance and Argote and Kane's understanding of knowledge governance (Chapter 8), or even between any of those four chapters. However, other chapters do seem to form more of a cluster; for example, Heiman, Nickerson, and Zenger (Chapter 2), Grandori (Chapter 3), Foss and Foss (Chapter 4), and Osterloh and Weibel (Chapter 5) all base their reasoning on a discriminating alignment framework, that is, the idea that the relevant knowledge-based unit of analysis is aligned with the governance structures or mechanisms that best handle the relevant activity or transaction. An efficiency principle is implicitly invoked as the mechanism that aligns transactions and structures/mechanisms. Although some of the chapters are explicitly critical of organizational economics in its transaction cost economics manifestation, there is nevertheless a significant debt owed to this approach. Another cluster of contributions seems to be formed through the chapters by Osterloh and Weibel, Argote and Kane, and Husted and Michailova, all inspired by organizational behavior theories and examining organizational behavior concepts as particular governance mechanisms (e.g., identity, socialization).

However, given the diversity of the contributions on knowledge governance, including the diversity of the chapters in this book, the more modest argument being advanced here is that we are witnessing the emergence of a relatively dense network of connected ideas called 'knowledge governance' (or the 'knowledge governance approach,' Foss 2007). Moreover, this 'network of ideas' goes beyond the overall and by now somewhat exhausted argument that the management of knowledge has become a critical issue for competitive dynamics, international strategy, the building of resources, the boundaries of firms, and many other issues. Specifically, we can see convergence on issues such as what knowledge governance should seek to explain; what is the unit of analysis; how that unit should be dimensionalized; and so on. The following sections identify such convergence. As a point of reference and orientation, the table below provides a mapping of the dimensions in which the chapters in this book differ and converge, respectively.[1]

[1] The chapter by Felin and Spender is left out because it is a confrontation between very different perspectives.

11.2. What Should Be Explained? Knowledge Governance *Explananda*

The notion that there is a unity to the various undertakings that can be classified under the knowledge governance umbrella may seem fragile in the face of the many phenomena that knowledge governance scholars seek to address and explain. This book has offered a series of seemingly very different *explananda*, many of which are entirely new to the literature. Examples include the following: how problem finding can be enabled by structured processes (Heiman et al.), how project acceptance depends on organization structure (Christensen and Knudsen), how distributed knowledge may be governed by managerial authority (Foss and Foss), how firms can cope with knowledge sharing dilemmas in interfirm alliances (Husted and Michailova), etc. (see Table 11.1). What unites these treatments in spite of the apparent diversity is the notion that management can design organizational arrangements and processes to facilitate knowledge processes—that is, the creation, transfer, sharing, integration, and use of knowledge—and that such design activities should take into account the distinct character of knowledge and knowledge processes (cf. also the Introductory chapter).

Assuredly, many scholars in organization, strategic management, and other fields in management as well as in economics and sociology have argued that organization is responsive to knowledge and that in turn organization may shape knowledge. The 'extended network' of knowledge governance scholars reaches far back in time. Thus, on a fundamental level the information-processing emphasis in the organization theory of the 1960s and 1970s illustrates the first causality (i.e., that organization is responsive to knowledge), and earlier, Hayek's (1945) famous argument concerning the need for decentralization when relevant knowledge is 'knowledge of time and circumstance' makes a similar point on an even more abstract level (as Grandori recognizes in her chapter). Less abstractly, the innovation management literature has long stressed that such organizational issues as role definition, team composition, the distribution of authority, etc. should be very much responsive to the nature of product development efforts.

However, organization also shapes knowledge: the organizational division of labor implies that processes of knowledge creation become path dependent. As Loasby (1976: 133) noted, an organizational structure '... not only determines where an organization's problems are worked on,

Table 11.1. Diversity across the chapters in this book

	Explanandum	Unit of analysis	Dimensions of unit of analysis	Microfoundations	Organizational alternatives
C2: Heiman et al.	Knowledge creation, 'problem solving and identification'	The problem	Complexity, degree of decomposability	Must take account of cognitive biases	Markets, authority-based and consensus-based hierarchy
C3: Christensen and Knudsen	Decision quality (i.e., search and evaluation processes)	The project	Project quality	Bounded rationality; motivational issues not treated	Organizational structures have differential evaluation properties
C4: Grandori	Knowledge creation	Innovation	Uncertainty	Agents are 'scientists'; they pursue valid knowledge through conjectures and refutations	'Associational' and 'polyarchic' governance are superior alternatives for governing knowledge creation
C5: Foss and Foss	Efficient governance of knowledge use when knowledge is distributed	Knowledge in a social system	How distributed is the relevant knowledge?	Conventional economic assumptions	Two types of authority are distinguished and contrasted with price-based allocation
C6: Osterloh and Weibel	Knowledge creation	Explorative knowledge production	Cognitive distance/overlap	Must include psychology research on motivation	High-powered incentives and 'unfriendly' monitoring are contrasted with low-powered incentives, institutional framing, etc.
C7: Argote and Kane	Knowledge creation and transfer	Innovation/idea	Degree of demonstrability	Must include identification processes	Building a superordinate identity may be a low-cost alternative to other mechanisms
C8: Husted and Michailova	Knowledge sharing	Shared knowledge	What knowledge, when, and why to keep in the organization, and what, when, and why to share externally?	Must include organizational members' identification and allegiance	Socialization tactics can efficiently substitute formal and more expensive governance mechanisms
C9: Scarbrough and Amaeshi	Governance of knowledge creation under open innovation	Shared knowledge	Tacitness, system embeddedness	Not explicated	Interplay between formal and relational mechanisms

but also helps to determine what problems they shall be, how they are defined, and what solutions will be attempted.' Thus, Clark and Fujimoto (1991) pointed out that building 'integrating mechanisms,' such as stage-overlapping product development processes, and embedding these organizationally would facilitate thick communication across departments. Ideas that, for example, alliances and joint ventures may be seen as vehicles for knowledge building (beginning perhaps with Hamel 1991); that high-performance HRM practices can drive innovation performance (Laursen and Foss 2003); that the 'differentiated multinational corporation' is a means of superior leverage of knowledge (e.g., Hedlund 1994); that knowledge creation and sharing are dependent on network relations (e.g., Hansen 2002); etc. all bear testimony to the fact that thinking about the relation between organization and knowledge processes can be found in several distinct quarters in management.

Still, knowledge governance scholars sharpen this overall focus in a number of ways. In particular, they seem to be taken up with designed, formal organization. Whereas this manifestation of organization has by no means been neglected in the knowledge movement at large, there has arguably been a tendency in recent research to focus more on 'informal organization,' that is, networks, culture, communities of practice, and the like, than on formal governance mechanisms.

The attempt to provide more room for such formal aspects of organization is by no means a denial that informal organization matters and it matters importantly. The attempt to explore how formal organization impacts knowledge processes is motivated by the recognition that formal organization, to a larger extent than informal organization, represents the levers that managers can actually pull. Even if it is granted that informal organization, for example, in the form of network relations, is a proximate cause of, say, the intensity of knowledge sharing in an organization, this informal organization may only be open to manipulation through changes in formal organization (e.g., changes in organizational structure may influence networks).

11.3. Knowledge-Related Units of Analysis and Their Dimensions

Knowledge-based work in management has worked with what appears to be a mind-boggling number of units of analysis, ranging from the transaction (e.g., Heiman and Nickerson 2002; Oxley 1997), the problem

(Nickerson and Zenger 2004), the routine (Nelson and Winter 1982), the knowledge asset (Winter 1987), dynamic capabilities (Teece, Pisano, and Shuen 1997), practices (Spender 2005), or 'knowledge units' (Contractor and Ra 2002; Simonin 1999). One can see an almost similar diversity reflected in this book. For example, Argote and Kane and Grandori take innovations as the relevant knowledge-based units of analysis; while Heiman, Nickerson, and Zenger focus on problems; and Christensen and Knudsen adopt the project as the unit. Compare this seeming confusion to transaction cost economics which consistently adopts the transaction as its unit of analysis, a strategy that has arguably strongly contributed to the success of TCE (as Williamson (1999) argued). One may be led to conclude that knowledge governance scholars will benefit from adopting an agreed upon unit of analysis.

However, disciplines, fields, or approaches are not necessarily characterized by unique units of analysis. Thus, the existing diversity in the knowledge movement may simply reflect that different research problems are involved. In general, what is the preferred unit of analysis should depend on the relevant research problems. The unit may differ depending on whether the focus is knowledge sharing or knowledge creation. Thus, Nickerson and Zenger (2004) construct a theory about the organization of knowledge creation, based on taking the problem as the unit of analysis. However, this seems primarily designed for understanding the governance of knowledge creation (i.e., solving problems by combining knowledge); it seems less well suited for understanding knowledge sharing or integration.

That being said, some units of analysis seem to be more generally applicable than others, and as a research strategy it may pay off to emphasize some units. The most generally applicable unit of analysis for the kind of problems that knowledge governance scholars are interested in is the knowledge transaction, that is, the transfer of an identifiable 'piece' of knowledge from one actor to another. While the chapters in this book do adopt different units (cf. Table 11.1), most of the reasoning in most of the chapters can be reconstructed in terms of taking the knowledge transaction as the unit of analysis. Thus, knowledge transactions are involved in knowledge sharing, integration, and creation. Of course, taking the knowledge transaction as unit of analysis has the added benefit of linking up with organizational economics and an established framework for linking transactions to alternative kinds of organizing ('alignment'). Indeed, about half of the chapters explicitly take organizational economics as an important source theory (i.e., chapters by Christensen and Knudsen,

Heiman, Nickerson, and Zenger, Grandori, Foss and Foss, Osterloh and Weibel).

However, the way of *dimensionalizing* transactions that has become dominant in organizational economics, namely, the transaction cost economics triad of frequency/uncertainty/asset specificity, is at best incomplete for the purposes of treating knowledge transactions (cf. also Grandori 2001; Heiman and Nickerson 2002; Nickerson and Zenger 2004). It is not clear how dimensionalizing a knowledge transaction in these terms assists the understanding of, for example, knowledge sharing where transactional problems may rather be caused by the degree of codification of the relevant knowledge than its 'uncertainty' (whatever that might mean in the specific context). The knowledge-based literature is unfortunately not clearly forthcoming with respect to dimensionalizing knowledge.[2]

An important exception is the Winter (1987) taxonomy, which has been the basis for much subsequent empirical work (e.g., Kogut and Zander 1993; Simonin 1999). Winter introduces the dimensions of tacitness versus explicitness, system-quality versus stand-alone, teachability versus non-teachability, and complexity versus noncomplexity. Although these dimensions have usually been applied to more aggregate knowledge constructs (such as routines and capabilities) in the empirical literature, they can also be used to characterize knowledge transactions. Accordingly, knowledge transactions can be dimensionalized in terms of the characteristics of the underlying knowledge.

The Winter taxonomy is implicitly reflected in a number of chapters. For example, Argote and Kane dimensionalize knowledge in terms of 'demonstrability' which seems close to the Winter notion of 'teachability.' The 'complexity' dimension is present in, for example, the Heimann, Nickerson, and Zenger chapter, etc. However, there is no need to stop the process of dimensionalizing with the Winter taxonomy; other dimensions may be relevant. For example, scholars working from a transaction cost economics perspective have suggested adding 'appropriability' as a relevant dimension (e.g., Oxley 1997),[3] and Contractor and Ra (2002)

[2] The many studies of interfirm imitation and intrafirm knowledge transfer (e.g., Maritan and Brush 2003) tend to develop dimensions of, say, capabilities in an inductive manner and the explicit or implicit dimensionalizations differ from study to study.

[3] Appropriability is to some extent derivative of, for example, the tacitness versus explicitness dimension, but not fully, as it also includes the legal framework surrounding the transaction.

suggest adding how 'novel' the knowledge is (knowledge with a higher degree of novelty is more costly to contract, absorb, assimilate, integrate, etc.). A number of contributions to this book suggest that transactions also need to be seen in a systemic context. For example, the chapters by Heimann, Nickerson, and Zenger, Grandori, and Foss and Foss argue that the degree of knowledge dispersal in an organization is a determinant of the governance mechanisms that can efficiently be adopted to govern this knowledge (although Grandori thinks that knowledge dispersal is a stronger constraint on governance choice than Foss and Foss do). Osterloh and Weibel introduce 'cognitive distance,' which also seems only partially overlapping with the Winter dimensions.

In the context of the knowledge governance approach, dimensionalizing the unit of analysis matters because the costs of sharing, transferring, integrating, using, and creating knowledge vary systematically with the relevant dimensions. The choice of governance mechanisms reflects these costs. If this principle is kept in mind, there is no reason to inherently prefer the transaction as *the* unit of analysis; other units may be (equally) appropriate. However, more aggregate or collective-level knowledge-based units of analysis, such as capabilities or competencies, may be less attractive to knowledge governance scholars because they tend to favor microanalysis.

11.4. Which Microfoundations?

As Teppo Felin notes in his dialogue with JC Spender in Chapter 10,

> . . . the KM literature would benefit from starting out from lower-level notions and systematically building theory upwards to understand how macro, knowledge-related outcomes emerge and form from these microlevel antecedents. This microfoundations program and intuition shares much with the social theory pioneered by James Coleman. (1990, cf. Felin and Foss 2006)

'Microfoundations' here implies that a starting point must be taken in explicit behavioral assumptions. Thus, explanation starts with the individual agent (even though it may be permissible to introduce more collective concepts, such as organization structure, in the analysis as shorthand). This implies modeling (i.e., making specific assumptions about) individual agents' preferences, knowledge, incentives, etc. For example, Christensen and Knudsen (this book) explicitly model individual agents' 'evaluation functions,' while Osterloh and Weibel (this book) provide a discussion of the psychological assumptions that need to be added to the characterization of individuals if one wants to understand the organization of explorative knowledge work.

However, the question is, which microfoundations? The general guideline is that this depends on the questions one tries to solve. Thus, economists have found that they have had to increasingly change the way they model individual cognition and motivation toward greater realism as they have moved from treating only market and macro-phenomena to also address contracts, organizations, networks, trust, and so on. As the contributions to this book suggest, the standard economics model of man as a cognitive superman that is only extrinsically motivated is inadequate for the building and development of knowledge governance theory. More realistic cognitive and motivational assumptions are needed. Moreover, a general rule is that the lower the level of analysis, the more fine-grained the description of the individual agent (Machlup 1967). Because the knowledge governance approach is all about how the deployment of specific governance mechanisms impacts knowledge processes (i.e., a low level of analysis), rather specific assumptions need to be made about individual agents, and these assumptions must 'allow for' the phenomena to which an explanation is sought.

While knowledge governance scholars are often sympathetic to the behavioral assumptions of transaction cost economics (e.g., Foss 2003; Mowery, Oxley, and Silverman 1996; Nickerson and Zenger 2004)—that is, bounded rationality and opportunism (Williamson 1996)—as these produce interesting organizational and exchange hazards, these behavioral assumptions may still be too coarse. 'Bounded rationality' means many things and 'opportunism' may manifest itself in multiple ways. Moreover, bounded rationality and opportunism are not given, but can be influenced by governance mechanisms. Relatedly, a more sophisticated view of motivation (e.g., as in Osterloh and Frey 2000) that is conventional in the economics of organization must be included. Indeed a number of chapters in this book call for a more nuanced view of motivation (e.g., Osterloh and Weibel, Argote and Kane), one that is informed by advances in social psychology and organizational behavior, and of cognition (e.g., Grandori). While much can perhaps be packed into the 'bounded rationality and opportunism' duo, many things, such as 'superordinate identity' (Argote and Kane) or 'allegiance' (Husted and Michailova), cannot.

11.5. Which Organizational and Governance Alternatives?

Knowledge governance may be seen as a sustained attempt to define the appropriate place for organization in the broader knowledge movement in management of which it is a part. The point is not that organization per se has been neglected here. The problems rather have to do with missing microfoundations (an issue explored by Felin and Spender in their conversation in Chapter 10), and with particularly formal organization being under-researched. With respect to the first point, precise and comprehensive inquiries of the causal links from governance mechanisms (macro) to individual knowledge-related behaviors (micro) to organizational knowledge-related outcomes (macro) are rare. By paying explicit attention to the level of individuals and individual interaction, knowledge governance scholars seek to open this black box of the causality from organizational arrangements to organization-level knowledge outcomes (e.g., organizational knowledge sharing). With respect to the second point, formal organization being under-researched, mechanisms such as the allocation of authority and decision rights, the provision of incentives, and the creation of organizational structure need to be given more explicit emphasis. The main part of the research that includes formal organization is work that deals with the influence of explicit incentives on knowledge sharing (starting in economics, see Bhattacharya, Glazer, and Sappington 1992), but clearly many other mechanisms of formal organization are relevant and should be included.

Bringing formal organization more explicitly into the analysis also means going significantly beyond the market–hybrid–hierarchy trichotomy of transaction cost economics, and explicitly considering the various governance mechanisms that can be combined within governance structures to support knowledge-related outcomes, and what exactly guides such combination. In other words, which governance mechanisms are substitutes and which are complements with respect to furthering knowledge-related outcomes? Which clusters of governance mechanisms should we expect to see for which kind of knowledge processes? Including also informal organization obviously complicates the picture. For example, it becomes pertinent to ask whether strong norms are, for example, knowledge sharing substitute for incentives to share knowledge, or may they rather complement them? What formal governance mechanisms complement the socialization tactics discussed by Husted and Michailova (Chapter 8) or the identities discussed by Argote and Kane (Chapter 7)? To what extent is management's ability to deploy formal governance mechanisms constrained or facilitated by the web of informal organization in place? Conversely, what kinds of formal mechanisms may harm informal mechanisms (e.g., relational ones), an issue treated by Scarbrough and Amaeshi and Osterloh and Weibel?

These issues are highly under-researched, no doubt because of their theoretical complexity and difficulties of empirical operationalization. In one of the few (theoretical) treatments that have a bearing on the issues, Grandori (2001) argues that scholars have managed to sidestep these complexities by simply deciding, in an essentially arbitrary fashion, that governance mechanisms cluster in discrete governance structures. If one examines the mechanisms that govern knowledge processes between and within firms, one finds that not only hierarchical or communitarian mechanisms are applied but also price-based (market-like) contracts, Grandori argues. The conclusion she draws from this is that the portfolio of mechanisms effectively employable between firms to link nodes of specialized knowledge can hardly be distinguished (in qualitative terms) from those mechanisms employable within firms. Grandori's (2001) discussion is refreshing and provocative, but not the last word on these intricate issues.

11.6. Toward Evidence-Based Knowledge Governance

In spite of the important strides forward that are contained in this-book, the knowledge governance research frontier is clearly an open one (if perhaps not a wide open one). Indeed, the above discussion of key themes in knowledge governance suggests that many important issues are not settled. Pfeffer and Sutton (2006) have recently made a general call for 'evidence-based management,' that is, the explicit use in management practice of the best available evidence in management decision-making (and social science in general). While many have observed that much, in fact, most, management decision-making takes places in complete isolation from any such evidence (e.g., Rousseau 2006), the other side of the coin is equally noteworthy: there are certainly important phenomena that concern managers about which precious little serious evidence actually exists. To exemplify, consider how much (little) we really know about the following two important and partly overlapping issues: the contribution of knowledge to competitive advantage (Grant 1996; Spender 1996) and the governance of knowledge-intensive firms (Starbuck 1992).

One of the first areas where knowledge-based views acquired prominence is strategic management (e.g., Grant 1996; Kogut and Zander 1992; Spender 1996). The field has seen a proliferation of approaches that (alternatively) place 'capabilities' (whether 'dynamic' or not), 'competencies' (whether 'core' or not), 'knowledge resources,' 'knowledge structures,' 'knowledge stocks,' etc. center stage. These are all firm-level knowledge resources. The key idea is that differential firm performance can be traced to differential capabilities (or competencies, etc.); successful firms control capabilities that result in more appropriable value-added than less successful firms. However, in spite of almost two decades of such 'knowledge-based' work in strategic management, the literature still suffers from a fundamental problem with connecting the (micro) level of individuals and their interaction to the (macro)level of capabilities (Felin and Foss 2005). In fact, the microlevel is usually bypassed. As Argote and Ingram (2000: 156) noted, to the extent that there has been progress in studying knowledge as the basis of competitive advantage, '... it has been at the level of identifying consistencies in organizations' knowledge development paths and almost never at the level of human interactions that are the primary source of knowledge and knowledge transfer.'

The issue of how knowledge that ultimately resides on the level of the individuals is somehow integrated through organizational means into organization-level capability is thereby obscured (Felin and Hesterly 2007). This is highly problematic, as it leaves completely in the dark, for example, whether knowledge-based competitive advantage is primarily caused by *ex ante* highly efficient, knowledgeable, etc. individuals self-selecting into certain organizational environments, or by superior interaction among employees that *ex ante* did not arrive with much human capital (or some mix between the two extremes). Moreover, because of its neglect of employee–firm-level links, the knowledge-based view also has difficulties finding room for organization: although capabilities are often taken to be *organizational* processes that enable managers to carry out certain key tasks, organization itself seems almost conspicuous by its absence in this kind of work. What knowledge governance can do here is to further knowledge-based work not only by placing the finger on the sore spots but also by more important actively work on the fundamental issue of the role of organization in the creation of knowledge-based competitive advantage.

The second example concerns knowledge-intensive firms, that is, firms where a significantly larger part of value-added can be ascribed to human than to physical assets. They range from R&D-intensive manufacturing firms to professional services firms. The increasing importance of such organizations have led many scholars to speculate that the very notion of firm boundaries is becoming increasingly problematic as (inalienable) human capital increasingly dominates (alienable) physical capital as the most important category of productive capital (see Foss 2002 for a critical discussion). Similarly, many have argued that the increased prevalence of knowledge-intensive firms has profound implications for the deployment of governance mechanisms such as the allocation (and exercise) of authority and the design of reward systems. In fact, according to a viewpoint that has almost acquired the status of conventional wisdom, human capital organizations may be differentiated from 'traditional' firms in terms of governance mechanisms by relying less on direction through the exercise of authority, eschewing high-powered performance incentives, and embracing 'culture' and 'clan' modes of organizational control (at least for the core group of employees) (e.g., Child and McGrath 2001). Organizational control is exercised through very different mechanisms in the two kinds of firms.

However, Teece (2003) develops a contrary view. Teece explains how the organization of his own firm (Law and Economics Consulting Group, LECG), a professional services firm, is very much different from the above portrayal of how human capital organizations are administered and controlled. In particular, while indeed the traditional blunt authority-mechanism (supervision, order-giving) is 'extremely weak' in this firm, very high-powered performance incentives are used (instead). The two features are related, for by setting compensation for 'experts' '. . . purely as a certain percentage α of the expert's own individual bill-out rate times hours worked (as accepted by the client)' (Teece 2003: 909), strong incentives are coupled with a small need for monitoring. Teece speculates that the specific organizational design of LECG (and there are other features in addition to those briefly mentioned here) '. . . may well portend the future for professional service organizations endeavoring to leverage top talent' (p. 914).

The point is, of course, not that Teece is right and those who argue differently are wrong, or vice versa; both may be right—for different kinds of knowledge-intensive firms or for different environments. However, we do not have a good theory that will allow us to discriminate between these alternative accounts in a clean manner. What does a 'good theory' mean here? It may mean something akin to the received transaction cost theory, that is, theorizing that begins from a knowledge-related unit of analysis and explains how the efficient deployment of governance mechanisms systematically varies when the unit of analysis varies, given assumptions about agents' knowledge and motivation and given assumptions about the principle (e.g., efficiency) that links the unit of analysis with alternative kinds of governance mechanisms (or combinations thereof). However, the theory may also include the notion that agents gradually learn what is the proper alignment of transactions and governance structures. It may take into account rich ideas on motivation and cognition from psychology, as suggested by a number of chapters in this book. It may be linked to environmental factors, etc.

The fact is that we only have parts and pieces of such a theory. To be sure, much is known about, for example, such issues as what kind of motivation works best for knowledge sharing or how network ties influence knowledge sharing and creation. The basic theory of governance choice is in fairly good shape and the last decade has witnessed important work that extends this theory to knowledge transactions (e.g., Heiman and Nickerson 2002, 2004; Oxley 1997). However, it is not clear how these ideas add up and connect. Clearly, for many management purposes, more partial views may be fully adequate. But for the Grand Questions we need something more than partial views. Among such Grand Questions are the relations between knowledge, competitive advantage, and economic organization. It is high time to not only aim at evidence-based management in the governance of knowledge processes but also make strides forward to actually build the theories and supporting evidence that can serve as proper decision support.

References

Argote, L. and P. Ingram. 2000. 'Knowledge Transfer: A Basis for Competitive Advantage in Firms,' *Organizational Behavior and Human Decision Processes* 82(1): 150–69.

Bhattacharya, S., J. Glazer, and D. Sappington. 1992. 'Licensing and the Sharing of Knowledge in Research Joint Ventures,' *Journal of Economic Theory* 56: 43–69.

Brown, J. S. and P. Duguid. 1998. 'Organizing Knowledge,' *California Management Review* 40(3): 90–111.

Cabrera, A., W. C. Collins, and J. F. Salgado. 2006. 'Determinants of Organizational Engagement in Knowledge Sharing,' *International Journal of Human Resource Management* 17: 245–64.

Child, J. and R. McGrath. 2001. 'Organizations Unfettered: Organizational Form in an Information Intensive Economy,' *Academy of Management Journal* 44: 1135–48.

Clark, K. B. and T. Fujimoto. 1991. *Product Development Performance: Strategy, Organisation and Management in the World Auto Industry*. Boston: Harvard University Press.

Coleman, J. S. 1990. *Foundations of Social Theory*. (Massachusetts)/London, Cambridge: The Belknap Press of Harvard University Press.

Contractor, F. J. and R. Wonchan. 2002. 'How Knowledge Attributes Influence Alliance Governance Choices,' *Journal of International Management* 8: 11–27.

Easterby-Smith, M. and M. A. Lyles (eds.) 2003. In *Handbook of Organizational Learning and Knowledge Management*. Oxford: Blackwell Publishing.

Felin, T. and N. D. Foss. 2005. 'Strategic Organization: A Field in Search of Microfoundations,' *Strategic Organization* 3: 441–55.

—— and W. Hesterley. 2007. 'The Knowledge-based View, Nested Heterogeneity, and New Value Creation,' *Academy of Management Review* 32: 195–218.

Foss, N. J. 2003. 'Selective Intervention and Internal Hybrids: Interpreting and Learning from the Rise and Decline of the Oticon Spaghetti Organization,' *Organization Science* 14: 331–49.

—— 2007. 'The Emerging Knowledge Governance Approach,' *Organization* 14: 29–52.

Grandori, A. 1997. 'Governance Structures, Coordination Mechanisms and Cognitive Models,' *Journal of Management and Governance* 1: 29–42.

—— 2001. 'Neither Hierarchy Nor Identity: Knowledge Governance Mechanisms and the Theory of the Firm,' *Journal of Management and Governance* 5: 381–99.

—— and B. Kogut. 2002. 'Dialogue on Organization and Knowledge,' *Organization Science* 13: 224–32.

Granovetter, M. 1973. 'The Strength of Weak Ties,' *American Journal of Sociology* 78: 1360–80.

Grant, R. M. 1996. 'Towards a Knowledge-Based Theory of the Firm,' *Strategic Management Journal* 17: 109–22.

Hamel, G. 1991. 'Competition for Competence and Inter-Partner Learning within International Strategic Alliances,' *Strategic Management Journal* 12: 83–103.

Hansen, M. T. 2002. 'Knowledge Networks: Explaining Effective Knowledge Sharing in Multiunit Companies,' *Organization Science* 13(3): 232–48.

Hayek, F. A. 1945. 'The Use of Knowledge in Society,' in idem. 1948. *Individualism and Economic Order*. Chicago: University of Chicago Press.

Hedlund, G. 1994. 'A Model of Knowledge Management and the N-Form Corporation,' *Strategic Management Journal* 15: 73–91.

Hedström, P. and R. Swedberg 1996. 'Social Mechanisms,' *Acta Sociologica* 39: 281–308.

Heiman, B. and J. A. Nickerson. 2002. 'Towards Reconciling Transaction Cost Economics and the Knowledge-Based View of the Firm: The Context of Interfirm Collaborations,' *International Journal of the Economics of Business* 9: 97–116.

Kogut, B. 2000. 'The Network as Knowledge: Generative Rules and the Emergence of Structure,' *Strategic Management Journal* 21: 405–25.

——and U. Zander. 1992. 'Knowledge of the Firm, Combinative Capabilities, and the Replication of Technology,' *Organization Science* 3: 383–97.

———— 1993. 'Knowledge of the Firm and the Evolutionary Theory of the Multinational Corporation,' *Journal of International Business Studies* 24: 625–45.

Kogut, B. and U. Zander. 1996. 'What Firms Do? Coordination, Identity, and Learning,' *Organization Science* 7: 502–18.

Lakatos, I. 1970. 'Falsification and the Methodology of Scientific Research Programmes,' in idem. 1978. *The Methodology of Scientific Research Programmes*. Cambridge: Cambridge University Press.

Laursen, K. and N. J. Foss. 2003. 'New HRM Practices, Complementarities, and the Impact on Innovation Performance,' *Cambridge Journal of Economics* 27: 243–63.

Liebeskind, J. P., et al. 1996. 'Social Networks, Learning, and Flexibility: Sourcing Scientific Knowledge among New Biotechnology Firms,' *Organization Science* 7: 428–43.

Lindenberg, S. 2003. 'The Cognitive Side of Governance,' *Research in the Sociology of Organizations* 20: 47–76.

Lippman, S. A. and R. P. Rumelt. 2003. 'The Payments Perspective,' *Strategic Management Journal* 24: 903–27.

Loasby, Brian J. 1976. *Choice, Complexity, and Ignorance*. Cambridge: Cambridge University Press.

Lyles, M. A. and C. R. Schwenk. 1992. 'Top Management Strategy and Organizational Knowledge,' *Journal of Management Studies* 29(2): 155–74.

Macher, J. T. 2006. 'Technological Development and the Boundaries of the Firm,' *Management Science* 52(6): 826–43.

Machlup, F. 1967. 'Theories of the Firm: Marginalist, Managerial and Behavioral,' in F. Machlup (ed.) 1978. *Essays on Economic Methodology*. New York: Wiley.

Maritan, C. A. and T. H. Brush. 2003. 'Heterogeneity and Transferring Practices: Implementing Flow Manufacturing in Multiple Plants,' *Strategic Management Journal* 24: 945–60.

Mayer, K. and N. Argyres. 2004. 'Learning to Contract,' *Organization Science* 15: 394–410.

Milgrom, P. and J. Roberts. 1990. 'The Economics of Modern Manufacturing: Technology, Strategy and Organization,' *American Economic Review* 80: 511–28.

Minbaeva, D., et al. 2003. 'MNC Knowledge Transfer, Subsidiary Absorptive Capacity, and HRM,' *Journal of International Business Studies* 34: 586–99.

Mowery, D. C., J. Oxley, and B. Silverman. 1996. 'Strategic Alliances and Interfirm Knowledge Transfer,' *Strategic Management Journal* 17: 77–91.

Nelson, R. R. and S. G. Winter. 1982. *The Evolutionary Theory of the Firm*. Cambridge, MA: Harvard University Press.

Nickerson, J. and T. Zenger. 2004. 'A Knowledge-Based Theory of the Firm: The Problem-Solving Perspective,' *Organization Science* 15(6): 617–32.

Osterloh, M. and B. Frey. 2000. 'Motivation, Knowledge Transfer and Organizational Form,' *Organization Science* 11: 538–50.

Oxley, J. 1997. 'Appropriability Hazards and Governance in Strategic Alliances: A Transaction Cost Approach,' *Journal of Law, Economics, and Organization* 13: 387–409.

Pfeffer, J. and R. I. Sutton. 2006. *Hard Facts, Dangerous Half-Truths, and Total Nonsense: Profiting from Evidence-Based Management*. Boston: Harvard Business School Press.

Rousseau, D. 2006. 'Presidential Address: Is There Such a Thing as "Evidence-Based Management"?,' *Academy of Management Review* 31: 256–69.

Simonin, B. L. 1999. 'Transfer of Marketing Know-How in International Strategic Alliances,' *Journal of International Business Studies* 30: 463–90.

Spender, J. C. 1996. 'Making Knowledge the Basis of a Dynamic Theory of the Firm,' *Strategic Management Journal* 17: 45–62.

——2005. 'Review Article: An Essay on the State of Knowledge Management,' *Prometheus* 23: 101–16.

Starbuck, W. 1992. 'Learning by Knowledge-Intensive Firms,' *Journal of Management Studies* 29: 713–41.

Teece, D. J. 2003. 'Expert Talent and the Design of (Professional Services) Firms,' *Industrial and Corporate Change* 12: 895–916.

——G. Pisano, and A. Shuen. 1997. 'Dynamic Capabilities and Strategic Management,' *Strategic Management Journal* 18: 509–34.

Tsai, W. P. 2001. 'Knowledge Transfer in Intra-Organizational Networks,' *Academy of Management Journal* 44(5): 996–1004.

——2002. 'Social Structure of "Coopetition" within a Multiunit Organization,' *Organization Science* 13: 179–90.

Williamson, O. E. 1996. *The Mechanisms of Governance*. Oxford: Oxford University Press.

——1999. 'Strategy Research: Governance and Competence Perspectives,' *Strategic Management Journal* 20: 1087–1108.

Winter, S. G. 1987. 'Knowledge and Competence as Strategic Assets' in D. Teece (ed.) *The Competitive Challenge*. Massachusetts, Cambridge: Ballinger.

Index

Note: page numbers in *italics* refer to figures and tables.